TOMASO ALBINONI

TOMASO ALBINONI

The Venetian Composer and His World

MICHAEL TALBOT

CLARENDON PRESS · OXFORD

1990

WITHDRAWN
LIBRARY MSU - BILLINGS

Oxford University Press, Walton Street, Oxford OX2 6DP
Oxford New York Toronto
Delhi Bombay Calcutta Madras Karachi
Petaling Jaya Singapore Hong Kong Tokyo
Nairobi Dar es Salaam Cape Town
Melbourne Auckland
and associated companies in
Berlin Ibadan

Oxford is a trade mark of Oxford University Press

Published in the United States
by Oxford University Press, New York

© Michael Talbot 1990

All rights reserved. No part of this publication may be reproduced,
stored in a retrieval system, or transmitted, in any form or by any means,
electronic, mechanical, photocopying, recording, or otherwise, without
the prior permission of Oxford University Press

British Library Cataloguing in Publication Data
Talbot, Michael, 1943
Tomaso Albinoni: the Venetian composer and his world.
1. Italian music. Albinoni, Tomaso, 1671–1751
I. Title
780.92
ISBN 0–19–315245–2

Library of Congress Cataloging in Publication Data
Talbot, Michael.
Tomaso Albinoni: the Venetian composer and his world
Michael Talbot.
Includes bibliographical references.
1. Albinoni, Tomaso, 1671–1751.
2. Composers—Italy—Biography.
I. Title.
ML410.A315T3513   1990   780'.92—dc20   89–49221
ISBN 0–19–315245–2

Typeset by Cotswold Typesetting Ltd., Gloucester
Printed in Great Britain by
St. Edmundsbury Press, Bury St. Edmunds, Suffolk

PREFACE

Asked to identify the composition by Albinoni that first sprang to mind, most music-lovers would probably name the Adagio in G minor for strings and organ, a piece originally published in 1958 and ever since a mainstay of record catalogues and chamber orchestra programmes. This is ironic, for the piece's actual composer, the musicologist and Albinoni scholar Remo Giazotto, has never claimed that the Adagio is based on more than a tiny original fragment; moreover, the existence of even that fragment has frequently been doubted since all efforts to trace it have failed. Whether this composition is minimally by Albinoni or not by Albinoni at all is of small concern; what matters is that its style is so totally unlike Albinoni's that it invites us to explore his music under false premises. Whereas the Adagio is unashamedly lachrymose, copying the idea of a pizzicato bass in striding octaves (evocative of sobbing) from a common way of performing Bach's so-called 'Air on the G string', Albinoni's real Adagio movements are dignified and classical in expression, even tending in his less inspired moments to dryness. The wonder is that Giazotto's Adagio has been so successful a catalyst in bringing Albinoni's instrumental works to the attention of the concert-going and record-buying public. Perverse as the basis of this achievement has been, it is none the less real.

When I first became an Albinoni enthusiast, also in the late 1950s, his sonatas and especially his concertos were well represented on record and in concert performances, and modern editions of his instrumental works were numerous. This heyday, which owed a lot to the advocacy of chamber orchestras such as I Musici and the Virtuosi di Roma, has now passed; in compensation, however, Albinoni's vocal music, which includes some of his greatest achievements, nowadays attracts more interest, particularly among the increasing number of singers who aspire to an authentic style of performance. If, as I hope, there is to be a second surge in Albinoni's popularity, it is likely to be the vocal music that leads the way.

My interest in Albinoni resulted first in a doctoral thesis (Cambridge, 1968) devoted to the instrumental music. Many years later, when I had revised some of my earlier conceptions and was far more familiar with the music of his contemporaries, I wrote a medium-length study of Albinoni's life and works. Circumstances caused it to appear not in English but in German, as *Albinoni: Leben und Werk* (Adliswil, Edition Kunzelmann, 1980). Eight years further on, I have continued, albeit more selectively, to develop and sometimes review my ideas; in the mean time, I have made a few discoveries that are presented in these pages for the first time in any book. I imagine there will not be many people reading these words who have also had the opportunity to consult my earlier Albinoni study, but I can at least reassure them that they will not find the present book merely a rehashed version of the one they already know.

Like its predecessor, this is a study that considers both Albinoni's life and his works. Quite deliberately, however, the emphasis falls on the music, since in a book of fairly modest dimensions aimed at a wide readership this has to be the first priority. All the same, one cannot overlook the fact that, as a Venetian composer, Albinoni lived and worked in a very distinctive social and cultural environment that inevitably left a strong mark on him. For this reason I have found it necessary to discuss the Venetian background in some detail.

Since this volume represents not so much a new project as one that has occupied me intermittently over a period of more than twenty years, the list of people who have at various times given me assistance and encouragement would run to several dozen names. If I may be allowed to be selective and confine my thanks to those who have helped me with the preparation for the book in the most recent period, I should like to record my gratitude to Carlo Guaita for his donation of a copy of his illuminating thesis on Albinoni's cantatas, to Brian Crosby for facilitating my study of manuscripts in Durham Cathedral Library and answering my many questions, to Gastone Vio for keeping me informed of his work in progress on Albinoni's biography, to Maurizio Grattoni for supplying photocopies of some arias, to Colin Timms for his comments on Chapter 5, to Carole Taylor and Thomas Walker for their comments on part of Chapter 8, and to my wife Shirley for relieving me of many chores that would otherwise have caused me to rise guiltily from the word-processor.

Liverpool   M.T.
1989

CONTENTS

LIST OF PLATES

(between pages 150 and 151)

1. First page of the autograph manuscript of Albinoni's violin sonata in B flat major, *So* 34 (*Sächsische Landesbibliothek, Dresden*)

2. Detail with the heads of Albinoni, Gizzi, and Colla from the engraving 'Parnaso italiano' after a drawing by Luigi Scotti (*Civica Raccolta Stampe 'A. Bertarelli', Castello Sforzesco, Milan*)

3. Anonymous oil painting of Albinoni (*private collection of Professor G. Mandel, Milan*: Artephot, J. P. Ziolo)

4. Title-page of the Violoncello part from the 1706 Sala edition of Albinoni's *Balletti a tre*, Op. 3 (*Musiksammlung der Grafen von Wiesentheid, Wiesentheid*)

5. Extracts from Albinoni's *Concerti a cinque*, Op. 10, included in Michel Corrette's *L'Art de se perfectionner dans le violon* (1782) (*Bibliothèque Nationale, Paris*)

6. Opening of the text of the comic intermezzi *Pimpinone* as it appears in the libretto of the original production (Venice, 1708) (*Civico Museo Bibliografico Musicale, Bologna*)

7. First page of the aria with obbligato oboe 'Cerco l'oggetto del mio furor' from the opera *I veri amici* (Munich, 1722) (*Bodleian Library, Oxford*)

8. Third page of the aria with obbligato archlute 'Con cetra più sonora' from the serenata *Il nascimento de l'Aurora* (*c.* 1710) (*Österreichische Nationalbibliothek, Vienna*)

to Paul Everett

FAME, OBLIVION, AND REVIVAL

TOMASO ALBINONI, a Venetian, was originally a maker of cards, but having an early propensity to music, and having been taught the violin in his youth, he became not only an excellent performer on that instrument, but also an excellent composer (Hawkins, 1776).[1]

Regarding the quality of his works, my study of some of his scores has shown me that his style is dry, his ideas dull or trivial, and the expression of the words in most of his operas almost nil (Fétis, 1835).[2]

Few musicians reveal such professional skill as composers. He wrote not a single movement which contains careless or even mediocre workmanship, and very few which fail to demonstrate an unusual command of organic form (Hutchings, 1961).[3]

As the above quotations illustrate, Albinoni's reputation over the last two centuries has described a curve whose shape is familiar from the posthumous experience of so many other composers of his generation. Indeed, the changes in the musical world's view of Albinoni after his death offer an exceptionally clear-cut example of the triad fame–oblivion–revival. The underlying reasons for these fluctuations deserve a brief discussion.

Most music of the eighteenth century and earlier was characterized by an inbuilt obsolescence. One reason for this was that the promotion of a composer's music was seen as primarily the responsibility of the composer himself in his role as performer or musical director. His removal from a locality might cause his works to disappear from the local repertory; his retirement from active performing might have a similar effect; and so, naturally, would his death.

A second reason was the subordination of the public's musical appreciation to a keen awareness of changes of fashion—changes that in Albinoni's middle and late years occurred very often. Speaking in particular of Italian operas, in which taste and style changed exceptionally rapidly to suit the demands of singers, an anonymous commentator in the *Mercure de France* observed in 1731 that such works 'die in the act of being

---

[1] Sir John Hawkins, *A General History of the Science and Practice of Music* (5 vols., London, 1776), ii. 678.

[2] François-Joseph Fétis, *Biographie universelle des musiciens* (8 vols., Brussels, 1835–44), i. art. 'Albinoni (Thomas)'.

[3] Arthur Hutchings, *The Baroque Concerto* (London, 1961), 136.

born and are never repeated, since the public always craves novelty';[4] a similar situation was described in 1739 by the French traveller Charles de Brosses, who wrote to his friend de Blancey after a meeting in Venice with Vivaldi: 'To my great astonishment I discovered that he is not as highly regarded as he deserves to be in this country, where everything has to be up-to-the-minute, where his works have been heard for too long, and where last year's music no longer brings in money'.[5] Stylistic evolution was less hectic in the domain of instrumental music, but its relevance to the present argument is illustrated by the reissue by the violinist-composer Francesco Geminiani in 1755 of comprehensively 'updated' versions of concertos (Opp. 2 and 3) that he had published only in 1732.

Both factors making for obsolescence, though no longer applicable to concert music, can be seen to operate with equal force today in the world of popular music, but a third important factor applies more exclusively to the period under discussion: the limited access of musicians and music-lovers to performing material. The high rate of perishability, through natural causes as well as neglect, of both manuscript and printed or engraved music meant that the most recently produced material was generally also the most accessible. One must remember that most music—including virtually all vocal music—circulated solely in manuscript, becoming reproduced in at most a few dozen copies; published music rarely sold in more than a hundred examples. For private individuals music for performance—even more so, music for study—was almost a luxury. De Brosses complained that in Italy 'music is never seen again, is never printed or engraved, with the result that the most famous pieces remain only in the memory; the rest is soon forgotten'.[6]

Of course, this rather gloomy picture admits of some qualification. Certain baroque composers, among whom Lully, Corelli, and Handel stand out, earned the status of 'classics' in their lifetime and continued to enjoy it for a considerable time afterwards. Many of their works remained in the active repertory, and their œuvre provided both approved models for younger composers and practice material for performers. Other composers maintained a place in the repertory by occupying special niches from which no successors sought to displace them. Benedetto Marcello's psalm paraphrases, the famous Estro poetico-armonico, and J. S. Bach's polyphonic motets exemplify this category. Composers with a reputation for being learned, like Bach, or for writing music of exceptional technical

---

[4] 'Dissertation critique sur l'état présent de l'Italie, concernant les sciences et les arts', Mercure de France, Dec. 1731, p. 2742.

[5] Charles de Brosses, Lettres familières écrites d'Italie en 1739 et 1740, ed. R. Colomb (2 vols., Paris, 1858), i. 193.

[6] Ibid. ii. 316.

difficulty, like Locatelli, also had greater than average chances of survival, if only in the pages of treatises and primers.

By 1800, however, none of the composers born between 1640 and 1710 (who may be regarded as Albinoni's contemporaries in the wider sense) could be said to retain a presence in the general repertory—with the notable exception of Handel in the British Isles. However, during the nineteenth century and the first part of the twentieth century there took place a remarkable process that ultimately transformed the concept of 'repertory': instead of consisting exclusively of works by living and recent composers, concert programmes began to contain works by the best (or most representative) composers of several generations, including ones at a considerable historical remove. Ultimately, the point was reached when a programme that failed to contain works from previous centuries was thought exceptional (which in some measure remains the case today).

One can distinguish several factors that combined to bring about this progressive revaluation of older music. Antiquarianism—the love of the old for the sake of its oldness—was the earliest strand to emerge; we find its beginnings, marked by the rise of concert societies such as the Academy of Ancient Music, already in the eighteenth century. A second strand was the rise, after Beethoven, of a concept of 'genius' that laid more stress on the individual attributes of a composer than on the style within which he worked; to a great extent this new concept neutralized the older idea of continuous progress and refinement in the art of music. Third, the study of musical history undertaken in universities and conservatories stimulated the not unnatural desire to hear the object under discussion *in vivo*. Ever since the nineteenth century musicology and music-making have interfered—most would say benignly—with each other. Finally, the growing permeation of culture by nationalist sentiment encouraged the revival of older music as a patriotic enterprise. In fact, the very remoteness in time of a Bach, a Rameau, or a Purcell made them all the more suited to be torchbearers of a national heritage. Not by accident, the great collected editions of the nineteenth century and the first part of the present century were without exception published in each composer's home country.

Since the 1950s we have moved by stages into a new phase characterized by the splitting off from the mainstream of most kinds of early music. Specialization—of instruments, ensembles, styles, and performing techniques—is now the order of the day. One interesting and not altogether welcome result of this process is that attention has increasingly become focused on the manner of performance rather than the matter performed, and this has in turn brought about diminution of regard for what one may call the 'genius factor'. In the words of Adorno's caustic comment on

enthusiasts for early music: 'They say Bach but they mean Telemann'.[7]
Laurence Dreyfus uses the expression 'a grand *nivellement* of value' to make
the same point.[8] One related development is that the initiative for the
revival of old music has now passed from critics, musicologists, collectors,
and concert-goers to the performing community itself. The consolidation
and further progress of the Albinoni revival must take account of this new
situation.

Valid in some degree for all composers contemporary with Albinoni, the
foregoing remarks constitute the background against which his rise to
prominence, subsequent disappearance, and more recent partial return to
favour have to be viewed. Let us now trace the story of his reception by
commentators, musicians, and the lay public.

Particularly when considering Albinoni's standing in his lifetime and
immediately afterwards, we have to take account of both explicit and
implicit testimony. Explicit testimony in written form has the advantage of
being concrete and mostly unambiguous but may, of course, be ill-
informed or tendentious. Implicit testimony, such as the volume of sales of
the composer's music, is less tangible but, if correctly interpreted, more
objective. Both kinds of evidence have to be sifted in parallel.

The earliest known reference to Albinoni's musical talents is the
compliment paid to his skill as a composer by the librettist of his very first
opera, *Zenobia, regina de' Palmireni* (Venice, Carnival 1694). In his foreword
to the printed libretto the poet Antonio Marchi addressed the public: 'You
will hear as a remedy for my deficiencies the accomplished and delightful
music of Signor Tomaso Albinoni, who through composing for delight
attains the goals of the foremost masters'. Here Marchi's use of the words
'dilettevole' and 'diletto' alludes openly to Albinoni's status as a *dilettante* (in
seventeenth-century usage this term means simply 'amateur' and has a
positive rather than negative ring). In similar vein, at the end of his
foreword to the libretto of *Il Tigrane, re d'Armenia* (Venice, Carnival 1697),
the poet Giulio Cesare Corradi praised 'the talent of Signor Tomaso
Albinoni, who causes one to wonder whether he should be honoured with
the title of *dilettante* alone or deserves instead that of perfect master of
music'. There is a hint of condescension in both eulogies, since librettists,
who themselves were nearly always *dilettanti*, belonged to a higher social
class (noble or citizen) than most musicians, who were members of the
general populace (*popolani*). By drawing attention to Albinoni's amateur
status, both poets flatteringly implied that he belonged to a higher stratum

---

[7] Quoted in Laurence Dreyfus, 'Early Music Defended against its Devotees: A Theory of Historical
Performance in the Twentieth Century', *The Musical Quarterly*, 69 (1983), 301–2.
[8] Ibid. 302.

than was in fact the case (Albinoni belonged to the rare category of *popolano dilettante*); however, by stressing that his accomplishment was on a fully professional level, they confirmed his worthiness to be their collaborator. Although the librettists were certainly not neutral commentators, their remarks testify to the recognition Albinoni had already attained in his early twenties.

The famous librettist Apostolo Zeno paid Albinoni an even more generous compliment in a letter of 24 February 1703 to his Florentine friend Anton Francesco Marmi. Zeno reported hearing that the première of his new drama *Griselda* in Florence had been a great success. Disclaiming all personal credit, he paid tribute to 'the excellence of the music provided by Signor Albinoni, whom I admire enormously' and to the fine singers.[9] Zeno had not witnessed the première personally, and in any case was notorious for his lack of musical sensibility, so this praise is probably a reflection of the general view of the Florentine audience.

By the early years of the next century Albinoni's sonatas, which were being republished in north-west Europe almost as quickly as they appeared in Venice, were beginning to make inroads into the transalpine repertory in the wake of Corelli's success. Jean Laurent Le Cerf de la Viéville, in his *Comparaison de la musique italienne et de la musique française* published in Brussels between 1704 and 1706, writes on the subject of sonatas (then a novelty in France): 'We are indebted to Italy for pieces of this kind; such men as Corelli, Albinoni, and Miquel [Mascitti], as well as many other great musicians, have produced works in this genre that will be immortal and within the attainment of only very few people, although a thousand others may wish to imitate them'.[10] The special significance of this praise is that it comes from a fervent partisan of the French style.

The German composer and critic Johann Mattheson found a similar vogue in his own country, noting with regret: 'Albinoni's sonatas are unjustly preferred to [French] overtures'.[11] Five years later, in 1722, Mattheson printed in his periodical *Critica musica* a report of the gala performance of Albinoni's opera *I veri amici* at the Bavarian court in Munich.[12] His correspondent comments glowingly on the production, though it is hard to establish what part of the praise refers to the music itself rather than to the performance and staging. The report refers to the composer as 'the real Albinoni'; in an amusing footnote Mattheson explains why. Apparently, an impersonator had not long before toured

[9] *Lettere di Apostolo Zeno* (2nd edn., 6 vols., Venice, 1785), i. 143.
[10] Quoted in Johann Mattheson, *Critica musica* (2 vols., Hamburg, 1722–5), i. 199–200.
[11] Id., *Das beschützte Orchestre* (Hamburg, 1717), 504.
[12] Id., *Critica musica*, i. 255.

Germany before departing from Rostock for Sweden. Besides showing that Albinoni was sufficiently eminent to be worth impersonating, this episode may have some relevance to the exceptionally high incidence of spurious instrumental works in manuscript today preserved under Albinoni's name in northern European collections—and particularly in Germany and Sweden!

In 1728 the organist Johann Gottfried Walther, who was well acquainted with some of Albinoni's early works since he had prepared scores of two sonatas in the latter's Op. 1 and had arranged for solo organ two concertos in his Op. 2, brought out the first instalment of his pioneering dictionary of music.[13] The entry for Albinoni is disappointing, since apart from terming him 'an excellent composer and violinist in the service of the Republic of Venice' (implying, incorrectly, Albinoni's holding of an official post), Walther merely lists in chronological order the nine published collections with opus number that had appeared up to then. This list proved very helpful to later lexicographers, who often reproduced it with minimal alteration, supplementing the information on instrumental collections with lists of Albinoni's operas culled from the famous bibliographies of libretti for Venetian productions published in 1730 and 1745 respectively by Bonlini and Groppo.[14]

In 1752 the wind player and theorist Johann Joachim Quantz acknowledged the importance of Albinoni to the history of the instrumental concerto, stating that although the actual inventor of the genre had been Giuseppe Torelli (1658–1709), it was Vivaldi, and, alongside him, Albinoni, who gave it 'a better form'.[15] It is worth noting that Quantz, too, was intimate with Albinoni's music, since, quite apart from his visit to Venice in 1726, he had served between 1718 and 1740 in the Saxon court orchestra at Dresden. During the late 1720s and the 1730s, under the leadership of the violin virtuoso Johann Georg Pisendel, this famous orchestra placed Venetian concertos and sinfonias at the heart of its instrumental repertory. In addition to playing oboe and flute, Quantz served Pisendel as an auxiliary copyist, which must have broadened his musical knowledge and aided his later development as a composer. He betrays his good recall of at least one Albinoni concerto preserved in the Dresden collection (today belonging to the Sächsische Landesbibliothek)

---

[13] Johann Gottfried Walther, *Musicalisches Lexicon oder musicalische Bibliothec* (Leipzig, 1732), art. 'Albinoni (Tomaso)'.

[14] [Giovanni Bonlini], *Le glorie della poesia e della musica contenute nell'esatta notitia de teatri della città di Venezia* (Venice, [1730]); Antonio Groppo, *Catalogo di tutti i drammi per musica recitati ne' teatri di Venezia* (Venice, 1745).

[15] Johann Joachim Quantz, *Versuch einer Anweisung, die Flöte traversiere zu spielen* (3rd edn., Berlin, 1789), 294.

by employing a close paraphrase of part of its unison opening as the fifty-third musical example in his treatise.[16]

Since we have already passed the year of Albinoni's death, it will be appropriate to retrace our steps for a moment to consider the implicit evidence relating to his reputation during his lifetime.

One can learn a great deal about Albinoni's success as an opera composer from plain statistics. The anonymous author of the previously mentioned *Dissertation critique* published in the *Mercure de France* for December 1731 reports a conversation in Venice with Albinoni, who told him that he never spent more than a month over the composition of an opera and had written more than 200 such works. This frankly incredible figure is belied by the claims printed, presumably with the composer's authority, in the libretti of Albinoni's operas *La Statira* (Rome, Carnival 1726) and *Candalide* (Venice, Carnival 1734), according to which these works were respectively his seventieth and eightieth operas. Italian composers of Albinoni's time were inclined, with little fear of being found out, to exaggerate their operatic productivity; it is possible that the true number does not exceed by much the figure of forty-nine operas whose existence is attested by libretti and in a few cases by surviving scores.

If we accept that a number around fifty is correct, Albinoni's tally is among the highest for its period. It falls short by some way of the totals achieved by his contemporaries Alessandro Scarlatti and Carlo Francesco Pollarolo, but approximately equals that of Francesco Gasparini and beats that of Antonio Vivaldi, his fellow Venetian, by a comfortable margin. Of course, the size of the figure has a lot to do with the quite exceptionally long duration (1694–1741) of his activity as a composer of opera. In the first four decades he averaged slightly over a dozen new works per decade; the only significant hiatus occurred between his penultimate (1734) and final (1741) operas.

Of the forty-nine known operas, thirty-seven were written for Venetian theatres and twelve for stages outside Venice. The predominance of Venice is a simple result of the fact that it was his permanent home, as well as being the acknowledged centre of Italian opera. Over the period his works were produced in six houses.

Sixteen operas, including a few revivals, were staged at the little Sant'Angelo theatre between 1698/9 and 1740/1. The double-barrelled form in which the year is given corresponds to the structure of the Venetian operatic season. This began in November, following the return of the nobility from their autumn vacation on the mainland, and continued until

---

[16] This is the concerto identified in my catalogue as *Co* 2. For an explanation of the cataloguing system see appendix A.

the middle of December; after an obligatory break for the Christmas festival, the theatres reopened on Boxing Day (St Stephen's Day) and remained active until the evening of Shrove Tuesday. Although this period was conventionally divided by the period of rest before Christmas into an Autumn and a Carnival (or Winter) season, it can be helpful to conceive the entire period as one 'grand' season straddling two years, especially since the cast of singers normally remained unchanged throughout.

A lively but rather unfashionable house, Sant'Angelo, which was named in the customary Venetian manner after the parish in which it was situated, was leased on a year-by-year basis to various impresarios (one of whom was Vivaldi); it therefore followed no consistent artistic policy and employed no 'regular' composer. In certain seasons (1700/1, 1717/18, and 1729/30) two operas by Albinoni were performed there. Since a normal season would accommodate up to three or (more rarely) four consecutive operas, one of which would be given before Christmas, these can be regarded as seasons in which Albinoni was the dominant composer.

Between 1696/7 and 1727/8 thirteen operas by Albinoni, including one (*Engelberta*) written jointly with Gasparini, were staged at the San Cassiano theatre owned by the Tron family. Albinoni was the leading composer there in the 1697/8 and 1698/9 seasons, and again in 1701/2. Gasparini, who had arrived in Venice in 1701 to take up the post of choirmaster at the famous institution for foundlings, the Ospedale della Pietà, almost immediately assumed the dominant position at San Cassiano, retaining it until his departure from Venice in 1713. During this period initially Antonio Lotti, first organist at San Marco, and subsequently Albinoni acted as his auxiliary. Between 1713 and 1724 the theatre opened only for one operatic season, but in the first phase of its renewed activity (1724–8) Albinoni once again was prominent. Of all Venice's theatres, the San Cassiano house was perhaps the most hospitable to him.

In the later part of Albinoni's career, between 1722 and 1732, the San Moisè theatre owned by the Giustinian family staged nine of his operas, including one (*Antigono, tutore di Filippo, re di Macedonia*) written in collaboration with Giovanni Porta, the new *maestro di coro* at the Pietà, who was the dominant composer there.

Albinoni also worked for three Venetian theatres owned by the Grimani family. He provided an opera for the Santi Giovanni e Paolo theatre in both the 1694 and 1695 Carnival seasons. In 1724 and 1727 he supplied the Ascensiontide operas at San Samuele. That was quite a distinction since only one or two theatres were allowed by the Council of Ten to open during the short season coinciding with the Ascensiontide fair, during which each produced no more than one opera. However, this success must be set against the fact that an Albinoni opera appeared only once, in Autumn 1717, at the San Giovanni Grisostomo theatre—Venice's grandest, most expensive to attend, and most fashionable. It was particularly at this theatre that the singers most in demand, such as Nicola Grimaldi, Carlo Broschi (Farinelli), Faustina Bordoni, and Francesca Cuzzoni, were accustomed to appeared on their visits to Venice; here too that the new wave of composers trained in Naples (Vinci, Porpora, Leo, etc.) made their breakthrough in the mid-1720s.

Mention should be made, finally, of a revival of Albinoni's *Ciro* in Carnival 1728 at the little Santa Margherita theatre managed by the impresario Fabrizio Brugnolo.

What general impression emerges from this mass of detail? It is clear that Albinoni, though never a composer of first resort for any sustained period, was a greatly respected figure in the world of Venetian opera. More successfully than any contemporary Venetian composer except Vivaldi (and without the latter's ability to secure commissions for himself through parallel activity as an impresario), he managed to keep abreast of changes in style and fashion, surviving for many years the challenge of the Neapolitans. All the same, one senses that he was valued more for his reliability, and perhaps also his speed of composition, than for the intrinsic qualities of his music.

An interesting comment on his style appears in an account of Albinoni included in Francesco Caffi's manuscript notes towards a history of Venetian theatre music, the intended sequel to his famous history of music in the ducal chapel of San Marco.[17] Caffi, who was writing around the middle of the nineteenth century, had an exceptionally good knowledge of documents from the previous century preserved in Venetian archives but was apt to elaborate fancifully on the information he derived from them. His statements must therefore be received with a degree of caution.

'Although his style lacked a certain finesse', Caffi wrote, 'it nevertheless met with much favour on account of its sinewy strength and popular quality.' And further on: 'Although his talent was smaller, he achieved greater success than his rival Gasparini.'

Concurrently with his operatic activity in Venice, Albinoni fulfilled commissions from theatres in other cities. The high points of this activity were the two operas he supplied to the Cocomero theatre of Florence in 1703 and the two for the Munich Hoftheater in 1722. He visited Florence and Munich at the invitation of their respective courts to attend these

---

[17] Venice, Biblioteca Nazionale Marciana, Cod. It. IV-747 (10465), fol. 39ʳ. Caffi's published history is the *Storia della musica sacra nella già cappella ducale di San Marco in Venezia dal 1318 al 1797* (2 vols., Venice, 1854–5).

productions. At various times he supplied scores also to Bologna, Brescia, Ferrara, Genoa, Piacenza, Prague, Rome, and Treviso, although it is not certain whether these operations took him away from Venice.

Into another category altogether come the forty-four known revivals of Albinoni operas both inside and outside Venice. On delivering their commissioned scores to operatic managements, composers effectively relinquished control over their subsequent use. For later productions the original score might be cut down, expanded, or rearranged by hands other than the composer's; choice arias might be extracted and used in pasticci, or patchwork operas stitched together from music by several composers. But however much Albinoni's music was altered for these new productions, and however little responsibility he had for these changes, the frequency with which his music was revived is an index of his reputation over a much wider area than that which he served directly through commissions. The earliest revival was a performance in Verona of his *L'ingratitudine gastigata* in 1701; his operas subsequently fanned out all over the Italian provinces. Even before 1710 his operatic music reached London, initially in the form of extracts appearing in pasticci but later extending to productions of his *Lucio Vero* at the King's Theatre in the Haymarket in 1715 and again in 1716. In the 1720s, after the Munich visit, his operas briefly enjoyed success north of the Alps in Prague, Breslau (Wrocław), Raudnitz (Roudnice), and Linz. There is some irony in the fact that during this period Albinoni, like Vivaldi, was able to conquer provincial and remote outposts of opera at the very time when his prestige was beginning to slip at home.

In a wide sense one may consider also as 'operatic' music Albinoni's comic intermezzi, represented by three known works. Such intermezzi were conceived as groups of between two and four linked comic scenes inserted for light relief into the interstices of the serious opera that they accompanied: preferably between the acts, but sometimes *faute de mieux* in the middle of one. Albinoni's intermezzi for the two characters Pimpinone and Vespetta, first performed with his *Astarto* in 1708, belong to the most successful examples from the first generation of comic intermezzi, being revived in association with different operas at least thirty times up to 1740. Sadly for the composer, however, they cannot have increased his reputation, since neither the many libretti nor the scores that have survived ever cite his name.

Three dramatic cantatas, or serenatas, by Albinoni are known. These were occasional compositions in operatic style generally commissioned by private individuals and performed in celebration of a joyful event such as a birthday or wedding. Their literary texts were not always published separately (even if they were, the composer was not always identified), and their scores have suffered an even higher rate of loss than those of contemporary operas, so the original total is likely to have been much higher. One work, *Il nome glorioso in terra, santificato in cielo*, was commissioned in 1724 by the Austrian ambassador to Venice to celebrate his Imperial master's name-day; an earlier serenata, *Il nascimento de l'Aurora*, celebrates the birthday of the emperor's wife Elisabeth Christine. The serenata *Il concilio de' pianeti* was written in 1729 for the French ambassador to Venice, in celebration of the birth of the dauphin. Earlier in the same decade it had been Vivaldi who supplied the French ambassador with occasional compositions; his absence from Venice in late 1729 may have given Albinoni this opportunity.

Albinoni's single known oratorio, *Maria annunziata*, which was performed by a Florentine religious confraternity in 1712, cannot represent a side of his activity recognized by contemporaries as important, but his forty-five or so extant chamber cantatas for solo voice were certainly regarded highly in some quarters during his lifetime. Such cantatas were an essential part of courtly life ('court' in the Italian context signifying a noble, not necessarily a royal, household); they were sung by professional singers in the service of the courts—very often the same singers appeared by permission of their employers on the operatic stage during the season—at private concerts attended by fashionable society. Judged by their style, Albinoni's cantatas all seem to date from the period 1695–1710, which is exactly the time when he had his closest links with Italian courts: in Rome, Mantua, and Florence. Twelve cantatas were published as his Op. 4 and dedicated to Francesco Maria de' Medici, brother of Grand Duke Cosimo III of Tuscany. Two of them became well known in England, where they were published with new texts in English paraphrasing the originals. The remainder are mostly preserved only in manuscript, either singly or in small groups. However, one very interesting manuscript in Berlin contains no fewer than eighteen cantatas for soprano by Albinoni, all in the same hand.[18] The copies were obviously prepared, probably with the co-operation of the composer himself, for a patron or collector who had a special fondness for the music of his cantatas.

In regard to instrumental music Albinoni depended for his reputation on his published collections to a quite unusual degree for an Italian composer (though Corelli provides a good precedent). Between 1694 and 1735 or 1736 nine 'authorized' collections, variously consisting of sonatas and concertos, were published—and a final collection of trio sonatas, Op. 11, may possibly have appeared around 1740, though this is uncertain. The nine collections, all containing 12 works, were each supplied with the

18 Berlin (West), Staatsbibliothek Preussischer Kulturbesitz, Mus. ms. 447.

appropriate opus number (leaving out Op. 4, belonging to the set of cantatas) and the customary dedication to a patron.

The quantity of these publications provides little evidence in itself of Albinoni's popularity, since all were probably subsidized by the composer, who will have hoped to recoup some of his costs from the dedicatee in the form of a valuable present. What speaks more eloquently for their reception is the frequency with which they were republished and the number of examples surviving today.

Opp. 1–5 were consigned to the most prominent local music printer, Giuseppe Sala. Rather unusually, all four instrumental collections in this group were reprinted by Sala. Op. 1 (1694) had a new edition in 1704, Op. 2 (1700) in 1702 and 1707, Op. 3 (1701) in 1704 and 1706, and Op. 5 (1707) in 1710. Since reprints were normally undertaken on the initiative of the publisher rather than the composer, their frequency testifies to the popularity of Albinoni's instrumental music in his native city during the first decade of the century.

All four collections were 'pirated' between 1697 and 1708 by the Amsterdam publisher Estienne Roger. Roger's engraved editions were both technically and aesthetically superior to the equivalent Italian editions printed, using a basically sixteenth-century technology, from movable type. Further, they were marketed more widely and efficiently, using an international network of agents. It was primarily through Roger that the sonatas and concertos of Albinoni and his fellow Italians reached the 'mass market' of northern Europe, where amateur music-making by the middle class as well as the gentry maintained a high level of demand.

The fact that Roger took these works is not itself very significant since during this period he was plundering the catalogues of Italian music printers (and especially Sala) wholesale. It is interesting however, that some time after 1722 Roger's successor Michel-Charles Le Cène issued a 'Nouvelle édition exactement corrigée' of Op. 5. Normally, engraved plates needed little more than the occasional retouching to remain serviceable over a period of several decades, so this new edition implies either that the original plates had been used so much as to become worn or that the concertos were so popular that it was worth the trouble to re-engrave them.

From Op. 6 (c. 1711) onwards Albinoni sent his works directly to Amsterdam for publication, following a trend general among Italian composers at the time (for instance, Vivaldi entrusted Roger with his Op. 3 concertos, L'estro armonico, also in 1711). Italian music publishers, whose industry was now in steep decline, made no attempt to practise reverse piracy, although as retailers they sometimes stocked Roger's publications.

However, Roger himself suffered piracy from competitors closer to home. In Amsterdam Pierre Mortier, who engaged Roger in a price war that Mortier eventually lost, published Albinoni's Opp. 3 and 5. In London, where Roger had an agent, he faced much greater and more sustained competition from John Walsh and his associates.

Walsh ventured very cautiously into the publication of Italian music. In 1702 he published extracts from Albinoni's Op. 3 *Balletti da camera a tre*, anglicizing the description of the works to 'Aires'. In 1704 he began a periodical publication, issuing to subscribers each month two (later three) Italian or italianate instrumental works, one of which was generally a 'solo' sonata for violin, while the other was a work for larger forces. The 'Instrumental Music for May' included the twelfth trio sonata in Albinoni's Op. 1, which was perhaps deemed especially attractive to English buyers on account of the ground-bass structure of its opening movement. In 1707 this work was reissued from the same plates, together with five other sonatas by different composers (including Purcell's so-called 'Golden Sonata'), as the anthology *Harmonia Mundi . . . the First Collection*.

The 'Instrumental Music for July' published in the 1704 series included a 'Sonata Concerto Grosse for Violins in 5, 6, and 7 Parts' by Albinoni. The garbled nomenclature reflects the fact that this composition was the first concerto by any author ever published in Britain. It was in fact the last concerto of Op. 2. In 1709 Walsh engraved the remaining five concertos in the set and published all six together; he omitted, however, the complementary group of six sonatas (also described as 'sinfonias') included in the original print. In the decades that followed Walsh issued the complete Op. 3, the sonatas of Op. 6, and selected concertos from Opp. 5 and 7.

Albinoni's first six collections must have sold extremely well. The number of examples for each of the two most popular sets, Opp. 3 and 5, preserved in libraries in Europe and North America runs to over twenty, taking into account all contemporary editions. This figure does not include the many manuscript copies of entire sets that are extant. Opp. 7–10 seem to have sold less well—indeed, no example of Op. 10 came to light in modern times until the 1960s. Part of the reason for the lower sales may have been the sheer bulk of the editions, a result of the greater average length of movements. Significantly, from Op. 7 (1715) onwards Albinoni followed a common practice of the time by dividing his concerto collections into two separate *libri*, each containing six works.

Parallel with the authorized series of publications ran an unauthorized one. In the early eighteenth century it became highly profitable for the first time to publish music, at least in such fashionable genres as the sonata and concerto. Publishers therefore had a motive for seeking out works by the most popular composers of the day to add to their catalogues without waiting for those composers to approach them first. One method, as we have seen, was piracy; but the point was soon reached when everything that was worth pirating had already been exploited. Further, it sometimes happened, particularly in France, that importers of music protected their wares through a royal privilege. And in any case, the sales of a pirated work were likely to be adversely affected by competition with the original, as Mortier had found.

Previously unpublished works were therefore at a premium. The most likely source for these lay in manuscripts containing works that had originally been put into circulation by the composers themselves, or perhaps by professional copyists, in fulfilment of private commissions. In the course of the transmission of these works knowledge of their authorship frequently became lost, and sometimes the names of well-known composers were added—or substituted—with varying degrees of inno-cence. Very often, too, compositions in manuscript formed sets containing fewer than the six or twelve works that were almost mandatory for a published collection.

Three collections of violin sonatas attributed to Albinoni illustrate the complexities of this situation. The first was a set of six so-called *Sonate da chiesa* brought out by Roger in 1708. Later issues of this set have the legend 'Opera quarta' inserted on the title-page—Roger was able to make this spurious identification since he had not republished the Op. 4 cantatas. Five of the sonatas are wholly Albinonian in style, though their lack of polish is typical of works written hurriedly for a specific commission and not intended by their composer for publication. The fourth sonata, however, differs from all the others in musical and notational style. In all probability it is a makeweight added to complete the half-dozen and has nothing to do with Albinoni. The collection was pirated by Walsh in 1710.

In 1717 Roger brought out under the imprint of his daughter Jeanne another set of violin pieces entitled *Sonate a violino solo e basso continuo . . . e uno suario o capriccio . . . del Sig. Tibaldi*. The final work in this collection was a set of variations, the 'Suario o capriccio' by the Modenese composer Giovanni Battista Tibaldi, the preceding five sonatas being attributed to Albinoni. But, here again, one work is anomalous in style—the fifth. Very likely, this is another unauthentic piece.

Finally, in *c.* 1740 the Parisian engraver Louis Hue published a set entitled *Six Sonates da camera* which he termed, very prematurely, the composer's 'Œuvre postume'. Two sonatas are undoubtedly genuine, but the remaining four (two of which may alternatively be played on the flute) are almost certainly by another composer. Further unauthentic works appeared under Albinoni's name in published anthologies—for instance the two concertos in Walsh's *Harmonia Mundi: The 2^d Collection* (1728).

The traffic in misattribution was not one-way, however, for as we shall see in Chapter 4, some early five-part balletti by Albinoni were published quite independently by Roger and Walsh in 1702 under the name of Ziani (presumably Marc'Antonio Ziani, deputy *maestro di cappella* to the Emperor).

Two genuine works by Albinoni are known to have been published without mention of their authorship. One was a sinfonia (*Si* 4) borrowed for the pasticcio *Cresco* (*Croesus*), which was performed at the Haymarket in 1714; Walsh included it in his *Six Overtures for Violins* (*c.* 1724). The other was a sinfonia-like composition (*Si* 3a) published by Roger in an anthology, *VI Sonates ou concerts à 4, 5 & 6 parties*, dating from *c.* 1710.

In a way, the unauthorized publications with their spurious attributions confirm Albinoni's leading position among composers of sonatas and concertos more eloquently than the authorized ones. They show that even towards the end of his life he retained a core of admirers, at least in northern Europe. Two contemporary English collectors of music, Frederick Ashfield and Charles Jennens, are known from sale catalogues of their libraries to have possessed virtually the entire series of his published works. The same is true of Nicolaas Selhof, bookseller at the Hague, whose music stock was sold at auction in 1759.[19]

From the relatively meagre amount of instrumental music by Albinoni that has come down to us only in manuscript form, it can be deduced that, unlike Vivaldi, he did not conduct a lively trade with private customers. The great majority of the manuscript compositions are early works from before 1700, linked by circumstantial evidence to his association at the time with the Mantuan court. Into this category come twenty-six works preserved among the Este manuscripts of the Österreichische National-bibliothek, Vienna, and a few further works in Oxford and Durham. The Sächsische Landesbibliothek contains three violin sonatas in Albinoni's own hand that were brought back from Venice by Pisendel in 1717 and miscellaneous sinfonias and concertos, some of which were copied into score by Pisendel during his Venetian sojourn, while others may have been acquired independently by the Dresden orchestra. Most of the few remaining compositions in manuscript, excluding concordances of works already mentioned, are today held by Swedish libraries in Stockholm, Uppsala, and Lund.

[19] On Selhof and the auction of his estate see Michael Talbot, 'Vivaldi in the Sale Catalogue of Nicolaas Selhof', *Informazioni e studi vivaldiani*, 6 (1985), 57–63.

For reasons that will be discussed further on, Albinoni's music was never a favourite vehicle for virtuoso performers. The composer himself did not tour as a violinist, though Zeno and Mattheson confirm that he was willing enough to undertake the normal duty of an opera composer to officiate, instrument in hand, on the first night. The *Post Man* of 22 August 1704, advertising the 'Sonata Concerto Grosse' mentioned earlier, reported its performance by the Cremonese violinist Gasparo Visconti at an unidentified London theatre. Pisendel certainly performed his concertos in Dresden, and the violinist Stefano Carbonelli, leader of Handel's opera orchestra, played a 'new concerto by Albinoni, just brought over' (almost certainly one of the Op. 9 concertos) at the Drury Lane theatre on 4 May 1722.[20] Roger Brown, the copyist of Telemann's *Pimpinone* (not to be confused with Albinoni's own setting of the original version of the same libretto seventeen years earlier), specified two concertos from Albinoni's Op. 9 as introductory and concluding music for the second intermezzo. But no Albinoni concerto was ever programmed at the Parisian Concert Spirituel, and we hear of no performances by violinists on the level of Veracini, Vivaldi, or Geminiani.

It seems that a modest market for manuscripts of Albinoni's music outlived him by a few decades. The Breitkopf catalogues issued in the 1760s list a few not very representative works that include, ironically, *Co* 1, a very primitive concerto that had already been in existence for over sixty years.

Taken as a whole, Albinoni's instrumental compositions made their greatest impact in the first decade of the eighteenth century. This was precisely the period when their style and form were freshest and most forward-looking. Interest in them within Italy seems to have started to decline at the point when their publication in that country ceased. Their cultivation north of the Alps held up well during the next decade but began to slacken in the 1720s. In fact, Albinoni remained fashionable as an opera composer for some years after his prestige had waned in the instrumental sphere. Making the same comparison in a different way, one can say that in Italy he was known and valued in his lifetime mostly for his operas, whereas in northern Europe he was appreciated more for his instrumental works.

This difference of focus comes out clearly in the critical evaluation of Albinoni in the half-century following his death. Up to Gerber (1790), if not beyond, commentators were able to base at least a part of their remarks

[20] Information from Edmund van der Straeten, *The Romance of the Fiddle: The Origin of the Modern Virtuoso and the Adventures of his Ancestors* (London, 1911), 196.

on information acquired during the composer's lifetime, sometimes at first hand.

We saw at the start of this chapter that Hawkins, writing in 1776, had a very favourable opinion of Albinoni, about whom an unidentified person who knew the composer personally had given him information. Hawkins singles out for comment the *Balletti a tre* of Op. 3, which, he says, 'at length became so familiar in England, that many of the common fiddlers were able to play them'. This observation is borne out by the frequency with which tutors and simple anthologies such as Walsh's *Select Preludes & Vollentarys for the Violin* (1705), Cluer's *Medulla Musicae* (1727), and Prelleur's *The Modern Music Master* (1731) delved into this collection, although the form in which the movements emerged—reduced to one or two parts and severely truncated—would have horrified their creator.

Charles Burney mentions Albinoni cursorily at various points in his *General History of Music*, but his most interesting comments come in the fourth volume (1789), where he speaks of the composer as 'well known in England about forty or fifty years ago, by some light and easy concertos for violins'.[21]

This description of the concertos as 'light and easy' merits discussion in the perspective of the apparent reluctance of the leading violin virtuosi of Albinoni's time to take his concertos into their repertory and, equally, of Hawkins's remarks on the 'familiarity' of the *Balletti a tre*. The truth is that whereas Albinoni's first collection of concertos (in Op. 2, published in 1700) represented, for both solo and orchestral players, the 'state of the art' in Italian writing for strings, successive collections lagged ever more behind contemporary technical developments. By Op. 7 (1715) Albinoni is markedly less demanding than Vivaldi; by Op. 10 (1735 or 1736) he struggles even to retain contact with the violinistic level of Tartini and Locatelli. By the same token, however, the relatively low technical demands of Albinoni's concertos made the perfect material for local and amateur orchestras, leading to their exceptionally wide diffusion in northern Europe.

In Jean-Benjamin Laborde's *Essai sur la musique ancienne et moderne* (1780) we meet the first adversely critical observations on Albinoni's style. Laborde first described the composer as 'habile' (able) but then goes on to write that in the judgement of musical experts his style lacks 'aisance' (facility).[22] What this means is perhaps that although Albinoni has mastered the elements of composition well, his music lacks a certain quality of

[21] Charles Burney, *A General History of Music from the Earliest Ages to the Present Period* (4 vols., London, 1776–89), iv. 77.

[22] Jean-Benjamin Laborde, *Essai sur la musique ancienne et moderne* (4 vols., Paris, 1780), iii. 162.

naturalness or gratefulness. Laborde's rather vaguely expressed reservation becomes the starting-point for a long tradition of more finely tuned criticism from later commentators. Another remark by Laborde—that Albinoni was more successful in the composition of operas than in that of church music—also becomes a favourite motif later on.

Esteban de Arteaga has an interesting brief mention of Albinoni in the second volume (1785) of his history of opera, including him among a small group of Italian musicians (the other names are Gaetano Greco, Antonio Caldara, Giovanni Bononcini, and Pietro Sandoni) who 'upheld with such dignity the glory of the Italian name in England amid all the stir that the compositions of Handel had deservedly raised in that island'.[23] Until very recently, when the prominence of Albinoni's music in the operatic productions of the 1710s in London became evident, this remark seemed enigmatic.

The entry for Albinoni in Ernst Ludwig Gerber's original *Lexicon* of 1790–2 (its sequel, the *Neues historisch-biographisches Lexicon der Tonkünstler* of 1812, does not concern us here) synthesizes the accounts of Walther and Laborde. The two remarks of Laborde already quoted are fleshed out and rather surprisingly brought into relation with one another to become: 'Connoisseurs claimed to find something stiff and dry in his manner of writing. This being so, it is all the more surprising that he worked exclusively for the theatre since he had no success with the church style.'[24]

A further elaboration of this commentary occurs in the history of Italian music by Count Grigori Orlov (1822), where we read:

But it must be said—the style of this composer is suited, on account of its gravity and slowness, more to church music than to that for the theatre; and through one of those contradictions that are no less common among artists than among less enlightened and philosophical men, he unswervingly preferred the second of those genres to the first; nevertheless, despite the severity and dryness of this style, redeemed as it was by science and neatness, most of Albinoni's operas were successful.[25]

The first report of substance on the character of Albinoni's music is that by the Belgian scholar François-Joseph Fétis in the first volume of his pioneering biographical dictionary. Fétis had the considerable advantage of possessing a little music by Albinoni, including the score of several arias from the opera *L'inganno innocente* (inherited after his death by the library

---

[23] Stefano Arteaga, *Le rivoluzioni del teatro musicale italiano* (3 vols., Bologna and Venice, 1783–8), ii (Venice edn.), 18.

[24] Ernst Ludwig Gerber, *Historisch-biographisches Lexicon der Tonkünstler* (2 vols., Leipzig, 1790–2), i, art. 'Albinoni (Thomas)'.

[25] Grégoire Orloff, *Essai sur l'histoire de la musique en Italie* (2 vols., Paris, 1822), ii. 295–6.

of the Brussels Conservatoire). Notwithstanding his direct access to the music, Fétis picks up with disappointing alacrity a theme already developed to excess by Laborde and his followers. 'Regarding the quality of his works', Fétis writes, 'my examination of some of his scores has shown me that his style is dry, his ideas dull or trivial, and the expression of the words in most of his operas almost nil.' But Fétis continues in a happier vein: 'Albinoni also wrote much instrumental music. He showed a greater gift for this type of music than for opera; one notes in his sonatas, and especially in his *Balletti da camera*, a certain charm and a solid workmanship that Corelli would not have disavowed.'[26]

The criticism of Albinoni's word-setting, which needs to be viewed in the context of the attitudes and usages prevalent in the Italy of his time, will be examined later. It is pleasing to see that two of the positive qualities recognized in the instrumental works by more recent commentators— melodic charm and structural cogency—already receive commendation from Fétis, although the clear distinction drawn between the relative merits of Albinoni's vocal and instrumental music may have served to prejudice future attitudes.

From the same year as the first volume of Fétis's *Biographie universelle* (1835) comes that of Gustav Schilling's *Universal-Lexicon der Tonkunst*. The facts in Schilling's account are drawn in the main from Gerber, except for a splendid *gaffe* that identifies *Gasparini* as one of Albinoni's operas. Schilling's final evaluation of the composer departs, however, from the heavily qualified approval of earlier critics to become an overblown paean of praise to Albinoni as a representative of the Protestant ethic: 'Thus Albinoni was not only fertile in invention and ideas but also great and possessed of genius in his art, and unremittingly active, indefatigable in his labours'.[27]

Some of this silliness lingers on in Hermann Mendel's *Musikalisches Conversations-Lexicon* of 1870.[28] It is typical of the superficial approach of such writers that Mendel ventures to describe *Didone abbandonata* as the best of Albinoni's operas—without, of course, having seen any of its music. Perhaps he thought that Metastasio's verse would inevitably have inspired Albinoni to unprecedented heights, or that the opera's productions north of the Alps were in themselves evidence of its high quality. Mendel records that, in addition to the familiar *Balletti*, Albinoni's 'VI sonate a violino solo con basso continuo' (probably to be identified with the unauthorized publication of 1708) were universally known and loved in Germany in

---

[26] Loc. cit.
[27] Gustav Schilling, *Universal-Lexicon der Tonkunst* (6 vols., Stuttgart, 1835–8), i. 127.
[28] Hermann Mendel, *Musikalisches Conversations-Lexicon* (Berlin, 1870), art. 'Albinoni, Tommaso'.

former times. It is impossible to tell whether this is a mere inference or stems from some unknown source of information.

A German scholar of more solid musicological foundations, Wilhelm Joseph von Wasielewski, brings Albinoni down to earth again in his influential historical study of violin music first published in 1869. Wasielewski belongs to a group of German scholars active in the second half of the nineteenth century who were strongly influenced by nationalist sentiment. Regarding Bach and Handel as the two seas into which all rivers flowed, such critics as Wasielewski, Rühlmann, Waldersee, and Spitta treated the immediate Italian predecessors of the two German masters in a very particular way. On one hand, they could not deny a certain merit, even an exemplary quality, to Albinoni and Vivaldi, since otherwise Bach would have wasted his time studying, transcribing, and borrowing themes from their works; on the other hand, their workmanlike virtues had to be distinguished from the creative genius of the German.

Nodding in the direction of the Protestant ethic again, Wasielewski first acknowledges the 'serious, thorough study' informing Albinoni's work and assesses his skill in manipulating form as second to none among his contemporaries. Then come the hammer blows: 'Albinoni's music is characterized by the most arid philistinism. He hardly ever manages even momentarily to rise above empty formal schematicism, but rather revels in it. Instead of melodic ideas we mostly find empty figuration, with which his allegro movements are copiously supplied, while adagios almost invariably occupy him only fleetingly.'[29]

Nationalistic bias apart, Wasielewski's failing lies more in evaluation than in observation. He unreasonably denies virtuosic passage-work its fundamental rôle in the emergence of the early concerto. It is also easy to see how the first generation of German musicologists were baffled by the un-Bachian lean textures and plain melodic lines of the slow movements (Rühlmann even thought that the orchestral musicians might have been expected to improvise middle parts!).

In his great study of Bach's life and works, first published in 1873, Philip Spitta notes his subject's special fondness for Albinoni's music. He mentions the keyboard realization of the continuo part of the violin sonata Op. 6 no. 6 prepared under Bach's supervision by his pupil Heinrich Nikolaus Gerber, father of the lexicographer; the manuscript, which contains corrections in Bach's hand, is preserved in the Deutsche Staatsbibliothek, East Berlin.[30] Unknown to Spitta but supportive of his case is a continuo

[29] Wilhelm Joseph von Wasielewski, *Die Violine und ihre Meister* (4th edn., Leipzig, 1904), 112.
[30] Philipp Spitta, *Johann Sebastian Bach* (2 vols., Leipzig. 1873–80), ii. supplement (*Beilage*) 1.

part for the second concerto of Op. 2 in Bach's hand today belonging to the Manfred Gorke collection of the Musikbibliothek der Stadt Leipzig.

Spitta discusses at considerable length two keyboard fugues that Bach based on subjects from Albinoni's Op. 1: BWV 950, based on the second movement of Op. 1 no. 3 in A major, and BWV 951a (in a later version, BWV 951), based on the second movement of Op. 1 no. 8 in B minor (he missed, however, the identification of the subject of a Bach fugue in C major, BWV 946, with that of the fourth movement of Albinoni's Op. 1 no. 12 in B flat major).[31] Comparing the originals with their Bachian counterparts, Spitta finds them deficient in development and not always free from triviality in their episodes. Once again, this criticism lacks contextual awareness. After all, Albinoni was writing the movements under discussion not as 'fugues' intended to stand on their own and exemplify fugal processes in a self-conscious manner but as moderately proportioned fast movements within a four-movement cycle.

The first critical examination of Albinoni's instrumental music in Italian musicography (for Caffi, and before him Emmanuele Antonio Cicogna, had been concerned mainly with biographical matters) was undertaken by Luigi Torchi in his famous long essay on Italian instrumental music from the sixteenth to the eighteenth century published at the turn of the present century in successive volumes of the *Rivista musicale italiana*. Torchi represents to a striking degree the once fashionable 'evolutionary' approach to music history in which what is good in music is equated *tout court* with what seems to look forward to future developments. This view admits only with great difficulty the concept of a composer as 'good but conservative'. Torchi has rightly been criticized for the superficiality of some of his investigations and the capriciousness of some of his conclusions, and it seems that he did not take much account of music that did not happen to be available for inspection at close hand in the Liceo Musicale (today the Civico Museo Bibliografico Musicale) of Bologna.

Discussing Albinoni alongside three contemporary minor composers— Giuseppe Aldrovandini, Francesco Manfredini, and Artemio Motta— Torchi finds fault with the predilection of each for 'abstract' (i.e. non-melodic) figuration, for sequences, and for conventional devices such as the measured tremolo. Echoing Wasielewski once more, he chides Albinoni and his colleagues for their neglect of the Adagio. This harshness corresponds to Torchi's view of the period around 1700 as one of decadence in Italian music, which only the arrival of Vivaldi, Veracini, Locatelli, and Tartini will regenerate. It is symptomatic of Torchi's unilinear concept of musical progress that he singles out for grudging approval a binary-form

[31] Ibid. 424.

finale in Albinoni's Op. 2 (to be honest, a rather over-brief and trivial movement) in order to use it as a stick with which to beat the mosaic-like or through-composed movements typical of the time.[32]

The four pages devoted to Albinoni's concertos in Arnold Schering's influential history of the genre first published in 1905 mark the beginning of well-informed analytical criticism of his music.[33] Schering is the meeting-point of the critical worlds of the nineteenth and twentieth centuries. He does not completely escape from the sterile terms of the debate about Albinoni's music inaugurated by Laborde but more than compensates by laying a fresh groundwork on which later commentators can build. For example, he is the first to note the rhythmic pregnancy of Albinoni's opening themes and their indebtedness to operatic style. Much of Schering's discussion is analytical in the narrow sense and does not concern us here, but one sentence will suffice to show how far Albinoni's rehabilitation goes in Schering's eyes: 'It [Op. 5] contains in its final movements masterpieces of fugal writing in five parts, and in its opening movements so much excellent and euphonious counterpoint that one well understands why Bach was drawn for a time to Albinoni.'

Briefer, but almost as perceptive, are Eugen Schmitz's comments on Albinoni's cantatas in his study of that genre, a companion volume to that of Schering. Schmitz finds Albinoni's recitatives dry and stereotyped but praises the melodic invention of his arias, which he finds predominantly elegiac in tone.[34]

It was during this period that modern editions of Albinoni's music began to appear. The first such edition was one by Alfred Moffat of the first work in the second unauthorized collection of violin sonatas; this was published c. 1909. In 1928–9 Nagels Archiv introduced three violin sonatas from Op. 6 and one trio sonata from Op. 1. In 1930 there appeared the first concerto—the work identified as Co 2 that has already been discussed in connection with Quantz—from the Berlin publisher Vieweg. Significantly, all these were instrumental works. Until the 1970s the stimulation of scholarly interest in Albinoni's instrumental music through the publication and performance of instrumental works—and its converse, the stimulation of performers' interest in the instrumental music through its recommendation in scholarly literature—conspired to keep the cantatas, serenatas, and operatic music well hidden.

In Andreas Moser's history of violin-playing (1923) the enthusiasm

[32] Luigi Torchi, 'L'arte musicale in Italia nei secoli XVI, XVII e XVIII: IX', *Rivista musicale italiana*, 6 (1899), 261–88.

[33] Arnold Schering, *Geschichte des Instrumentalkonzerts* (Leipzig, 1905), 73–7.

[34] Eugen Schmitz, *Geschichte der weltlichen Solokantate* (Leipzig, 1914), 150–1.

shown by Schering for the concertos is carried over into the domain of the sonatas. Like his predecessor, Moser is a campaigning scholar whose lavish praise for individual works reads like an imploration to publish and perform. It is notable that Moser regards the sonatas and balletti of Albinoni's Op. 8 as his most significant collection, though one is amused at his mention of their 'many quite masterly canons and fugues', which hints at a far too automatic respect for academic counterpoint.[35]

The next substantial contribution to Albinoni criticism was Remo Giazotto's major study of the composer's life and works, completed under very unfavourable conditions during the Second World War and published in 1945. The impact of this book obviously cannot be summed up adequately in one paragraph, but a distinction must be made between the value of its biographical, analytical, and critical parts. The biography introduced a wealth of new facts based on documentary evidence; although several details have needed to be corrected and much new evidence has come to light since 1945, it has deservedly remained the central repository of facts on Albinoni's life. The analysis, though rather pedestrian, is useful, even if spoilt by a failure to weed out obviously unauthentic compositions. The criticism, however, is disfigured by a rhetorical excess and a degree of pointless abstraction that must perplex even the Italian reader, long inured to these tendencies. What is one to make of a paragraph like the following, which forms part of Giazotto's final summing-up?

Albinoni, the Venetian, roams broad-winged over the musical horizons of the eighteenth century. Composed and dignified, he alternately swoops down and soars up; the first action enables him to search on the ground for his daily nourishment, which will give him the fresh strength that will then carry him up towards the highest peaks, whence he will gaze with his razor-sharp eyes into the furthest distances. On the ground he finds true substance and a sure source of regeneration: Corellian substance; reality. And up on high, towards the sky, there resides the unknown, the untried, the beckoning call of things that have never been seen before; distant, ever so distant spectacles, full of mystery and romantic temptation.[36]

For all its exaggerations, Giazotto's advocacy placed Albinoni once and for all in the central area of the map of late baroque Italian music. It inspired Marc Pincherle, who had earlier reviewed Giazotto's book, to devote considerable space to a comparison between Albinoni and his more eminent Venetian contemporary in his great study *Antonio Vivaldi et la*

---

[35] Andreas Moser, *Geschichte des Violinspiels* (Berlin, 1923), 78–9.

[36] Remo Giazotto, *Tomaso Albinoni: 'Musico di violino dilettante veneto' (1671–1750)* (Milan, 1945), 299.

musique instrumentale (1948). Developing a point made less forcefully by Schering, Pincherle portrays Albinoni as a composer who exerted an important formative influence on Vivaldi and was in turn influenced by him, although somewhat hindered in this by a natural conservatism and a less bountiful imagination.[37] Albinoni is turned into the 'second string', as it were, of the Venetian team.

The musical twinning of Albinoni and Vivaldi becomes a constant feature from now on. William S. Newman wrote an important article in 1952 in which he compared the sonatas of both men.[38] One ironic aspect of this article is that by mistranslating a sentence of Giazotto in which Vivaldi was held 'to surpass Albinoni in the frequency of what are today defined as romantic emotions' so that the position of the two composers was reversed, Newman was led to justify and exemplify this difficult thesis. Unfortunately, his principal piece of evidence, the rhapsodic third movement of the fifth sonata in the unauthorized 1717 set (*So* 39), is most probably not by Albinoni.

Undoubtedly the most influential advocate of Albinoni's music in the English-speaking countries has been Arthur Hutchings, whose book *The Baroque Concerto* discusses him in the context of a Venetian 'school' comprising not only Vivaldi and Albinoni but also the two Marcello brothers, Alessandro and Benedetto. Hutchings regards Albinoni as 'ridiculously undervalued', and in lively prose that is often provocatively assertive (the quotation heading this chapter is typical) seeks to win over his readers to the cause. His persuasiveness is increased by detailed and uncommonly perceptive reference to the music.

The favourable climate induced by the studies of Giazotto and Hutchings, and secured at a less exalted level by the extraordinary success of the Adagio in G minor, stimulated the publication and performance of Albinoni's music (still, however, primarily the instrumental music) during the 1960s and 1970s. What progress has been made can be judged from the discussion of modern publications in appendix B.

The equilibrium that Albinoni's reputation has experienced over the last twenty-five years has had the effect of directing the attention of scholars towards the question of his historical position and the finer details of his style and away from questions of aesthetic value and musical importance. This trend is clearly seen in the fine survey of his concertos and sonatas contained in the chapter devoted to him in Eleanor Selfridge-Field's

---

[37] Marc Pincherle, *Antonio Vivaldi et la musique instrumentale* (2 vols., Paris, 1948), i. 228–9.

[38] William S. Newman, 'The Sonatas of Albinoni and Vivaldi', *Journal of the American Musicological Society*, 5 (1952), 99–113. In condensed form much of the material in this article reappears in the same author's *The Sonata in the Baroque Era* (Chapel Hill, 1959).

Venetian Instrumental Music from Gabrieli to Vivaldi. [39] Even Carlo Guaita's recent dissertation on the cantatas rarely poses the question: 'How good?'[40]

To a certain extent, my own writings on Albinoni during the same period have put forward a 'revisionist' thesis that the present book attempts to continue and refine. I remain mindful of the need to guard against what Adorno cruelly but accurately termed the 'Kleinmeister-compulsion'—the temptation to build up relatively minor composers to a level where it seems that their achievement challenges that of a Bach or a Handel. Although I consider that Albinoni wrote much excellent and original music that fully deserves a place in modern concert life, I feel that it is no less important to point out his limitations and to differentiate scrupulously between his stronger and weaker works. Much of his best music is not instrumental but vocal, so my most energetic advocacy will be reserved for work in the second category.

Albinoni's originality as a composer is rooted in the very untypical circumstances of his life, to which we turn next.

[39] Eleanor Selfridge-Field, *Venetian Music from Gabrieli to Vivaldi* (Oxford, 1975).

[40] Carlo Guaita, 'Le cantate di Tomaso Albinoni (1671–1751): Studio storico-critico e bibliografico', dissertation (University of Milan, 1986).

2

LIFE AND CAREER

THE members of the Albinoni clan resident in Venice from the second half of the sixteenth century, if not earlier, were all immigrants originating from Castione della Presolana near Bergamo, in the north-western corner of the Venetian state. Many of the Venetian Albinonis retained links with their place of origin through their inheritance of landed property.[1]

Already by the early years of the seventeenth century the Venetian members of the clan had divided into different branches that increasingly moved apart from each another, so that it soon becomes impossible to speak any longer of a single Albinoni family. In the parish of San Zaccaria there were spicers; in San Canciano and Santa Maria Nova there were mercers; in Santa Maria Formosa, ironmongers. Yet other Albinonis traded in luxury goods and attempted to move up the social scale into the Venetian citizenry (to use this term in its narrow, legal sense).

Tomaso Albinoni, however, belonged to a branch of the Albinonis that had settled in the capital only one generation earlier. His father Giovanni Antonio (c. 1634–1709), later known more simply as Antonio, came to Venice in his youth together with a brother, Ardengo. The latter became a pasta-maker, while Antonio became around 1651 an apprentice in a stationery business owned by the widow Angela Pasinato née Mina. Angela's son Bartolomeo committed suicide in 1667, leaving her without natural heirs. As a result Antonio, who had served her loyally and efficiently, became a kind of adoptive son. He was the principal beneficiary of her will, drawn up on 19 October 1671. On her death in 1684 he inherited her shop, which included a workshop in which playing cards were manufactured, together with all the tools and stock. He retained the shop-sign (a diamond) of his benefactress and carried on her business very successfully.

Another beneficiary of Angela Pasinato's will was Antonio's wife Lucrezia (c. 1645–87), daughter of the bootmaker Stefano Fabris. Their marriage, which had been celebrated in 1668, produced eight children.

---

[1] Most of the biographical details in the present chapter already appear with appropriate reference to documentary evidence (often supported by reproductions or transcriptions) either in Remo Giazotto's book *Tomaso Albinoni* or in Gastone Vio's article 'Per una migliore conoscenza di Tomaso Albinoni: documenti d'archivio' (*Recercare*, i. 1988, forthcoming). In order to keep footnotes to a reasonable number, I will cite primary sources only where they provide information not given in either of these two works.

Three sons survived into adulthood: Tomaso (named after Antonio's father), born on 8 June 1671, Domenico (1675–1726), and Giovanni (1679–1718); a fourth, Giovanni Pietro (born 1686), died early.[2] Of the four daughters, the first-born, Margherita (born 1670), was no longer alive at the time when Antonio drew up his own will on 16 November 1705, but this will mentions two married daughters, Angeletta (born 1673) and Giustina (born 1677), and an unmarried daughter, Caterina (born 1680).

Although his wealth was acquired suddenly and providentially, it would be misleading to term Antonio Albinoni a 'nouveau riche'. True, he became wealthy enough to dower each of his daughters with 5,000 ducats (twelve-and-a-half times the annual stipend of the *primo maestro* at San Marco), but his will shows him to have remained a man of sober habits who was prudent in his affairs and punctilious in his religious observance. Touchingly, Antonio refers many times in his will to the generosity of Angela Pasinato, as if to disclaim all personal credit for his good fortune.

However, Antonio could not avoid being faced with a dilemma familiar to successful tradesmen: how to allow one's children to enjoy the benefits of a rise in family income, in particular through educational opportunity, while at the same time ensuring the continuance of the business in family hands.

Tomaso, the first-born, was marked out initially as his father's successor. Following the traditional pattern, he became first an apprentice (*garzon*), then a master (*maestro*). As a master in his own right he held and exploited the licence to manufacture packs of playing cards with his name printed on the Two of Spades.

Nevertheless, Tomaso was able at the same time to receive musical training with the apparent blessing of his family. Caffi informs us, no doubt on good authority, that he first learnt the violin, then turned his attention to singing, and finally studied composition (which this historian, following older usage, calls 'counterpoint').[3] There is no information on Tomaso's teachers. It has been suggested that Giovanni Legrenzi, *primo maestro* at San Marco from 1685 until his death in 1690, was one of his teachers, but this is an inference unsupported by firm evidence. It is interesting to note, however, that Legrenzi's birthplace, Clusone, lies very close to the ancestral home of the Albinonis, Castione della Presolana; their common

---

[2] Venetian given names and surnames normally exist in both dialectal and Tuscan forms. This explains variations such as Tomaso (Venetian) and Tommaso (Tuscan), Anzoleta (Venetian) and Angeletta (Tuscan), Zuane (Venetian) and Giovanni (Tuscan), Dolfin (Venetian) and Delfino (Tuscan). For practical convenience I will give names in only one form, Venetian or Tuscan as seems most appropriate.

[3] Venice, Biblioteca Nazionale Marciana, Cod. It. IV-747 (10465), fol. 39ʳ.

Bergamask origin might well have brought the old maestro and the young learner together.

The tradition recorded by Laborde that Tomaso's first, unsuccessful, essays in composition took the form of sacred vocal music receives support from a single surviving composition in this genre: a short a cappella Mass for two tenors and bass.[4] There is no absolute certainty of this work's authenticity, but it leaves a strong impression of immaturity, besides providing a good measure of the dryness and stiffness for which, as we saw, Albinoni was chided by his first critics.

Meanwhile, Domenico, the second son, received a thorough academic education that earned him a doctorate (probably in civil law) and the status of 'citizen'. In the dedication of his Op. 1 (1694) Tomaso refers to a unnamed brother in the service of the Ottoboni family in Rome. This must be Domenico, whom the nineteenth-century historian Cicogna identifies as an honorary page of Anna Maria Ottoboni (wife of the Venetian nobleman Antonio Ottoboni and mother of Cardinal Pietro Ottoboni) and the author of a volume of *Poesie divise in rime eroiche, morali, sacre, ed amorose*, published in Venice in 1707.[5] It is evident from Antonio's will and the subsequent fortunes of the family that Domenico's status precluded his direct involvement in the business, although the will reserves for him a general supervisory role after Antonio's death.

By 1705 Tomaso had clearly given up—or been forced by his father to give up—his activity as a 'maker of cards' (to use Hawkins's expression). The terms of the will exclude him from inheriting his father's stationery shop in the Frezzaria (a principal Venetian shopping street, in the San Moisè parish not far from the Piazza San Marco), the adjoining shop rented out to a tailor, or the first-floor and second-floor apartments above them. Nor is he to occupy the family's house and estate in Prata di Pordenone on the mainland without his two brothers' permission. His share consists solely of the premises of another shop in the Frezzaria (occupied by a wigmaker) and a third of the income from the stationery business. Giovanni is to take over the stationery shop and the management of the business with Domenico as adviser; he also inherits the first-floor flat. Domenico's portion is the tailor's shop and the second-floor flat. The two younger brothers are likewise entitled to a third of the proceeds of the business, and there are elaborate provisions in the will for 'buying out' the interest of any of the brothers.

Further evidence of Tomaso's neglect of his trade is found in the files of

---

[4] Venice, Biblioteca Nazionale Marciana, Cod. It. IV-1336 (11616).

[5] Giovanni Maria Mazzuchelli, *Gli scrittori d'Italia* (2 vols., Brescia, 1753–63), i/1. 335; also Emmanuele Antonio Cicogna, *Delle inscrizioni veneziani* (6 vols., Venice, 1826–53), ii. 171. The volume of poetry by Domenico remains untraced.

the state magistracy known as the Giustizia Vecchia. In 1708 the head of the guild representing painters and stationers in Venice (*Arte dei Depentori*) brought an action against Antonio Albinoni for non-payment of his dues in respect of an apprentice (presumably Giovanni) and two workers; worse still, Tomaso had not yet paid his initial membership fee of five ducats although he had practised as a *maestro* for several years. After a protest from Antonio that Tomaso had retired altogether from active involvement in the manufacture of cards the second complaint was resolved by making Giovanni officially *maestro* in place of Tomaso.

Before returning to the eldest son's real career, it will be interesting to trace briefly the fortunes of the business after Antonio's death on 23 January 1709. It seems that under Giovanni's stewardship it fell into decline, acquiring bad debts in the Aegean islands whose recovery may have been impeded by Venice's war against the Ottoman Empire (1714–18). Giovanni's death in 1718 removed the only member of the family intimately involved with the business. On 28 July 1721 a former creditor of Antonio, Zorzi Stamatello, became the legal owner of the three shops and two apartments inherited by Tomaso and Domenico, in settlement of the outstanding sum of 6,895 ducats and 23 *grossi* owed to him.

While this event seems not to have affected Tomaso's life too seriously, Domenico's situation deteriorated badly. He died a pauper in 1726, leaving six children aged from 6 to 15. His heir was Caterina, still unmarried. It was perhaps in his capacity as Caterina's brother rather than in his own right that in 1726 and in 1727 Tomaso was among the signatories of a petition to the senate of the paper-makers' guild, the *carteri*; the petition asked that the guild be allowed to levy the duty on playing cards manufactured in the territory of the Republic.

Until his father's death Tomaso punctiliously styled himself 'Dilettante veneto' or sometimes 'Musico di violino dilettante veneto' on the title-pages of his publications, thereby insisting (perhaps at his family's behest) on his amateur status. Neither then nor later did he obtain membership of the official instrumentalists' guild, the *Arte de' Sonadori*, which would have enabled him to earn money by performing in public. This must have been through choice and not merely because he already exercised the profession of *carter*; the case of the printer-musician Lorenzo Basegio shows that simultaneous membership of two guilds was possible. He remained aloof, too, from the Società Santa Cecilia, the charitable-cum-social organization of Venetian musicians.

After 1709 the tell-tale word 'dilettante' disappeared from Tomaso's title-pages, but it would be wrong to infer that he became a professional musician in the ordinary sense of the term. Apparently by choice, he never (with one possible exception) sought a salaried post at any Venetian institution. The basilica of San Marco, the numerous other Venetian churches, the four *ospedali*: none of these engaged his services. In fact, his status as a musician depended, very unusually for the time, on his activity as a composer and little more.

In 1705 Tomaso followed a practice common among Venetian opera composers of his day by marrying a professional singer. His bride, Margherita Raimondi, is identified as 'Veronese' (a native of the city or province of Verona) both in the cast-lists of operatic productions found in libretti and in documents relating to her marriage; however, one libretto (that of Caldara's *Le equivoci nel sembiante*) nicknames her 'La Salarina', which suggests a connection, by birth or upbringing, with the little town of Salara about 60 kilometres south-east of Verona and just north of the Po.

Margherita's first known appearances on the stage occurred during the 1699/1700 season at the Venetian theatre of San Salvatore, where she had parts in three consecutive operas. In 1703 she sang in the Caldara opera just mentioned at Casale Monferrato, where the Mantuan court had taken refuge as a result of military reverses suffered during the War of the Spanish Succession (of which more shortly).

When and how Tomaso and Margherita met is not known. Their common connection with the Mantuan court could have brought them together, but since they both resided in Venice and moved in operatic circles perhaps no special explanation is needed.

The celebration of their marriage in Milan rather than Venice hints at parental opposition, perhaps even at an elopement. On 26 February 1705 two witnesses testified to the Venetian Curia that Margherita, whose age was given as 21, was eligible for marriage. One was Antonio Biffi, *primo maestro* at San Marco and perhaps also Margherita's singing teacher, who confirmed that he had followed her progress between the age of about 10 and the previous October (the time of her departure for Milan). A similar deposition was made for Tomaso on 5 March, his month of departure from Venice being identified as November 1704. The wedding took place, exceptionally, in Lent, on 17 March. One of the two witnesses on that occasion was Don Federico Millo, Resident (i.e. official diplomatic representative) of the duchy of Mantua at the court of the viceroy of Milan.

On their return to Venice the couple moved into an apartment in Corte Palmarina close to the Eremite church in the parish of Saints Gervasius and Protasius (known in the vernacular simply as 'San Trovaso'). Their annual rent, 80 ducats, suggests a fairly comfortable but hardly luxurious existence.

Seven children were born of the marriage. The first, Antonio Francesco (born 22 March 1707), was apparently named after Margherita's father; the second, Giovanni Antonio (born 11 November 1708), commemorates Tomaso's father. The third-born, Francesco Donato (born 4 December 1710), was named after his godfather Giovanni Donato Correggio. This nobleman, a secular priest, was a member of Venice's most important musical society, the Accademia Filarmonica, which flourished in the second decade of the eighteenth century; Albinoni later dedicated to him his Op. 7 concertos (1715). Then came two daughters, Lucrezia Antonia (born 29 March 1712) and Francesca Maria (born 5 June 1713); the first had as godfather Leonardo Delfino (Dolfin), another member of the Accademia Filarmonica. Michele Gerolamo (born 29 September 1716) had as godfather a third *accademico*, Giovanni Civran, while Leonardo Delfino acted a second time for the final child, Francesco Antonio (born 12 June 1718).

Not too much should be made of the fact that the Albinoni children all had noble godparents. The Republic's laws, designed to prevent the formation of large coalitions based on family ties among the ruling élite, forbade members of the patriciate to act in this capacity to one another; they became perforce all the more available as godparents to children from lower social strata. Nevertheless, the noble status of the children's godparents shows that as celebrated musicians the Albinoni parents were well received in patrician circles.

The lives of the seven children are so far unresearched, except for that of Francesco Donato, who took holy orders and finally became chaplain of the Eremite almost opposite the house of his birth.

Her maternal duties caused Margherita's career to be suspended for long periods. However, she resumed her activity between the births of Francesca Maria and Michele Gerolamo, singing at Parma in spring 1714, Verona in summer 1715, and Brescia in Carnival 1716. After Francesco Antonio's birth she achieved her greatest successes, singing in Pietro Torri's *Lucio Vero* at the Munich court theatre in October 1720 and at the Pergola theatre in Florence the following Carnival. Shortly after these triumphs she died in Venice on 22 August 1721 of an illness diagnosed as 'fever and intestinal inflammation'.

Fragmentary though her singing career was, Margherita evidently attracted considerable notice. The literary historian Francesco Saverio Quadrio lists her among the operatic singers 'who began to flourish from 1720 to 1730'.[6] What is remarkable is her total artistic independence from her husband: no management, it seems, ever engaged her to sing in one of

---

[6] Francesco Saverio Quadrio, *Della storia e della ragione d'ogni poesia* (5 vols., Bologna amd Milan, 1741–52), iii/2. 537.

Tomaso's works. This situation contrasts in striking manner with the relationship of Antonio Lotti and his wife Santa Stella, Johann Adolf Hasse and his wife Faustina Bordoni, or—notoriously—Antonio Vivaldi and his friend Anna Girò.

Caffi claimed that Tomaso ran a very successful school of singing in Venice that produced several distinguished pupils including an unnamed niece (or granddaughter—Italian uses the same word, *nipote*) who achieved great fame.[7] This report is probably well founded, except that Caffi may have confused Margherita herself (whose career 'peaked' when her husband had already turned 50) with the alleged niece. If true, this activity as a private teacher may explain Albinoni's lack of need to involve himself in the institutional musical life of Venice.

Something of the composer's career objectives can be gleaned from the choice of dedicatees for his published collections. Opp. 1–5, spanning the period 1694–1707, look beyond Venice to the courtly society of the Italian mainland. It may well be that Albinoni entertained hopes in his early career of obtaining a permanent position in the court of an Italian ruling house. In contrast, Opp. 6 and 7 (*c.* 1711 and 1715 respectively) are dedicated to minor Venetian patricians, which implies a lowering of aspirations, a reconciliation to making the best of local opportunities. Significantly, it was during the same decade that five of the seven Albinoni children were born. Opp. 8–10 represent a new phase in which the centre of gravity of Albinoni's career, particularly as regards his instrumental music, shifts away from Italian soil.

Cardinal Pietro Ottoboni (1667–1740), to whom Op. 1 was dedicated, belonged to the socially not quite accepted 'new' patriciate of Venice. His great-grandfather Marco (1554–1649), who had obtained the highest office open to the Venetian citizenry, that of Grand Chancellor, seized the opportunity to buy himself and his family into the nobility for 100,000 ducats in 1646, when the Republic, anxious to obtain additional funds to finance its war against the Ottomans over Crete, opened its Golden Book. Marco's son Pietro (1610–91), a cardinal since 1652, was elected pope in 1689, taking the name of Alexander VIII. In the sixteen months of his reign Alexander provided an object lesson in nepotism. His *nipote* Antonio (1646–1720), son of his deceased elder brother Agostino, was summoned to Rome to become a prince of the papal throne and a general of the Church, having already been honoured in his native city (as a close relative of a Venetian pope) by being made a supernumerary procurator of San Marco and a hereditary knight (*cavaliere della stola d'oro*). A greater honour was reserved for Antonio's son Pietro, who was raised to the purple and given

---

[7] Venice, Biblioteca Nazionale Marciana, Cod. It. IV–747 (10465), fol. 39^r (marginal note).

appropriate benefices and offices that enabled him, as vice-chancellor of the Church, to occupy the Cancelleria palace in the Vatican.[8]

His Roman honours proved something of an embarrassment for Antonio, who could see the wisdom, as a relative newcomer to the patriciate, of not contravening the Venetian law forbidding patricians to serve foreign powers (which included, naturally, the papacy). After Alexander's death in 1691 Antonio renounced his generalship of the Church and returned to Venice, though he remained in the closest contact with his son, whom he visited periodically. Notwithstanding this renunciation, Ottoboni senior remained under a cloud for several years. His return to official favour is shown by his service as a governor of the Pietà from 1702 to 1710, a period almost coinciding with the first phase of Vivaldi's employment there as violin master.

Antonio was doubtless musically inclined but his main interest was poetry. His poetic compositions designed to be set to music (as oratorios, cantatas, etc.) alone number over 260. One of Albinoni's cantatas, *Partenza di Filli* ('Sorgea col lume in fronte'), is a setting of a text by him. What would be interesting to learn is whether this cantata was intended for performance at a *conversazione* in Antonio's Venetian residence in the parish of San Severo or whether its real destination was Rome. It may be significant that another of Albinoni's cantatas, which begins 'Donna illustre del Latio' (Illustrious lady of Latium), is an econium to a Roman noblewoman, while *In alta rocca, ove d'un genio amico* contains a reference to the seven hills of Rome. One suspects that Albinoni, like his fellow Venetians Antonio Biffi and Carlo Francesco Pollarolo, played his part in a regular cultural exchange that involved the procurement by Antonio of Venetian compositions for performance at his son's court in Rome.

For his part, Pietro combined a similar activity as a poet with generous musical patronage. He employed Corelli as a household musician with special privileges from 1690 until the composer's death in 1713. The church of San Lorenzo in Damaso adjoining the Cancelleria of which he was patron boasted as its *maestro di cappella* during the same period Giuseppe Ottavio Pitoni. Through his control of appointments at Santa Maria Maggiore Pietro was able to further the careers of Alessandro and Domenico Scarlatti. Many other great musicians such as Handel and Vivaldi enjoyed his patronage more fleetingly but hardly less significantly.

Although Pietro's court was also to cultivate orchestral music

---

[8] On Antonio Ottoboni see Michael Talbot and Colin Timms, 'Music and the Poetry of Antonio Ottoboni (1646–1720)', in Nino Pirrotta and Agostino Ziino (eds.), *Händel e gli Scarlatti a Roma: Atti del convegno internazionale di studi (Roma, 12–14 giugno 1985)* (Florence, 1987), 367–438. *Partenza di Filli* is listed as item 228 in the catalogue of Ottoboni's *poesie per musica* that concludes this article.

extensively in the 1720s, its focus of attention at the turn of the century was on chamber music. In the very year that Albinoni dedicated his first opus to the cardinal Corelli did the same for his Op. 4 chamber sonatas. Similar collections were dedicated to Ottoboni by Michele Mascitti (Op. 5, 1714) and Giovanni Battista Somis (Op. 4, 1726). Ottoboni, it seems, drew dedications as a honey-pot draws bees.

Albinoni's links with the Ottobonis, initially created, perhaps, by his brother Domenico's connection, are unlikely to have persisted beyond the end of the first decade of the eighteenth century. In 1709 Pietro accepted the title of Protector of the Affairs of France at the Vatican in succession to Cardinal Francesco Maria de' Medici, who had become laicized in preparation for marriage to Eleonora di Guastalla in a desperate effort— vain as it turned out—to provide an heir for the Medici dynasty. This flagrant contravention of the law prohibiting the service of Venetian nobles with foreign powers outraged Venetian opinion and provoked a rupture of diplomatic relations between Venice and France. The Republic wreaked vengeance on the Ottobonis by erasing them from the Golden Book and confiscating their Venetian property; in January 1712 Antonio and his household went into permanent exile in Rome.

Relations with both France and the Ottoboni family were repaired in the 1720s, and the cardinal paid an ostentatiously triumphant visit to his native city in 1726. It was during this decade that Vivaldi and Giovanni Porta, among Venetian musicians, enjoyed his special favour. Albinoni, however, does not appear to have been a beneficiary of the *rapprochement*. The very extensive fragments of the orchestral repertory of the cardinal's court preserved today in the Henry Watson Music Library, Manchester, contain only one concerto attributed to Albinoni, and this is probably spurious.

The patron to whom Albinoni's Op. 2 was dedicated was Ferdinando Carlo di Gonzaga, duke of Mantua and father of Eleonora di Guastalla. Born in 1652, Ferdinando Carlo succeeded to the duchy in 1665. His reign was marked by extravagance; his twin passions for women and the opera, on show during his regular visits to Venice, became notorious. The outbreak of war in 1700 between the French Bourbons and the Austrian Habsburgs over the question of the Spanish succession placed the duke in a delicate situation. Mantua was, legally, a fief of the emperor, to whom it owed automatic allegiance. However, confronted with the advance of French troops on the city of Mantua and seduced by the promise of huge French subsidies if he allied himself with the invaders, Ferdinando Carlo took the bold and for him ultimately disastrous step of changing sides. The fortunes of war oscillated for a while, but the Imperial armies finally prevailed, occupying Mantua in 1707 in accordance with the Treaty of Milan. In 1710 the duchy became a hereditary possession of Austria and between 1737 and 1750 suffered the final indignity of being governed as part of Lombardy. Ferdinando Carlo ended his days in 1708, a pathetic exile in his beloved Venice.

A peculiarity of the organization of the musical life at the Mantuan court under both Ferdinando Carlo and the Habsburg governor who succeeded him, Prince Philip of Hesse-Darmstadt, was that there were two posts of *maestro*: a *maestro di cappella di chiesa* looked after the ducal church of Santa Barbara, while a *maestro di cappella di camera* oversaw the opera and secular music generally. Another peculiarity of the court was to grant the status of honorary *maestro* to non-resident musicians.

On the title-page of Op. 2 Albinoni styles himself the duke's 'servo', which literally means 'servant'. Imprecise as this description is, it does not belong to the language of pure convention and must refer to some kind of established relationship. Unfortunately, records for the employment of musicians at the Gonzaga court preserved in the State Archives of Mantua are incomplete for the years immediately preceding 1700. In 1687–8 Carlo Grossi held the title of 'maestro di cappella universale' responsible for both sacred and secular areas, though this post was probably honorary since he concurrently held posts in Venice. He may either have replaced, or merely supplemented, Marc'Antonio Ziani, who had been appointed *maestro di cappella di chiesa* in September 1686. The next *maestro* of whom we hear is the Roman musician Francesco Navarra, who was in post during 1696–7. The Op. 1 (1697) of the Ferrarese musician Paolo Antonio Bassani (son of the more famous Giovanni Battista Bassani) identifies him as 'Maestro di Cappella d'Onore dell'Altezza Serenissima di Mantova'. There follows another uncertain period until the appointment of Antonio Caldara in May 1699 followed by Giuseppe Boniventi in 1707.

In this strangely fluid context it is easy to visualize how Albinoni may have been able, without either forsaking his playing cards or infringing the prerogatives of a permanent *maestro*, to act as an occasional 'purveyor of music' to Ferdinando Carlo. Indeed, his direct contact with the duke may have been limited to the times of the latter's visits to Venice. More about the repertory to which he contributed will be said in Chapter 4.

Behind Albinoni's decision to dedicate his next collection to Grand Prince Ferdinando of Tuscany lay a special consideration. Ferdinando's father, Cosimo III, had been born in 1642 and had reigned in Florence as grand duke since 1670. Aware that on his succession the grand prince would be known as Ferdinando III, at least four composers—Torelli (1687), Albinoni (1701), Gentili (*c*. 1706), and Vivaldi (1711)—paid their homage in advance, so to speak, by dedicating to him their third publication. (Their expectations were not to be fulfilled, since Ferdinando died in 1713, Cosimo in 1723.)

Whereas Cosimo had no particular interest in music, Ferdinando, who was an accomplished harpsichordist, made its cultivation a central part of his life, maintaining a court of his own that included a private theatre housed in his villa at Pratolino, near Florence. Ferdinando also deserves credit for promoting the early development of the piano in the hands of Bartolomeo Cristofori.

The dedication of Albinoni's Op. 3 hints strongly at a previous encounter with Ferdinando, since it includes the phrase 'a debt of gratitude that I profess towards your royal patronage'. If a meeting had taken place, it was most probably in Venice, which the grand prince visited often (and where he is said to have contracted the venereal disease that ended his life prematurely).

In his role of patron Ferdinando could be fickle, as the two Scarlattis, once his protégés, were to learn. It seems, however, that Albinoni's *Balletti a tre* struck home, for their sequel, the twelve cantatas, were dedicated, as we saw, to Ferdinando's uncle, Cardinal Francesco Maria de' Medici (1642–1711). He too was a music-lover, who in his younger years had established the 'Conversazione del Casino di San Marco' that staged operas annually from 1678 to 1682.

The Florentine dedications later bore fruit in the operatic commissions of 1703, *Griselda* and *Aminta*, and possibly in Albinoni's subsequent commission for the oratorio *Maria annunziata*, already preceded in 1703 by a contribution to the pasticcio-oratorio *I trionfi di Giosuè*.

Another frequent visitor to Venice was Carlos Felipe Antonio Spinola Colonna (1665–1721), marquis of Los Balbases. He was in fact the dedicatee of Corradi's libretto to *Il Tigrane, re d'Armenia* (1697) for which Albinoni had supplied the music. Although Genoese by origin, Spinola Colonna was a grandee of Spain. At the time (1707) when Albinoni dedicated to him his Op. 5, he had become viceroy and captain-general of Sicily, then a Spanish possession. Albinoni's dedication leaves no clues to the nature of the relationship. One must always take care not to infer too much from the mere fact of a dedication, since composers might choose a dedicatee entirely speculatively in an attempt to profit from the presence close at hand of a suitably eminent person (a prime example of this kind of opportunism is Vivaldi's Op. 2, which, having already been at press for some while, was dedicated to Frederick IV of Denmark during the brief period that this monarch spent in Venice at the beginning of 1709).

Certainly, however, the dedication of Op. 6 to the Venetian nobleman

Giovanni Francesco Zeno (born 1686) bespeaks personal acquaintance. Having first paid an orotund compliment to the publisher Estienne Roger ('Well may I make the most accurate presses groan under distant Batavian skies'), the composer declares that Zeno can 'with his hand add ornament to the harmony'. By implication, therefore, the dedicatee is a skilled violinist, perhaps even a pupil of the composer. (The word 'fregio' (ornament) should perhaps not be interpreted in a technical sense as 'gracing'; it may simply convey the banal idea that a skilled performance can enhance the work of the composer.)

In similar vein, the dedication of Albinoni's Op. 7 praises the connoisseurship and musical prowess of his son Francesco Donato's godfather Giovanni Donato Correggio (1689–1738), who, with his 'polite plectrum', will revive and embellish the flaccid notes of the concertos. The cithara and its plectrum are used in the language of the time as pseudo-classical metaphors for a violin (or similar stringed instrument) and its bow, so one gathers that Correggio, too, was a string player.

The dedication of the *Balletti e sonate a tre*, Op. 8 (late 1721 or early 1722), is the most interesting in biographical respects. Its recipient was Christian Heinrich von Watzdorf (1698–1747), a cabinet minister at the electoral court of Saxony whom Mattheson singled out in 1722 as a 'great patron of music', noting that he was residing in Rome at the time.[9] In the catalogue of the publisher, Jeanne Roger, Op. 8 was allotted the number 493, which comes immediately before the pair of numbers for the two volumes comprising Albinoni's Op. 9 (494–5). This implies that its engraving had been held up for a while. Ordinarily, one would expect a dedication to be penned at a late stage in the process of publication, which may still be the case here, although the other possibility certainly exists. Albinoni refers in the undated dedication to 'the welcome approval that Your Illustrious Lordship gave to my theatrical compositions [*note the plural*] this year in Venice'. The puzzling fact is that on the evidence of the contemporary opera registers and surviving libretti only one Albinoni opera, *Gli eccessi della gelosia*, was staged in Venice in 1721/2—and the previous three Carnival seasons are entirely void of his operas. The 1717/18 season, however, included three operas by him.

Although it seems unlikely, on the face of it, that the publication of Op. 8 was held back for as long as four years, the very close resemblance of one sentence in Albinoni's preface to a sentence in the preface to the libretto of his own opera *Cleomene* (Venice, Carnival 1718) written by the author of the drama, Vincenzo Cassani, suggests that the latter's text was fresh in his mind at the time. Cassani has: 'Se altra volta m'accordasti il tuo

<hr />

[9] *Critica musica*, i. 118.

compatimento per sola benigna inclinazione, questa mel devi per convenienza, e giustizia' (If on another occasion you granted me your indulgence solely out of kindness, this time you owe it to me out of propriety and justice). Albinoni has: 'Se altre volte l'ottenni [il tuo compatimentol della tua ben' inclinata natura questa mel deve la tua generosa giustizia' (If on other occasions I obtained it [your indulgence] from your natural kindness, this time your generous sense of justice owes it to me). The closeness of style and content seems too great to be coincidental. On the other hand, one then has to explain why Estienne and Jeanne Roger, having delayed the publication for so long, gave the composer no opportunity to bring the letter of dedication up to date.

Albinoni's choice of Maximilian II Emanuel, elector of Bavaria, as the dedicatee of his Op. 9 (1722) was a logical outcome of factors both recent and long-standing. The Wittelsbach dynasty, which ruled over a part of Catholic Germany close in geography and spirit to Italy, were frequent visitors to Venice. Max Emanuel, born in 1662, became elector in 1680. As governor of the Spanish Netherlands he spent a good deal of the first part of his reign in Brussels, where he acquired a taste for French music. Returning to Munich in 1701, Max Emanuel rashly entered the War of the Spanish Succession on the French side. After being driven out of Bavaria, he took refuge first in the Netherlands and later in France. Only in 1715, following the Treaty of Rastatt, was he able to re-establish his court in Munich, where he was joined by his wife Kunigunde, who had lived in Venice between 1705 and 1715, and his daughter Violante Beatrice, widow of Ferdinando de' Medici. With Giuseppe Antonio Bernabei and Pietro Torri as his directors of sacred and secular music respectively, and the Veronese violinist-composer Evaristo Felice Dall'Abaco as his concertmaster, the elector was soon able to restore musical life in Munich to its former glory. Though his senior musical personnel were all Italians, their style was attractively cosmopolitan, admitting some French and German elements.

The Albinonis may first have come to the notice of the Bavarian court through Tomaso's acquaintance with the grand princess in Florence early in the century or during Kunigunde's ten-year exile in Venice. Or perhaps they met Max Emanuel's son Karl Albrecht when he paid a semi-official visit to Venice in 1716. We may assume that Tomaso accompanied Margherita to Munich in 1720 for her singing engagement; it was most likely then that he received the favours from the elector and his sons briefly acknowledged without further elaboration in the dedication of Op. 9. This dedication also refers to the elector's love of recreation on the 'cithara' and to the dexterity with which he wields the sword and the plectrum alike. In this instance, the ancient Greek instrument stands for the bass viol, of which Max Emanuel was an expert player.

When Albinoni came, after the lapse of some fourteen years, to dedicate his next instrumental collection, Op. 10 (1735/6), Italy was once again undergoing political and military convulsions. The War of the Polish Succession had resulted in the conquest of Naples by a Spanish force, which placed the Infant of Spain, Don Carlos, on the throne. In northern Italy French and Spanish troops were engaged in a less decisive campaign against Imperial forces. Venice, as usual, observed an impotent neutrality, unable to prevent violations of her sovereignty by both sides.

One of the military leaders on the Spanish side was Don Luca Fernando Patiño, marquis of Castelar. In his dedication of the concertos to Patiño Albinoni mentions an earlier meeting at which he had been honoured to 'kiss the hand' of the marquis. Presumably this refers to a diplomatic or pleasure-seeking mission paid by Patiño to Venice. Albinoni flatters Patiño's musical accomplishments by depicting the relaxation of a knightly soldier, instrument in hand, after the rigours of battle.

An unusual feature of this dedication is the frank expression of political partisanship with which Albinoni opens his eulogy. 'Italy breathed again', he writes, 'when she saw the victorious standards of Catholic [i.e. Spanish] arms, for which she had so long yearned, unfurled on her soil.' This sentiment is typically Venetian, for Venice regarded herself as the only true successor of the Roman Republic within the Italian peninsula and as the custodian of the idea of Italian independence and eventual reunification. What distinguished Bourbon rule in Naples in Venetian eyes from the Habsburg rule it displaced was that Charles III, though installed by a foreign army, reigned as an independent monarch, not subservient, as the Austrian viceroys had been, to an external power.

A few years later Albinoni sent a collection of trio sonatas to Le Cène for engraving. In a letter to Padre Martini of 1 May 1739 the publisher, apologizing for his delay in bringing out the former's keyboard sonatas, mentions a long backlog of works awaiting engraving, some of which he has had for over a year; he gives as examples 'Monsieur G. Tartini solo' and 'Monsieur Albinoni trio'.[10]

Le Cène's sluggishness was due partly to his own ill-health, partly to a decline in motivation brought about the the death of his son, who was to have carried on the business. He did eventually publish the Martini sonatas in July 1742, giving them the catalogue number 592, and the Tartini sonatas (Op. 2) in October 1743 with the catalogue number 594. Since the catalogue of Le Cène's publications brought out shortly after his death in 1743 by the purchaser of his stock, the Amsterdam bookseller Emmanuel Jean de La Coste, lists an unbroken series of publications numbered from 1

---

[10] Bologna, Civico Museo Bibliografico Musicale, I.19.2.

to 594, among which no 'Op. 11' of Albinoni appears, it must be presumed that the intended engraving of the trios did not in fact take place.

Among the manuscripts offered for sale in 1759 as part of the bookseller Nicolaas Selhof's estate was a work of Albinoni described as 'VI [Sonate] a Tré, ut supra [due Violini è Cembalo], Violoncello, opera XI'.[11] The title looks credible, especially since the cello and continuo parts are separate (this being a normal practice of Albinoni that was less common among his contemporaries). It may well be that this item was the 'publisher's copy' of the lost collection (Selhof had a historical connection with Le Cène, having earlier been his agent in The Hague).

After his wife's death Albinoni had moved to a new apartment situated in the Calle Longa in the parish of San Barnaba. This unfashionable district of the city was one known for its large population of impoverished nobles, the so-called *Barnabotti*. The composer's own financial circumstances cannot have been good, for his apartment, which in 1750 he was sharing with three of his children, was rented for only 28 ducats per annum—not enough to make him liable for a charge in respect of Venice's newly introduced public street lighting. Between the production of his opera *Artamene* at the end of 1740 and his death in 1751 we hear no more of Albinoni except for one slightly puzzling reference that deserves to be discussed in some detail.

During the 1730s musical standards at the Venetian charitable institution known as the Ospedale dei Derelitti (or more simply as the 'Ospedaletto') had been slipping. On 7 September 1739 the governors responsible for the chapel, the *deputati sopra le figlie*, reported in a memorandum to their colleagues that attendance at services had fallen.[12] This was serious news since donations and endowments from external benefactors provided the Ospedaletto with valuable income. The report blamed a decline of interest in music as such, modern social habits inimical to church attendance, the poor health of the female residents of the Ospedaletto (from whom the *coro* was exclusively drawn), and above all the devolution of much of the responsibility for musical instruction upon the older members of the *coro*, which resulted in the perpetuation of bad or obsolete practices. Soon afterwards, the musical staff suffered depletion through the death of the *solfeggio* master (responsible for teaching the rudiments of singing) and the

[11] *Catalogue d'une trés belle bibliotheque de livres . . . deslaissez par feu, Monsieur Nicolas Selhof* (The Hague, 1759), lot 2233.

[12] I am grateful to Gastone Vio for information relating to this episode of Albinoni's life. The documents on which the present account draws are all preserved in the section of the archive of the Istituto di Ricovero e di Educazione, Venice, containing material originating from the Derelitti. Reference is made to the documents shelfmarked B. 11 (Notatorio 1732–1748), fols. 194 and 197, and G. 2 no. 48, fasc. 'Musica', insertions nos. 13, 35, 42, 45, and 47.

dismissal of the singing master. This left only a *maestro di suono* responsible for instrumental music, Antonio Martinelli, and the *maestro di coro*, Antonio Pollarolo. However, the lack of a stipendiary singing teacher was largely overcome by the generous intervention of Nicola Porpora, a former *maestro di coro* at the Ospedale degli Incurabili recently appointed to the Pietà, who in July 1742 began to give instruction to selected members of the *coro*. On 13 May 1743 the *deputati* reviewed the situation. Their report lamented once again the meagre attendance at services and pointed the finger at Pollarolo, whose music was old-fashioned and who no longer enjoyed the confidence of the *coro*. Obligingly, Pollarolo resigned his post soon afterwards, giving as reasons his old age and onerous responsibilities as *primo maestro* at San Marco.

On 20 September 1743 the *deputati* wrote a memorandum expressing their thoughts on the selection procedure to be followed in the appointment of a new *maestro di coro*. Whereas in the past a public competition had often been held, they believed that this was no longer an effective method, since eminent masters would not risk their reputations against lesser figures. They recommended, instead, the taking of discreet soundings. The governors decided to follow this advice and instructed the *deputati* to inform themselves of the musical ability and moral suitability of possible candidates. By combining the posts of *maestro di coro* and singing master, it would be possible to offer an attractive salary of 300 ducats per annum.

The first of two nominations received by the *deputati* was that of Albinoni. It is unclear from the documentation whether Albinoni advanced his own candidature or was proposed by a supporter within the ranks of the governors. The second candidate was Porpora, in whose favour the governors voted on 20 January 1744.

How Albinoni came to be considered at all is a mystery. There is no surviving evidence of any involvement by him with sacred vocal music after his brief and reportedly unsuccessful flirtation with it in his youth. The only sacred vocal composition attributed to him apart from the Mass mentioned in Chapter 1 is a setting of the Magnificat for solo voices, choir, and strings included in a manuscript anthology in the Deutsche Staatsbibliothek, East Berlin.[13] This source is dated 1720 and identifies Albinoni as a *Kapellmeister* in Venice. Since the style of this Magnificat is so different from that of Albinoni's other music—particularly in the lyrical solo sections, where one would expect some affinity with his secular vocal music—its authorship must be challenged. On the other hand, Albinoni's

---

[13] Shelfmark Mus. ms. 30088. The work was published in 1968 by Edition Eulenburg in an edition by Felix Schroeder that accepts Albinoni's authorship as genuine.

experience as a teacher of singing may have been a recommendation in view of the amalgamation of the two *maestro* posts.

His life ended quietly on 17 January 1751. The parish necrology gives his age rather inaccurately as 'about 84' (he was in fact 79) and identifies the cause of death as 'diabetes, fever, and catarrh', noting that he had been confined to bed for two years. He was evidently not living in the direst poverty, since his funeral was to be held with the full participation of the chapter of the church of San Barnaba.[14]

Testimonies to Albinoni's personality have not been uncovered. The best one can do is to make inferences from the handwriting and musical notation of the three surviving musical autographs.[15] Albinoni's hand is neat and stylish, though devoid of unnecessary flourishes (see Plate 1). His note-heads are small and the attached stems long, so that his notation has a slightly spidery appearance. The beams uniting groups of quavers and shorter values tend to undulate smoothly in gentle ripples, a feature reminiscent of J. S. Bach's musical handwriting. The restrained, almost businesslike appearance of the music, which contains relatively few corrections although it appears to be in first draft, gives an impression of practised efficiency and great calmness. It makes a striking contrast to the impression of manic impulsiveness and brusque impatience conveyed by Vivaldi's autograph manuscripts.

Only two pictorial representations of Albinoni are known. The more familiar one is a profile appearing on one of twenty-four medallions arranged at various levels around the slopes of Mount Parnassus in a fanciful drawing by Luigi Scotti entitled *Parnaso italiano*; an engraving of this drawing was made by the studio of Francesco Rainaldi in Florence in the period 1801–5. Albinoni shares his medallion with the composer Giuseppe Colla (1739–1806) and the famous castrato Domenico Gizzi (*c.* 1680–1758); the three profiles overlap, with the result that only the front part of Albinoni's head is visible (Plate 2).

Less well known is an anonymous painting in oils of the composer (Plate 3) in the private collection of Professor Gabriele Mandel.[16] It shows him full-faced and holding in his hands a piece of vocal music, possibly an

[14] Sources that give 1750 as the year of Albinoni's death fail to take account of the peculiarity of the Venetian calendar. In this calendar the year advanced on 1 March, two months later than in modern practice. Thus 17 Jan. 1750 'more veneto' is the same as our 17 Jan. 1751.

[15] These autograph works are the three violin sonatas So 32–4, preserved in the Sächsische Landesbibliothek, Dresden, under the shelfmarks Mus. 2199-R-1, Mus. 2199-R-5, and Mus. 2199-R-6. The first, inscribed to Pisendel, has been published in a facsimile edition with a commentary by the present writer (Leipzig, 1980).

[16] I am grateful to Professor Mandel for information concerning this painting. I have not, however, been able to trace a contemporary engraving reportedly based on the portrait in question.

operatic aria. It is not possible to say how old Albinoni was at the time of the sitting.

The salient features of both portraits are the long, undulating nose, receding forehead, and heavy jowls. The physiognomy they represent is very typical of north-east Italy.

We can end this chapter by considering in broad terms what influence Albinoni's highly unusual career had on the kind of music he wrote. He was certainly not a typical *dilettante di musica* of his day in that he belonged to a low social stratum, was not drawn to cultural pursuits outside music (so far as we can judge), and lacked the zest for experimentation and interest in theoretical problems that we find, for instance, in the Marcello brothers. On the other hand, it was only in the sphere of composition and perhaps teaching that his pattern of life resembled that of a professional musician, for he performed little in public and held no official posts. There is something almost hermetic about his musical language that corresponds to the privacy of his life. He found a personal voice early on—it is already evident in his first opera, *Zenobia, regina de' Palmireni*, and his first instrumental collection, both of 1694. His language evolved steadily during the remainder of his career but relied more on its inner resources than on external stimuli. For this sturdy independence Albinoni paid a price in his later compositions, which would have benefited from a closer look at what his contemporaries were doing. But without the same independence the 'Albinoni style', which can lend attractiveness to even his more ephemeral works, would not exist.

3

ALBINONI'S MUSICAL STYLE

SOME composers are instantly recognizable, no matter from which period of their career or musical genre the work to be identified is chosen. Musicological detectives of the future would have little hesitation in attributing an anonymously preserved composition to Fauré or to Martinů on the basis of style alone since the mature musical language of each of these two composers is both so individual and so consistent in its elements as to be practically unmistakable. We are dealing, of course, with a matter of degree: Fauré and Martinů merely stand at one end of a continuum of 'recognizability' that has at its other end such protean figures as Busoni and Frank Bridge.

It is important to realize that stylistic consistency has little intrinsic musical value. For a work to be readily identifiable as by a given composer is no guarantee against shallowness or even technical incompetence. In fact, the greatest composers seem often to have been the ones most responsive to external musical stimuli, with the result that their stylistic range becomes wider; in return for a small sacrifice of individuality (conceived narrowly), their works achieve the quality of universality that enables them to be admitted more easily to the musical 'canon'.

Nevertheless, many music-lovers clearly derive satisfaction from their association of a composer with a personal style—and are prepared to listen sympathetically even to his weaker works for the sake of experiencing it. The style becomes, as it were, reified; it can appear the most important aspect of all, taking precedence over the cogency of the musical argument and even the originality of the composition within the composer's own œuvre. The artwork is valued above all because it points to the artist. Many will consider this basis for appreciation primitive and even perverse, but few will deny its existence.

As one of the most distinctive composers not merely of his generation but of all time, Albinoni is a major beneficiary of this 'style' factor. His distinctiveness is all the more remarkable for occurring within a musical language possessing far fewer resources than those available to a more recent composer. In fact, the basic melodic, harmonic, rhythmic, and instrumentational ingredients of Albinoni's music are all shared with his contemporaries; his originality begins to manifest itself only at the stage when those ingredients start to be mixed and combined.

The price Albinoni pays for his originality *vis-à-vis* other composers is the undeniably repetitive nature of his music. What is vital and striking about one of his fugal movements is likely to be precisely the same set of features encountered in another of his fugal movements written twenty years earlier (or later). It is the same kind of repetitiveness that one notes in, say, Mendelssohn scherzos and Shostakovich passacaglias. To exaggerate just a little: Albinoni is a composer with a single vision (or, perhaps better, set of visions) refracted in different ways on separate occasions to produce a number of formally distinct but intimately related pieces.

This is not to say that Albinoni's musical style is static over time. On the contrary, it evolves continuously, partly in response to its inner dynamic and partly in response to changing musical fashion. But a bedrock of fundamental principles remains obstinately unchanged, restraining the extent of this evolution and channelling its form.

Albinoni's artistic inflexibility may well be related to his background as an amateur musician and his relative isolation after he acquired quasi-professional status. One can easily imagine that, having learnt his craft largely through his own efforts and perhaps very laboriously, he did not have the confidence or the energy to jettison tried and tested methods. Nor does it seem that his clientele wished him to do so: they too may have wished always to have the Albinoni whom they knew from previous experience. Ironically, it was Vivaldi rather than Albinoni who was censured by contemporary critics for his idiosyncrasies and solecisms (Goldoni refers to his 'incorrect' basses and Avison to his 'defective' harmony). But Vivaldi's liability to criticism must be related to the high profile that he himself wished to cultivate as a musician–cum–entrepreneur. A figure working with quiet industry at the margins of Venetian musical life, Albinoni was not likely ever to become a subject of similar public debate.

Before I review his compositions according to their chronology and genre in the chapters that follow, it will be useful to examine the salient features of this very personal musical language.

Except for his shortest movements with the function of simple transitions, all Albinoni's movements can be divided into a number of periods, which are then divisible further into phrases. Following the contemporary definitions of Scheibe (1745) and Eximeno (1774), a period, which is the counterpart of a prose sentence, can be described as a passage of music occurring between two clearly marked cadences. The means by which the cadence concluding a period in the manner of a full stop is distinguished from less emphatic cadences occurring earlier in the period (equivalent to punctuation marks such as the comma and semicolon) are various; they include, for example, the prolongation of the dominant chord over a greater number of beats than in the preceding perfect cadences. The identity of that period is confirmed in addition by its syntactical unity: it and its sub-units can be broken down into paired statements having the character of proposition (antecedent) and response (consequent). Antecedent and consequent are rarely exactly equal in length, except in shorter or less sophisticated movements (such as most gavottes); in individual phrases the consequent is frequently extended by the use of sequence or a similar device, while at the higher level of organization relating to the period as a whole the consequent is often shorter than the antecedent. Whatever its particular syntax, the period forms a well-balanced whole to which the final cadence provides a satisfying and expected conclusion.

The first point to note about Albinoni's periods is how clearly articulated they are. The end of one period is with only rare exceptions separable from the start of the next despite the frequent identity of the last chord of one and the first chord of the other. In other words, Albinoni makes remarkably little use of the common technique of 'interlocking', by which the final chord of one period and the opening chord of its successor are made the same. This characteristic distinguishes him from Vivaldi, Bach, and Handel, all of whom make ample use of interlocked periods. Equally noticeable is Albinoni's avoidance of any form of syntactical ambiguity, through which a phrase can serve simultaneously as the consequent of a preceding phrase and the antecedent of a following one (which may indeed belong to a new period). In his construction of a movement he sets a premium on clarity and simplicity.

The cadences, actual or implied, that end the phrases making up a period have to be well varied in order to give definition to the antecedent–consequent relationships. Leaving aside the possibility of modulation within the period, which enables the composer to contrast cadences of identical type in different keys, there are four cadential varieties from which to choose: plagal, interrupted, imperfect, and perfect. Albinoni avoids the ordinary form of plagal cadence (chords IV–I) almost entirely, even in its traditional role as a solemn conclusion to the movement, although he quite often ends phrases with a rather archaic-sounding IIb–Ia cadence that can be regarded as an unusual variety of the plagal form, offering a way of harmonizing the melodic progression II–I without resorting to a conventional perfect cadence.[1] Interrupted cadences—not merely to the sixth degree of the scale

[1] The letters a, b, c, and d following a chord (identified by a Roman number representing the degree of the scale occupied by its root) stand for root position, first inversion, second inversion, and third inversion respectively. The IIb–Ia cadence can be seen in bar 2 of Ex. 11.

but also to more exotic chords such as the subdominant in first inversion with the root chromatically raised—are uncommon in the early works but occur quite often in the later works, where they help to postpone the arrival of the clinching cadence that brings the period to an end. Imperfect cadences (V preceded by any approach chord) are as common as one would expect throughout Albinoni's music. Perfect cadences, the most frequently encountered type, are also the most differentiated. 'Weak' types of perfect cadence, in which the duration of the dominant chord is short or inversions of either chord (V or I) are employed, are so distinct in effect from 'strong' types (exemplified by the cadence concluding the period) that they function almost as a separate cadential species; the antecedent–consequent relationship can be expressed as satisfactorily by the succession perfect (weak)–perfect (strong) as by the succession imperfect–perfect.

The internal structure of Albinoni's periods tends to conform to a standard plan that conditions important aspects of their melody, harmony, phrasing, and thematic development. This plan is seen most clearly in homophonic movements, where one part alone carries the melody, but exists equally in contrapuntal ones. Typically, it entails the division of the period into three segments which we will term the opening, middle, and closing segments respectively.

The opening segment presents the most characteristic and memorable material, usually delivered as a series of short, balanced phrases. It tends to emphasize primary triads (I, IV, V) and often has a reiterative quality. That of the first period often functions in whole or part as a requotable 'motto' used to introduce subsequent periods, thus imparting thematic unity of a simple kind to the movement.

The middle segment is more continuous in style, utilizing techniques of extension such as sequence and phrase-repetition. It may develop intensively motives derived from the opening segment or draw on the large fund of thematically neutral figures used for passage-work by countless composers of the time. In either case, the material is episodic in character and not intended for independent restatement. This segment is harmonically the most varied, making full use of secondary triads (those on degrees II, III, VI, and VII).

The closing segment leads purposefully towards the final cadence. Like the opening segment, it often emphasizes primary triads; its reiterative character may be even more strongly marked. In certain cases (for example, in the opening period of the first movement of the seventh concerto of Op. 5) it reintroduces in varied guise the motivic substance of the opening segment, giving the impression almost of a reprise. The build-up to the final cadence may be lengthy, entailing a gradual melodic and harmonic intensification, but the cadence itself is nearly always stereotyped and impersonal in form. Not for Albinoni the strikingly original and thematically significant melodic approaches to the cadence found in Bach and sometimes also Vivaldi: rather, he seems to regard it as a necessary but in itself unimportant punctuation mark that serves to clarify structural divisions.

Naturally, the basic plan just outlined admits of some variation. For instance, an internal period may actually begin with passage-work corresponding to the style of the middle segment. In such cases the whole preceding period is perceived as the antecedent to which the new period supplies the consequent. Or the middle and closing segments may be fused in such a way that the passage-work itself leads directly to the cadence.

Despite these variations, one feature remains constant: the differentiation of structural function between the segments making up a period is absolute and rarely permits any interchangeability. Whereas in a Vivaldi movement three segments initially appearing in the order A-B-C may emerge later in the order C-A-B or B-A-C, this hardly ever happens in Albinoni. Instead of the more agglutinative, therefore more pliable, musical syntax favoured by the younger composer (and most other contemporaries) we find a preference for a more seamless, more expansive, flow of musical thought. The price paid for this approach is a certain rigidity and uniformity, as well as a diminished capacity for springing dramatic surprises. But there is a corresponding gain in musical flow and transparency of form.

The orchestral ritornello to the tenor aria 'Se incontrate tempeste o procelle' from Albinoni's serenata *Il nascimento de l'Aurora* (Ex. 1), will illustrate these characteristics. The opening segment comprises bar 1 and the first three beats of bar 2. It introduces a scale-motive in both a full form spanning an octave (bar 1) and an abridged form spanning a fifth (bar 2), as well as descending broken chords in quavers following each. A weak perfect cadence (VIIb–Ia) in bar 1 is answered by an imperfect cadence in bar 2; the second cadence marks the end of a higher-level antecedent to which the middle segment, bars 3–6 (discounting upbeats), responds. This opens with a two-bar sequence descending by step in which first IV (G) and then III (F) are 'tonicized'. The sequential unit is formed from a combination of the abridged version of the scale-motive and the descending third with which the opening segment concludes; the development is hence rigorously thematic. A second part of the middle segment (bars 5–6) ingeniously recombines the same two elements in a new sequence ascending by step; the previously descending third is now inverted to become an ascending third or (through octave-displacement) a

Ex. I

descending sixth. This segment ends, as did the first, with an emphatic imperfect cadence in D minor. The repetition of this cadence-form is made possible by the series of intervening 'weak' perfect cadences, which supply tonal variety. It remains for the closing segment, bars 7–10, to supply the consequent to the two preceding segments taken together. This segment inverts the abridged scale-motive and complements it with pairs of quavers that in their preference for larger intervals (especially the fifth) refer back to the second beat of bar 2. The drive to the cadence produces first a harmonic intensification (the Neapolitan Sixth—one of Albinoni's favourite chromaticisms—in bar 8) and then a melodic intensification as the line surges up to g'', $c\sharp'''$, and finally d''', before plunging down and decelerating to reach the terminal cadence.[2]

Although one must concede that this period is fashioned in a way that may seem a little calculated, it achieves a marvellous sense of continuity and logical unfolding that fully deserves to be described as 'classical'. The parts mean nothing: the whole everything.

Periods can be classed as either 'closed' or 'open'. A closed period ends in the key in which it began. It is therefore static in a tonal sense (although it may include incidental modulation as found in Ex. 1), serving to affirm or re-establish a single key-centre. In contrast, an open period ends in a key different from its starting key and is therefore tonally dynamic. Since, in a baroque movement, the group of related keys that may be visited is small, a high incidence of closed periods tends to increase the movement's length by turning what might have been (to use a topographical metaphor) narrow peaks into broad plateaux.

Unlike most of his Italian contemporaries, Albinoni prefers to use only open periods for the central portion of the movement in which most of the structurally essential modulation takes place. In orchestrally accompanied arias and the outer movements of concertos employing one or two oboes he includes as standard a short ritornello in the dominant or equivalent related key (for minor tonalities), but that is as far as his use of closed periods outside the area of the tonic goes. On the other hand, both at the beginning and the end of the movement closed periods in the tonic are normal. Sometimes, in fact, there are two or three closed periods in succession at either end of the movement; this happens notably in the outer movements of the oboe concertos. So considerable are these stretches of unrelieved tonic that monotony is not easily averted. A few movements, particularly in his early works before 1700, open with a period that modulates immediately from the tonic to the dominant. This practice, inherited from

[2] Pitches are indicated with strokes and upper-case or lower-case letters according to the Helmholtz system. Middle C is represented as c', and the C two octaves lower as C.

the seventeenth century, works well as long as the dimensions of the movement are kept very compact but is incompatible with the increase in average movement length that characterizes most musical genres in the late baroque.

In his sonata and concerto movements, though not in his vocal arias, Albinoni regularly includes a coda that constitutes a period on its own or takes the form of a lengthy extension to the final period. The stereotyped, unemphatic nature of his cadential formulae may lie behind Albinoni's insistence on a coda, which commonly achieves a sense of finality more through constant reiteration of a cadential phrase than through the adoption of a device such as the reduction of harmonic rhythm (the rate of chord-change) or the move to a slower tempo. Rather remarkably, only one movement in the whole of Albinoni's instrumental music (the opening Allegro of the concerto Op. 9 no. 9) borrows the end of its final period from that of its opening period. (This feature is, however, absolutely normal in Vivaldian ritornello form.)

In discussing Albinoni's handling of modulation one must distinguish between self-contained movements that are 'closed' in the sense defined above and those, more transitional in nature, that are 'open'. Recitatives are the prime examples of open movements, but some interior movements in sonatas and concertos have a similar structure. With rare exceptions, the closed movements restrict themselves to a group of six keys comprising the tonic, subdominant, and dominant, plus the relative major or minor keys of each. Another way of defining this group is to say that it consists of all the keys whose key signature differs by no more than one accidental (in modern notation) from that of the principal tonality. Since the tonic chord of all the keys in the group exists as a diatonic triad in the home key, the process of modulating to, from, and between them is extremely smooth and straightforward.

Some of Albinoni's early major-key movements venture beyond the dominant to the supertonic major key. This is a primitive trait that looks back to the earlier part of the seventeenth century; it does not appear in the mature works.

The late works, on the other hand, begin cautiously to exploit 'transmodal' modulation—that between keys in different modes (major or minor) sharing a tonic. Traditionally, Italian music, unlike French, did not recognize as intimately related two 'parallel' keys such as C major and C minor. Until well into the eighteenth century modal contrast in interior movements was far more frequently achieved by the adoption of the relative minor or major key than that of the parallel major or minor. By the second decade of that century transmodal modulation, already present embryonically in the form of chromatic harmony, was beginning to be exploited systematically within individual movements. In 1739 Charles de Brosses could report, speaking of Italian composers: 'Nearly all their arias are written in the major mode; but they intersperse in these without warning certain phrases in the minor mode that surprise and arrest the ear'.[3] Most of the surviving examples of transmodal modulation in Albinoni's music—always from major to minor and back—come from Op. 10 (1735/6). They are not especially frequent or prominent and sometimes lack conviction; one feels that their introduction was due more to the external pressure of fashion than to inner need.

The order in which the modulations to various keys occur in an Albinoni movement is governed, first, by the conventions observed generally during his lifetime and, second, by a number of additional, self-imposed practices. With one important exception to be described shortly, Albinoni adheres to the widely shared principle that each foreign key should be visited only once in the course of a movement. The keys that the music visits can thus be likened to a series of destinations on a circular tour beginning and ending at the same point: the tonic. (This principle does not apply in a simple way to fugal movements, however, since these are apt to oscillate continuously between tonic and dominant.)

In major-key movements Albinoni never deviates from the normal practice of striking out first to the dominant. In binary movements this is the key in which the cadence before the first repeat-sign takes place; in arias, the key in which the first vocal period ends. This accomplished, the music travels to the minor keys in the group. In particularly elaborate movements all three may be visited in turn, and in very concise ones only one. Often, however, Albinoni selects two—an especially popular procedure is to go first to the submediant, then the mediant. At this point the music returns to the home key, either directly (in which case the hiatus is often emphasized by a rest in all the parts) or via a short linking passage equivalent to what the theorists of sonata form call the 'retransition'. This passage often takes the form of a sequence descending by step and employing passage-work of neutral thematic character; it is among the most recognizably Albinonian of any of the formal features we are discussing. The absence of the subdominant key from the standard plan is striking; unlike Bach and many other contemporaries, Albinoni obviously felt no pressing need to compensate for the earlier emphasis on the 'sharp' side of the home key by touching on the 'flat' side before the close.

In minor-key movements Albinoni's practice is less uniform. However, it is normal for the relative major and dominant keys to be visited first in

---

[3] *Lettres familières*, ii. 333.

that order before other keys are reached. In the first section of binary movements and the first vocal period of arias Albinoni has the unusual habit of passing to the dominant key via the relative major key, in which a transient cadence is made earlier in the same period. This often anticipates a modulation to the relative major key later in the movement (in the second section of a binary movement or the 'B' section of a da capo aria) and so appears to violate the principle of visiting each key only once. It is surprising that Albinoni remained so wedded to what other composers might well have regarded as a fundamental design fault!

None of these restrictions applies to 'open' movements, whose tonal organization follows no set plan. One particular device of which Albinoni is fond is to roam to and fro along the circumference of the circle of fifths in the minor mode. This is illustrated in concise form by Ex. 2, the brief central movement of the second concerto of Op. 7 (1715). Beginning in C minor, it passes through G minor to D minor in bar 3, deftly retracing its steps in the following two bars. One cannot refrain from remarking in passing how naturally and beautifully this movement develops the melodic idea of a descending fourth: variously diatonic and chromatic, syncopated and naturally accented.

Melody is indeed the point on which to champion Albinoni without reservation. Were one to find nothing else of merit in his music, one would be bound to acknowledge his great natural gifts as a tunesmith. His melodic ideals are vocal in inspiration: almost invariably, his melodic lines close by descending gracefully to the tonic note, decelerating as they do so (this is the design favoured since earliest times in vocal music, since it makes allowance for the singer's growing shortage of breath as a phrase ends). The starting-point of Albinoni's melodies is more variable, but they often begin close to the base, so giving the line as a whole the profile of a rising arch. Naturally, the arch is rarely smooth or simple: its apex is not placed centrally (a favourite location is just before the final descent to the cadence, as in Ex. 1), and the line is given individuality by being broken up into a series of shorter curves.

How beautifully Albinoni can mould a line even in a movement without pretensions to sophistication can be seen from Ex. 3, the Corrente from the third of the early *Balletti a quattro*. Each of the four-bar phrases making up the little dance forms its own version of the curve: the first begins near the mid-point, the second a little higher, the third near the base, and the fourth at the very apex. Although the highest note, b''', occurs once in each of the three last phrases, repetitiveness is avoided by making the context different every time.

The vocal inspiration of Albinoni's writing for instruments persists even

Ex. 2

when the melody includes a high quotient of leaps, some of which may entail (on the violin or cello) skipping over intermediate strings. Wide intervals often result from an implied polyphony: the assimilation in a single line of two or more notional strands occupying different registers. Angularity necessarily occurs when the composer temporarily abandons one strand to attend to the other. This is illustrated by Ex. 4, the closing bars of the opening movement of the second sonata in the 1717 collection. Beneath the original solo violin line I have supplied a paraphrase in which the polyphony is made explicit by dividing the line into two, as if for two

Ex. 3

Ex. 4

violins in a trio sonata. (Notes required for completion of the sense but not present in the original are printed small.) Bars 8–10 of the extract are especially interesting as they exemplify the common feature of a 'self-imitating' line in which, so to speak, a single instrument engages in dialogue with itself. Note as well the effective deflection of the expected cadence six bars from the end which by prolonging the phrase enables the line to sweep up once again to *c"'* and achieve an impressive climax.

The handling of rhythm in Albinoni's early works is rather unadventurous. Simple formations of crotchets, quavers, and semiquavers, varied by the occasional dotted group, constitute the entire rhythmic vocabulary in many works. His predilection for 'sewing-machine' rhythms is not, however, a wholly personal one: it informs most Italian music in the years around 1700. But even during this period Albinoni achieves in a few slow movements of cantatas and sonatas a greater degree of suppleness, assisted by a generous admixture of demisemiquavers. The opening of the third movement of the fourth sonata in Op. 2 (the seventh work in the collection) is a case in point (Ex. 5).

Ex. 5

Gradually, during the 1710s, Albinoni's rhythm loosens up and acquires new resources. Syncopation—in particular, the figure formed by a crotchet flanked by quavers—first becomes prominent in Op. 7 (1715). In Op. 8 (*c.* 1722) triplet groupings make a belated but welcome appearance. Appoggiaturas become more common—the languorous slow movement of the concerto Op. 9 no. 7 is filled with them to saturation point. The intricate, indeed sometimes rather precious, rhythmic nuances associated with the 'Neapolitan' style introduced to Venetian music in the mid-1720s are taken up by Albinoni in time to figure prominently in the Op. 10 concertos (1735/6). In the first violin line of the first period of the opening movement of the ninth concerto from this collection (Ex. 6) we first find 'Lombard' (or *alla zoppa*) rhythms produced by inversion of the familiar dotted group relieved by fierce *tirate* (upward sweeps of quick notes); these yield later on to tripping semiquaver triplets that evoke the world of *opera buffa*.

While the rhythmic resources of Albinoni's melodies steadily expand, those of the accompanying parts and particularly the bass remain almost as

Ex. 6

if in a time-warp, harking back to the 'walking' and 'running' patterns of equal notes that are a hallmark of the Corellian style. The one concession to modernity seems to be the more frequent insertion of rests, which do a little to break up the monolithic succession of notes. Albinoni's late works can be criticized as a whole for a curious disharmony between the keen rhythmic alertness of their upper parts and the leaden-footed tread of their basses.

One special rhythmic device that Albinoni employs with superb effect throughout his career is that of hemiola. This occurs when accents are shifted so that two groups of three notes become three groups of two notes, or vice versa. Hemiola entails no change in note-durations; all that changes is the pattern of stress (though this will of course have some effect on harmonic movement).

Most cases of hemiola in Albinoni's music entail the displacement of triple division to a higher level. Ex. 7, the opening of the finale of the oboe concerto Op. 7 no. 6, momentarily adopts the stress pattern of 3/4 metre (replacing that of 6/8) in bar 4. The displacement can, however, also

Ex. 7

vl unis.

proceed downwards, as one notes from the solo passage quoted as Ex. 8, which is taken from the finale of the concerto Op. 9 no. 10.

Particularly in fast fugal movements, Albinoni likes to make the hemiola patterns in the different contrapuntal lines non-coincident. This injects an exhilarating rhythmic dimension into the mêlée of the parts.

He is no less original in the style of melodic phrasing he favours. Instead of 'phrasing forward' from accented notes, he generally prefers to phrase in units that begin immediately after a note on the beat and conclude on an accented note. Conventional systems of beaming, which break beams before accented notes, tend to obscure the patterns in Albinoni's music that are founded on this style of phrasing. The opening of the first violin part in the Allemanda of the first balletto of Op. 3 is instructive (Ex. 9). The choice of c'' (rather than g') and d'' (rather than b') as the last notes of the first two semiquaver groups respectively would seem over-fastidious, were the composer not so insistent on carrying the phrasing forward to the ensuing accented note. In the third bar of the extract it is important to make a separation in thought between the opening c''', which concludes a phrase, and the following c'', which embarks on a new phrase that is repeated sequentially.

'Upbeat' phrasing patterns often start, as here, on the very first note of the melody, but Albinoni may also begin them on the second note, leaving

Ex. 8

vl pr

Ex. 9

Allegro

vl 1

the first note isolated on the strong beat as a kind of metrical marker calling the listener to attention.

Sequence forms the backbone of episodic and figurational writing in Albinoni's music. Arguably, he used the device too frequently and for too long stretches at a time—but then so do the great majority of his Italian contemporaries, Vivaldi included. Most of his sequences are strictly linear, moving up or down the scale one note at a time. Not many follow the 'zig-zag' pattern, in which the sequential unit moves alternately by a fifth and a fourth in the opposite direction (this can be regarded merely as an elaboration of the linear model that features stepwise movement at two pitch-levels instead of one); the other possibility, progression by rising or falling thirds, is hardly encountered at all.

Albinoni's sequences are normally 'total': they embrace all the parts at once. In some contrapuntal movements, however, the composer counter-poses a sequential line to a non-sequential one, creating an effective tension between different kinds of musical logic. Take, for example, the opening of the fugal second movement of the sonata Op. 2 no. 7 (Ex. 10). The subject ends on the first note of bar 4 and is followed without a pause by the countersubject, which, anticipating the answer in bar 5, proceeds upwards in a strict sequence for two-and-a-half bars.

Ex. 10

This passage illustrates Albinoni's liking for a type of counterpoint that emphasizes the independence of two lines heard simultaneously rather than their interrelationship, as in conventional imitative procedures. The music examples provided so far show with what relish he allows lines to intertwine, even when it means that an accompanying line rises above the principal line for a few notes. This very distinctive criss-crossing movement between the upper parts can be observed in the brief ritornello opening the bass aria 'Guarda un poco in quest'occhi di foco' from *Pimpinone* (Ex. 11). From bar 2 onwards the two violins have a relationship that one could describe as 'quasi-imitative'; the lines have similar contours

Ex. 11

and are bounded by the same notes, yet literal imitation does not occur.

Orthodox imitation does, of course, occupy a significant place in Albinoni's music. Snatches of canonic writing at the unison or the octave occur throughout his works, and in the sonatas of Op. 8 all the quick movements are in canon throughout. The prominence of fugal writing, which is employed not only in sonatas but also in certain concertos and even solo cantatas, was recognized, as we saw, by Schering and Moser.

Yet even in his fugues Albinoni exhibits many distinctive, indeed idiosyncratic, features. The subjects themselves tend towards an 'ideal' design following the arched shape described earlier in the discussion of Albinoni's melody; most end in time-honoured style on the tonic note preceded by the supertonic. A *reductio ad absurdum* of this design is provided by the subject of the fourth movement of the sonata Op. 1 no. 12 (taken over by Bach for BWV 946), which ascends by step from the tonic to the submediant, with just one ornamental 'kink' on the way, and then descends again to the tonic scalewise. The voice proposing the subject often continues with a codetta modulating to the dominant, in which key the answer is then heard.[4] This modulating link enables Albinoni to substitute a

---

[4] In the special case of Ex. 10 the codetta is identical with the opening of the countersubject.

'real' answer for the 'tonal' answer that the subject would conventionally require. The relative rarity of tonal answers accords with Albinoni's view of a fugue subject as a melodically significant theme whose integrity should be violated as little as possible.

The traditional fugal artifices interest Albinoni hardly at all. Discounting a number of 'stretto' fugues (in which subject and answer overlap), he employs stretto as a special device in only a handful of movements, among them the second movement of Op. 1 no. 9; its appearance there is almost mandatory, given the choice of a very traditional subject resembling the opening of the famous *Non nobis, Domine* canon. Inversion, augmentation, and diminution are not exploited in a formal manner. Strangely, although Albinoni is in other contexts fond of pedal-points over which dominant, dominant seventh, and tonic chords alternate (see Ex. 2 earlier), he does not employ these in his fugues—as Vivaldi, among others, regularly does—to create expectancy towards the end of the movement.

He betrays a conservative side by being reluctant to present the subject in the opposite mode. Thus in a movement in C major one will hear the subject in G major and possibly (but not necessarily) F major, but almost never in D, E, or A minor. Such a 'monomodal' approach is normal in the generation of Buxtehude, Legrenzi, and Purcell, but surprising in a contemporary of Vivaldi. One effect of this restriction is to confine visits to the keys of the opposite mode to the freely derived episodes separating groups of entries of the subject. The reappearances of the subject thus correlate with the re-establishment of the tonic and dominant keys. Inevitably, a rondo-like effect is produced, in which the return of the subject has the appearance of the restatement of a refrain. Indeed, Albinoni often accentuates this impression by repeating the opening exposition almost literally (i.e. except for added accompanying strands) near the end of the movement.

One peculiarly Albinonian type of imitation should be mentioned. It occurs in movements when one part, generally the first violin, holds the melodic interest. Since Albinoni's style of writing is highly articulated, there will be frequent points when this instrument pauses between phrases. These interstices give other instruments the chance to dart in. The interpolations very often take the form of 'pre-echoes' anticipating the continuation of the melody. They can be highly comic in effect, as in the opening of the Corrente of the seventh balletto from Op. 3 (Ex. 12). Here metrical displacement adds to the piquancy.

Albinoni remains true to his Corellian model in his preference for a style whose normal language is diatonic, chromaticism being reserved for special expressive effect. Passages such as the one quoted earlier as Ex. 2,

Ex. 12

which utilizes linear movement in semitones (the *passus duriusculus*, as it was called by the theorists of musical rhetoric), are not exactly rare; but they are absent from the majority of his works. Much of the chromatic inflection, such as that seen in bars 6 and 7 of Ex. 6, results from the 'tonicization' of triads and the consequent raising of the third in the chord serving as 'dominant'. The Neapolitan Sixth, however, is a resource that appears very frequently in minor keys, as does the diminished seventh over the raised subdominant in both modes. The Italian Sixth makes a token appearance in the late works. Unusual intervals are normally eschewed in the part-writing. In his early and middle-period works, Albinoni, like Corelli, avoids the augmented second as a melodic interval within the same phrase, though he freely uses its inversion, the diminished seventh (see Ex. 10, bars 1–2). The augmented second is at last admitted as a legitimate melodic interval in Op. 10 (Vivaldi had been exploiting it since the first decade of the century).

Eleanor Selfridge-Field makes an interesting series of observations about Albinoni's Op. 1 that by implication apply to his works in general. She writes: 'Suspensions are relatively few. Dissonances and diminished sevenths are also generally avoided. Long series of flawless consonances seem to be much preferred'.[5] The first two statements perhaps need a little qualification, but the third alludes accurately to a remarkable penchant of Albinoni for 'passing' chords. Most composers of his time allow passing notes in the bass travelling between the root of a chord and its third (or vice versa) to dissonate. Albinoni, however, likes to harmonize these notes, the upper parts moving smoothly in similar or contrary motion, with the result that a six–three or eight–three chord is formed. (A six–three chord is, of course, merely a triad in first inversion, but an eight–three chord is more ambiguous, functioning either as a first-inversion chord lacking the root or as a root-position chord lacking the fifth.) Since a high proportion of notes between the beats carry a chord, the music is extremely active harmonically and at a times produces an almost mesmeric effect when the same small group of chords is heard over and over again in various permutations. The

---

[5] *Venetian Instrumental Music from Gabrieli to Vivaldi*, p. 200.

opening of the tenth concerto of Op. 7 (Ex. 13) illustrates this. This example also shows another typically Albinonian feature: the full harmonization of a short upbeat note with an anticipation of the chord that arrives on the main beat (see also Ex. 12).

Ex. 13

Albinoni's use of seventh chords is conservative. Sevenths are rarely employed to enrich dominant chords at cadences. One must point out, however, that this restraint was shared by other Italian composers; it was the French and the Germans who liked to use dominant seventh chords in the cadential position. Albinoni always prepares the seventh by having the same note in the same part in the previous chord or, at the very least, by introducing it by step. Totally unprepared sevenths, such as one encounters in Vivaldi, are shunned. Once or twice one finds long successions of seventh chords on the Vivaldian pattern—for instance in Ex. 14 taken from the Allemanda of the eleventh balletto of Op. 3.

The most problematic and difficult to justify of all Albinoni's stylistic idiosyncrasies is the device that, for want of a better name, I shall call the 'transposed bass'. It is a radical extension of a practice that first came into being in the late seventeenth century, probably in opera. For the sake of variety all the bass instruments, including the continuo, were suppressed

Ex. 14

during certain passages, and the bass line was transferred to violas or violins playing in a register one octave higher than normal. These 'basses' in a high register were known by the diminutive form *bassetti*.

In a psychological sense, though in defiance of acoustic reality, *bassetti* were commonly treated as if the upward transposition from 'eight-foot' to 'four-foot' pitch had not occurred. Significantly, *bassetto* passages for violin or viola are often notated (though, strangely enough, never by Albinoni) in the bass clef one octave lower than sounding pitch. That is, they read at eight-foot pitch but sound at four-foot pitch. It became customary to tolerate the occasional second-inversion (six–four) chord in places where a root-position chord would be grammatically more correct, provided that it could be perceived as resulting from the transposition of the bass from its theoretical 'normal' register. A good example is provided by the Vivaldi slow movement that appears both as the opening movement of the violin sonata RV 12 and the middle movement of the concerto RV 582.[6] In the sonata the bass is for continuo, while in the concerto, apparently a later work, it is assigned as a *bassetto* to the first violins of the first orchestra. No changes are made to the lower part in the concerto despite the creation of some extraordinary inverted intervals (an augmented sixth, for instance, becoming a much harsher diminished third).

Such licences did not go unchallenged. In the introduction to the second part of his *Versuch über die wahre Art, das Clavier zu spielen* (1762) Carl Philipp Emanuel Bach voices disapproval of the use of the violin as an accompanying instrument precisely because of the confusion (his term) brought about by the crossing of parts.[7] Nevertheless, chord inversions introduced in this manner remained idiomatic well beyond the middle of the century. Early Haydn quartets often have the *basso* (played on the cello) momentarily rising above the viola to produce six–four chords. Their

---

[6] RV numbers are taken from the standard catalogue of Vivaldi's works by Peter Ryom.

[7] C. P. E. Bach, *Essay on the True Art of Playing Keyboard Instruments*, tr. and ed. William J. Mitchell (2nd edn., London, 1951), 173.

intolerance of this effect led some modern scholars to hypothesize that the composer intended a double-bass to come to the rescue of the cello by doubling the notes of the *basso* in the lower octave—which then led to speculation that these quartets were conceived for orchestral forces. However, Haydn makes his intentions clear beyond all doubt in the Trio of his String Quartet Op. 9 no. 4 (Hob. III: 22), which is scored for the two violins alone; in the cadential dominant chord at the end of the first section he has the first violin double-stopping the notes *b* and *g♯′*, while the second violin supplies the 'bass' note *e′*.

Albinoni extends the customary use of the 'transposed bass' in two different ways, each of which is highly distinctive and, to modern ears at least, questionable. He seems, first, to have regarded the second inversion of a chord as an acceptable substitute for its root position in all textures from which the continuo was absent. We find six–four chords used casually in this manner in the juvenile *Messa a 3* and in many fugal expositions in sonata and concerto movements up to the point when the continuo enters and the normal rules of counterpoint start to apply. It is not always possible to explain the inversions by reference to the presence of a *bassetto*. In Ex. 15, showing bars 64–6 of the first movement of the second concerto in Op. 10, neither of the accompanying parts is identifiable from its outline as a 'bass' part; the six–four chords (identified by asterisks) arise haphazardly from the free interweaving of the orchestral violins.

Ex. 15

But even where the chord-inversions are clearly attributable to the upward transposition of the bass, Albinoni sometimes introduces long chains of six–four chords that can seem quite disconcerting. Nowhere is this effect more marked than in the slow movements of three of his Op. 5 concertos (nos. 2, 5, and 8). In Ex. 16, scored for principal (solo) violin, second violin, and cello occurring in bars 15–17 of the second movement of the second concerto, the 'bass' on second violin would have to descend by not one but two octaves to restore harmonic orthodoxy. Had the cello part, which was probably intended for a solo instrument, been assigned instead to a voice, the effect would not be so strange, since solo voices accompanied instrumentally are never actually heard, in subjective terms, as lowest parts (which is why Schubert songs for contralto can pass easily into the bass repertory without regard for the changed pitch–relationship of the voice and the piano). In a homogeneous ensemble of instruments, however, this illusion is less easily sustainable.

Ex. 16

Albinoni's contrapuntal textures fall into two main classes. On one hand we have the 'trio' style, whose *locus classicus* is the trio sonata. Here the structural voices comprise two parts interacting contrapuntally plus a bass which may either participate in the contrapuntal discourse or provide a mere harmonic support. On the other hand we have the 'solo' style, seen at its simplest in violin sonatas and solo cantatas accompanied by continuo alone. This is founded on only two voices: a treble and a bass.

Naturally, these basic texture-models derived from the most economical forms of chamber music become modified in music for larger ensembles by the addition of 'filling' voices that give extra body and weight to the sound, although they make little or no individual contribution to the harmony, rhythm, or melody. Paradoxically, the 'trio' style is recognizable as such even when the voices are reduced to two, provided that these two are treated as equal contrapuntal partners. Many specimens of this kind of texture occur in the *cavate* of the solo cantatas (the term 'cavata' is explained in Chapter 5), and the instrumental music furnishes one splendid example in the shape of the fugal second movement of the sixth sonata from the 'unauthorized' 1708 collection. Inverting the paradox, it is equally possible for the 'solo' style to be represented by a three-strand texture. This often happens in orchestral writing when the violins play in unison, leaving the viola to contribute a solitary middle strand (as in Ex. 1 above); it is also found in the *Balletti a tre* of Opp. 3 and 8 in those movements where the first violin is permitted to sustain a continuous melody.

The instruments responsible for supplying the 'filling' are most often strings: one or two violas and the second violin. Even the first violin can sometimes take a filling part when it has to accompany a violin or oboe soloist. Wind instruments in Albinoni's music are accorded a prominent solo role most of the time, but in more heavily scored passages involving the full ensemble they too may have to yield to the upper strings and retreat into the background.

The use of solo instruments—variously violin, cello, trumpet, and one or two oboes—inevitably introduces greater complexity. Nevertheless, it is rare not to be able to discern either the 'trio' or the 'solo' style as a point of reference for these more elaborate textures. For example, in the concertos with two obbligato oboes in Opp. 7 and 9 one often finds that each pair of treble instruments, violins or oboes, operates as a more or less homophonic unit; the contrapuntal opposition consequently occurs between paired instruments rather than single instruments; in all other respects, however, the texture conforms to the simple 'trio' model.

Unison writing is employed very sparingly by Albinoni in his orchestral music. Nearly all the works in which orchestral unisons appear belong to the period in Albinoni's career—from Op. 7 (1715) to Op. 9 (1722)— when the influence of Vivaldi is most evident. The opening period of the first movement of the concerto in C major remembered by Quantz is a prime example. Strangely enough, the early trumpet sonata used as the sinfonia to *Zenobia, regina de' Palmireni* (1694) also features unison writing—it must actually be one of the first examples of this characteristic texture in orchestral literature. Between this work and Op. 7, however, one searches in vain for any similar passages. A few of the unisons are 'impure' in the sense that the viola inserts foreign notes (without, however, subverting the general unison effect); Albinoni's reasons for allowing the viola to deviate so inconsequentially remain obscure.

It is noteworthy that Albinoni employs unison writing only in the major mode and overwhelmingly in C major and D major, the keys of the natural trumpet. Whether by design or accident, the thematic character of the unison passages more often than not alludes to the *stile tromba*. Significantly, unison writing is absent altogether from movements in slow tempo—from which trumpets by tradition (and for their own comfort) were normally excluded.

In passages featuring a solo instrument Albinoni follows the general practice of his time by lightening the orchestral texture. Rather surprisingly, the simplest form of accompanimental texture—a single strand on continuo or a substitute such as violin—is relatively uncommon in the instrumental music. We find it used to support the solo instrument in its dialogues with the string ensemble in some early trumpet sonatas. In one third movement (in Sonata IV) from Op. 2 and four central movements (in Concertos II, V, VIII, and XI) from Op. 5 it appears in the context of a stylistic allusion to the texture of the trio or solo sonata. The most frequent recourse to it occurs in the concertos with one or two oboes (though not those for strings alone) in Op. 7, which in this respect as in many others is the least 'unorthodox' of Albinoni's concerto collections. Thereafter it becomes rarer.

A two-strand accompaniment (generally on violins) becomes common in the later works. Ex. 15 shows its most typical form. This is a mode of accompaniment associated in particular with Tartini, although Vivaldi also adopted it frequently in the 1730s. Albinoni's abundant use of it in Op. 10 reflects his concern to remain abreast of contemporary fashion in small details—without, of course, changing the fundamentals of his style.

Many other forms of lightening that entail the elimination of certain instruments are employed, and it would be tedious to list them all. Mention should be made of the frequent suppression of the continuo—not only in the later works but even as early as Op. 2. In operatic arias the viola is often omitted in passages where the voice has to sing, but in this case there may be an additional, practical motive that is not strictly musical in inspiration. It frequently happened that an extra system could be fitted on to a page of score, with a consequent saving in paper, if two of the parts could be made to share a single staff. A convenient way of doing this was to 'double up' the viola and the voice, which would otherwise occupy adjacent staves. It was even unnecessary to supply cues, since the presence of an underlaid text would show where the voice entered and the viola paused, and vice versa.

The omission of parts must not be confused with their doubling, which serves not to lighten but to strengthen the texture. Albinoni employs unison violins not for accompaniment to a soloist in the fashion of Vivaldi but for vigorous enunciation of the primary material. Where the average size of orchestras was small, the effect of massing the violins on a single line was correspondingly greater. In order to achieve weightiness Albinoni elects to concentrate his forces horizontally (multiplying the number of players on each strand) rather than vertically (multiplying the number of strands).

Strange as it may seem, the textures in Albinoni's music that feature the greatest number of separate strands are found in accompaniments to solo passages for the principal violin. Albinoni must be the only Italian composer of his generation who does not equate a light texture with a lean one. Naturally, he has to guard against 'swamping' the soloist; this he does by keeping the accompaniment strictly homophonic and its rhythm absolutely regular, and by interposing rests at frequent intervals. It is instructive to compare the 'presto' inserts occuring in some of his concerto slow movements with their counterparts in Torelli's concertos (on which they may have been modelled). Whereas the older composer sheds all instruments except the continuo, Albinoni retains a multi-strand accompaniment containing up to six parts (two violins, two violas, cello, and continuo). Although they are thoroughly untypical of the Italian tradition, 'full' accompaniments of this kind are quite often encountered in concertos by northern European composers (including Handel), some of whom may have drawn inspiration from Albinoni's widely circulated Opp. 2 and 5.

As we have seen, the viola figures prominently in Albinoni's accompanimental textures. Indeed, it rarely has any other role in his music than to accompany, except in fugal movements. Even there, its obbligato status lapses as soon as it has finished presenting the subject or countersubject. It rarely contributes anything essential to the harmony; the dissonances found in the viola parts of northern composers such as Purcell and Albicastro are eschewed almost completely. Nor does it have any rhythmic independence except in those few cases where it enlivens the middle of the texture with repeated semiquavers. Unlike some of his contemporaries, Albinoni never explicitly describes a viola part as 'ad libitum'. Nevertheless, many of his works remain perfectly viable when shorn of violas, as some contemporary arrangements as trio sonatas of his *Balletti a cinque* show.

Up to Op. 5 (1707) Albinoni almost always has two viola parts rather than one (the twelve *Balletti a quattro* are the great exception). But from the operatic scores of 1708 onwards viola parts come singly. This abrupt change reflects accurately an evolution undergone by Venetian music in the years around 1710 that in turn fits into a much wider pattern of development.

To understand it we have to go back to the early seventeenth century, when the first works for a 'consort of violins' were written. Quite understandably, ensembles formed from instruments of the violin family, like viol consorts before them, were modelled on vocal ensembles. At this time five voices constituted the norm in compositions such as madrigals and polyphonic motets, the SSATB and SATTB dispositions being especially common. Adopting the same dispositions, the violin consort could be made up either from two violins, two violas (playing respectively in alto and tenor ranges), and a bass violin (*violone*), or from one violin, three violas, and a bass violin. The second disposition, common until the end of the century in France, gave way to the first in Italy at an earlier stage.

The reduction from five parts to four, which entailed the loss of the second viola part, was pioneered in Roman music in the 1670s during the periods of Stradella's and then Corelli's ascendancy. The whole of Corelli's surviving orchestral music is scored for a large ensemble (*concerto grosso*) in four parts, to which a small ensemble (*concertino*) comprising the players needed for a trio sonata is added.

Although the Roman-style division of the orchestra into a *concerto grosso* (or *ripieno*) and a *concertino* never took root elsewhere in Italy (as distinct from northern Europe), the reduction to a single viola part gradually became universal. Venice resisted a little longer than most other Italian centres but eventually bowed to fashion. The last collection of concertos by a Venetian composer to require two viola parts is Vivaldi's *L'estro armonico*, Op. 3, published in 1711.

When not simply termed 'Viola prima' and 'Viola seconda', the two viola parts commonly took the name of the register that they occupied, being styled 'Alto viola' and 'Tenore viola' or 'Violetta alto' and 'Violetta tenore'. In either case the same type of instrument and the same tuning was employed. (This remark is needed to counter a lingering belief that there existed for this repertory a separate tenor instrument of the violin family played in the manner of a cello!) When instruments for a consort of violins were manufactured as a set, the size of viola intended for the alto part was sometimes made slightly smaller than that of its tenor partner, but that does not alter the basic identity of the instruments.

In his early works Albinoni handles viola parts rather awkwardly. At the best of times filling parts have to be written with care in order to avoid proscribed consecutive fifths and octaves; monotony on one hand and angularity on the other are almost impossible to avoid completely, though their worst effects can be mitigated. During his musical apprenticeship Albinoni seems to find viola parts an embarrassment. He has difficulty in controlling their register, allowing them either to drift wide apart and encroach on the territory of the violins and the bass respectively or to tangle unnecessarily with each other. Often, too, they double notes that are already sufficiently strong at the expense of weaker or absent harmony notes. Around the time of Op. 5, however, he begins to show a surer touch; from that point onwards his viola parts, though as unambitious as ever in their intentions, are skilfully written and largely free of solecisms.

The ordinary bass instrument for which Albinoni wrote, at least in his mature works, was not the original bass violin, often called *violone piccolo* to distinguish it from the *violone grosso*, the double-bass instrument. It was the *violoncello*, the smaller, more effective version of the same instrument that the invention of wire-wound strings in Bologna during the 1660s had made a practical proposition.[8] It is true that the *Trattenimenti armonici per camera*, Op. 6 (*c.* 1711), specify a *violone* as the bass stringed instrument, but the conservatism here is probably one of nomenclature rather than actual performance practice. (In similar fashion, the violin sonatas of Corelli's Op. 5 (1700) also call for *violone* rather than *violoncello*; it seems that the first term was still employed for preference in cases where the stringed instrument, as here, merely reinforced the continuo line.)

Without exception, Albinoni's authorized published music in three or more real parts always includes a separate partbook for cello. The extra partbook is even found, most surprisingly, in the balletti of Opp. 3 and 8— in a genre where by tradition the bass for the stringed and keyboard instruments was identical, allowing performance of the music without continuo (or, alternatively, without the support of the stringed instrument). In the compositions preserved only in manuscript, however, the provision of a separate cello part is less common, and is not found at all in the mature works.

The reason for the distinction can perhaps be found in the nature of the difference between the cello and continuo parts when it occurs. Discounting those relatively few instances in concertos where the cello has brief solo passages, either independently or in dialogue with the principal violin (as in Ex. 16), its line diverges from that of the continuo in simple ways familiar from the tradition of improvised 'divisions': some longer notes are broken into figures employing smaller notes, and octave-variants (generally, but not invariably, in the upper octave) occur frequently. In

<hr>

[8] The origin of the *violoncello* and the reasons for its success are discussed in Stephen Bonta, 'From Violone to Violoncello: A Question of Strings?', *Journal of the American Musical Instrument Society*, 3 (1977), 64–99.

many cases the difference between the cello and continuo parts is too trivial to be perceived by the listener and in that respect is redundant musically. However, it is evident to the performers and may give the cellist a sense, albeit a rather illusory one, of making an independent contribution. Perhaps Albinoni insisted on separate cello parts in his published works more as a social gesture aimed at the gratification of his customers than as a genuine enrichment of the music.

In many modern performances of Albinoni's concertos the *violoncello* part is taken by the entire cello section, leaving the continuo line to harpsichord supported by double-basses playing in the lower octave. This distribution produces absurd results when the cello part is written an octave higher than the continuo part, since cellos and double-basses are now two octaves apart, leaving only the harpsichord in the middle. Since cues for 'solo' and 'tutti' are not used to mark out those passages for cello that are clearly for a soloist, it is probably correct to assume that the *violoncello* part is intended in its entirety for a single player. Additional cellos must therefore join the harpsichord on the continuo line, reinforcing the eight-foot tone. If this deduction is well founded, the player of the *violoncello* part assumes a role in relation to his fellow cellists comparable with that of the principal violin *vis-à-vis* the first violins.

The Italian editions of Albinoni's instrumental music from Op. 1 to Op. 5 distinguish carefully between 'Organo' (Op. 1) and 'Cembalo' (Opp. 3 and 5) as the harmony instrument to be employed for the continuo. Op. 2, which mixes sonatas and concertos, employs the neutral term 'Basso continuo'. The Dutch and English editions, however, replace *cembalo* by *organo*, employing the second term in its more general contemporary meaning of a keyboard instrument of any kind (organ or harpsichord) playing from a figured bass. Albinoni nowhere specifies the archlute or theorbo as the harmony instrument for the continuo; in fact, his serenata *Il nascimento de l'Aurora* is the only place in the whole of his extant music where a plucked stringed instrument is mentioned. Nevertheless, the cultivation of these instruments was so extensive in the Venice—indeed, the Italy—of his time that it is difficult to imagine their exclusion from contemporary performances of his music.

Albinoni's approach to writing for the violin deserves a few preliminary comments (more will be said in later chapters). He is notably conservative in his exploration of high positions, scarcely ranging further than the fifth position (f'''), which even Corelli reached in his second Op. 6 concerto. This may be compared with Vivaldi's exploitation of the twelfth position in the cadenza to the third movement of the concerto RV 212 (to which one manuscript ascribes the date 1712) and Locatelli's recourse to the sixteenth position (five-stroke C♯!) in his twenty-second Capriccio (1733). On the other hand, he is inventive in his use of double and multiple stopping, whether polyphonic or homophonic in character. Some of his *brisures* are pleasingly idiomatic (take for example the arpeggiated chord *b–d'–f"* used in the fourth bar of Ex. 8). Signs of articulation such as staccato dots or wedges, found in profusion in Vivaldi's music, appear very rarely. In fact, the only performance direction worthy of note occurring in any of Albinoni's violin parts is the instruction 'sopra il manico arpeggio' over a solo passage in the first movement of Op. 7 no. 10. This tells the player to move his left hand over the fingerboard, thus into a higher position, in order to play a series of broken chords that, although not in a high register, would be difficult to negotiate otherwise.

His bowing patterns mostly belong to the simplest and most widely used types. Slurs generally begin on an accented note and finish on an unaccented one, though 'syncopated' patterns cutting across metrical divisions are occasionally found (as in the third bar of Ex. 5 above). The vast majority of notes are intended to be separately articulated, although it must be pointed out that this style of articulation does not necessarily entail a constant see-sawing of the bow, since the technique of 're-placing' the bow without changing direction ('craquer', in the terminology of the composer Georg Muffat) was a recognized method of preserving the 'rule of down-bow'.

Although it cannot be considered an aspect of his style, Albinoni's attitude to borrowing from his own music and that of others is a general question that can conveniently be discussed at this point. How widespread borrowing from pre-existing music was in the early eighteenth century needs no stressing. For some composers it was a solution to the problem of shortage of time or inspiration; for others it was an opportunity to refine or enlarge on what they (or others) had said in earlier works; it could even be conceived as an act of homage. The motives for borrowing were doubtless often mixed. Who is to say whether Vivaldi's two adaptations of a 'Cum sancto spiritu' fugue by Giovanni Maria Ruggieri for his own settings of the Gloria were occasioned by a rapidly advancing deadline, a lack of confidence in his own ability to compose in the 'strict' style, or a genuine admiration for a movement in which he discerned attractive possibilities of improvement? Perhaps all three factors played a part.

No cases of a direct borrowing by Albinoni from another composer have come to light. He was certainly wise not to attempt this, for in a style as individual as his any 'imported' material would easily have been recognized as a foreign body. In his dramatic music he occasionally re-used movements. The final movement of the sinfonia to *La Statira* (1726) is a transposed and rescored version of that concluding the sinfonia of the serenata *Il nome glorioso in terra, santificato in cielo* (1724). Some arias reappear with changed literary text. In view of the very incomplete preservation of his vocal music it would be premature to estimate how great his 'propensity to borrow' was, but the signs are that he borrowed sparingly—certainly by comparison with Vivaldi, Bach, and Handel.

Within the corpus of his instrumental music published in authorized collections no borrowings at all—not even of individual movements—are evident. This is not surprising, since such music was exposed to particularly close scrutiny by the public, which would have frowned upon any hint of laziness; even Vivaldi—almost—refrains from self-borrowing in his authorized published collections. However, the two unauthorized collections of violin sonatas (1708 and *c.* 1717) show that certain movements underwent a long gestation before they achieved their definitive shape. Different versions of one particular movement serve as the second movement of the opening sonata in both those collections as well as appearing in a more refined guise as the second movement of Op. 6 no. 4. No doubt, the composer regarded the 'unauthorized' versions as work in progress that he would not ideally have wished to present to a wide public, although they may at the time have met the needs of a particular customer.

Where one or both works have only 'manuscript' status, he has fewer inhibitions about extracting and re-using individual passages. Surprisingly, he does not adopt a procedure of which Vivaldi was especially fond: namely, the retention of the primary material of a movement (e.g., the 'tutti' sections) and the recomposition of the subsidiary material (e.g., the 'solo' sections). Perhaps he felt that the identity of incipit made such borrowings too indiscreet. However, he delights in a process of transformation in which the primary material is paraphrased, changing its melodic outline but retaining its harmonic sense, and the subsidiary material is reproduced exactly as before. The process can be illustrated by comparing (in Ex. 17) bars 9–13 of the first violin part in the first movement of the fourth concerto of Op. 7 with the corresponding bars in a sinfonia of perhaps slightly later date preserved in Dresden. The gently flowing lines of the 'motto' phrase in the concerto are transformed into a more stridently assertive shape capable of hushing an operatic audience.

Vivaldi, too, employs this device, albeit relatively infrequently. However, in his hands it is less consistently successful, since his subsidiary material tends to be derived more closely from the primary material than is usually the case in Albinoni's music. In the outer movements of the concerto RV 582, for instance, all the solo episodes of the concerto RV 210 (Op. 8 no. 10) reappear. But since some of these episodes develop the

Ex. 17

primary material of RV 210 in a very purposeful manner, the fragmentary reference to the same material in the context of RV 582 (where it has not been stated in its full, original form) is puzzling and incongruous. Since Albinoni's episodic material tends, in contrast, to be neutral in character, containing no specific reference to primary material, it is more suited to transportation from one work to another.

Like all composers of his time, Albinoni reverts again and again to a few favourite turns of phrase and, especially, harmonic formulae. These occur particularly at the beginning of movements, where, so to speak, they serve the composer as a starting-handle, cranking his imagination into motion. One only has to examine the preludes of Bach's '48' to realize how natural

Ex. 18

and blameless such formulae are. There is not space to list all of Albinoni's opening routines, but Ex. 18 shows one of his favourite harmonic designs, taken from the second movement of Op. 6 no. 8. The specifically 'Albinonian' touch is the tonicization of the subdominant (A) in bar 3, following a conventional I–V–V^7–I progression.

So much for Albinoni in general: we turn now to a more detailed consideration of his works arranged by period and genre.

4

THE EARLY INSTRUMENTAL
WORKS (TO 1700)

THE division of a composer's works into early, mature, and late periods is such a conventional exercise that one really has to consider whether it has not become a mere artifice arising more out of the need to organize a book into manageable chapters than in accordance with the stylistic evolution of the music. Fortunately, a threefold division suits our examination of Albinoni's music very well. All the instrumental music of his that survives up to Op. 2, conveniently placed at the turn of the century (1700), can be accurately described as 'early' not merely in a chronological sense but also in the sense of 'not fully mature'. Typically for music of a composer's apprentice years, it starts by oscillating unpredictably between a cautious schematicism, in which the strong influence of composers of a previous generation is discernible, and a reckless experimentalism. As Albinoni gains experience, a middle course emerges, and the characteristic features of his style that will be carried over into the mature period gradually become set. His technical mastery, at first insecure, steadily improves and gains in fluency. In biographical terms the period beginning shortly before 1694 and ending in 1700 also forms a unity, since it appears to correspond to his association with the Mantuan court.

Very little of this music deserves to be revived today, except as a historical curiosity. One can make an exception for some of the Op. 1 and Op. 2 sonatas, one or two of the *Balletti a quattro*, and possibly the last of the Op. 2 concertos. The difference in quality between works prepared for the press and those left in manuscript, evident throughout Albinoni's career, is especially marked in this period.

The genre most strongly represented among the early works is that conveniently but not quite accurately described as the 'church' sonata (a more historically authentic term would be 'sonata' *tout court*). Besides the twelve sonatas of Op. 1 and the six in Op. 2 there is a manuscript set of six that can be assigned to the years leading up to 1700 on account of certain borrowings from it that appear in the second printed collection. In addition, there is an anonymous five-part sonata in Durham Cathedral Library which on stylistic grounds, with some support from circumstantial evidence, can be considered a very strong candidate for attribution to Albinoni.

Next, there are two sonatas for strings and trumpet (identified respectively as *So* 1 and *Si* 1 in my catalogue) that require consideration as a separate group on account of their instrumentation and their concerto-like features; to these can be added three anonymous sonatas with similar scoring in Durham Cathedral Library.

The concertos surviving from this period comprise only the six in Op. 2 plus one very primitive work (*Co* 1) in manuscript.

Finally, we have a set of six five-part balletti and another of twelve four-part balletti. These are works which, again using terminology rather too loosely, can be described as 'chamber' sonatas consisting primarily of dance movements.

In no other period of his career are so many of Albinoni's works in manuscript misattributed in the sources. Indeed, in several cases the incorrect attributions outnumber the correct ones. The explanation is a matter for guesswork, but I would suggest that Albinoni's lack of celebrity in his early years was partly responsible. In contemporary manuscript collections of music by several composers (the Durham volumes offer an illustration) unattributed pieces are common, and composers unfamiliar to the copyist must have run a more than average risk of having their authorship omitted from the heading of a work. When new copies of the same collections were prepared, there was always a temptation for the names already appearing in the attributed works to be transferred willy-nilly to the anonymous ones. Indeed, modern librarians have often been guilty of precisely the same act, and for similar motives. So laziness, or a misplaced concern for uniformity, lies at the root of many of these misattributions—not any desire to falsify, or to improve one composer's reputation at the expense of another's.

At this point it is appropriate to review the nature and state of the sources for these fifty-five works. Little time need be spent on the twenty-four works constituting Opp. 1 and 2. The history of their publication has been outlined in Chapter 1, and their extant manuscript sources all seem to be derived directly from the versions printed in Italy or subsequently engraved in Holland and England.

With five exceptions, the remaining works are all preserved in correctly attributed and fairly accurate non-autograph parts preserved among the Este manuscripts (Estensische Musikalien) of the Österreichische National-bibliothek, Vienna. Most of this large and important collection, whose separate catalogue was published in 1927, was originally owned by the Obizzi family, who resided in the castle of Delizia in Catajo near Padua.[1] The 'courtly' character of many of the Albinoni works, in particular the

[1] See Robert Haas, *Die estensischen Musikalien: Thematisches Verzeichnis mit Einleitung* (Regensburg, 1927).

balletti, encourages a suspicion that these are secondary copies of works originally destined for Mantua.

The contested attributions arise from concordances preserved elsewhere. The *Balletti a quattro* (Vienna shelfmark EM 94/94a) are preserved anonymously in an arrangement for three recorders and bass in the Library of the Counts of Schönborn at Wiesentheid, West Germany (catalogued as no. 406); a first-violin part in the Library of the University of California at Berkeley (Ms. It. 63) ascribes them, however, to Corelli and carries the date (of copying?) 1728. The case of the *Balletti a cinque* is even more complicated. A score of them in Christ Church Library (Ms. Mus. 3) originates from the collection of Henry Aldrich (1648–1710), Dean of Christ Church. This source lacks the Sarabanda of the fourth balletto. In comparison with the Vienna parts, the notation has undergone some modernization in regard to key signatures, and the alto clef has replaced the tenor clef for the second viola part. (Such modifications are common in northern European copies of Italian music; whereas Italy possessed professional copyists whose brief was merely to reproduce their exemplars in neat and regular form, without any thought of editing or arrangement, the northern Europeans had to resort for this task to professional musicians or musically literate amateurs who would naturally be free from such restraints.)

The Christ Church score names 'Ziani' as the composer. Presumably, the reference is not to Pietro Andrea Ziani, a Venetian musician who died in 1684, but to his nephew Marc'Antonio, who died in Vienna in 1715. The younger Ziani's involvement, as *maestro di cappella*, with the Mantuan court has been mentioned in Chapter 2. It is therefore possible that the confusion between Albinoni and Ziani has its origin in the inclusion of music by both men in collections devoted to the repertory of that court. Or else it may be related to their common operatic activity in Venice in the years leading up to 1700.

Even if the Vienna source were not, objectively, the *codex optimus* on account of the presence there of the Sarabanda for the fourth balletto, a stylistic comparison between the music of Albinoni and both Zianis leaves no room for equivocation: the *Balletti a cinque* are as characteristic of Albinoni's style as they are foreign to that of either Pietro Andrea or Marc'Antonio.

A further English source, textually very closely related to the Oxford score (from which it may even have been copied), is preserved in Durham Cathedral Library (MS M193/1 and 2–7).[2] It consists of both a score and separate parts, attributed as before to Ziani. The manuscript formerly

---

[2] Fuller information on the MSS in Durham Cathedral Library and their diverse provenance can be found in Brian Crosby, *A Catalogue of Durham Cathedral Music Manuscripts* (Oxford, 1986).

belonged to the collection of Bamburgh Castle, Northumberland, and its first owner appears to have been the Hon. Edward Finch (1664–1738), who took his MA at Oxford in 1679, remaining as a Fellow of Christ Church until 1700, when he was ordained a deacon at York. The association of both Aldrich and Finch with Christ Church undoubtedly has something to do with the many common works in their respective collections, although the exact nature of the connection has not yet been established.

In 1702, very shortly after issuing extracts from Albinoni's Op. 3 as *Albinoni's Aires in 3 Parts for Two Violins and a Through Bass*, Walsh and Hare brought out a companion collection that they entitled *Ziani's Aires or Sonatas in 3 Parts for Two Violins and a Thorow Bass*. This collection contains twenty-two separate movements. The first twelve, amazing to relate, are the first three *Balletti a cinque*, lacking their viola parts. They retain the key signature of the Vienna source (which means that they do not belong to the same line of transmission as the Durham and Oxford manuscripts) and remain in other respects faithful to its text, except that the introductory movements are described as 'Aria' instead of 'Introdutione'. From movement thirteen onwards the style is different and could indeed be that of Marc'Antonio Ziani. Perhaps Walsh declined to publish the last three Albinoni balletti because in the fourth and fifth the violas, although not indispensable, make a modest contribution to the contrapuntal activity. Hence the 'co-option' of movements from an altogether different source in order to produce a collection of acceptable length.

To add to the complexity, there is a further published concordance, of which I became aware only recently. In 1702 Estienne Roger issued a collection entitled *VI Sonates à due violini col basso per l'organo del Sig. A. Ziani*. Only its bass part survives, preserved in the Bodleian Library, Oxford (Mus. 179. f. 1^{1-6}). All six balletti are included, although the fourth still lacks its Sarabanda. In places the bass line has been modified. Key signatures have been modernized in a more thoroughgoing manner than in any other source (for example, two flats are used for F minor in Vienna and by Walsh, three in Durham and Oxford, and four by Roger).

The five sources just discussed point to a very complex pattern of transmission that indicates the existence around 1700 of many further sources that are now lost. Since only one source (fortunately, the best!) gives the composer's name correctly, this case reminds us that establishing a work's authorship amid conflicting attributions is never a matter simply of counting heads and awarding it to the person whose name appears most often in the sources: it also has to take into account their various textual and contextual relationships.

Even more variety of attribution is shown by the trumpet sonata in D major *Si* 1. In my Albinoni catalogue it is classed as a sinfonia, since it appears as the overture to Albinoni's first opera, *Zenobia, regina de' Palmireni* (Carnival 1694).[3] However, I have now come round to the view that it originated as an independent sonata and only subsequently served as an operatic sinfonia. Certainly, its form, which will be discussed further on, places it squarely in the tradition of the trumpet sonata, while distancing it from that of the Venetian *sinfonia avanti l'opera*.

Only one of the four separate manuscript sources of the sonata names Albinoni as the composer. This is a set of parts in Warsaw University Library (Mf 8). The owner (who was possibly also the copyist) is identified on the title-page as a certain Franciscus Hintzinger associated with a church of St James ('Chori S. Jacobi'), and the manuscript is dated 1711. The work is titled *Sonata di concerto â VII vocibus* and comprises parts for solo trumpet (called 'Clarino' in the German fashion), first and second violins, alto and tenor violas, cello, and continuo ('Violone o Cembalo').

A score of the work is also found in the former Aldridge collection in Christ Church Library, where it is called *Sonata con violini e tromba a 6* and attributed, like the balletti, to 'Ziani'. There is obviously some connection between the similar misattributions. Perhaps the sonata belonged to the same, possibly Mantuan, repertory.

A set of parts in the Zentralbibliothek, Zurich, names the work (lacking its tenor viola) as *II. Sinfonia a 6* and identifies its composer as 'Bornozini'. Perhaps this is a corruption of 'Bononcini'; it may be significant that in 1685 the young Giovanni Bononcini (1670–1747) published in Bologna a set of *sinfonie*, Op. 3, for five to eight instruments, some of which include parts for one or two trumpets. Here 'sinfonia' has the meaning not of 'operatic overture' but rather of 'sonata'; in Italy the term was widely used to refer to heavily scored sonatas employing violas (of which those in Albinoni's Op. 2 are perfect examples).

The final source, which names no composer, is in the possession of the University Library, Uppsala (Instr. Mus. i hs. 66:4). It was copied out by Joachim Daniel Gudenschwager, who was a violinist in the Swedish court orchestra from 1727 to 1777 and a strong partisan of Italian music.

No problems of attribution surround the trumpet sonata in C major (*So* 1), the concerto *Co* 1, and the six *Sonate a tre* (*So* 20–5). These are preserved only in Vienna and are shelfmarked EM 96, EM 110b, and EM 73 respectively. It is interesting that the concerto is listed in the Breitkopf *Supplemento I dei catalogi delle sinfonie . . . che si trovano in*

---

[3] The Library of Congress, Washington DC, holds the only score of *Zenobia* (M1500.A72Z4) whose location is known today. Another score, which once belonged to the collection of Pietro Ottoboni and was auctioned at Sotheby's in 1918, presumably survives in private ownership.

manoscritto (Leipzig, 1766) as a 'Sinfonia a 6'. Once again we glimpse the confusion regarding the identity of the concerto during the formative years of the genre.

It is difficult to decide on what basis the music of the four anonymous compositions in Durham Cathedral Library can properly be discussed in this chapter. One may plead that their vocabulary, grammar, and syntax are thoroughly Albinonian—right down to idiosyncratic details—and that many passages in them are extraordinarily similar to ones found in Albinoni's authenticated music of this period. But it is unwise to rely on evidence of style alone. All four works appear in MS M175, a miscellany of sonatas and similar compositions in score; separate parts for three of them are contained, alongside those of the six *Balletti a cinque*, in MS M193.[4] The presence in the same volumes of two five-part *sinfonie* by Francesco Navarra, one of which is dated 1697 and identifies this composer as 'Maestro di Cappella di Sua Altezza Serenissima di Mantova', hints at a Mantuan provenance, although it has to be admitted that no other composers among those whose names are given support this connection.

In the circumstances it is safest to resist the temptation to use these four anonymous works to demonstrate stages in Albinoni's evolution as a composer, since this would beg the question of their authenticity. However, I consider it permissible to show how they would fit into the pattern already established by the authenticated works, pending a final verdict on their authorship.

We have seen that, both quantitatively and qualitatively, sonatas are the most significant product of this early period. When Op. 1 appeared in 1694, inaugurating Albinoni's long series of published collections, the sonata was already over 100 years old. It had emerged in the late sixteenth century as a genre specifically designed for instruments (the word 'sonata' and its variant 'suonata' mean 'played' [piece], in the same way that 'cantata' means 'sung' [piece]). Unlike some other purely instrumental forms such as the ricercar and fantasia, the early sonata had no prescribed form or texture. It was, however, abstract in nature, tolerating no overt description of extra-musical ideas and avoiding too close a reference to the dance, and it was normally shaped as a single long movement consisting of a succession of sections contrasted among themselves in metre, tempo, texture, and tonal inclination. The principle of alternating these elements in a regular fashion—for example, following imitative sections with passages of homophony or inserting *tripla* sections as a relief from the prevailing common time—became established very early on. Typical of the sonata in

---

[4] The titles, thematic incipits, and full shelfmarks of the four works are given at the end of appendix A.

its first phase, near the beginning of the seventeenth century, are the examples by Giovanni Gabrieli and Salamone Rossi.

On its way to its 'classic' design, established by Corelli in the 1680s, the sonata underwent one important transformation. Towards the middle of the century what had previously been merely different sections within the same continuous movement evolved into discrete movements. Willi Apel sees the *Canzoni a tre*, Op. 2 (1642), of the Bolognese composer Maurizio Cazzati as a watershed in this development (the *canzone* or *canzona*, though by origin generically distinct from the sonata, was by this time hardly distinguishable).[5] After the separation of the movements was achieved, their nature and organization underwent a gradual process of rationalization that tended to reduce their number and increase their length, ending in the Corellian four-movement design (following the tempo sequence slow–fast–slow–fast) that became almost normative towards the end of the century.

Vestiges of the sonata's origin as a single-movement form are still visible in the Corellian sonata at the turn of the eighteenth century. Internal movements—particularly the second slow movement—are often 'open', ending either in a new key or with a half-close. The type of imperfect cadence that introduces the dominant chord with a subdominant chord in first inversion, commonly termed a Phrygian cadence on account of its coincidence of form (though not of function) with the old regular cadence in the Phrygian mode, is a hallowed Corellian cliché. Since a half-close at the end of a movement presupposes an *attacca* continuation, the music in effect reverts to the continuous style of construction found in the primitive sonata.

Another throw-back to the origins of the sonata can be seen when 'cyclic' connections between the thematic material of different movements occur. In early sonatas it was common for a reprise of the opening material to be made towards the end as a signal to the listener that the movement was about to draw to its close (Monteverdi's *Sonata sopra Sancta Maria* affords a good example); in addition, *tripla* sections often used the primary material in paraphrase. By the end of the seventeenth century such connections appear only sporadically. Nevertheless, they can be very striking where they occur. In the fourth sonata of Albinoni's Op. 1 all four movements open with different versions of the basic shape D–E♭–D–C–B♭–A–G (see Ex. 19).

Whether one chooses to call the type of sonata that has just been described a *sonata da chiesa* (church sonata) depends on whether analytical or

[5] See Willi Apel, *Die italienische Violinmusik im 17. Jahrhundert* (Wiesbaden, 1983), 96–9.

Ex. 19

(i)

(ii)
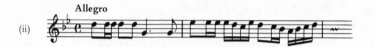

(iii)

(iv)

historical considerations have priority. For analytical purposes, it has been very convenient in the past to establish a bipolarity among baroque sonatas, assigning to the *da chiesa* category those containing only abstract movements, and to the *da camera* category those consisting wholly or largely of dance-movements, while regarding as 'composite' or 'mixed' the many examples, particularly in the literature of the solo sonata, which contain abstract movements and dance-movements in equal measure.

The first problem arising from this classification is that it corresponds only very approximately to terminological usage during the seventeenth and eighteenth centuries. The label 'da chiesa' first appears, alongside 'da camera', in the Op. 12 collection (1637) of Tarquinio Merula. Thereafter, it is used only occasionally. Ironically, the church sonatas *par excellence*, the Opp. 1 (1681) and 3 (1689) of Corelli, are described on the original title-pages merely as 'Sonate a tre'; their familiar definition as 'Sonate da chiesa a tre' is a well-meant falsification introduced by their first modern editors, Joseph Joachim and Friedrich Chrysander.

The 'da camera' label occurs with greater regularity, but a further complication arises from the fact that the label is sometimes applied to works that, although employing binary form in the manner of dance-movements, retain an abstract character. The Op. 5 (1687) of Pirro Albergati and the Op. 4 (1697) of Giovanni Maria Ruggieri consist entirely of abstract movements; so, too, do the *Trattenimenti armonici per camera*, Op. 6, of Albinoni.

The other problem with the 'church' and 'chamber' labels is that they can all too easily seem too narrowly prescriptive. It is true that a sonata containing only abstract movements (whether or not expressly called 'da chiesa') would be suitable for use at Mass or Vespers—as introductory or concluding music, or as a solemn accompaniment to a relatively slow-moving part of the service such as the Elevation of the Host. But its uses did not stop there. Abstract sonatas were also popular as purely recreational music played in private homes and at academies. To equate so-called church sonatas with performance in church would be as unreasonable as to restrict an *étude de concert* to the recital room.

Suonate a tre, Op. 1

It was not by accident that Albinoni made his début in instrumental music with a set of trio sonatas. The trio sonata had long enjoyed the same kind of prestige that the string quartet was to earn in the next century. It put on display the most typical contrapuntal language of the age: a three-part texture that was light enough to allow the contrapuntal voices to interweave freely but weighty enough to produce a resonant, full sound. Accordingly, many young composers chose the trio sonata as the vehicle for their initial exposure to a wide public. The first collections of Bonporti, Caldara, Gentili, Torelli, Valentini, and Vivaldi—all contemporaries of Albinoni—belong to this medium.

Albinoni uses twelve different keys for his sonatas. The six major keys among them range from B♭ major to A major; the six minor keys, from F minor to B minor (omitting C minor). This rather narrow tonal span, which many of his contemporaries were beginning to enlarge, will suffice him right up to the end of his life (not counting the rare appearance of E major). The principle of avoiding duplication of any key within a collection is one he shares with most of his fellow composers. (He will relax it, however, in some of the concerto collections, and in particular those including oboes, where practical constraints apply.)

All twelve works follow the slow–fast–slow–fast plan. In adhering so relentlessly to this 'Corellian' formula, Albinoni shows himself to be 'plus royaliste que le roi', since his mentor deviates from it four times in Op. 1 and three times in Op. 3! In general, Albinoni likes to keep the external plan of works in the same group or subgroup identical, while naturally varying the internal details.

The first movements in slow tempo all have a formal, stately character befitting their introductory role. They are all in common time and run to twenty bars on average. Their form is through-composed, each period developing a different idea. The absence of any element of reprise is typical of short slow movements of the period.

One notes many devices that come straight out of the Corellian copybook. The opening gambit of a short phrase ending with a half-close that is repeated in the dominant after a general pause (nos. 8 and 10) is the purest Corelli; so, too, is the 'leap-frogging' imitation of the violins at the start of the sixth sonata. Several movements open in typical Corellian fashion with chains of parallel thirds on the violins that soon give way to a more imitative treatment.

The two most distinctive opening movements are those of the last two sonatas. The eleventh sonata begins with an eloquent fugato. The twelfth employs a modulating ground bass after the fashion of a 'ground'. However, it makes no attempt to make the phrase-structure of the free parts different from that of the ostinato bass, as comparable movements by Purcell regularly do; its attractiveness derives more from the lively exchanges between the treble instruments than from any contrapuntal sophistication.

The second movements are all fugal. Within that general definition some interesting varieties of treatment are apparent. The first and sixth sonatas have 'permutational' fugues, in the sense that not one but two regular countersubjects are employed; this means that successive entries of the subject and its countersubjects present essentially the same material redistributed among the instruments through inversion of the counterpoint. Such fugues are uncharacteristic of Corelli, though they are common in the music of certain other composers of the late seventeenth century, for example Purcell and Buxtehude.

The subjects of the fugues of the seventh and eleventh sonatas belong to a characteristic type, also found in Corelli, that one might term 'reduplicative'; they consist of a string of short phrases, some of which repeat or paraphrase earlier phrases. A different, though related, kind of repetition is found in the eleventh sonata, whose countersubject imitates the subject canonically.

In the second sonata we encounter a 'stretto' fugue; together with the second movement of the ninth sonata, referred to in Chapter 3, it represents the more academic side of Albinoni's counterpoint.

Two of the fugues (nos. 9 and 12) are 'accompanied'; that is, the subject is partnered by the continuo (without the cello) from the outset. Again, this is a type of fugue familiar from Corelli's sonatas.

The third movements resemble the first movements, except that their character is more informal. Ten out of twelve adopt either triple or compound metre. Interestingly, five remain in the main key of the work. This is fairly unusual for Corelli, but becomes an important feature of Vivaldi's style. Such 'homotonal' treatment can do much to reinforce the dominant mood of a work but introduces a danger that the sameness will engender monotony. In later published collections of sonatas Albinoni shows less partiality for homotonality, usually selecting the relative major or minor key for the internal slow movement.

The second Grave of the third sonata stands apart from the other slow movements. It is structured in an unusually formal manner, reintroducing its principal idea first in the dominant and then, by way of reprise, in the tonic. It handles chromaticism (the *passus duriusculus*) in a poignant but dignified way. Especially impressive is the preparation for the reprise, in which two harmonic clichés normally heard in different contexts (identified as 'x' and 'y' in Ex. 20) are juxtaposed to produce a novel effect. Note that the chromatically rising bass of this progression is an inversion of the descending line of the opening. The sudden rise of the bass to a higher octave for the start of the reprise is another telling stroke.

It is very hard to gauge the extent to which these bars—and this entire collection—draw on a native Venetian tradition. Eleanor Selfridge-Field cites the chromatic bass line of this movement as a specifically Venetian feature.[6] Indeed, the introduction to the last movement of Legrenzi's trio sonata *La Benaglia* from his Op. 4 (1656) is strikingly similar. However, it would be quite wrong to assume that Venetian composers of music in universally cultivated genres such as the trio sonata lived in a self-contained world, especially since composers from all over northern Italy had their music printed in Venice during the seventeenth century.

Nine of the final movements are fugal in the manner of the second movements. Lighter and racier than the latter, they are nearly all in triple or compound metre, making copious and highly effective use of hemiola. The other three are cast in binary form. Those of the sixth and tenth sonatas strongly resemble the last movement of Corelli's sonata Op. 3 no. 11: their opening section ends with a half-close, and the second section then opens with a restatement of the initial idea in the dominant. The quasi-canonic entries appearing in quick succession in the three voices are likewise found in the Corelli movement (and also in similar movements by Stradella). The finale of the second sonata adheres to a more primitive version of binary form in which both sections end in the tonic key with the same cadential phrase. This type of movement, common in the instrumental music of

---

[6] *Venetian Instrumental Music from Gabrieli to Vivaldi*, p. 201.

Ex. 20

Legrenzi's generation, does not appear in Corelli's Opp. 1 and 3. However, specimens can be found in that composer's chamber sonatas: for instance, the Allemanda of Op. 2 no. 3, whose bass gave rise to the famous 'Quarrel of the fifths'.

As a *coup d'essai*, Albinoni's Op. 1 is very creditable. It demonstrates a sure grasp of form, a genuine feeling for counterpoint, and the beginnings of a personal style. On the whole, the treatment of the material is more interesting than the material itself. Sometimes, as in the long sequences that dominate the episodic writing, even the treatment lapses into banality. Undeniably, the third sonata is the strongest work of the twelve, but the first sonata deserves praise for the density of its counterpoint, the fifth for its vigour and gaiety, and the twelfth for the imaginative use of a 'basso ostinato' in its opening movement.

Six Trio Sonatas (*So* 20–5)

Although in all their externals these very homogeneous works conform rigorously to the ground plan laid down in Op. 1, they exhibit some interesting differences that can be viewed as evidence of stylistic progress. Their textures are much more open: each violin part has long pauses that allow its partner to present material alone, so that in place of the closely wrought imitative patterns of Op. 1 one encounters real dialogues. Ex. 21, taken from the third movement of the first sonata (*So* 20), is typical. Its relaxed harmonic rhythm finds no precedent in the earlier set.

In the fugal movements that occupy second and fourth place the episodic sections expand greatly, so that the total length of each movement grows by about a fifth on average. The passage-work in these episodes is more demanding for the violinist, suggesting the type of figuration employed in concertos (significantly, Albinoni exploits the fifth position in these sonatas, whereas Op. 1 had observed Corelli's limit in his trio sonatas of the third position). In fact, in the years around 1700, when the generic and stylistic distinction between sonata and concerto had not yet become firmly established, we find several Venetian composers writing sonatas with concerto-like features. The *Sonate a tre*, Op. 1 (1701), of Giorgio Gentili, the principal violinist at San Marco, have this quality; so, too, do the five-part sonata by Caldara published by Walsh in August 1704 and Vivaldi's slightly later sonata for violin, oboe, and obbligato organ (RV 779). Once the concerto had emancipated itself fully from the sonata and achieved recognition as the proper vehicle for virtuosity, the latter soon became—at least, in Italy—a repository of conservative style and technique, substituting a classic poise for its former exuberance.

Ex. 21

For all their innovative qualities, the six *Sonate a tre* fail to attain the degree of refinement seen in the best of the Op. 1 sonatas. They are typical transitional works, wrestling with a new idiom that their composer still has fully to master.

Sinfonie (sonate) a cinque, Op. 2

The idea of interweaving compositions of different kinds within a single collection was not Albinoni's invention. Indeed, an unmistakable precedent for the *Sinfonie e concerti a cinque* exists in Torelli's *Sinfonie a tre e concerti a quattro*, Op. 5 (1692), a pioneering collection in the history of the concerto. The principle of forming a regular pattern in 'hybrid' collections of this sort through the strict alternation of the different genres was universally followed. Vivaldi's Op. 3, in which the twelve concertos divide into four units that each comprise first a concerto for four violins, then one for two violins, and finally one for a single violin, offers a famous instance. In his Op. 2 Albinoni divides the set into six units, each comprising first a sonata and then a concerto. The sequence is therefore: Sonata I, Concerto I,

Sonata II, Concerto II, and so on. Within their separate groups the sonatas and the concertos alike feature six different keys, although three keys (C, G, and B♮ major) appear in both series.

One question immediately looms large. Were the sonatas of Op. 2, like the companion concertos, intended for orchestral performance (with more than one instrument to a part)? For twenty or more years after the Second World War, during a period when some of these works were being published and performed, the answer seemed self-evident: the presence of two viola parts clearly indicated orchestral performance. This attitude is rightly seen today as simplistic, and the pendulum has more recently swung towards performance with one instrument to a part.

But perhaps this trend has been reactive rather than carefully considered. It is interesting that manuscript sources of Sonata IV preserved in the Sächsische Landesbibliothek (Mus. 2199-Q-4(4)) and the University Library of Lund (Engelharts Samling 407) both have the two violin parts in duplicate; the Dresden source also supplies an extra part for the *violoncello* and reinforces the continuo with two bassoons. Arguably, the Dresden evidence is untypical since the musicians of the Saxon court orchestra regularly amplified the instrumentation of Italian works that came into their possession, but the Lund source cannot be so easily dismissed. It is significant that the *alto viola* and *tenore viola* parts remain undoubled. The priority of the musicians was to increase the weight and sonority of the outer parts even at the price of leaving a 'chamber-music' texture in the middle.

It is wisest to be undogmatic over this issue. The seventeenth and early eighteenth centuries were less interested than we are today in the difference of timbre between solo and doubled instruments. Provided that a satisfactory balance and adequate clarity are achieved, Albinoni's sonatas and balletti in four and five parts can be—and doubtless were in their own time—performed successfully in either fashion.

Two borrowings from the manuscript *Sonate a tre* appear in the Op. 2 set. A lengthy episode occupying bars 17–39 of the fourth movement of the fifth trio sonata (*So* 24) turns up again, lightly retouched and with violas added, as bars 20–42 of the corresponding movement in Sonata I. Practically all the episodic material from the second movement of the second trio sonata is re-used in that of Sonata V. The refinements made to these passages in the published sonatas confirm the direction of borrowing beyond any doubt.

The slow movements of the Op. 2 sonatas (occupying first and third place as before) are noticeably more tightly structured than their predecessors. Some reprises are found (e.g. in the first movement of Sonata

II), and even when they do not occur, the motivic substance introduced at the beginning of the movement is likely to persist. Two opening movements (in Sonatas II and V) feature an ostinato bass. The most original of the slow movements is the third movement of Sonata IV, whose opening has been quoted in Chapter 3 as Ex. 5; here Albinoni pits a 'concertino' of two violins and cello against the full ensemble—a type of lyrical *concertato* writing that will be exploited more thoroughly and in a less unexpected context in his Op. 5 concertos.

As well as being longer than his earlier fugal movements (a feature that the participation of the two violas makes almost inevitable), the second and fourth movements of Op. 2 impress by the strongly melodic quality of their fugue subjects. Some are highly dynamic, exploiting broken chords played across the strings. All are lengthy except for the textbook subject of the second movement of Sonata I (a dry 'stretto' fugue of pronounced academic cast). Countersubjects imitating the subject canonically (and thus drawing attention to its harmonically 'reduplicative' nature) are used often, most strikingly in Sonata V.

The most novel and interesting of the subjects is the one opening the second movement of Sonata II (see Ex. 22). The quiet lyricism of its melodic line (which does not, however, preclude an exceptionally fast harmonic rhythm) is vocally, even operatically, inspired. An ecstatic, almost hypnotic effect is produced by the rhythmic conformity of the countersubject and other accompanying parts, which lends particular emphasis to the 'dactylic' rhythmic unit of a quaver followed by two semiquavers.

The liveliness of the episodes in these sonatas continues a trend remarked on in the discussion of the *Sonate a tre*. In a few instances one might even imagine the rapid passage-work, considered in isolation, to have come from one of the concertos, but the contrapuntal activity of the accompanying parts soon reveals the identity of the genre.

Op. 2 contains some of the finest ensemble sonatas that Albinoni was to write. Only the first and fifth sonatas (perhaps significantly, the two which borrow from earlier music) fall below this high standard—and then not in every movement. In stylistic terms, these works stand on the threshold of maturity.

The Anonymous Five-part Sonata in Durham

If the sonata in G minor listed in Brian Crosby's catalogue of the Cathedral manuscripts as 'anon 97' is indeed by Albinoni, it offers striking evidence of the progress made by the composer in the few years that elapsed between

Ex. 22

Op. 1 and Op. 2. It marries the five-part texture of the Op. 2 sonatas to the style and form of the Op. 1 trio sonatas. Indeed, the technical insecurity of the Durham work suggests that it predates 1694.

The opening bars of its first movement, featuring 'leap-frogging' violins à la Corelli, are almost identical (allowing for the change of key and the addition of viola parts) with those of Op. 1 no. 6. The principal subject of its second movement is a variant of that used for the second movement of the Op. 1 sonata in the same key (no. 4). There is a clear melodic and harmonic relationship between the opening of its third movement and that of the second movement of both the eighth *Balletto a quattro* and the third *Balletto a cinque*. These three correspondences offer strong evidence not only of authorship but also of date.

The most remarkable movement is the second. Here the composer adds to the principal subject four different countersubjects, all treated (though not with equal success) as invertible. This is the *ne plus ultra* of a 'permutational' fugue! Actually, to call the movement a fugue is stretching a point, since all twelve entries of the full subject (in the space of only fifty-one bars) appear in the tonic; modulation is confined to a few brief and thematically nondescript episodes. Numerous contrapuntal solecisms (such as chains of consecutive octaves) suggest that in this movement the composer has bitten off more than he can chew.

The Trumpet Sonatas

The sonata for trumpet and strings was not the progenitor of the instrumental concerto but can fairly claim to have been its midwife since the string textures and the type of melodic writing developed in response to the special conditions of the first genre exercised a decisive formative influence on the second.

The earliest examples of the trumpet sonata were written for performance in San Petronio, Bologna, by musicians who were members of its large orchestra. The Op. 35 (1665) of Maurizio Cazzati, at that time the *maestro di cappella* of the basilica, contains the first dated specimens. Cazzati's colleagues and successors at San Petronio, who included Torelli, Manfredini, Perti, Bononcini, and Alberti, built up a substantial corpus of works. Corelli made a contribution to the genre, probably after he had left Bologna for Rome, and a surprisingly large number of trumpet sonatas by German and English composers (including Biber and Purcell) survive.

Most Bolognese trumpet sonatas eschew the fine-grained counterpoint of the conventional sonata in favour of broad effects designed to be clearly audible in the large space within the basilica (which with a length of 132 metres, a width of 60 metres, and a height of 44 metres is one of the most capacious churches in Christendom). In their fast movements the trumpet, accompanied by continuo, engages in *concertato* dialogue with the first violin, which is supported by the rest of the strings, the two partners joining forces at moments of climax.

This tossing to and fro of successive phrases, which is what *concertato* treatment entails, presupposes that the partners have identical, or at least recognizably similar, material. The trumpet was limited by being a 'natural' (i.e. valveless) instrument. Its usable repertory of notes consisted in the first octave of a tonic triad (for an instrument in C this would be the notes c', e', and g'), and in the second octave of a scale, diatonic in its first half and chromatic in its second. Hence the prominence of broken-chord and repeated-note figures, and of passage-work in diatonic, conjunct intervals. In order to partner the trumpet effectively, the violin had to appropriate features of the *stile tromba*. In time, these features became so thoroughly assimilated into violin style that they were perceived as authentically violinistic in their own right. By this route they became an essential ingredient of the early concerto.

Albinoni's two extant trumpet sonatas, to which the three anonymous works in Durham can cautiously be added, exemplify this process. Not only is the trumpet handled in a *concertante* manner, thus foreshadowing the use of a soloist in a true concerto: we also find the violins treated *ante diem* in a fashion typical of the concerto.

The more primitive of the two authenticated works is the *Sonata a sei con tromba* in C (*So* 1) belonging to the Este collection. An original *alto viola* part is missing, but as a 'filling' part similar to the extant *tenore viola* it is not vital to an understanding of the work. The slow first and third movements are for strings alone. Both modulate unusually widely and include some audacious chromaticisms but the pattern of modulation seems arbitrary and conveys an impression of inexperience. The third movement consists of a long series of chords in chugging quavers—a relative of the 'athematic' type of slow movement found in many of Albinoni's early concertos.

In both quick movements the trumpet dialogues with the string body in the manner described above. The second movement makes much use of repeated semiquavers (*note raddoppiate*) on the strings; this rather facile means of generating excitement is another feature common to the trumpet sonata and the early concerto.

The trumpet sonata in D major serving as the introductory sinfonia to *Zenobia* is altogether a more competent work. Like a concerto or an operatic sinfonia it adopts a three-movement plan (fast–slow–fast), with the refinement that the central movement is tripartite, enclosing a 'presto' section within a 'grave' and an 'adagio'. Although the outer movements employ a certain amount of *concertato* dialogue between trumpet and strings, much of the musical argument is carried by the two violins or even the first violin alone, the trumpet being content to punctuate the texture with sparse notes. The opening movement even has a brief unison ritornello entrusted to the strings alone.

The tripartite central movement belongs to a type familiar from Torelli's sonatas and concertos, to which Albinoni may have been directly indebted. After five introductory bars of solemn, quasi-vocal counterpoint the 'presto' begins. During this nineteen-bar section the first violin has semiquavers almost throughout (when it pauses, the second violin takes over the semiquaver movement); from time to time the obbligato cello adds short counterpoints that are also in semiquavers. Following a dramatic pause, four bars of 'adagio' round the movement off.

But for the fact that the first violin part in the central section is not expressly described as a solo part (and there is no separate part for orchestral first violins), this movement corresponds in all its details to movements on the same plan in Opp. 2 and 5.

However, one of the Durham compositions, which likewise features a tripartite central movement, actually uses a solo violin for the quick middle section and in so doing supplies a 'missing link' to the concerto. This is the work oddly (and doubtless inexactly) titled 'Serenatto' by its English copyist; Crosby lists it as 'anon 99'. The three violin parts (elsewhere there are only two) are not named, but with Albinoni's Opp. 2 and 5 as models it is possible to identify the uppermost part in running semiquavers as the solo part (which Albinoni will initially call 'violino primo', and later 'violino primo principale' or simply 'violino principale'), the next part down as the orchestral first violin ('violino di concerto') in its characteristic role as a 'reinforcing instrument' picking out prominent notes of the solo part, and the third part as the orchestral second violin. The movement is brief enough to quote in its entirety (see Ex. 23).

It will be noted that its harmony is extremely simple, hardly ranging beyond the tonic and dominant chords of the scale degree that at any given point is 'tonicized'. However, it employs the first inversion of chords fastidiously, even fussily. All this is typical of early Albinoni. Between the ninth and tenth bars we see an elided form of the progression indicated by bracketed 'x' and 'y' in Ex. 20. In its more direct version shown in Ex. 23 this progression is even more audacious.

Albinoni's authorship is further suggested by the march-like gait of the opening movement, which for nine notes follows exactly the melody of the Gavotta from the third *Balletto a quattro* (So 10).

Ex. 23

One of the remaining trumpet sonatas ('anon 98') imitates the pattern of *Si* 1 very closely, except that it has no independent cello part and has a unitary slow movement of only three bars. The other ('anon 93') retains the tripartite central movement but does without the tenor viola and cello parts.

None of this music has great artistic pretensions, but it must have given

Ex. 23 [CONTINUED]

its composer invaluable experience in the handling of an obbligato wind instrument and the use of homophonic, treble-dominated string textures.

An Early Concerto (*Co* 1)

The term 'concerto' originated as an abstract idea: that of a combination of different elements in a spirit of co-operation or friendly competition. This meaning is preserved in the Concert Spirituel, the Parisian concert series. Whereas the term 'symphonia', in its abstract sense, conveys the notion of a homogeneous ensemble, 'concerto' suggests the bringing together of more disparate forces.

In its more concrete application 'concerto' could signify: a set of instruments of different sizes (as in a five-piece 'concerto di viole'); a group of players for those instruments (as in English 'consort' and Italian 'concerto grosso'), an occasion on which these players performed (a concert); and, finally, a composition designed for such an occasion.

In the last-mentioned sense, the first 'concertos' were vocal pieces with instrumental accompaniment. It was the addition of an ensemble of instruments to the voices that justified the term. Monteverdi's seventh book of madrigals is entitled *Concerto*. However, such compositions were generally sacred in character, hence their description as 'concerti sacri' (in German, 'geistliche Konzerte').

The purely instrumental concerto emerged in the last decade of the seventeenth century as a progressive offshoot of the sonata intended specifically for orchestral performance. It might be argued, on the evidence of Georg Muffat's recollection of Corelli's performances in Rome in the early 1680s (imitated by Muffat in his *Armonico tributo* sonatas of 1682), that the new genre originated earlier and that Corelli was its inventor. However, we have no evidence that the works Muffat heard resembled those later published posthumously as Corelli's Op. 6 (1714). Even the latter—most of the time—have the appearance of amplified trio sonatas adapted to the peculiarly Roman institutions of the *concertino* and *concerto grosso*; where they go beyond this simple conception, one suspects that they have absorbed influences from the mainstream of the concerto in northern Italy. Such influences are certainly manifest in the concertos of Corelli's Roman colleague Giuseppe Valentini, whose *Concerti grossi*, Op. 7, appeared in 1710.

The concertos published in Italy during the 1690s, which must obviously represent a much larger repertory that remained in manuscript, comprise four collections:

> 1692: Giuseppe Torelli, *[6] Sinfonie a tre e e [6] concerti a quattro*, Op. 5 (Bologna).
>
> 1696: Giulio Taglietti, *[6] Concerti e [4] sinfonie a tre,* Op. 2 (Venice).
>
> 1698: Giovanni Lorenzo Gregori, *[10] Concerti grossi a più stromenti*, Op. 2 (Lucca).
>
> 1698: Giuseppe Torelli, *[12] Concerti musicali a quattro*, Op. 6 (Augsburg).

It will be noted that although Taglietti entrusted his concertos to a Venetian printer, none of these pioneer composers was a Venetian. Albinoni may in fact have been the first native-born Venetian to cultivate the concerto.

In the details of their style and structure these compositions are very varied. The concertos in Torelli's Op. 5 and Taglietti's Op. 2 have frequent recourse to binary form, whereas Torelli's Op. 6 prefers a unitary structure and includes several loosely fugal movements. Echoes of the trumpet sonata are found in Gregori's Op. 2 and Torelli's Op. 6 but not in the two earlier collections. What these works have in common, however, is a bias towards treble-dominated homophony, a preference for broad rather than subtle effects, and—most novel of all—a conception in orchestral rather than chamber-music terms. In their prefaces the composers alert their readers to the desirability of doubling the parts (but warn them, naturally, to revert to a single instrument for passages marked 'solo').

In this connection the definition Mattheson gives of the concerto in 1713 is interesting. He writes:

Concertos, in a wide sense, are musical gatherings and *collegia musica*; but in a stricter sense this word is quite often used for chamber music employing both voices and instruments (i.e., a composition by that name); more strictly still, it refers to works for violin [i.e., instruments of the violin family] that are composed in such a way that at the appropriate moment each part comes into prominence and vies with the other parts. Hence it is also used for works of this kind and others in which only the first [violin] part dominates, and where among many violins one, called *Violino concertino*, stands out by virtue of its especial rapidity.[7]

This is a description which betrays by its vagueness and cumbersome language the novelty of the genre as well as an uncertainty whether the use of a solo violin was intrinsic or extrinsic. An examination of the first generation of concertos shows that the appearance of a solo violin (and, occasionally, of a second solo violin and a solo cello) is an exceptional occurrence. Further, its function is decorative rather than structural. All solo passages could (hypothetically) be rescored for the tutti without undermining the form. The essence of the concerto lies in the energetic writing for the dominant part (usually the first violin but on occasion the second violin), not in solo–tutti contrast as such.

There was, however, a factor that in the long run favoured the introduction of solo parts. The larger the ensemble, the more diverse the level of ability among its members was likely to be. This applied with particular force to ensembles, such as those formed by academies and *collegia musica*, in which amateur and professional musicians mingled

[7] Johann Mattheson, *Das neu-eröffnete Orchestre* (Hamburg, 1713), 193–4.

indiscriminately, but it was true also of the fully-professional *cappelle* of churches and courts—in particular, the large ensembles employing supernumeraries recruited for the celebration of anniversaries and major festivals. By differentiating parts making high technical demands (for soloists) from those making low technical demands (for the rank and file), a composer could at a stroke gratify the leading players, allowing them to prove their mettle, and accommodate those of lesser ability.

Even when a solo player is employed, however, the idea of 'opposing' him to the rest of the ensemble in the spirit of a modern concerto is foreign to baroque practice. The realities of the situation, including the factor of status, dictated that when a single violin soloist was needed, he would normally be the *maestro de' concerti*, or concertmaster. For a second violin soloist the composer would have recourse either to the leader of the second violins or to the second-best player among the first violins. In other words, the recruitment of soloists was entirely internal. But these were the very players who in normal circumstances had the responsibility of controlling and inspiring their less gifted colleagues. It made sense, therefore, to allow the concertmaster and the other solo performers to play continuously throughout a concerto, just as they would do for other genres. Consequently, 'solo' textures arise when *ripieno* instruments temporarily drop out or have a separate part—not when soloists re-enter after an absence.[8]

As we saw in Chapter 3, most composers chose to lighten the texture during solo passages by excising middle parts. It was therefore economical to combine the principal violin and the orchestral first violin in a single volume, instructing the latter to pause at the cue 'solo' and re-enter at the cue 'tutti'. For Albinoni, who preferred to retain a full accompaniment during solo passages, this arrangement was obviously inappropriate. Right from the beginning, he employed a quite separate orchestral first violin part that was the sole occupant of a stave in a score and was given its own partbook. He may not have been quite the first composer to do this, since Gregori supplies a special *ripieno* part for the final movement of his fourth concerto, but he was certainly the first to regard a separate first violin part as a normal feature in a concerto.

In Torelli's Op. 6 we find the opening moves towards establishing a characteristic form for the fast movements of a concerto. In certain movements—notably in the outer movements of the sixth concerto, which is one of only two employing a soloist—Torelli opens each period with the restatement in the appropriate key of a 'motto' heard at the outset. This is

---

[8] This observation does not always apply to slow movements, where the soloist may pause during ritornelli. Nor is it true of the oboe parts in Albinoni's concertos—as distinct from those of Vivaldi.

not a ritornello in the Vivaldian sense, since it is syntactically incomplete and continues differently every time. But it does at least establish the difference between requotable and incidental material, and between material that is necessarily for the full ensemble (the motto) and that which can optionally include solo passages. Albinoni uses this simple motto technique from the very beginning—indeed, he rarely advances beyond it.

Now and then the earliest concertos adopt the three-movement plan of the operatic sinfonia, though the four-movement plan of the contemporary sonata is still more common. Albinoni is the first composer to cast his concertos regularly in three movements—a pattern from which he will not deviate once in the whole of his career.

The early date of the concerto in D major (Co 1) preserved in the Este collection has to be inferred from its style since the non-textual evidence provides no clues. Its scoring is for principal violin, first and second violins, alto viola, and continuo (a *violone* part, like several such parts in the same collection, gives the appearance of having been added—none too skilfully—by a later hand). The three violin parts are not given their familiar names but are instead identified as *violino primo, violino secondo*, and *violino terzo*; this nomenclature, which may well originate with the composer himself, is what one would expect to find in an ordinary sonata with three violin parts. It furnishes another hint that the work belongs to a period—perhaps around 1695—when the generic identity of the concerto was not fully established.

The work could be described as a trumpet sonata without the trumpet; in addition to its quota of episodic passage-work, which one would expect to find in a trumpet sonata after the model of *Si* 1, the principal violin takes on the trumpet's rôle of dialoguing with the string ensemble. In fact, the opening motto of the first movement, requoted at intervals, is fashioned in *concertato* style, the strings responding to an initial phrase on the principal violin alone. This movement is long and, for Albinoni, uncharacteristically rambling. It is pieced together from short, mostly one-bar, phrases and employs *note raddoppiate* without respite. Its plan of modulation is haphazard: both near the beginning and near the end of the movement Albinoni travels out to the supertonic major key via the dominant and then retraces his steps. The overall 'sharpward' bias is so pronounced that the movement fails to establish a satisfactory tonal equilibrium.

The harmony rarely ventures beyond the alternation of tonic and dominant chords illustrated by Ex. 22. Albinoni is obviously seeking the maximum simplicity and transparency and using extreme means to achieve it. To us the result seems crude, but to his contemporaries it may have seemed exciting and refreshing.

The tripartite central movement follows the design described earlier. The last movement contains three repeated sections instead of the two found in binary form. This design can best be viewed as a variant of binary form that has the virtue of spinning out a short movement a little longer. Throughout his career Albinoni uses it now and again in place of binary form, particularly in final movements such as gavottes.

The last movement, in which the principal and first violins join forces, is cast in a quickish minuet rhythm. This rhythm, notated in 3/4 metre, is encountered again in the finale of the trumpet sonata *So* 1 and in that of the 'Serenatto' in Durham. There was a vogue in Italy for the minuet, introduced from France, in the late seventeenth century—the Venetian composer Benedetto Vinaccesi included minuets as a novelty in his trio sonatas published in 1687. The fashion seems briefly to abate after 1700, and we have to wait until the finale of the sixth concerto of Op. 9 (1722) for Albinoni to employ this rhythm again in his instrumental music.

Although *Co* 1 is undeniably an unsatisfactory work, its experimental features and the basic ingredients of its musical language clearly look forward to Op. 2 and beyond.

Concerto a cinque, Op. 2

If one were asked to pick out a group of works by Albinoni that could claim a historical importance, it would have to be the six concertos in Op. 2. These were the first concertos by any composer to make a great impact north of the Alps. In Chapter 1 we saw how Bach copied out the second concerto of this collection, how his cousin Johann Gottfried Walther transcribed two of the concertos for organ (the fourth and fifth), and how Walsh published the sixth concerto as a 'sampler' for the new genre. Their technical simplicity and light (but not too overtly dance-like) character made them suitable for performance by amateurs or professionals, in churches or courts.

For his concertos Albinoni adds to the partbooks already required for the companion sonatas a volume for 'Violino de concerto' ('de' is merely dialectal for 'di'). This is the orchestral first violin part as distinct from the *violino primo*, which is reserved for the principal instrument. Throughout the concertos there is much doubling between the three violin parts: the *violino primo* and *violino de concerto* frequently go in unison, and sometimes the *violino secondo* joins them as well (as in the whole of the opening movement of the first concerto). The violas, too, occasionally double up, as in most of the first movement of the sixth concerto. In contrast to the sonatas, which preserve the polyphonic independence of the parts

Incidence of solo writing for the principal violin (approx. %)	Op. 2	Op. 5	Op. 7	Op. 9	Op. 10
55	—	11	—	—	12
50	8*, 12	12*	—	4, 7	8
35	—	2, 5	10	1, 10	10
20	—	1*, 6, 7, 9, 10	—	—	4, 6
5	4, 10	3, 4*, 8	—	—	2
nil	2, 6	—	1, 4, 7	—	1, 3*, 5, 7, 9, 11

throughout, this is 'orchestrated' music that seeks to vary the texture according to the effect desired.

The purely decorative role of 'solo' passages has already been remarked on in connection with the concertos of Albinoni's predecessors. Albinoni continues in this spirit—and will not depart radically from it for the rest of his career, even after Vivaldi has shown a way in which the contrast between solo and tutti can be turned with advantage into a structural element. The unpredictability of Albinoni's use of 'solo' writing in concertos can be seen from the table, which charts the incidence of such passages in the first movements of the concertos for strings alone in the five published collections. The numbers in the columns refer to individual concertos identified by their position within the respective opus (in the case of Op. 2 the numbers take account of the sonatas as well, so that '10', for example, refers to Concerto V). Asterisks identify movements in which passages for solo cello occur. The table shows that the average incidence of solo writing does not rise as Albinoni's style matures.[9] Even as late as Op. 10 he is willing to write true *concerti ripieni* (to borrow Vivaldi's term): works that eschew solo writing altogether.

Further, the extent of solo writing in the first movement does not allow one to predict how much solo writing there will be in the rest of the work. The second and third movements may either increase or decrease it as the composer's inspiration—or caprice—dictates.

In five of his opening movements (the exception being the binary-form movement found in Concerto III) and two of his finales Albinoni takes

---

[9] Pincherle claimed (*Antonio Vivaldi et la musique instrumentale*, i. 228) that Albinoni's Op. 5 had less solo writing than his Op. 2: 'Il y a même . . . régression, de son op. II (1700) à son op. V'. Close examination does not bear out this statement; in average terms, the later collection is slightly better endowed with solos.

over and expands the 'motto' technique used in Torelli's Op. 6. In the middle periods of a movement he is apt to present the 'motto' twice in succession: first in the key of the previous cadence and then in the key that is his next destination. The first period having closed in the tonic, the second period is likely to open with a form of the motto ending with a half-close that is often identical with the first phrase of the movement; this will be followed by a literal restatement in the dominant, after which the middle segment of the period begins. In subsequent central periods a form of the motto closing with a perfect cadence may be presented first in a foreign key and then in the tonic. Exceptionally, the motto may be heard three or four times in succession (as in bars 13–18 of the first movement of the fourth concerto in Op. 2). The effect of this distinctive technique, which juxtaposes different keys abruptly instead of passing smoothly from one to the other, is to concentrate modulation in the opening segment of a period rather than in the middle segment where one would normally expect to find it. Other composers will bring back a motto in a double statement now and again, but only Albinoni turns this into a standard feature.

Solos, where present, usually emerge imperceptibly from 'tutti' writing and merge back again in time for the cadence with equal unobtrusiveness. The last period of the first movement of Concerto VI (bar 27 onwards) conveys the flavour (see Ex. 24). Appropriately for a concerto in D major, this movement—and especially its motto (here bracketed)—evokes the trumpet quite unashamedly.

Albinoni does not yet—in his concertos—regard the slow movement as a possible vehicle for lyrical expression. In Op. 2 the first, third, and fourth concertos have as their central movement a short, modulating series of chords exactly as in some of the early trumpet sonatas. Concerto V has a similar movement, differing only in that it replaces the quasi-vocal polyphony with a patterned series of homophonic chords. Concertos II and VI adopt the familiar tripartite scheme, though now with slightly more generous dimensions.

The finales are all in triple or compound metre. In baroque compositions consisting of several movements the greatest weight normally falls on the first quick movement, the remaining movements becoming progressively lighter in character and often shorter in length as well. This tendency is seen most clearly in operatic sinfonias and chamber sonatas, but to some extent it also affects 'abstract' sonatas and concertos. One common sign of 'lightness' is the choice of a 'short' metre such as 3/8 or 2/4.

The first and fourth concertos end with simple binary movements in the rhythm of a *giga*. The finales of the second and sixth concertos, both in 3/4, reproduce the form of the first movements; in both of them the two

Ex. 24

vl pr
vl 1
vl 2

vla unis.

vlc/bc

etc. for 4
more bars,
leading to

alto vla

tenor vla

etc. for 3
more bars.

orchestral violin parts continually toss material to one another, but this is more a case of repetition with voice-exchange (a commonplace in sonatas) than genuine *concertato* treatment. The third concerto has a curious *perpetuum mobile* for the principal and first violins in unison; in three repeated sections, it is over in only fourteen bars. By far the most forward-looking and attractive finale is that of the fifth concerto. This is a concise binary movement in a fleet-footed 3/8 that could have sprung from the pages of an operatic sinfonia. Its alert rhythm, which places the main accent by turns on the first and the second beat, anticipates the subtleties of Albinoni's later music. The opening bars shown in Ex. 25 provide an excellent illustration of Arthur Hutchings's pertinent observation that 'if nothing by Vivaldi had survived, Albinoni would be admired as the man who most notably brought the forms and much of the expression of the opera into the concerto'.[10]

In the opening movement of Concerto IV Albinoni includes two short solo flights for cello. However, these are not melodically independent lines, such as we will find from Op. 5 onwards, but simply elaborations in semiquavers of the bass part.

Ex. 25

[10] *The Baroque Concerto*, p. 160.

The quality of the Op. 2 concertos is very uneven. Walsh made a wise choice in 1704 when he picked the sixth concerto for his anthology, for this is clearly the strongest work overall, even if its finale is rather dull. The most attractive aspect of the six works is the incisive, memorable character of their main themes. Not only did Vivaldi derive inspiration from them (compare, for instance, the opening of Albinoni's E minor concerto (no. 2) with that of Vivaldi's Op. 4 no. 2): so, too, did many other Italian composers in the first decade of the new century—among them, Gentili in Venice, Torelli in Bologna, and Valentini in Rome.

Balletti a cinque (So 2–7)

Dance-music for ensembles comprising instruments of the violin family with or without continuo was written down and published during the whole of the seventeenth century. Doubtless, most of the dance-movements that survive in notated form were conceived more as music to be listened to than as a practical accompaniment to dancing. Not only did dances such as the allemande retain their popularity as quasi-abstract compositions long after they had disappeared from the ballroom floor, but most of the popular dance-types are found in a great variety of alternative stylizations, some of which would have been ill-suited to a practical context on account of their implied tempo or their rhythmic character.

Throughout most of the seventeenth century Italian dance-forms were not grouped cyclically in the manner of a late baroque suite. In published collections we usually find dances of the same kind grouped together, one type after the other. If he wished to make up a cycle, the performer had to select and order the pieces himself, taking care to preserve congruity of key and style.

The idea eventually arose, in the second half of the century, of forming two or three dances into a fixed cycle along the lines of a sonata in several movements. The term 'da camera' already existed as an indication of the preferred secular destination of certain sonatas; this description was now appropriated for the new dance-suites, which very soon became the dominant type of sonata da camera. Giovanni Maria Bononcini, the father of Giovanni Bononcini, was the first composer to use this expression in its new sense, in his Op. 9 of 1675; the second known example is the Op. 2 (1685) of Corelli. It was always possible to refer to the chamber suite by other names; Albinoni always labels his suites 'balletti' (a rather unusual term), even when they contain no actual dance entitled 'balletto'.

Apart from the chaconne, which was commonly structured as a series of continuous variations, the dances of the Italian chamber sonata were organized in two or more repeated strains. Bisectional (or binary) form predominates, but the trisectional form commented on earlier is a possible alternative. *Rondeau* form, which was favoured by the French baroque tradition, scarcely appears. Italian composers differ from their French counterparts in another important respect: they maintain modal as well as tonal unity in the cycle, whereas the French like to shift (between movements) from minor to major or vice versa.

One problem faced by Italian composers in the composition of chamber sonatas was that none of the standard dances had a truly slow tempo. Even the saraband, which in France and Germany during the age of Bach and Handel was sometimes taken very slowly, moved at a brisk pace. For this reason it became common to co-opt, as it were, the stately opening movement of the church sonata and call it a *preludio*, *aria*, or *introduzione*. On occasion, a composer might insert an abstract slow movement into the interior of a chamber sonata, as in Corelli's Op. 4 no. 1.

In comparison with the 'church' sonata, the chamber sonata favoured a lightish texture and often allowed the first violin to monopolize the melodic writing. Imitative counterpoint is much used, especially for the opening of sections, but its nature is playful rather than erudite. One notes that even in their preludes, and still more so in the dance-movements themselves, chamber sonatas employ dotted rhythms distinctly more often than church sonatas—perhaps since such rhythms were associated with the 'springiness' of dance steps. This comparison should naturally be understood only in a relative sense: plenty of dance-movements are entirely devoid of dotted rhythms. And, in any case, rhythmic character-istics derived from dance-music permeate nominally abstract music so thoroughly that the ear alone cannot detect which passage comes from a gavotte, which from a sonata movement headed 'Tempo di gavotta', and which from an abstract movement in common time simply headed 'Presto'! Italian dances tend in a less extreme manner than their French equivalents towards a homorhythmic style (in which the accompanying parts reproduce the rhythms of the melody), but this bias nevertheless makes itself felt, particularly in fast movements such as gavottes.

A problem confronts anyone wishing to write about the dances of the Italian chamber sonata in English. The familiar terms are the French ones encountered in the suites of Bach and Handel. The equivalent Italian terms (e.g. *allemanda*, *giga*) look odd in English, particularly when they go into the plural. However, the distinction is not merely a linguistic one, since Italian forms of the dances often differ in their range of possible stylizations from their French counterparts. A *corrente* is not the same as a *courante*: the former is usually written in a quick 3/4, while the latter proceeds at a more leisurely pace in 6/4. (There remains a vestigial similarity in that both types employ pre-cadential hemiolas corresponding to the *pas de courante*.)

This troublesome issue will be resolved by a compromise. The dances will be given their French names when used in the plural or in a general context (except that 'corrente', plural 'correnti', will be preferred to 'courante', 'saraband' to 'sarabande', and 'jig' to 'gigue'); in reference to specific movements, however, the Italian forms will be retained.

Shunning novelty for its own sake in his usual manner, Albinoni restricts himself to the five dance-types that occur most often in the Italian repertory: the allemande (including its close relative, the balletto), the corrente, the saraband, the jig, and the gavotte.[11] The allemande, a processional dance in a slow, moderate, or quick common time that originated in Germany around the middle of the sixteenth century, is the longest and traditionally the weightiest of these. Albinoni always includes an allemande (or a balletto) in his chamber sonatas and places it without exception at the head of the dances. (It should be pointed out that Italian composers were in general less rigid than their French and German colleagues over the order in which the dances appeared; Corelli and Vivaldi, for instance, often positioned the allemande later in the cycle.) More often than not, the allemande is succeeded by a corrente, but in four of the Op. 3 *Balletti a tre* its place is taken by a saraband. Three of the balletti in Op. 8 and two of the five-part balletti follow the allemande with a jig. The final dance of the three (Albinoni extends the cycle to four dances only in the two balletti for solo violin in Dresden, *So* 33 and 34) may be either a jig, a gavotte, or a saraband. The presence of an introductory abstract movement varies from collection to collection.

In early collections of dance-music such as the suites in Johann Hermann Schein's *Banchetto musicale* (1617) associated dances are often thematically linked. In extreme cases one dance may be derived *in toto* from another through rhythmic manipulation. Dances by composers of Albinoni's generation feature such relationships more haphazardly, and the resemblances often do not persist beyond a few bars. On the whole, these links are more frequent in Albinoni's earlier balletti than in his later ones.

It is impossible to determine from their musical style whether the six *Balletti a cinque* predate or postdate the twelve *Balletti a quattro*. A direct comparison is difficult, because the five-part pieces are generally written in the 'trio' style described in the previous chapter, whereas the four-part ones favour the 'solo' style. One little clue, however, hints at the priority of the former. In the two five-part balletti in minor keys the Picardy Third is used

---

[11] The minuet appearing in the first of the sonatas published in Paris *c*. 1740 (*So* 40) should be discounted, since the authenticity of this work is doubtful.

regularly at the end of each movement. This device is found in no other authenticated works by Albinoni (though it appears, perhaps significantly in regard to dating, in the G minor five-part sonata in Durham). It may be a legacy, soon discarded, of his attempts to compose church music at the very start of his career.

In using the term 'balletto' to denote a complete four-movement cycle rather than one specific dance, Albinoni is resorting to the same kind of synecdoche that in France turned an *ouverture* into a whole suite headed by the overture proper: with the difference, here, that no 'balletto' movements are actually present. The *introdutioni* prefacing each work are remarkably similar to the opening movements of Op. 1. That of the first balletto reproduces, in a slightly altered rhythm, the first ten notes of Op. 1 no. 2 transposed from F major to B♭ major, while the third balletto opens with yet another version of the 'leap-frogging' violins.

All the allemandes except the third make some conspicuous show of counterpoint; indeed, the second and fifth employ fugal textures. The first and sixth both adopt the obsolescent type of binary form in which both sections end with a perfect cadence in the tonic. Sadly, the contrapuntal effort is spoilt in places by untidy details, particularly in the viola parts.

In the correnti, which are present in the second, fourth, fifth, and sixth works, Albinoni gives us the kind of vigorous violin writing later turned to good effect in his concertos. The corrente of the fifth balletto contains a remarkable passage of sustained close imitation in three parts, the third part being (unexpectedly!) the alto viola. That of the sixth balletto is titled, enigmatically, 'Corrente alla francese'. In Italian music of the time one ordinarily expects the description 'alla francese' to allude to the use of sharp saccadé rhythms after the manner of the Lullian overture—this seems to be the case in the 'Sarabanda alla francese' that follows the present corrente— but the earlier movement contains scarcely any dotted notes. Perhaps the term refers to its see-sawing syncopations reminiscent of a hornpipe.

The sarabands in the second and fourth balletti are homophonic movements in a fast tempo that suggests 'one in a bar'. Momentarily putting in abeyance his contrapuntal ambitions, Albinoni turns his attention to pure melodic writing and, perhaps for the first time in his music, shows what a superb tunesmith he can be.

The jigs in the first and third works both exemplify the typical Italian 'leaping' style that captures the grotesque and parodistic nature of this solo dance in compound metre which originated in the British Isles.

The gavottes closing the first, third, and fifth balletti are all march-like, every crotchet beat receiving a certain emphasis. The notation of all three begins on the first crotchet of the bar; the Italians were less insistent than the

French that a gavotte should begin two crotchets before the start of the first bar, but the difference concerns only the eye, not the sense, since the main stress is simply displaced on to the third crotchet in the bar.

Like other Italians, Albinoni is not concerned to achieve arithmetical perfection in the proportions of his dance-movements. The allemande, corrente, and jig are in principle symmetrical movements, but considerable discrepancies in length between the two sections are tolerated. The actual content of the second section may be briefer than that of the first if it reaches its required length only by repeating the last phrase in the manner of a 'petite reprise'. In some dances in quadruple metre, such as allemandes and jigs, 'odd' half bars are occasionally left at the end of sections. This is less unsatisfactory in practice than it may appear in theory, since such long bars function as 'double-length' bars that lend themselves easily to bisection. In other words, a strain of an allemande that occupies twelve-and-a-half bars is no less acceptable than a strain of a corrente that occupies twenty-five bars. Sarabands and gavottes are normally asymmetrical—gavottes very pointedly so, since their first strain normally comprises a mere four bars, while the second strain may run to more than a dozen bars.

The degree of thematic integration shown by these balletti is neither more nor less than one would expect from music of this time. When both strains close with a perfect cadence, the opportunity exists to match the endings, working back as far as the composer deems suitable. When the first strain cadences in or on the dominant, it is also possible to match the openings of the two strains. Examples of both procedures are found, but they do yet not occur in the regular, organized (and, let it be said, often facile) manner normal in late baroque music.

These early dance-movements have one interesting rhythmic feature that they share with some of the finales *alla giga* in Albinoni's trumpet sonatas: they like 'feminine' phrase-endings whose penultimate note, rather than the final note, is in the metrically stressed position (as seen in Ex. 3 in Chapter 3). This is, for Albinoni, a primitive trait that soon drops out of his vocabulary.

Balletti a quattro (So 8–19)

The make-up of these twelve works is fixed: a brief Grave in common time occupying between six and twelve bars introduces a balletto, a corrente, and a gavotte. However, this outward uniformity harbours a welcome variety of rhythmic and melodic stylizations.

The opening movements are so condensed that in a few cases they comprise only a single period. Nevertheless, some of the longer examples—in particular, those of the third and seventh works—show an admirable thematic consistency that marks an advance over the purely episodic construction of the introductions to the five-part balletti.

In the balletto movements that come second Albinoni evinces more strongly than anywhere else in his music a real gift for humour. The first balletto, with its fiercely dotted rhythms and abrupt stops and starts, is positively quirky, while in the opening bars of the second strain of the fifth balletto, where all four parts have striding octaves simultaneously, an almost riotous effect results. Best of all is the opening of the ninth balletto (shown in Ex. 26). The two violins start the fun with a game of tag, which gives way in the next period to a hocket of the middle parts.

Ex. 26

The correnti, variously homophonic and contrapuntal in texture, impress once again by their sensitive melodic shaping. In the eighth corrente we see for the first time in Albinoni's music an example of 'rounded' binary form, in which a reprise of the opening occurs mid-way through the second strain. This again indicates a growing concern with thematic signposting.

The gavottes generally resemble those of the five-part balletti, although their proportions are more variable. Some very pleasing asymmetries of phrase-length are found in them. The eleventh gavotte departs from the usual model, moving in quavers instead of crotchets (which implies a slower crotchet pulse); this new type, in which the first beat really does carry the main accent, will eventually come to supplant the older one in Albinoni's music.

For the first time, Albinoni uses the contrast between 'forte' and 'piano' as a structurally relevant device. Some of the echo-repeats possess real wit, enhancing the gaiety that is such a pronounced feature of the collection.

Notwithstanding the freshness and rhythmic inventiveness of these little works, a certain laxity in their part-writing lets them down all too often. Taking all their movements into consideration, the best works in the set are the first, third, eighth, tenth, and twelfth.

5

THE CANTATAS

SCHOLARS and musicians have been slow to appreciate not only the quality of Albinoni's chamber cantatas for solo voice but also the extent of his contribution to this extremely important genre. Eugen Schmitz's otherwise well-judged observations on them, mentioned in Chapter 1, include a remark that for Albinoni, as for Vivaldi, the solo cantata was to some extent only a subsidiary activity.[1] Schmitz was not to know that their true number (as measured by surviving examples) was double that of the works he was able to examine in Berlin. The total—upwards of forty-five works—is fairly impressive in absolute terms, although it will naturally not bear comparison with the vast production, running into hundreds, of such cantata specialists as Alessandro Scarlatti and Benedetto Marcello. Within Albinoni's own œuvre solo cantatas easily outnumber their closest instrumental equivalent, solo violin sonatas. More significantly, they appear to have been composed over a relatively short period of perhaps at most fifteen years, within which they can be seen, in both numerical and artistic respects, as occupying a dominant position.

Although this time-frame (1695–1710) straddles the boundary between what we have defined for the instrumental works as Albinoni's 'early' and 'mature' periods, his cantatas show no perceptible stylistic discontinuity. The earliest extant examples, which must date from the years immediately before 1700, are already recognizably mature in style. The inference to be drawn is that Albinoni ripened as a composer of cantatas—and possibly of vocal music in general—at a time when he was still finding his feet in the world of the sonata and concerto.

Three years before Schmitz's study appeared, Hugo Riemann had recognized the worth of Albinoni's cantatas by making *Vorrei scoprir l'affanno* the fifth work in his anthology *Ausgewählte Kammer-Kantaten der Zeit um 1700* (Leipzig, 1911). There was then a gap of sixty-eight years before the next modern edition of a complete Albinoni cantata (an edition, in fact, of the entire Op. 4 set) same out.[2] This neglect in the early part of the present century is less astonishing than it might seem, for whereas a

---

[1] *Geschichte der weltlichen Solokantate*, p. 151.
[2] Under the title *Tomaso Albinoni: Twelve Cantatas, Opus 4*, this set was published in an edition by the present writer as vol. xxxi of the series 'Recent Researches in the Music of the Baroque Era' (A–R Editions, Madison, 1979).

baroque violin sonata, its bass elaborately realized for the keyboard, could be co-opted into the literature for violin and piano, and find a small place in recital programmes, a baroque solo cantata was too remote in style, technique, and even the language of its literary text from the tradition of the *Lied* or the *mélodie* to be absorbed naturally into the repertory for voice and piano. In these conditions the demand from performing musicians for editions of cantatas was too low to make them a commercial proposition. So this truly vast repertory remained largely unknown, even to scholars. The modern renaissance of the baroque cantata, which is still only in its early stages, could not begin until ensembles created specifically for the performance of works in that genre came into being—and this did not happen on an appreciable scale until the 1960s.

There are two principal sources that between them contain over half Albinoni's extant cantatas: Mus. ms. 447 in the Staatsbibliothek Preussischer Kulturbesitz, West Berlin, which contains eighteen works, and the *Cantate da camera a voce sola*, Op. 4, which has twelve (two of which are also found in the Berlin source). In Chapter 1 we saw that the published cantatas were dedicated to Francesco Maria de' Medici. We know this fact and the year of publication (1702) only from the report in Walther's *Lexicon*, for the sole known example, presented by Edward J. Dent to the library of the Fitzwilliam Museum, Cambridge, in 1907, lacks the initial gathering containing the title-page and dedication. By a curious mischance, the title of the work forming part of the gathering signature at the foot of the first page of music identifies the collection incorrectly as 'Opera Sesta' (all subsequent gatherings have, correctly, 'Opera Quarta'). This mistake was perpetuated in the catalogue of the music in the Fitzwilliam Museum, and has more recently found its way into the *British Union-Catalogue of Early Music* and the *RISM* catalogue.[3]

One isolated solo cantata by Albinoni, *Là dove il nobil Giano*, was included in an anthology entitled *Cantate a I e II voci con tromba e flauti e sensa* brought out by Estienne Roger in 1702. The collection contains in addition one work each by Caldara, C. F. Pollarolo, and Carlo Marini, and two works by a certain 'Sig. S. D. K.' (the final initial does not necessarily betray a Germanic origin, for the Venetian title denoting knighthood was customarily spelt 'Kavaliere'). It may be that Roger 'pirated' the collection from an earlier Italian edition, since he borrows for the title-page an emblem associated with the Bolognese publishing house of Monti: a violin accompanied by the motto 'UT RElevet MIserum FAtum SOLitosque LAbores'

---

[3] See Edith B. Schnapper (ed.), *The British Union-Catalogue of Early Music printed before the Year 1801* (2 vols., London, 1957), i. 17, and Karlheinz Schlager (ed.), *Einzeldrucke vor 1800* (11 vols. to date, Kassel, etc., 1971–), i. 43.

(the mnemonic devised by the theorist Angelo Berardi for the six solmization syllables).

Besides Mus. ms. 447, the West Berlin Staatsbibliothek and its counterpart in East Berlin, the Deutsche Staatsbibliothek (which is heir to the same pre-war library), possess five further cantatas by Albinoni, all of them known from other sources. The most important locations of his manuscript cantatas outside Berlin are Ostiglia and Naples. The Biblioteca Musicale Greggiati of Ostiglia possesses a manuscript (Mss. Musiche B 260) whose twenty-two items include five cantatas by Albinoni. Two of them, *Questa è l'ora fatale* and *Fileno, caro amico*, differ in greater or smaller part from the corresponding settings in Berlin, Mus. ms. 447, while another, *Senza il core del mio bene*, diverges at one point from its concordance in Naples (the two remaining cantatas are unique to Ostiglia). Carlo Guaita, who brought to light these cantatas in Ostiglia, argues convincingly from an analysis of their style, both in general terms and in comparison with the concordant works in Berlin and Naples, that they are among the earliest settings of cantata verse by Albinoni to survive.[4] The Conservatorio di Musica 'San Pietro a Majella' in Naples has three manuscript volumes of cantatas that between them contain six cantatas.

It would be tedious to list all the libraries throughout the world that possess manuscripts of Albinoni cantatas. Suffice it to say that in addition to those already mentioned they number at least twenty—in Austria, Belgium, Great Britain, France, East and West Germany, Italy, Sweden, and the United States. Of the forty-five cantatas with continuo accompaniment accepted as authentic in Carlo Guaita's catalogue,[5] twenty-one have multiple sources. One cantata, *Da l'arco d'un bel ciglio* (Op. 4 no. 2), is preserved in no fewer than five different manuscript sources.

The problem of attribution in the case of solo cantatas is acute, particularly since their characteristic form of preservation is in long anthologies containing works by a variety of named composers—and, very likely, anonymous compositions as well. Many misattributions to other composers occur in the manuscripts of Albinoni cantatas authenticated by reference to other sources. The composers to whom the works are incorrectly attributed include Attilio Ariosti, Francesco Mancini, and Alessandro Scarlatti. Logically, there should be a similar number of misattributions to Albinoni of cantatas by other composers. Guaita identifies two of these: *Per un volto di gigli e di rose*, which is attributed in the Österreichische Nationalbibliothek, Vienna, to Francesco Antonio

---

[4] See 'Le cantate di Tomaso Albinoni', pp. 77–91.
[5] The catalogue takes the form of a set of appendices occupying pp. 356–494 of the dissertation.

Pistocchi and in the library of the Royal Academy of Music, London, to Alessandro Scarlatti, and *Volto caro del mio bel sole*, attributed in the library of the Convento di San Francesco, Assisi, to Giacomo Antonio Perti.[6] On stylistic grounds a case can be made for questioning the authenticity of two further cantatas (whose authorship is not thrown into doubt, however, by any conflicting attribution in the sources): *Al fin m'ucciderete, o miei pensieri* and *Io non amo altri che voi*. These 'contested' works must be distinguished clearly from settings of the same cantata text by a different composer altogether (such as Pier Francesco Tosi's version of *Io che per colpa sol del fato rio*, also set by Albinoni). Just as operatic libretti could be set to music over and over again, so cantata texts could pass from composer to composer, often in a spirit of friendly competition encouraged by the poet. Sometimes, of course, the poets borrowed from one other—which makes it unwise in the extreme to assume that two texts are the same merely because their first lines coincide!

The information so far gathered on the paper-types, staving, hands, and provenance of the manuscripts is insufficient to offer any help with dating. A *terminus ad quem* for the Op. 4 cantatas and for *Là dove il nobil Giano* is the year 1702, in which the two published collections in question appeared. Ironically, the only source to offer a further clue to chronology is one of two containing Albinoni's only extant solo cantata with an instrumental accompaniment in addition to continuo: *E dove, Amor, mi guidi*. The two evidently related sources of this work, one in the Bodleian Library, Oxford (Mus. Sch. E. 393), and the other in the Guildhall Library, London (G Mus 400), both take the form of a short score comprising the vocal line with its bass but no upper instrumental parts (except, in this case, for a violin part in one ritornello). Short scores of this kind were used by singers, who would learn and practise their part from them; they were often supplied by copyists to their less demanding customers in preference to a complete score. The index to the volume in Oxford containing the cantata concludes with the note 'achevé a Londres 1700 Charles Babel'. Babel (or Babell) was a French oboist and bassoonist who at the time was in the service of Queen Anne's consort, Prince George of Denmark; his son William became a well-known harpsichordist and composer. This source establishes, at least, that Albinoni's composition of cantatas preceded the turn of the century. The reason for believing that all the cantatas were composed before 1710 is that the vocal writing of continuo arias in Albinoni's operas begins around that time to undergo a stylistic evolution that finds no parallel in the cantata arias, previously very similar.

[6] I am not as certain as Guaita, from an examination of style, that *Per un volto di gigli e di rose* is by another composer, although I too find no positive indications of Albinoni's authorship.

It would be surprising if Albinoni's cantatas for Rome, and in particular for the Ottoboni court, were not among his first (though he went on to write others for Florence and Venice as well). In the second half of the seventeenth century and for long afterwards Rome was easily the leading centre of the cantata in Italy. The suggestion that this was because the periodic papal interdicts concerning opera diverted singers and their patrons into safer channels is perhaps too ingenious:[7] it has not been shown that the cultivation of the cantata (as opposed to the oratorio) varied inversely with the provision of opera in the Holy City, and in any case the operatic season occupied only a small part of the year. The reason for Rome's pre-eminence lies more in the structure of its large aristocracy, divided into a multitude of petty courts including those of high prelates, who, on account of their extensive education, were especially well equipped intellectually for the refined, classicizing world of the cantata. Among their house musicians several of these courts retained singers who would circulate among the courts in accordance with the social calendar of the aristocracy. The characteristic form of cultural activity within the courts was the *conversazione* or 'academy' held on a fixed day of the week, to which fellow nobles and men of letters were invited. A typical *conversazione* would include the performance of chamber music, instrumental and vocal, and the recital of prepared or extemporized poetry. De Blainville describes, a little maliciously, such an evening *chez* Ottoboni that took place during May 1707:

His Eminence . . . keeps in his Pay, the best Musicians and Performers in Rome, and amongst others, the famous Arcangelo Corelli, and young Paolucci, who is reckoned the finest Voice in Europe; so that every Wednesday he has an excellent Concert in his Palace, and we assisted there this very Day. We were there served with iced and other delicate Liquors; and this is likewise the custom when the Cardinals or Roman Princes visit one another. But the greatest Inconveniency in all these Concerts and Visits, is, that one is pestered with Swarms of trifling little *Abbés*, who come thither on purpose to fill their Bellies with those Liquors, and to carry off the Crystal Bottles, with the Napkins into the Bargain.[8]

Not only erudition but also topicality and spontaneity were qualities valued in this milieu. Antonio Ottoboni wrote the text of a duet, *Chi più gode nel mondo di noi*, which (in his own words) 'was done on the spot at the behest of two ladies while on horseback, was immediately set to music by

---

[7] This view is advanced by Hans Joachim Marx in vol. vi of *The New Oxford History of Music* (Oxford and New York, 1986), 99.

[8] M. de Blainville, *Travels through Holland, Germany, Switzerland, and other Parts of Europe, but especially Italy*, tr. G. Turnbull and W. Guthrie (3 vols., London, 1757), ii. 394.

Signor Angelo Farina, and was sung by the same ladies [the last two operations presumably after the return!]'.[9]

Poets and musicians were likely to be very unequal partners in the composition of cantatas, since the first, who were usually *dilettanti* from the noble or citizen classes, might well be the employers of the second. It cannot have happened often that a composer was in a position to prevail on the poet of a cantata to make modifications in the interest of the music. On the other hand, there was such a strong social consensus on the nature of a cantata—its subject-matter, length, and structure—that there was little scope for originality on either side. When we do come across a truly original cantata, such as Benedetto Marcello's setting of Antonio Conti's *Il Timoteo* (which is an Italian paraphrase of Dryden's ode *Alexander's Feast*), a special factor is usually responsible. In that particular case, the fact that the two men were intimates and social equals—each the promoter of *conversazioni* in his own right—obviously afforded them exceptional latitude. The greatest scope for inventiveness on the composer's part lay in the handling of melody and harmony, which could take on extreme, even bizarre, forms in order to express a 'conceit' or an *affetto* with particular force (as in Alessandro Scarlatti's setting of *Andate, o miei sospiri* 'con idea inumana'). Unlike the audience of an opera house, which on the whole desired merely to be pleased, that of a *conversazione* was prepared on occasion to be surprised as well.

One question on which the poet and the musician could differ was the relative weighting given to aria and recitative. To state matters succinctly: for the poet, an aria was a lyrical interpolation in the middle of recitative; for the musician (whether composer or performer), a recitative was a passage preparing for an aria or connecting two arias. The German dramatic poet Carl Wilhelm Ramler (1728–98) put it even more bluntly when he wrote in 1754: 'the arias are only for the musician, but the recitatives are for the poet'.[10] On the whole, modern opinion takes the musician's side. A subordination of recitative to aria is implicit in Willi Flemming's famous dictum (referring to opera but equally applicable to the cantata): 'The recitative loads the gun, the aria fires it'.[11]

A typical 'poet's cantata' is one that both begins and ends with recitative verse. Using the letter R and A to stand for recitative and aria respectively, we can define the structures that result from this approach as RAR, RARAR, RARARAR, and so on. Antonio Ottoboni, a poet confident enough of his skill

---

[9] The music of this duet is lost, but the text is preserved in Venice, Museo Civico Correr, Cod. Correr 466, pp. 577–8.

[10] Letter to Johann Wilhelm Ludwig Gleim, dated 24 June 1754.

[11] Quoted in Donald Jay Grout, *A Short History of Opera* (New York, 2/1965), 187.

to acknowledge authorship of his *poesia per musica* (as so many—perhaps wisely—did not), shows a distinct preference for structures of this kind. The RARAR layout occurs more frequently than any other in his cantata texts, and the RARARAR layout is surprisingly common.

Opening a cantata with a recitative allows the poet to set the scene before embarking on the first aria. This arrangement is not so inconvenient for the composer, if he is able to follow the pattern described by Flemming and use the recitative to build up tension. In cantatas employing the popular RARA layout, having an initial recitative in fact confers an important musical advantage, since it enables the first aria, as an internal movement, to be in a different key from the last one, and hence makes it easier to differentiate their respective *affetti*.

Ending a cantata with a recitative allows the poet to 'wrap up' the action more satisfactorily and perhaps conclude with a moralistic aphorism. Here the composer has an apparent problem, for this final recitative has no aria to introduce and risks ending the work in too colourless and perfunctory a manner. But a ready solution was to hand. It was always possible for a composer, at his discretion, to set one or two lines of recitative verse lyrically, either in a florid, aria-like style (*arioso*) or as a synthetic aria extracted (*cavata*) from the rest of the stanza. So a final recitative can end in a suitably climactic way with one of these devices. We will discuss the *cavata* and Albinoni's notable contribution to this form later on.

The 'musician's cantata' tends to minimize the recitative element by opening and closing with an aria. The two most common layouts are ARA and ARARA. Increasingly, during the eighteenth century, audiences came to prefer recitatives to be not only few but also brief; even so enlightened a commentator as Quadrio recommends brevity,[12] echoing a view of Alessandro Spagna at the start of the century. In 1751 Georg Philipp Telemann could assert that because of an aversion towards recitative, Italian cantatas had gone out of fashion in Germany, their place being taken by single arias.[13]

As the eighteenth century progresses, one also becomes aware of a pressure towards reducing the number of arias to two, whereas previously some cantatas had possessed four or more. This tendency stemmed partly from the greater average length of individual arias (and can therefore be likened to the process that reduced the number of movements in a sonata first to four and eventually to three), and partly from a decline of interest in the genre's poetic possibilities (which are naturally better served by having

---

[12] *Della storia e della ragione d'ogni poesia*, ii/2. 334.
[13] Letter to Carl Heinrich Graun dated 15 Dec. 1751.

	Scarlatti (b. 1660)	Albinoni (b. 1671)	Vivaldi (b. 1678)	Porpora (b. 1686)	Hasse (b. 1699)
RARARA	67	1	—	—	1
ARARA	49	4	—	—	1
RARA	248	24	17	77	36
ARA	60	5	12	55	20

greater length in which to develop); but it reflects above all a fear of tedium.

The threefold shift in fashion—towards the musician at the expense of the poet, towards the aria at the expense of the recitative, and towards brevity at the expense of poetic expression—is clearly evident from the table, which charts the incidence of four common layouts (RARARA, ARARA, RARAR, and ARA), as they occur in the extant cantatas for solo voice and continuo of five composers (Alessandro Scarlatti, Albinoni, Vivaldi, Porpora, and Hasse).[14]

All of Albinoni's solo cantatas employ either a soprano or an alto voice. The forty-five cantatas considered authentic by Guaita divide into thirty-four for soprano and eleven for alto. The preponderance of the soprano voice is even greater if one discounts Op. 4, in which the two voices are used for alternate works. From the register of the voice alone one cannot identify the intended singer as male or female; a soprano is as likely to have been a castrato as a high female voice, while an alto part might have been sung by a falsettist (counter-tenor), a castrato, a juvenile male singer (such as the young Annibale Pio Fabri), or a female contralto. Although the singer normally represents a character who is clearly either male (a shepherd) or female (a nymph), one should not make assumptons about gender on that account, since the indifference with which principal operatic roles were assigned to *virtuosi* and *virtuose* proves that it was the quality of the voice that counted, not the verisimilitude of the impersonation.

The total absence of cantatas for tenor and bass should not surprise. These natural male voices were in any case less highly regarded in the late baroque period, and their presence in cantatas is virtually confined to works with string accompaniment.[15]

[14] The statistics for Scarlatti, Porpora, and Hasse are taken from information in Everett L. Sutton, 'The Solo Vocal Works of Nicola Porpora: An Annotated Thematic Index', University of Minnesota, 1974; those for Vivaldi are derived from Colin Timms, 'The Dramatic in Vivaldi's Cantatas', in Lorenzo Bianconi and Giovanni Morelli (eds.), *Antonio Vivaldi: Teatro musicale, cultura e società* (Florence, 1982), 97–129.

[15] An interesting exception is a lost set of cantatas for solo bass voice and continuo by Pietro Scarpari (c. 1682–1763), a priest and singer at San Marco who was active as a singing teacher at several Venetian institutions including the Pietà, the Mendicanti, the Ospedaletto, and the convent of San Lorenzo. An ms of these works is listed in the sale catalogue of Nicolaas Selhof's stock (1759).

About the choice of instruments for the continuo there can be some doubt. Whereas C. P. E. Bach's *Essay* is adamant that 'the most complete accompaniment to a solo [hence, presumably, to a solo cantata], to which nobody can take any exception, is a keyed instrument in conjunction with a violoncello', this injunction gives the impression of being prescriptive rather than descriptive.[16] In any case, it refers to the practice of a different country in a somewhat later period. There is ample evidence from contemporary references that, as in the Italian solo sonata, the keyboard instrument and the stringed instrument could be regarded as alternatives. The critic Johann Adolph Scheibe makes this point in 1745, when he observes that in cantatas without obbligato instruments the voice is accompanied either by cello alone or by the keyboard.[17] The harpsichord alone must have been used in the celebrated self-accompanied performances of cantatas by Emanuele D'Astorga and Domenico Alberti. Incidentally, one is surprised to see little reference to the plucked stringed instruments, the archlute and the theorbo, for these were otherwise much used for continuo performance in Rome and Venice around 1700.

Very occasionally in Albinoni's cantatas the bass momentarily divides into what is obviously a slower-moving part for harpsichord and a livelier part for cello (as shown in Ex. 30 below). But it would be unwise to infer from this rare occurrence that both instruments are mandatory for every cantata.

Another vexed question concerning the performance of the instrumental accompaniment is whether the long pedal-notes for the bass that characterize most of the recitative apart from the cadences should be performed as they stand or shortened. Gasparini's advice to the keyboard player in *L'armonico pratico al cimbalo* (Venice, 1708) is to hold the keys down after striking them—in other words, to allow the sound to decay naturally.[18] But most other theorists advocate short attacks followed by a rest. Contemporary descriptions of recitative suggest that a 'dry' (*secco*) performance was the normal one. Pierre-Jacques Fourgeroux heard it performed in this way at the King's Theatre in the Haymarket in 1728, and Joachim Christoph Nemeitz similarly in Venetian opera houses in 1721.[19] Vivaldi's use of the direction 'arcate lunghe' (long bows) in certain continuo passages occurring in his operas and sacred vocal music implies

[16] Quoted in Frank T. Arnold, *The Art of Accompaniment from a Thorough-Bass as Practised in the XVIIth and XVIIIth Centuries* (2nd edn., 2 vols., New York, 1965), i. 328.

[17] *Der critische Musikus* (2nd edn., Leipzig, 1745), 395.

[18] Quoted in Dale E. Monson, '*Semplice o secco*: Continuo Declamation in Early 18th-century Italian Recitative', *Studi pergolesiani*, 1 (1986), 107.

[19] See Winton Dean, 'The Performance of Recitative in Late Baroque Opera', *Music & Letters*, 58 (1977), 392, and Joachim Christoph Nemeitz, *Nachlese besonderer Nachrichten von Italien* (Leipzig, 1726), i. 425.

that this form of performance was the exception. One wonders, nevertheless, whether a more sustained style was permissible in solo cantatas, to which the rapid, conversational tone of operatic dialogue was foreign.

The subject-matter of cantata texts very rarely departed from the Arcadian conventions that dominated Italian lyric poetry from the sixteenth to the eighteenth century. The fashion for Arcadian subjects dates back to Jacopo Sannazaro's *L'Arcadia*, completed around 1490, and received a powerful boost from Torquato Tasso's *Aminta* (1573). A remote, wooded, and mountainous area of the central Peloponnese, Arcadia was conceived as the idyllic home of nymphs and shepherds. Love, and love alone, was the proper occupation of these fortunate denizens. The patent artificiality and, above all, the triteness of Arcadian poetics was recognized even by some who had no option but to work within its parameters. In his cantata text *Povera Poesia, quanto sei stitica*, which is a semi-serious reproach addressed to the prevailing poetic conventions, Antonio Ottoboni (who was born early enough to have been familiar with a more robust and varied type of poetry) observes:

La farfalletta,	The little butterfly,
la tortorella,	the little turtle-dove,
la lucciolletta,	the little fire-fly,
la rondinella,	the little swallow,
son frasi armoniche	are harmonious phrases
del tuo cantar.	of your songs.
Quel ruscelletto,	That little brook,
quel praticello,	that little meadow,
quell'augelletto,	that little bird,
quell'arborello,	that little tree,
son grazie o croniche	are adornments or tales
del tuo scherzar.	of your jests.[20]

Other critics were less gentle. The critic and traveller Giuseppe Baretti conjured up for his English readers the horrifying vision of nothing being heard 'from the foot of the Alps to the farthermost end of Calabria but descriptions of purling streams rolling gently along flowery meadows situated by the sides of verdant hills shaded by spreading trees, among whose leafy branches the sad Progne with her melancholy sister Philomela warbled their chaste loves, or murmured their doleful lamentations'.[21]

This fantasy-world carried over into the fabric of very institutions that

---

[20] Carlo Cesarini's setting of this amusing text, which can be dated *c.* 1710, is preserved in London, British Library, Add. MS 34057, fols. 97–100.

[21] Joseph [Giuseppe] Baretti, *An Account of the Manners and Customs of Italy, with Observations on the Mistakes of some Travellers, with Regard to that Country* (2nd edn., 2 vols., London, 1769), i. 251.

promoted the poetry. In 1690 a group of former participants in the *conversazioni* of Christina, the exiled Queen of Sweden, founded in her memory the Radunanza degli Arcadi, or Arcadian Academy. The new society took as its symbol the pipes of Pan and adopted the Christ-child as its tutelary deity (the shepherds of the Nativity story supplying the connection with Ancient Greece). All members were required to take 'Arcadian' names (that of Antonio Ottoboni was Eneto Ereo). During the spring and summer of every year the Academy held six literary-cum-musical sessions. Very quickly, so-called colonies of the Roman parent society sprang up all over Italy; indeed, some societies already in existence such as the Accademia degli Animosi in Venice became voluntary affiliates.

If the subject-matter and imagery of Arcadian poetry are limited, its themes are hardly less so. The texts of Albinoni's cantatas bear this remark out fully. Their dramatis personae are almost without exception nymphs (Clori, Filli, Irene, or Dalinda) and shepherds (Clizio, Elmindo, Fileno, Florindo, Lidio, or Tirsi). The vast majority of poems complain of love unfulfilled—either because of the absence or departure of the beloved, or because of her (more rarely, his) unresponsiveness or infidelity. Many texts invoke the god Amor (Cupid), either to blame him for kindling the lover's passion, or to enlist his support in reuniting the couple. Just a few escape this stereotype. *Dubbio affetto il cor mi strugge* (which has the separate title *Amante timido*), *Il bel ciglio d'Irene*, and *Vorrei scoprir l'affanno* are a lover's confessions of shyness. *Fileno, caro amico* is a lover's protestation, made to a friend, of his fidelity. *Mi dà pena quando spira* (Op. 4 no. 8) accuses Zephyr, the West Wind, of having amorous designs on Chloris. *Donna illustre del Latio* and *Io non amo altri che voi* sing the praises of two ladies (who naturally wear an Arcadian disguise). Perhaps the least hackneyed theme (albeit marred by clumsy expression) is the 'amorous lesson' given to Phyllis by a far from disinterested teacher in *Filli, chiedi al mio core* (Op. 4 no. 6). It opens with these lines:

Filli, chiedi al mio core	Phyllis, you ask my heart
che t'ami e t'idolatri,	to love and worship you,
ma ciò che più s'apprezza	but to what is most highly prized
in amor non osservi.	in love you pay no heed.
La fede, la costanza,	Fidelity and constancy,
che di macigno ancor i cori spezza,	which melt even hearts of flint,
sono a te nomi ignoti.	are words unknown to you.
Eppur fede, costanza,	Now, fidelity and constancy,
quando insieme non regnano in un'alma,	when they do not reign together in a soul,
perde amor la sua forza,	cause love to wane,
nè mai d'amor può riportar la palma.	nor can one ever carry off the palm of love.

Most of the texts set by Albinoni conform to a general pattern by remaining throughout in the 'lyric' mode (to use Aristotle's terminology): the poet speaks directly to the audience in the first person. Once or twice, however, recitatives are cast in the 'epic', or narrative, mode, in which the poet describes events in the third person. The opening of *Da l'arco d'un bel ciglio* (Op. 4 no. 2) is typical:

Da l'arco d'un bel ciglio,	By the bow of a fair eyebrow,
sagittario d'Amore,	whence issued Cupid's arrows,
semplicetto garzon languia trafitto,	a simple lad lay pierced,
nè trovando pietade	finding no sympathy
nell'adorata Irene	from his beloved Irene
delle sue acerbe pene	for his bitter pangs
e del suo immenso ardore.	and his great passion.
Sospiroso e dolente,	With sighs and tears
un giorno in tali note	he complained one day
si lagnò con l'arcier nume inclemente.	to the pitiless archer-god in these accents.

The metrical and rhyming conventions of cantata verse can best be illustrated by examining one complete text. The chosen example is *Lontan da te, mia vita*, sixth of the cantatas in Berlin, Mus. ms. 447.

Lontan da te, mia vita,	Far from you, my life,	
s'ancor viva son io,	if I am still alive,	
o che del viver mio	either the quivered archer	
il faretrato arcier forma un portento	conjures up the likeness of my life,	
o per anima in seno ho il mio tormento.	or the feeling I have in my breast torments me.	5
No, che viva non sono	No, for I am not alive	
se il mio cor, la mia vita è sempre teco,	if my heart and my life remain with you always,	
sì che viva son sempre	so that alive I am always	
a la mia morte a canto,	close to death,	
se mi scorge ch'io vivo il duolo e il pianto.	and if I am aware that I live in grief and sorrow.	10
Senza voi, care pupille,	Without you, dear eyes,	
s'io mi viva ancor non so;	I know not if I am still alive;	
così esangue è questo core	this heart is so drained of blood	
che nel pianto e nel dolore	that in tears of grief	
vivendo il mio morir vita non ho.	I am lifeless living my death.	15

Deh, se i pianti e i sospiri
pon destarti a pietade,
biondo nume di Delo,
rischiara l'aura e il cielo
e porta, oh Dio, quel giorno
ch'a me l'anima mia faccia ritorno.
Affretta il tempo e l'ore
perché rieda il mio core
e s'al corso men lenti
coi tuoi dardi, Amor, sferza i
   momenti.

Chi mi rende il mio tesoro

vita all'alma renderà;

Chi mi dà chi tanto adoro
del mio core il cor sarà.

Alas, if tears and sighs
can move you to pity,
blond god of Delos,
lighten the breeze and the sky
and bring, o God, that day   20
when my soul returns to me.
Hasten the time and the hour
of my heart's return
and with your darts, Cupid,
lash the seconds into quicker
   motion.   25

Whoever returns my beloved to
   me
will restore life to my soul;

Whoever gives me the one I
love so much
will be the heart of my heart.

The RARA layout employed by this text, which represents a compromise between literary and musical priorities, is the one favoured by poets of Albinoni's generation. The type of expression appropriate for a recitative is carefully distinguished from that of an aria. As the essayist Pier Jacopo Martello recommends, the first type of setting is reserved for 'everything that is narration or temperate expression',[22] while the second is proper for more intense statements. The RARA scheme being fixed in advance, the poet obviously has to alternate the two types of expression accordingly.

The recitatives (lines 1–10 and 16–25) are written in *versi sciolti*, lines of either seven or eleven syllables intermingled freely. These two metres, profiting from their uneven number of syllables, have variable stress patterns that make them especially suited to long stanzas, where too much regularity of accent could produce monotony. Ordinarily, *versi sciolti*— like their English equivalent, blank verse—are not obliged to have end-rhymes. An exception is made for the last line of the stanza, which is almost always rhymed with the line preceding it, or, less often, a line further back. A rhyme in this position can act as a signal that the recitative is at an end and so create anticipation for the start of the aria. Guaita's painstaking examination of the cantata recitatives set by Albinoni turned up only one that did not feature this terminal rhyme.[23] In fact, each of the present examples also includes a number of end-rhymes earlier in the stanza (e.g.

[22] *Della tragedia antica e moderna* (Rome, 1715), 285.
[23] 'Le cantate di Tomaso Albinoni', pp. 53–4. The recitative in question is the one opening *Fileno, caro amico*.

between lines 2 and 3) in addition to some internal consonantal rhymes (e.g. 'rischiara' and 'l'aura' in line 19) and assonance (e.g. between 'vita' in line 1 and 'viva' in line 2).

Virtually all recitatives employ exclusively *versi piani*—lines ending with a stressed syllable followed by an unstressed one. When set to music, this strong–weak pattern gives rise to a characteristic 'feminine' ending that is often represented in notation by a pair of repeated quavers (although in performance the first of these may be replaced by an appoggiatura on a different note). To scan a line correctly one has to take account of the possible coalescence of adjoining vowels either in different words (*sinalefe*) or within the same word (*sineresi*), and, conversely, of their separation (*iato* and *dieresi*), following the elaborate rules of Italian prosody. Line 25, for instance, requires coalescence of the 'oi' in 'coi', the 'uoi' in 'tuoi', and the 'ai' in 'sferza i', but a hiatus between the last vowel of 'dardi' and the first of 'Amor'. These niceties usually, but not invariably, survive musical setting.

Aria stanzas were normally divided by the poet, as here, into two syntactically independent semistrophes. The purpose of this division was to enable the composer to repeat his setting of the first semistrophe in da capo fashion. This practice, which largely ousted the strophic form of organization common in the early cantata, had already established itself firmly by the time Albinoni began to compose; we find Giuseppe Salvadori advocating it already in 1691.[24] The use of repetition, common to the da capo aria and its strophic predecessor, enabled singers to display their ability to embellish a vocal line. Nemeitz relates how he heard Faustina Bordoni, later to become Hasse's wife, sing arias at the San Giovanni Grisostomo theatre entirely without ornamentation the first time round but richly embellished on the repeat. (The truth of his statement that composers often preferred the singer's version to their original conception must remain in doubt, however.)[25]

When the number of lines in the semistrophes is not absolutely equal, the second is commonly the longer. This compensates for the fact that the B section of the aria has its portion of text stated only once (disregarding the repetition of individual words and phrases), whereas the A section regularly includes two separate, consecutive statements of the text. Lines containing an even number of syllables are on the whole favoured for arias, as they tend to have a regular stress-pattern and therefore conform easily to the symmetries of the music. The eight-syllable line (*ottonario*), employed in both the present arias, is for obvious reasons the most common of all.

---

[24] *Poetica toscana all'uso dove con brevità e chiarezza s'insegna il modo di comporre ogni poesia* (Naples, 1691), 76.

[25] *Nachlese besonderer Nachrichten aus Italien*, i. 426.

Certain lines—in particular those concluding a semistrophe—may be *versi tronchi*; these lack a final unstressed syllable (e.g. lines 27 and 29 in the example). In Italian prosody such lines are counted as equivalent to *versi piani* containing one more syllable. They are well suited to emphatic, 'masculine' cadences whose last note arrives on a strong beat.

End-rhyme is employed systematically in aria stanzas, following simple schemes such as AABB, ABBA, and ABAB. As a matter of principle, the poets usually include *versi chiave*—'key' rhymes that link the different stanzas (or, as here, semistrophes). In the second aria *versi chiave* are employed exclusively; in the first, they are limited to lines 12 and 15. When a strict metrical pattern imposes order on the aria verse by purely rhythmic means, it is possible to leave one or two lines unrhymed, as in the case of line 11.

No translation can disguise the poverty of vocabulary and imagery voluntarily accepted by the Arcadian poetic tradition. Not one word, phrase, or sentiment in this cantata text does not connect it with hundreds of similar texts. The 'quivered archer' (Cupid), the 'blond god of Delos' (Apollo), the *pupille* and *luci* (both metonymical expressions for 'eyes'), the symbiotic relationship of life and death: all these are more than familiar to the student of baroque cantatas. Even the difference of mood between the two arias—the first lachrymose and self-pitying, the second cautiously hopeful—conforms to a stereotype.

Although such poetry often appears to us quite unworthy of the notes in which it came to be clothed, it has to be taken seriously in its own right. One cannot overlook the fact that contemporaries regarded *poesia per musica* as a kind of literary work subject to many special constraints but nevertheless possessing an artistic value quite independent of any musical setting. Albinoni had no greater a lien over a poem by Antonio Ottoboni than Alessandro Scarlatti, Carlo Francesco Pollarolo, or whoever was invited or commanded to set it. This relative autonomy of the literary and musical spheres on one hand reduced the composer's freedom of action, but on the other diminished his complicity in the shortcomings of the poem. In this sense, the music of a cantata is not a recreation, still less an enhancement, of the poetic content, but rather a kind of analogue that remains true to its own laws. It is therefore possible—fortunately—for an exquisite musical setting to be allied to the most banal and technically incompetent verse, which imposes on it a number of important stylistic conventions but does not inevitably infect it with its own ineptitude.

This point comes out in Albinoni's setting of the opening recitative of *Lontan da te, mia vita*, shown in Ex. 27. The external correspondences between text and music are obvious. The composer marks the line-endings

Ex. 27

Soprano

Lon - tan____ da te, mia vi - ta, S'an - cor vi - va son

i - o, O che del vi - ver mi - o Il fa - re - tra - to ar -

- cier for - ma un por - ten - to, O per a - ni - ma in se - no ho il mio tor -

- men - to, ho il mio tor - men - - to. No, che vi - va non

so - no. Se il mio cor, la mia vi - ta è sem - pre te - co,

with cadences (or their equivalent) followed by a rest, even drawing attention to the division between the two hemistiches in line 4 by pausing on a crotchet. But the patterns formed by the melodic and harmonic progressions do not coincide neatly with those present in the verse (such as rhymes). Albinoni's characteristic chromatic 'slithering' from a six–four–two chord to a seven–five chord in bar 2, reproduced quasi-sequentially in bars 3–4, corresponds rather untidily to lines 1–3 and the first hemistich of line 4. An opportunity to reproduce the rhyme of 'io' (line 2) and 'mio' (line 3) in musical terms is not merely spurned but deliberately averted through the prolongation of the bass $F\sharp$ by an extra bar. The four harmonic progressions that follow, all of which involve a bass descending by step ($F–E\flat, E\natural–D, (B)–A–G, (c)–B–A\sharp$) and a vocal line rising, mostly chromatically, also by step ($b'–c'', c\sharp''–d'', d\sharp''–e'', e''–f\sharp''$) make admirable musical sense (they are in fact a varied continuation of the initial sequence); the accelerated motion of the last two progressions is an effective climactic touch. But in this instance Albinoni decides to draw attention to the relationship, through assonance, between 'seno' (ending the first hemistich of line 5), the preceding 'portento', and the following 'tormento', by placing each of the three words at the end of the musical unit repeated in sequence.

Word-painting is employed selectively and always in conformity with purely musical logic. We meet it in the setting of the very first word, 'Lontan', whose two syllables span a sixth. The repetition of 'ho il mio tormento', which is set almost in *arioso* fashion with a writhing melodic line accompanied by 'anguished' diminished thirds (c–(B)–$A\sharp$, G–$E\sharp$) in the bass, occurs, appropriately, before a point of articulation: the end of the first sentence, which is also the end of the first musical period. Such writing has its counterpart in Albinoni's purely instrumental music. The other passage of melismatic writing, which is applied to the second hemistich of the final line, illustrates the word 'duolo' first with a harsh diminished third (perhaps a little mitigated by the substitution of an appoggiatura for the first $g\sharp'$) and then with upward and downward leaps of a seventh, before going on to convey the idea of 'pianto' with a short cantillation on the neighbouring notes a', b', and c''. Once again, the opportunity for heightened expression coincides perfectly with the urge towards pre-cadential elaboration found in any type of music, as the poet no doubt intended it to do. However, the conspicuous rising major seventh marking the end of the line 'No, che viva non sono' in bar 10 has no extra-musical justification. Arguably, it conveys an appropriate sense of agitation—but the same effect could have been introduced just as successfully in the previous bar or the next bar.

One can therefore speak of a 'counterpoint of intentions' between poet and composer. Albinoni's success as a writer of cantatas (in fact, of vocal music in general) cannot simply be measured by the fidelity with which he transfers to his own language the sounds, feelings, and meanings of another language; it needs also to take account of the skill with which he reconciles this possibility with the autonomous claims of his art-form, which from time to time lead him along a parallel rather than identical path.

Schmitz disparages Albinoni's recitatives in no uncertain terms, describing them as very dry and stereotyped ('ganz trocken und stereotyp'), in contrast to those of Vivaldi, which he finds excellent.[26] He criticizes them for failing to take advantage of opportunities for descriptive writing. Ex. 27 shows that this judgement needs some qualification. However, it must be admitted that the recitative chosen for the illustration is one of Albinoni's most resourceful and varied, both in melody and harmony; many others are indeed little more than efficient. In cantatas it

---

[26] *Geschichte der weltlichen Solokantate*, p. 151.

was always possible to introduce refinements inadmissible in operatic recitative, since the scale was smaller, the audience more attentive and cultivated, and the singer under less pressure since the part did not have to be memorized. It does seem, however, that Albinoni's immersion in opera from an early stage in his career inclined him to compose cantata recitatives in a relatively straightforward, even bland, manner that allowed him to pay close attention to overall design but inhibited him from lingering over details. Only fifty years further on C. P. E. Bach was to advocate precisely this approach: 'Not so long ago, recitatives used to be crammed with endless chords, resolutions and enharmonic changes. A special kind of beauty was sought in these harmonic extravagances, without there being the slightest excuse for their employment. . . . But today, thanks to our intelligent taste, exceptional harmonies are introduced into the recitative only rarely, and then with sufficient motivation.'[27] Whatever the shortcomings of Albinoni's cantata recitatives, they did not lag behind the times.

One peculiarity of Albinoni's word-setting in recitatives should be mentioned. In *versi sciolti* the first accent may fall on any of the first four syllables. Line 4 of *Lontan da te, mia vita* opens with 'il faretrato arcier', where the stress arrives on the second syllable, 'fa'. One might have expected Albinoni to place this syllable on the third beat of bar 4, preceding it with an unstressed quaver for 'il'. Instead, the weak opening syllable is accorded the stressed position. The violence to the natural accentuation of the words is not great—particularly if the singer exploits the rhythmic freedom permissible in recitative with the aim of disguising it—but it is none the less perceptible. In the context of Albinoni's cantatas taken as a whole unnatural stress occurs too often at the opening of phrases to be ascribed to negligence or insouciance. We therefore have to accept it as yet another of his mannerisms.

One interesting additional fact about the rhythm of Albinoni's vocal lines in the recitatives of both his cantatas and his operas may have a bearing on the matter just discussed. In syllabic passages, of which recitative mainly consists, the low incidence of dotted notes, quavers and crotchets alike, is a striking feature of his music. A dactylic rhythmic module, consisting of a quaver followed by a pair of semiquavers, is his favourite means of injecting animation into what would otherwise be a plain series of quavers. But the contraction brought about by the conversion of a pair of quavers into a pair of semiquavers has to be compensated for by adding a quaver elsewhere. Albinoni's preferred solution is to displace what would

---

[27] *Essay on the True Art of Playing Keyboard Instruments*, pp. 420–1.

otherwise be the 'upbeat' quaver forwards and extend the rest preceding it by a quaver, so that this rest now lasts a full crotchet. Perhaps that is the underlying reason for the accented openings of lines 4, 7, 8, 9, and 10 in the example.

When we turn to the arias, Schmitz takes a much more generous view. He calls Albinoni 'a very powerful inventor of vocal melody' ('ein sehr potenter vokaler Melodieerfinder')—an opinion that the evidence bears out fully. He puts the matter into an interesting perspective when he goes on to declare that Vivaldi does not measure up to Albinoni as a composer for the voice.[28] There are perhaps virtues in Vivaldi's melodic writing (very different, admittedly, from those of Albinoni) that Schmitz does not acknowledge, but one understands what he means: essentially, Albinoni has a holistic view of melody that subordinates the details to the overall design, whereas for Vivaldi the whole tends to be no more and no less than the aggregate of the details.

It will be useful to start by describing the structure of a typical Albinoni aria with da capo. This scheme applies to all his known cantata arias bar two.[29] In its externals it conforms absolutely to the standard plan followed without exception by Albinoni's Italian contemporaries. To that extent, his handling of form is less original in vocal than in instrumental music. But there are still plenty of personal touches in the detailed execution of the plan. The basic plan can be summarized as follows:

A *section*:
1 Introductory ritornello (optional)
2 *Devise* period (optional)
3 First vocal period
4 Second vocal period
5 Coda
6 Concluding ritornello

B *section*:
7 Third vocal period
8 Fourth vocal period (or extension of 7)

The reasons for having purely instrumental ritornelli are several. By providing pauses in the solo line more extensive than those naturally occurring between phrases, ritornelli offer the singer some relief and a welcome opportunity to prepare mentally for the next passage. They give the accompanist (or accompanists) the chance to emerge from the shadows.

[28] *Geschichte der weltlichen Solokantate*, p. 150.
[29] The exceptions are 'Dunque sì vago' from *Clori nel ciel d'amor lucida stella* and 'Fa che al labro giunga il riso' from *Senti, bel sol, deh senti*. Both are simple, dance-like movements without ritornelli.

Their alternation with vocal sections provides a convenient peg on which to hang two contrasted types of thematic material (recurrent and non-recurrent) and tonal character (modulating and non-modulating). They can be used to create dramatic opposition between the voice and its accompaniment. Most practically of all, they set or adjust the tempo for the singer and help him to find his starting note.

Whereas ritornelli in instrumentally accompanied arias can extend over many bars, those of continuo arias are always terse, since a bass line devoid of all support except (possibly) a continuo realization will not bear a more ample treatment. The melodic style of a bass ritornello is *sui generis*, though not unrelated to that of an orchestral unison. The single line has to be a melody and a bass rolled into one: from traditional melodic writing it derives its clear articulation, regular phrasing, and purposeful contouring; from traditional bass writing, its fondness for wide leaps and constant changes of register, and the practice of marking cadences with solid root-progressions.

It may surprise that nearly one third of Albinoni's da capo arias lack an introductory ritornello. Part of the explanation lies in the historical development of the ritornello, which during most of the seventeenth century was conceived more as a link between two vocal sections or as an epilogue than as an opening gesture. Naturally, none of the arias opening cantatas employing the ARA layout dispenses with this ritornello, which is essential if the singer is to pitch his first note accurately. Otherwise, the absence of an initial ritornello correlates positively (though not as strongly as one might imagine) with the features associated with lightness such as an A section in binary form or a 'short' metre such as 2/4 or 3/8. Since the quality of lightness is most appropriate for the final aria (it fits both the normal baroque aesthetic preference for a cheerful resolution and the brighter mood so often introduced at this point by the poet), arias without an introductory ritornello are more often than not the concluding movement of the cantata.

The presence or absence of an introductory ritornello has important implications for the character of the ritornelli appearing later in the movement. If the bass enters before the voice, it has the chance to present germinal ideas that, in more fragmentary form, can be retained in accompaniment to the voice and may even influence the shape of the vocal line itself. If, on the other hand, the voice enters right at the start of the movement, it has the opportunity to impress its thematic character on the bass, so that the ritornelli, when they arrive, may be no more than simple paraphrases of the vocal incipit. Basses that are thematically independent of the voice—employing, say, characteristically 'instrumental' figurations such as broken chords—tend to occur in arias with an initial ritornello, whereas those that have less independence and accompany in a more discreet fashion are more often found in arias lacking it. These tendencies should not be understood as rigid laws; nor should it be assumed that material appearing later necessarily 'develops' out of similar material appearing earlier. Looking at Ex. 28 below, who can say whether the ritornello or the vocal incipit was composed first? Neither is obviously derived from the other: they are simply formed from the same primary material.

Devise is German for 'heraldic device'. Hugo Riemann was the first to use the term to describe a particular kind of motto-opening that briefly became popular in arias written around 1700. It gives the impression of a false start by the voice, which, having given out an opening phrase, abruptly breaks off, leaving the accompaniment to complete the period. The voice then resumes, usually with the identical opening phrase, and this time continues normally. The second part of the *Devise* period, supplied by the accompaniment, is normally an abridged version of the initial ritornello—most commonly, its concluding portion.

This opening gambit, which is too much of a routine to be capable of producing a genuinely dramatic effect, has at least the virtues of expanding the dimensions of the movement a little and allowing the singer and the audience briefly to take the measure of each other before the main business of the movement commences. It is best suited to arias of the more formal, imposing kind. Albinoni employs it in considerably more than a third of his cantata arias. Its incidence in the different groups of cantatas preserved in the sources varies a little, but unfortunately not so greatly as to provide an aid to dating. (In Albinoni's operas the *Devise* becomes less common at the end of the first decade of the eighteenth century and virtually disappears during the second decade, so its infrequent appearance would suggest a later date.)

In the first vocal period the singer takes the music from its home key to the main subsidiary key of the A section. In major-key movements this is invariably the dominant, but one is pleased to see that in minor-key movements Albinoni varies his choice, sometimes even selecting the subdominant.

The second vocal period, which repeats the words of the first semistrophe, follows on almost immediately. In arias with instrumental accompaniment it is normal to interpose at this point a short ritornello in the key reached at the end of the first period, but this is unusual in arias accompanied only by a bass. Since the singer has to pause briefly before embarking on the second vocal period, there is at least time for the accompaniment to insert a short connective passage of, say, half a dozen notes, which may refer to ritornello material. This period takes the music back to the home key. Its thematic relationship to the first vocal period is not laid down by convention, but the openings are often matched in some way. Very often the vocal writing becomes more florid in the course of this period, producing a sense of climax.

To prolong the vocal display and reinforce the finality of the return to the home key, the composer often appends a coda to the second vocal section that may constitute a period in its own right. This may merely take the form of a *petite reprise* of the cadential passage preceding it, but is more likely, in Albinoni's hands, to become an extended paraphrase of it.

In strictly functional terms, the concluding ritornello does not need to differ at all from the introductory one. Nevertheless, Albinoni quite often varies it, extending or contracting it a little, or even displacing its rhythm to produce an altogether new version. A striking displacement of this kind is seen in the aria 'Che tu m'abbia incatenato' from *Da l'arco d'un bel ciglio*.

The B section, which sets the words of the second semistrophe, normally contains two vocal periods, although as few as one or as many as three can be found in individual cases. At least one of the principal cadences in this section is likely to be in the mode 'opposite' to that of the home key, but there are otherwise no firm rules. The style, *affetto*, and thematic content are unlikely to depart significantly from what has gone before, although there is no obligation to refer back to the material of the A section in literal fashion. Albinoni shows a pleasing willingness to make his B sections substantial in length and content. This point is worth making, since so many of his contemporaries have a habit of 'skimping' on the B section, treating it as a formality to be satisfied as economically as possible.

No single musical example can encompass the great variety of style and treatment found in these arias, but in Ex. 28 the A section of the second aria from *Lontan da te, mia vita*, which follows on immediately from the recitative quoted in Ex. 27, demonstrates some of their virtues. Albinoni's sense of line and proportion is admirable; the unexpected turn to F minor (in place of F major) just before the cadence marking the end of the first vocal section is a typical harmonic finesse that has no counterpart in the instrumental music he was writing at around the same time.

This example illustrates the high degree of thematic integration that Albinoni was able to achieve, in an entirely fresh and natural way, in these movements. Here there is an obvious link between the ritornello and the vocal line, which take turns to reiterate or develop the figure presented in the opening bar. In other arias the voice and bass imitate one another. Elsewhere, the thematic substance of the two parts is kept quite distinct,

Ex. 28

each part undergoing motivic development separately. The extent to which Albinoni reutilizes elements of the ritornello in the accompaniment to the vocal sections varies enormously. At one extreme we have the fairly numerous arias built over a ground bass, which may either be maintained strictly throughout the movement, modulating for the B section, or else confined to the A section. In these arias the ritornello becomes merely the preliminary, unadorned enunciation of the ostinato pattern. At the other extreme stand those arias in which the accompaniment begins by quoting from the ritornello but soon abandons the connection, retreating into a more purely functional supportive role. Albinoni has a favourite trick of appearing to ignore the material of the ritornello until close to the end of the second vocal section, when it is suddenly introduced in counterpoint to the voice (a good example is the aria 'Impara a serbar fede' from *Filli, chiedi al mio core*). Appearing unexpectedly at this point, it signals the impending return of the ritornello to conclude the A section, and so builds up excitement.

Another effective device is to borrow a characteristic motive from the ritornello and use it as a kind of motto to be inserted where appropriate between caesuras in the vocal part. This technique is applied most elaborately in 'Amor ch'è tenero', from *Bella, perché tu forsi*. In Ex. 29 below the motto is identified by a bracket. The same extract gives an idea of the rhythmic suppleness that Albinoni was able to achieve in his writing for the voice. The division of the dotted crotchet into four instead of three equal notes which occurs in the seventh bar is a refinement totally foreign to Albinoni's instrumental music—and none too common in the music of his time in general.

Schmitz finds Albinoni's arias rather one-sidedly inclined to a slow

Ex. 29

tempo and an elegiac mood.[30] Even in relation to the Berlin cantatas this impression is too superficial; it becomes downright misleading when applied to the Op. 4 works. The truth is that Albinoni is something of a specialist in the writing of simple, dance-like arias that are emphatically cheerful. Arthur Hutchings was thinking of the concertos when he wrote that Albinoni was 'one of the few musicians in all history who could produce . . . entirely gay movements as admirable as other men's serious movements', but the observation is equally true of the cantatas.[31] Such arias often reinforce the connection with the dance by having the A section in binary form with the first or both vocal sections repeated. They recall the tradition of dance-songs represented by such collections as Giovanni Lorenzo Gregori's *Arie in stil francese*, Op. 1 (Lucca, 1698).

Where a sombre and a bright aria coexist within a single cantata, Albinoni often uses a contrast in tonality to underscore the difference. Since recitative can modulate at will to distant keys (Ex. 27 is very unusual in being a tonally 'closed' recitative that returns to its point of departure), internal arias are able to appear in keys that are quite remote from the principal tonality. For example, *Dubbio affetto il cor mi strugge*, in C major, has its second aria in G minor; *Fatto bersaglio eterno*, in E minor, has its first aria in F major. Such a wide tonal ambit will occur only much later in Albinoni's instrumental music.

Albinoni's use of coloratura decoration strikes a perfect balance between the potentially conflicting imperatives of virtuosity and good taste. While his word-setting is open to criticism on occasion, he never overtaxes the voice or forces it into unnatural contortions. As Mattheson wrote of Vivaldi, he knows how to keep violinistic leaps away from his vocal pieces (and, one might add, to remember to insert pauses for breathing). One feels that, with a wife at hand to demonstrate, or offer advice on, *fioriture*, he possessed a true insider's knowledge of the singer's art.

The most memorable parts of Albinoni's cantatas are not, however, the arias but the cavatas. Quadrio defines a cavata as an artificial aria that has not been designed as such by the poet but is manufactured from recitative verse by the composer. He adds that such arias are usually 'extracted' from the last line or pair of lines in a stanza of *versi sciolti*.[32] The presence of a cavata is almost mandatory if the cantata text finishes with recitative verse; however, it occasionally appears after a recitative in an earlier part of the work, as happens twice in Albinoni's cantatas.

Numbering thirteen, his extant cavatas all take the form of fairly extensive through-composed sections in strict time appended to conven-

---

[30] *Geschichte der weltlichen Solokantate*, p. 150.   [31] *The Baroque Concerto*, p. 158.

[32] *Della storia e della ragione d'ogni poesia*, iii/2. 335.

tional recitative. Their texture is consistently imitative in a fugal or canonic manner, and they exploit invertible counterpoint to the full. Their tempo may be either quick or slow, depending on the *affetto* required. With one exception, all the cavatas move from the unvaried common time of recitative into triple or compound metre. This gives Albinoni the opportunity to indulge his penchant for hemiola, which he likes to apply to the two lines independently, so creating a fascinating mêlée of conflicting accents.

The longest and most impressive of the cavatas is that of seventy bars ending *Sorgea col lume in fronte*. In the four preceding stanzas, set alternately as recitatives and arias, Antonio Ottoboni's eloquent text depicts the departure by sea of Phyllis, who leaves her lover, the poet, uncomprehending and disconsolate. In a final stanza the poet gives vent to his despair:

Misero, all'aura sorda, al mare insano	Wretchedly, I scatter my prayers in vain
spargo le preci invano:	to the deaf breeze, the wild sea:
anzi, accresce a chi parte il mio tormento	but my torment over her departure is only swelled
col pianto l'onda, e coi sospiri il vento.	by the wailing of the waves and the sighing of the wind.

Albinoni sets the first three lines straightforwardly as recitative, reserving cavata treatment for the very last line. His principal subject and countersubject respond sensitively to the text, for the latter part of the subject has 'billows' that illustrate the motion of the waves, while the countersubject conveys the idea of sighing in time-honoured fashion with suspensions. The two ideas recur intermittently throughout the cavata, relieved by episodes on cognate material. The tonal plan of the section describes an appropriate wave-form, first travelling sharpwards from the home key of B minor via D major to F♯ minor, then veering flatwards to E minor and D minor, and finally restoring equilibrium by returning to B minor through the circle of fifths. An emphasis on minor keys accentuates the bleakness of the music. The opening is quoted in Ex. 30. In order to bring out the hemiola effects, I have added accent marks (-) where appropriate.

It is unlikely that Albinoni's cantatas ever became a great talking point at the *conversazioni* under whose auspices they were first performed. They do not pretend to be innovative in any conspicuous way and avoid extravagant gestures. Their great merit lies, rather, in the stylistic integrity and sheer musicianship with which familiar materials are cast and recast. The longer one's acquaintance with them, the greater one's appreciation of

Ex. 30

their little touches of individuality and the subtle points of differentiation among them. Whereas there are obvious practical and aesthetic problems affecting the revival of his operas, there is no reason why, given the steady growth of interest in the Italian baroque cantata, this branch of Albinoni's vocal writing, at least, should not come to occupy a respected place in recital programmes.

6

THE MATURE INSTRUMENTAL
WORKS, 1701–1714

WHAT does maturity mean? It means, first, that an artist has achieved a
reconciliation between originality and tradition: he speaks in his own voice
within a shared language. Its second meaning is that he has reached the full
measure of technical competence of which he is capable.

Between Op. 3, published in 1701, and Op. 6, published *c.* 1711,
Albinoni produced a series of balletti, sonatas, and concertos that satisfy
both criteria perfectly. They show a composer working within his natural
means, combining imagination and good workmanship without apparent
effort or strain. During this period Albinoni's instrumental works
represented a progressive (though not in any sense revolutionary) current
in Italian music and were regarded as exemplary north of the Alps.

Balletti a tre, Op. 3

If the sonatas of Albinoni's Op. 1 were Corellian, these trio balletti could
aptly be called 'neo-Corellian', for although they faithfully follow the
model of Corelli's Opp. 2 and 4 in their general design, they are far closer in
spirit to Albinoni's own concertos published a year earlier. Their
independent cello part sets them apart from chamber sonatas of the same
period (such as Vivaldi's Op. 1, published in 1705, and Bonporti's Opp. 2
and 4 from 1698 and 1703). It is rare, too, to find a composer of chamber
trios using imitative counterpoint quite as intensively as Albinoni does in
some of their movements.

Four of these balletti (nos. 2, 5, 8, and 11) dispense with an initial *preludio*
and begin straight away with the allemande. In compensation, this
movement is written in a slow tempo, 'largo' or 'larghetto', in place of the
more usual 'allegro'. The preludes themselves, also 'largo', are brief
versions, occupying a mere 8–16 bars in common time, of the customary
opening movement in a church sonata. Their texture is sometimes
predominantly homophonic, sometimes more contrapuntal.

The allemandes, which constitute the opening dance in every balletto,
are generously proportioned and follow a great variety of rhythmic
stylizations. Two of them, nos. 9 and 11, employ fugal texture in a manner
recalling the *Balletti a cinque*; however, imitation is now handled much

more deftly. Several allemandes, notably the eleventh, contain elaborate passage-work that would not be out of place in a concerto. Even when the second violin has essentially a filling part, Albinoni never neglects to give it brief bursts of activity that keep the player on his toes and preserve a modicum of contrapuntal interest.

The corrente and saraband, both in a quick triple metre, are treated as alternatives, except in Balletto VII, which includes one of each. Here again, Albinoni uses a mixture of imitative and homophonic textures. In the Sarabanda of Balletto VI Albinoni adds to an already complex texture an elaborate 'division' of the bass line in running quavers for the obbligato cello.

The jig and gavotte are likewise alternatives. The Giga of Balletto VIII is notable for its independent cello part in running quavers. In the gavottes Albinoni oscillates between the older march-like type, found in nos. 1, 3, and 6, and the newer type employing semiquavers, found in nos. 9 and 11.

The restatement of the opening idea at the start of the second repeated strain is now a standard feature. The ends of the strains are also sometimes matched, but not yet as a matter of course. Unity is still more a matter of stylistic consistency than thematic manipulation.

When the average quality is so high, it is hard to single out pieces for special commendation. Perhaps the most rewarding works in the set are those in the middle, from Balletto V to Balletto IX—which is not to say that the others should be ignored.

Without doubt, the *Balletti a tre* were in their day Albinoni 's most successful compositions for the trio medium. A perverse but none the less eloquent tribute to their popularity is paid by an ostensible 'church' sonata in a contemporary English manuscript, which has been assembled from the seventh balletto, stripped of its allemande, into which the prelude of the sixth balletto, transposed from F major to D major, has been imported as a slow third movement.[1] To complete the illusion, the saraband ending the work is superscribed 'Fugue'—not wholly inappropriately, since this movement does indeed make fugal gestures.

Sad to relate, cannibalizations of this kind are not unknown even in modern publications of Albinoni's music. In 1964 Ricordi published an arrangement by Giazotto (entitled *Sonata a 4*) of the first three movements of the second sonata from Albinoni's Op. 6, to which was added, in place of the suppressed fourth movement, the finale of the fourth of the so-called *Sonate da chiesa* (So 29)—a work, moreover, of dubious authenticity. The misery was compounded by the invention of inner parts for second violin and viola.

[1] London, British Library, Add. MS 34074–5.

Concerti a cinque, Op. 5

The simplest way to describe this set of concertos is to imagine a combination of the most attractive features of the sonatas and the concertos of Op. 2 respectively: from the sonatas they derive their fluent contrapuntal writing, but the old tendency to stiffness is gone; from the concertos they derive their dash, energy, and opportunities for solo display, but their material is now more complex and finely nuanced. Their indebtedness to the sonata tradition comes out most clearly in their finales, which are all fugal movements conforming to the general plan of the fast movements in the Op. 2 sonatas, except for the appearance of solos for the principal violin in certain episodes. Albinoni's Op. 5 is in fact a pioneer of the integration of the fugal principle within the solo concerto, looking forward to works by Bach and Leclair. The debt to the sonata is almost as evident in those slow movements, to be described below, which continue the tradition of the fourth sonata in Op. 2 by presenting several contrasted textures in succession. The fact that four out of the twelve works are in a minor key suggests the world of the sonata more than that of the concerto—in no other concerto collection does Albinoni allow the minor mode such strong representation. On the other hand, the status of these works as true concertos is confirmed by their three-movement plan, the incisive quality of their themes, and the presence of solos for the principal violin in every single work.

Three types of slow movement appear in the collection, succeeding one another in what appears to be a planned regular pattern. Concertos I, IV, VII, and X have short, transitional movements. Concertos III, VI, IX, and XII follow the familiar tripartite plan, though with larger dimensions and more inventive figuration than previously. Concertos II, V, VIII, and XI have the mosaic-like form borrowed from Op. 2 no. 7, but this time with three separate violin parts (*violino primo, violino de concerto,* and *violino secondo*) instead of two.

The form of the first movements follows the principles introduced in Op. 2. Statements of the opening motto in internal periods tend to appear in duplicate, as described before. It is noteworthy that Albinoni insists on retaining an identifiable coda even when, as in the seventh concerto, the opening period had enough weight and character to have served, if the composer had wished, as a ritornello in the Vivaldian sense, rounding off the movement exactly as it began it. In certain opening movements Albinoni adds interest to the restatements of the motto by supplying new countersubjects; in Concerto II the principal violin introduces shimmering broken chords (later on, roles are exchanged, when the principal violin has the motto theme and the other violins accompany), while in Concerto XII a solo cello enters in support of the chain of parallel thirds on the principal and first violins.

Op. 5 is an apotheosis of running semiquaver figuration. Every conceivable type of linear or chordal shape composed of semiquavers seems to find a place, and simultaneous semiquaver figures in two or more parts create dense swirls of sound that have a powerful effect in performance. Only in this collection does Albinoni often resort to the parallel motion in thirds for the upper parts that Purcell identified as a typically Italian device worthy of imitation in the 1694 edition of John Playford's *Introduction to the Skill of Music*. Torelli shares a fondness for this device, which naturally risks becoming facile or trite if used too much. On the whole, Albinoni does not abuse it; one particularly successful instance of its use occurs in the first four bars of the twelfth concerto, where fifty unaccompanied consecutive thirds on principal violin and first orchestral violin build up tremendous expectancy in preparation for the entry of the rest of the ensemble in the fifth bar.

In these chains of continuous thirds the principal violin is always accompanied by the *violino de concerto*. If one were to follow the lead of the slightly later concertos preserved in Dresden manuscripts, which in Pisendel's arrangement have the lower part allotted to a *violino secondo concertato* in similar passages, one would reduce the *violino de concerto* to a single player in order to match the tone of the principal violin more exactly. However, the composer gives no sign that this is his intention.

The opening movements of the first, fourth, and twelfth concertos contain short passages of semi-virtuosic writing for obbligato cello. Albinoni has no wish to create a 'double' concerto for violin and cello or even the mere impression of one; these rare solo flights exist merely to gratify the player and surprise the listener.

The obbligato cello also plays a prominent part in the four slow movements in 'mosaic' style. Its solo at the start of the Adagio of Concerto XI, accompanied in a similar register by the two violas (see Ex. 31), is

Ex. 31

without doubt the most adventurous piece of instrumentation that had appeared in any concerto up till then.

These four movements are the most elaborately 'orchestrated' pieces of music that Albinoni was ever to write, and the most *concertante* in spirit. It is strange that he abandoned this type of writing in his later concertos. Perhaps he considered, in the wake of the Vivaldian revolution, that the solo interest in them was too diffused, too even-handedly distributed, to be justifiable in a concerto.

The most interesting feature of the concluding fugues is not, as one might have expected, their inclusion of solo passages (which are brief enough), but their long, finely chiselled subjects, most of which are so attractive in their own right that one looks forward to their return as if they were catchy rondo refrains. Five of the subjects (in the first, third, ninth, eleventh, and twelfth concertos) are formed from pounding quavers interspersed with semiquavers; the seven quavers on the same note that open the subject in Concerto IX may have been in the back of Handel's mind when he started the subject of the second movement of his Op. 6 no. 7 on a monotone. Concertos IV, V, VI, and VII have fleet-footed subjects in triple or compound metre that countersubjects will later enliven with hemiola cross-rhythms. The finale of Concerto V is a 'stretto' fugue, while that of Concerto VI introduces stretto a third of the way through the movement in such a euphonious way that the skill behind the device is easily overlooked. Concerto X has a lilting, cantabile subject that seems to have stepped out of the pages of a cantata. Only Concertos II and VIII have traditional, vocally inspired subjects—and that of the second concerto is mocked with amusing effect by a syncopated countersubject.

When Op. 5 was first published by Sala in 1707, Handel was newly arrived in Italy. The coincidence is not without significance, for everywhere in this collection one finds passages that are 'pre-echoes' of familiar Handelian gestures. It may have been Albinoni who suggested to Handel the rhetorical device of breaking off dramatically on a seventh chord and making a short general pause before lurching into the final cadence. Pre-Handelian, too, is the oscillation between chords VIIb and I seen in the coda of the first movement of Concerto II, shown here in Ex. 32.

Hutchings's opinion that Albinoni's last concertos (by which he meant those of Opp. 7 and 9) are 'simply his longest, most highly organized and best' is more than a little unfair to Op. 5, for which the same writer claims merely 'energy and vitality'.[2] The very compactness of the earlier works is an asset, for even in Op. 7 Albinoni is beginning to stretch his structures beyond the point of comfort. Unquestionably, Op. 5 is the most inventive

[2] *The Baroque Concerto*, pp. 157, 163.

Ex. 32

of all Albinoni's concerto collections in terms of scoring. If these works have a weakness, it lies in their rather limited rhythmic imagination. Whoever coined the expression 'sewing-machine rhythms' could well have had them in mind.

'Sonate da chiesa a violino solo e violoncello o basso continuo' (So 26–31)

In Chapter 1 the background to this, the first of three 'unauthorized' published collections of violin sonatas by Albinoni, was discussed. When Roger first brought them out in 1708, they were not given an opus number; but when the sonatas were reissued from the original plates some years later, the line OPERA QUARTA was inelegantly squeezed in between TOMASSO [sic] ALBINONI and A AMSTERDAM. Needless to say, the works' description as church sonatas does not necessarily originate with the composer; although dance-titles do not appear, the allemande, corrente, or jig are clearly the rhythmic and formal models for most of their fast movements.

Roger's engraver allowed an unusually large number of errors to creep into this publication, perhaps because the composer (one assumes) did not have the opportunity to read the proofs. These inaccuracies are sometimes hard to distinguish from instances of genuine clumsiness, particularly in the setting of the bass. In view of the rather unpolished quality of the set, Moser and Newman are surprisingly complimentary towards it. It has its virtues, too, of course: energy, passion, and (in some slow movements) lyricism.

The probably inauthentic fourth sonata (So 29) betrays its separateness in several ways. To begin with, it is completely untypical of Albinoni, in a set of six sonatas for a stringed instrument, to include two works in the same key (G minor)—and side by side, into the bargain (as Sonatas IV and V).[3] Sonata IV is the only work in the set to use a cross to denote a trill; the remainder all use the letter 't', which is normal for Italians and for Albinoni himself elsewhere. This transalpine notational feature accords with the style of the work, which reminds one of such northerners as Loeillet and De Fesch writing in an italianate style, or Italian émigrés working in northern Europe such as Dall'Abaco and Mascitti. The second movement of *So* 29 is anomalous in another respect: it is through-composed, whereas all the other fast movements in the set are in binary form.

All the sonatas follow the slow–fast–slow–fast plan. The first is fairly undistinguished, being a preliminary draft, as it were, of closely related works published in Op. 6 (as no. 4) and in the 1717 set (as no. 1). The second sonata features a particularly lovely nine-bar Largo as its second slow movement. This shows the influence of recitative and is a good example of the 'semi-ornamented' style that was just beginning to become current in the solo parts of sonatas and concertos. In this style certain embellishments are written out in minute detail by the composer (cf. bars 1–3 of Ex. 33 below), while in other places phrases are left plain in

Ex. 33

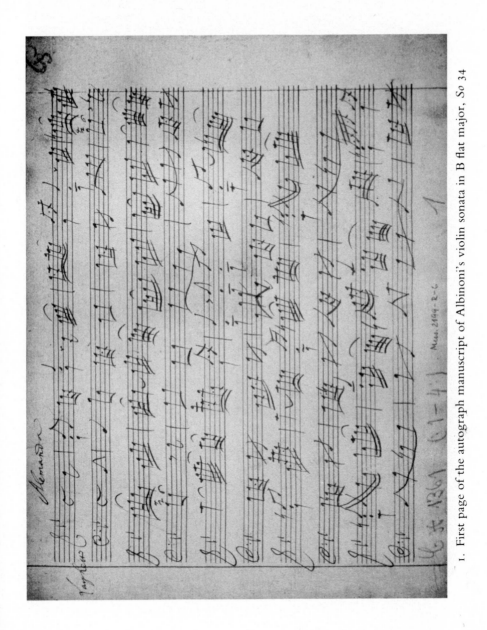

1. First page of the autograph manuscript of Albinoni's violin sonata in B flat major, So 34

2. Detail with the heads of Albinoni, Gizzi, and Colla from the engraving 'Parnaso italiano' after a drawing by Luigi Scotti

3. Anonymous oil painting of Albinoni

Violoncello:

BALLETTI

A Trè due Violini, Violoncello, e Cembalo

CONSACRATI

ALL' ALTEZZA REALE DI

FERDINANDO III.

GRAN PRENCIPE DI

TOSCANA

DA TOMASO ALBINONI DILETANTE VENETO

OPERA TERZA.

IN VENETIA. Da Gioseppe Sala. M. D. C C VI.

Si Vendono à S: Gio: Grisostimo All'Insegna del Rè David.

4. Title-page of the Violoncello part from the 1706 Sala edition of Albinoni's *Balletti a tre*, Op. 3

5. Extracts from Albinoni's *Concerti a cinque*, Op. 10, included in Michel Corrette's *L'Art de se perfectionner dans le violon* (1782)

INTERMEZZO
PRIMO.

Vespetta, e Pimpinone.

Ve. CHi mi vuol? Son cameriera.
Fo di tutto. Pian. M'intendo
Di quel tutto che conviene.
Son dabbene, son sincera:
Non ambisco, non pretendo,
E mi aggiusto al male e al bene. Chi co.
Cerco la mia ventura,
Ma per le vie onorate. Un po di dote
Farmi vorrei col mio sudor. Ma viene
Il Signor Pimpinone.
Nobil non è, ma ricco a canna, e sciocco.
Che buon Padron saria per me. Vediamo.
Pi. Guai a chi è ricco, guai. Per ogni parte
Ogn'un mi vuol rubar. Più tanta gente
Non voglio in casa mia. Sia benedetto
L'uso delle servette. Una di queste
Per me saria un tesoro...Uh! qui Vespetta.
Ve. Se costui mi accettasse...
Pi. Se volesse costei...
a 2 Seco pur volontier mi aggiusterei.)
Pi. Vespettina gentil, come si sta.
Ve. Vossignoria illustrissima perdoni.
Io non l'avea veduta in verità.
Pi. Che belle riverenze!
Ve. Dal maestro di ballo
Ch'insegna ov'io serviva, io l'ho imparate.
Pi. Gran Dama la Padrona esser dovea.
Ve. Che gran Dama? oggidì l'uso non falla.
Adesso il mi la sol, il la la la la,
Troppo è comune. Ognuna canta, e balla.
Pi. A che giova, a che serve un tal diletto?

A 2　　Ve. Se

6. Opening of the text of the comic intermezzi *Pimpinone* as it appears
in the libretto of the original production (Venice, 1708)

7. First page of the aria with obbligato oboe 'Cerco l'oggetto del mio furor' from the opera *I veri amici* (Munich, 1722)

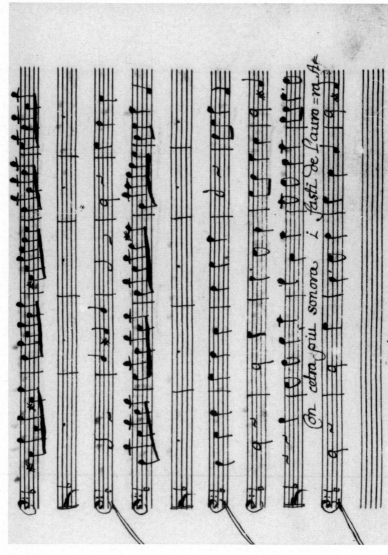

8. Third page of the aria with obbligato archlute 'Con cetra più sonora' from the serenata *Il nascimento de l'Aurora* (c. 1710)

traditional fashion so that the performer can work his fancy on them (cf. bars 4–6 and 8–9).

After a rather colourless third sonata, the fifth and sixth make ample amends. The first contains, in the passage-work of its second movement, almost the highest note (g″′) to appear in Albinoni's music. Both of its slow movements are highly charged, full of yearning leaps and chromatic alterations. The finale, a virtual *perpetuum mobile* for the violin, is singled out by Moser.[4]

Unquestionably the finest sonata overall is the sixth, in B minor. It is the only one (disregarding Sonata IV) not to exploit double stopping, and its lowest note for the violin part is a curiously high e♯′. Although B minor is not a typical recorder key, the sonata can be played successfully on that instrument. Since solo sonatas for treble recorder were certainly being composed around then by Venetian composers—Benedetto Marcello published a set of them *c*.1715 as his Op. 2—one cannot rule out the possibility that this sonata began life as a recorder sonata. The transverse flute is a less likely candidate, since Venetian composers apparently did not begin to write for it until many years later (which does not mean, of course, that modern flute players should be debarred in all circumstances from taking it into their repertory). The high point of the sonata is its second movement, a two-voice fugue very reminiscent of the cavatas in Albinoni's cantatas, but here quintessentially instrumental in style, with wide leaps and intricate passage-work.

Trattenimenti armonici per camera a violino, violone e cembalo, Op. 6

'Trattenimento' means 'entertainment'—in a more etymological sense, something that detains one from more serious activities. As a title for a set of sonatas, it is merely ornamental. A few collections described similarly as *trattenimenti* had appeared in the decades preceding the publication of Albinoni's collection. Perhaps our composer modelled his title directly on a set of *Trattenimenti musicali di sonate da camera a violino, violone o cembalo*, Op. 1, brought out by a certain Stefano Macarani in 1709.

The *Trattenimenti armonici* belong to the subsidiary but distinctive tradition of chamber sonatas that have no overt connection with the dance. In fact, their form is exactly the same as that of the so-called *Sonate da chiesa* of the previous collection: two through-composed slow movements introduce two quick movements in binary form. The first quick movement is in Op. 6 always in common time, vaguely after the fashion of

---

[4] *Geschichte des Violinspiels*, p. 79.

an allemande; the second quick movement adopts triple or compound metre. The first slow movement is always in common time; the second is in a variety of metres, with 3/4 predominant. Outwardly, therefore, Albinoni is uncommonly rigid even by his own standards in the shape he gives these works.

This time Roger, who had come by the sonatas more legitimately, did their composer proud. The engraved edition is a model of beauty, clarity, and accuracy. It provides, incidentally, an early example of notation that takes the temporal relationship as the criterion for vertical alignment (according to the older system, the symbols in each stave were grouped equidistantly within the bar regardless of the sequence of sounds). However, the precision masks a small but not unimportant problem. Italian composers writing out violin sonatas in score were accustomed to figure the bass very sparingly. They could do this because performers in Italy were experienced in the realization of unfigured basses (provided, of course, that they could refer to the obbligato parts while they played). In northern Europe, where there were large numbers of technically proficient but theoretically uneducated amateur performers, such parsimony did not suffice. If one compares Roger's editions of solo sonatas such as Vivaldi's Op. 2 and Valentini's Op. 8 with the Italian originals, one notices that most of the bass figures are newly added. On the whole, the supplementary figures are uncontroversial, but sometimes they seem badly chosen. Since no earlier print or manuscript of Albinoni's Op. 6 exists, it is impossible to know for sure which, if any, of the suspect figures go back to the original. All that the modern editor can do is to follow his own instinct, in defiance of the figuring, when not to do so would be musically unsatisfactory.

The care taken over the bass part is one pleasing feature of these sonatas. From time to time the bass has little snatches of imitation or animation of a type not found in the unauthorized collections. It is possibly for this reason that Albinoni specifies the *violone* (i.e., for practical purposes, the cello) as additional rather than alternative to the harpsichord. Without a stringed instrument, the imitative passages will be out of balance; without harpsichord, the texture may sound thin.

The melodic writing is notably linear, even vocal, in character. Where characteristically violinistic writing occurs, which is predominantly in the quick movements, the ostensible angularity is in reality a simultaneous linearity at two or three different pitch levels, as explained in Chapter 3. Within each movement Albinoni now begins to diversify the rhythmic activity, moving away from the prevailing uniformity found in the binary-form movements of his earlier balletti. The endings of the two strains in the fast movements are now quite often matched, although this procedure is not yet a routine.

The *Trattenimenti armonici* are the very epitome of classicism in music. Hutchings writes very aptly that Albinoni's energy 'glows' where Vivaldi's 'flames'.[5] A steady glow is precisely what he is aiming for. This is music that will satisfy even more in the memory after a performance than during the act of listening to it. Everything is in place: after the enunciation of an initial idea, the music merely has to follow its prescribed course, deftly steered by the composer.

Of course, the classical coolness does not preclude moments of great poignancy. The Largo of the second sonata (G minor) is a case in point. Its key is E♭ major, in vocal music associated with tenderness and mellow feelings. As melody, this is entirely through-composed music, but Albinoni imposes discipline and unity on the movement by employing a sequential ostinato pattern in the bass almost all the way through, departing from it only to make a cadence or move to a new key. Each of the three periods forming it is superbly contoured, rising and falling with the build-up and release of tension.

Op. 6, which came out *c.* 1711, was a seminal work that did much to re-establish the separate identity of the sonata genre after all the stylistic confusion brought about by the rise of the concerto. Its influence can be seen in Valentini's *Allettamenti per camera*, Op. 8 (1714), and the four solo sonatas in Vivaldi's Op. 5 (1716). The tuneful sixth sonata, whose bass was realized by H. N. Gerber under the watchful eye of Bach, was successfully adapted (with the sacrifice of its double-stops) by a contemporary as a recorder sonata, in which guise it is preserved in the Biblioteca Palatina, Parma, and the Fürstenberg collection in Schloss Herdringen, West Germany;[6] in this version it was published in 1935 in a modern edition ostensibly for flute.[7] It is not impossible that the version for recorder was actually the original one.

Four sinfonias (*Si* 2–5)

From many history books one might gather that the baroque sinfonia and the classical symphony were different genres altogether. Indeed, this belief is implicit in our very usage, which retains the original Italian word for the first, and substitutes an anglicized form for the second. In reality, however, the sinfonia, best known in its function as the overture to the first act of an opera, is the direct ancestor of the concert symphony of the late eighteenth century. What changes are apparent (beyond the evolution from a baroque to a classical musical language) have nothing to do with the influence of the

---

[5] *The Baroque Concerto*, p. 162.
[6] The shelfmarks are respectively CF-V-23 and Fü 3614a.
[7] As Nagels Archiv 74, edited by Ludwig Schäffler.

concerto, as some writers would have it: they stem, rather, from the increasing use of the sinfonia as pure concert music and its gradual differentiation from the overture, which moved in the direction of a closer integration with the stage work that it preceded.

Of course, the baroque sinfonia, as 'functional' music, was not found only in operas and serenatas. It was widely used as introductory or concluding music in solemn church services, exactly in the manner of the sonata. The surviving fragments of the Pietà's repertory include sinfonias by Vivaldi and Lampugnani dating from around 1740 which are identical in all their features to an operatic overture of the time.

The sinfonia was perfectly suited to use as concert music on account of its wholly abstract character. Mattheson, Quantz, and Algarotti all expressed the wish that something of the character of an opera should be foreshadowed by its overture, but this advice went unheeded until Rameau's *Zoroastre* (1749). When the scores of Italian operas were copied out, the overture customarily occupied a separate quire. This detachability was turned to good account by composers, who were apt to transfer the sinfonia of one work to another. (It may well be for this very reason that the scores of five Vivaldi operas otherwise preserved complete lack an overture.) Visitors to Italy often included the overture among operatic extracts bought from professional copyists, which is why northern European libraries today possess so many sinfonias by Albinoni, Vivaldi, and their Italian contemporaries. Italian sinfonias were very soon being performed as independent concert works and even commissioned from composers on that basis: take, for example, the five *Sinfonie a 4* by Benedetto Marcello supplied to a certain Mr Drex, which in general stylistic terms are extraordinarily similar to Albinoni's sinfonias.[8]

Only two of the Albinoni sinfonias considered here can be traced back to an identified stage work: *Si 2*, which opened *Engelberta* (Venice, San Cassiano, Carnival 1709),[9] and *Si 4*, used in 1714 as the sinfonia to the London pasticcio *Creso* (*Croesus*), and no doubt taken from one of Albinoni's operas staged in Italy during the years immediately preceding.[10] *Si 3* and 4 are both preserved among the Este manuscripts (as EM 109b and 109a respectively); manuscripts of *Si 4* and 5 exist in the library of the

---

[8] London, British Library, Add. MS 31579.

[9] The source of *Si 2* in Vienna (EM 124) names Gasparini as the composer. This misattribution obviously arose from the fact that Gasparini was the composer of the last two acts of the opera in addition to the comic intermezzi that were included in the original production. Although the opera registers of Bonlini and Groppo remain silent about Albinoni's contributions to *Engelberta*, the distribution of responsibility between the two composers is clearly explained in the score of the opera in the West Berlin Staatsbibliothek (Mus. ms. 445) and borne out by the musical style.

[10] In partnership with John and Joseph Hare, Walsh brought out the *Croesus* overture in the collection *Six Overtures for Violins* (c. 1724). Its composer is not identified in the published source.

Royal Academy of Music (Kungliga Musikaliska Akademiens Bibliotek), Stockholm. Their stylistic features as well as their association in the sources suggest that *Si* 3–5 are roughly contemporaneous works belonging to the period 1710–15.

Although the Italian sinfonia for strings and concerto for strings without soloist overlap stylistically to some extent, the typical sinfonia possesses a few distinctive traits. It strives to achieve a great weight of sound and to convey the impression of vigorous activity with a minimum of technical difficulty and does not allow the lure of counterpoint to subvert the dominating position of the highest part. All the movements are brief, but the second and third may be so short that their presence is hardly more than token. Albinoni writes sinfonias of the purest type. Indeed, their slow movements are so fragmentary that they here take the form of short codas to the opening Allegro movements, which lead straight into them. The finales are lightweight binary movements in 3/8 metre.

One must admire these works for their slick efficiency, which certainly makes a good advertisement for Albinoni's technique. All the same, they are distinctly unmemorable. The deliberate repetitiveness noted in Chapter 3 in connection with Ex. 13 is strongly in evidence; Albinoni shows the first signs of a malady which will blight much of his later music—a desire to draw out a period by artificial means to a length that it cannot easily sustain.

The sinfonia labelled *Si* 3a is a curiosity. Between 1709 and 1712 Estienne Roger brought out an anthology of instrumental works for four-part strings that he entitled *VI Sonates ou concerts à 4, 5 & 6 parties composées par Mrs. Bernardi, Torelli & autres fameux auteurs*. None of the individual works, unfortunately, is identified by composer, so all attributions have to be made on the basis of concordance with authenticated works preserved elsewhere. It so happens that the third sonata, besides being thoroughly Albinonian in style, is closely related to *Si* 3. Its first movement differs only by having a 'motto' which is a paraphrase (using the very same bass) of that in the cognate work and a concluding slow section that is rhythmically modified and slightly extended. The finale, however, is a bouncing fugal movement unknown from any other source. At first sight one might wonder whether Albinoni would compose a sinfonia (as distinct from a sonata or a concerto) ending with a fugue. The proposition is not so impossible, however, for the sinfonia to his serenata *Il nascimento de l'Aurora*, which dates from the same period around 1710, has a fugue as its first movement; further, a four-part sinfonia preserved separately in Dresden (my catalogue lists it as 'VII, 4a' on account of its close relationship to the concerto Op. 7 no. 4), ends with a similar movement. In eighteenth-century music fugue is not regarded solely as a learned or 'heavy' component; it has a lighter, playful side that can be used to express high spirits. The present movement can be seen, *mutatis mutandis*, as a forerunner of the finale to works such as Haydn's Symphony no. 3 and (despite the indecency of the comparison) Mozart's 'Jupiter' Symphony.

7

THE MATURE INSTRUMENTAL WORKS, 1715–1722

WERE one to measure the importance and value of Albinoni's works by their critical reception by modern scholarship and the extent of their publication and performance in recent years, there is no doubt that the instrumental works between Op. 7 (1715) and Op. 9 (1722) would win most of the prizes. To be sure, their reputation is unevenly distributed: only one of the eight violin sonatas belonging to this period is well known, and the position of the six orchestral works surviving only in manuscript is little better. Op. 8, despite the many compliments paid to it in the literature and the existence of two complete modern editions, has so far made little headway in recital programmes.[1] Only Op. 9 and the concertos with one oboe in Op. 7 have had a really wide exposure—but the extent of their popularity places them in a quite different category from all the rest of Albinoni's music (the spurious but indestructible Adagio in G minor naturally excepted).

Some of this success in modern times—and to some extent also in their own day—is a by-product of the vogue for Vivaldi's concertos, which Albinoni's concertos from this period resemble more than either his earlier ones (of Opp. 2 and 5) or his later ones (of Op. 10). Vivaldi started composing concertos at some point in the first decade of the century, and manuscript copies of them started circulating no later than 1709.[2] He first achieved prominence with the publication of his Op. 3 collection (*L'estro armonico*) in 1711; his international reputation was consolidated by the publication of three further collections (Opp. 4, 6, and 7) in the next few years.

The essence of Vivaldianism lay partly in a distinct musical style, partly in a distinct musical form (ritornello form). Foreign imitators, who saw Vivaldi's music as encapsulating all that was most progressive in contemporary Italian music, found it easy to assimilate both the style and the form as a coherent 'package'. Telemann, who was only three years

---

[1] Under the slightly misleading title of *Tomaso Albinoni: Sonatas and Suites, Opus 8*, the *Balletti e sonate a tre* have been published, in an edition by C. David Harris, as vols. li and lii of the series 'Recent Researches in the Music of the Baroque Era' (A–R Editions, Madison, 1986).

[2] A German musician named Franz Horneck made copies of some cello concertos by Vivaldi during a visit to Venice in Carnival 1708–9.

younger than Vivaldi, was writing concertos of unmistakably Vivaldian cast by the second decade; Bach soon followed.

Italian composers found it harder to become 'Vivaldians' for two important reasons. In the first place, the Roman school, represented first by Corelli and later by Valentini and Mossi, proved well-nigh impervious to Vivaldian influence because of the peculiar structure of Roman orchestras, with their *concerto grosso* and *concertino*. It therefore provided a competing source of influence, at least in central and southern Italy. Second, habits had grown up during the first two decades of concerto composition (roughly, 1690–1710) that were not so easy to shake off. Albinoni and Gentili, both older than Vivaldi, were not suddenly going to throw overboard all the technique and experience they had gained simply because the Red Priest had stolen their limelight. It was a younger composer altogether, Giuseppe Matteo Alberti (1685–1751), who was to become Vivaldi's first—and almost only—Italian acolyte.

So we should not be surprised to find Albinoni imitating Vivaldi only very selectively, almost grudgingly. The type of ritornello form described in textbooks is ignored completely (with one curious exception in Op. 7, to be discussed later), although one can see that Albinoni is obviously endeavouring, using his own methods, to achieve a comparable degree of thematic concentration. A few stylistic traits absent from his earlier music betray Vivaldian influence: the occasional grouping of phrases in threes instead of twos (or its equivalent, the inclusion of phrases occupying three instead of two metrical units, as in the opening of Ex. 35 below); a penchant for bold unison passages; a more lyrical treatment of the solo instrument (though not yet in the quick movements of string concertos).

Above all, Albinoni strives to match Vivaldi for length. Ritornello form, in which closed and open periods alternate, is calculated to spin out the length of a movement to the maximum extent, since all new keys visited are consolidated in a closed period before the tonality changes again. This is the basic reason why the fast movements of *L'estro armonico* are so much longer than their counterparts in the earlier concertos of Albinoni, Torelli, and Gentili—and the reason why, for the first time in the history of the concerto, Vivaldi found it necessary to divide the twelve works making up the collection into two *libri*.

Since Albinoni on the whole remains faithful to the principle of forming the central part of the movement from consecutive open periods, he denies himself this simple means of achieving greater length. Instead, he expands the dimensions by making each individual period significantly longer. How he does it can be seen in Ex. 34, the opening period of the first movement of the string concerto Op. 7 no. 1. It is striking how much

Ex. 34

repetition is contained within these eleven and a half bars—and how many different kinds of repetition. The six repeated notes heard at the outset (bracketed figure 'a') are repeated at a different pitch half-way through bar 9 and in rhythmic if not melodic outline prefigure the 'hammered' quavers in bars 3, 8, and 9. The little figure 'b', consisting of a descending scale in semiquavers (with its introductory and terminal notes, both quavers), describes a triad and can therefore be repeated at the appropriate pitch whenever the harmony remains the same for half a bar; this occurs in bars 2 (twice), 8, and 9. Figure 'c', first stated in bar 3, is heard three times in succession. This type of repetition, which is different from echo repetition since the restatement does not function as a response to the original statement, is aptly termed by Hutchings 'kinetic recurrence': the musical unit seems to repeat itself through the force of its own inner energy. More kinetic recurrence occurs in bars 7–9. In bars 10–11 an ostinato figure ('d') breaks up the line g''–$f\sharp''$–e''–d''–g''–$f\sharp''$ into two-note segments, retarding its progress. Finally, in bars 5–7 we see stepwise sequence of a familiar kind.

By judiciously mixing forms of repetition that are immediate and non-immediate, that occur at the same pitch and at different pitches, and that involve short units and long units, Albinoni manages to avoid any suggestion of *naïveté* or obviousness. One has to admire the adroitness of his pattern-making. However, there are two dangers in this technique of expansion. One is that it draws attention to itself by becoming too overt and subverts the naturalness that, in his earlier music, was one of his great assets. The other is that through miscalculation the repetitiveness is overdone, leading to stodginess or even monotony. Ex. 34 is free of those defects, but from now on Albinoni's concertos and sinfonias (less so, his sonatas and his vocal music) suffer increasingly from a flabbiness born of prolixity.

Concerti a cinque, Op. 7

Anyone who, in 1715, purchased this collection from Roger in the belief that it corresponded in its general specifications to the *Concerti a cinque* of Opp. 2 and 5 must have experienced a great surprise. Gone are the tenor viola and the separate partbook for *violino de concerto*. Instead, there is a part for *haubois primo* in eight of the concertos and one for *haubois secondo* in four concertos. Only the concertos with one oboe are *concerti a cinque* in the ordinary meaning of the term: those without oboes are *concerti a quattro*; those with two oboes, *concerti a sei*.

As in Op. 5, but now more overtly, the works are divided into four groups. Each group consists of a work for strings alone (Concertos I, IV, VII, and X), followed by a work with two oboes (Concertos II, V, VII, and XI) and one with a single oboe (Concertos III, VI, IX, and XII). Whereas within the group of string concertos, and, again, within the group of oboe concertos, the keys are all different, the concertos with two oboes comprise three in C major and one in D major. This restriction of key, which is not imposed by the obbligato instrument itself (the single-oboe concertos use B♭ and F major in addition to C and D major), points to the interesting fact, confirmed by many points of style, that Albinoni is here deliberately harking back to the tradition of the trumpet sonata: the oboes have become, so to speak, *ersatz* trumpets.

The string concertos in the set are disappointingly shallow works that, particularly in their first movements, stretch the listener's patience with over-long sequences. Giazotto is perhaps a little harsh when he describes their themes as 'almost invariably infantile';[3] it is true that the wholesale assimilation of features from the sinfonia lends them a certain blandness (which will be overcome in the string concertos of Op. 9), but Ex. 34 shows that their principal themes can, under the surface, achieve a high degree of sophistication. The first concerto, by far the best of the four, betrays its connection with the sinfonia very obviously, for its first and second movements are fused together exactly as in *Si* 3–5. Its finale, a cheerful binary-form movement in 2/4 metre, is the first example in

---

[3] *Tomaso Albinoni*, p. 169.

Albinoni's instrumental music of a type that will prove very successful in his later works.

The fourth concerto has a kind of slow movement new to Albinoni but familiar from Vivaldi's Opp. 3 and 4: the treble part (here the *violino primo* is not assigned expressly to a solo instrument, although solo performance would be effective) weaves a continuous, ornate line made up of repeated short figures to which simple patterns of block chords on the remaining instruments give support. The outer movements, however, are most undistinguished.

A manuscript of this work in the library of the Royal Academy of Music, Stockholm, replaces the three upper parts by flute, first violin, and second violin respectively. As an ostensible flute concerto it was published in this form in 1957.[4] The fact that the upper part (for flute) is totally independent from start to finish ought to have alerted the editors to the improbability of this version's being other than an *ad hoc* arrangement. (Sadly, Albinoni composed no concertos with obbligato wind parts other than the sixteen with one or two oboes.) The sinfonia related to this concerto, briefly mentioned at the end of the last chapter, will be discussed further on in this chapter.

Of the seventh concerto there is little to say: the vacuous bustle of its outer movements is redeemed a little by an Adagio similar to that of the fourth concerto but less developed.

Concerto X, whose opening has been quoted as Ex. 13 in Chapter 3, appears to be a slightly adapted version of a concerto with principal violin. Since Op. 7 does not provide separate partbooks for principal and first violins, all solo passages have to be cued in exactly as in the earliest published concertos. Another version of this concerto, this time with separate principal and first violin parts, is preserved in a manuscript copied out by Pisendel, presumably during 1716–17.[5] This is one of Pisendel's so-called *Reisepartituren*, or 'travelling scores', which were written on Venetian paper of unusually small dimensions, presumably in order to facilitate their transport back to Dresden. However, this version ('VII, 10a') cannot be the original one either, since it contains clear evidence of reworking by Pisendel: inner parts are frequently reorganized and some solos are extended. Moreover, the original finale, which has no solo passages, has been replaced by a briefer movement in binary form. One suspects that the author of this movement is Pisendel himself, since in a transposition to C major it reappears in a version of the Vivaldi violin concerto RV 192 also preserved (uniquely) in Dresden.[6]

---

[4] Edited by Johannes Brinckmann and Jan Pontén (Sikorski, Hamburg, 1957).

[5] Dresden, Sächsische Landesbibliothek, Mus. 2199-O-5.

[6] Dresden, Sächsische Landesbibliothek, Mus. 2389-N-7b.

An unusual feature of the opening movement of this concerto is that solo passages are inserted as early as the first period.[7] This is a further demonstration of Albinoni's wish not to counterpose the principal violin to the rest of the ensemble in *concertante* fashion but instead to exploit its agility for colouristic purposes. The slow movement, framed by short tuttis, alternates single bars of tutti chords (to which the principal violin also contributes) with passages of one to four bars for the principal instrument, lightly supported. The irregular length of these solos lends this movement a pleasing capriciousness reminiscent of the slow movements in Vivaldi's *La stravaganza*, Op. 4.

A variant of this concerto that has no separate part for principal violin ('VII, 10b') is preserved in two manuscript sources in the University Library, Uppsala.[8] One set of parts is in the hand of J. D. Gudenschwager, mentioned earlier; the other bears the name of J. Carlberg. This variant differs from the published version in having a new 'motto' for the first movement; this phrase has elements in common with the opening of the third concerto of the Op. 7 set.

It will be useful to preface our discussion of the oboe concertos in Op. 7 with some remarks on the cultivation of the oboe in Venice and the early history of the oboe concerto in general.[9] A recent article by Alfredo Bernardini sheds considerable light on the first question.[10] Perfected in France shortly after 1650, the oboe had reached Venice by the last decade of the century; it is required in the scores of two operas (C. F. Pollarolo's *Onorio in Roma* and Perti's *Furio Camillo*) produced there in 1692. Apparently, Venetian oboe playing did not grow out of an indigenous tradition of shawm playing in the context of folk or military music, and it is significant that for a long time after its introduction many of the eminent players were of non-Venetian origin.

The first oboist of note was a Milanese player, Onofrio Penati (*c.* 1662–1752), who is named as one of the supernumerary players engaged for the celebration of Christmas 1696 at San Marco (another 'extra' on that occasion was the young Antonio Vivaldi, making his first known public appearance). In 1698 Penati was admitted to the ducal *cappella*, which he served until his retirement in 1748; in the former year he also became attached to the doge as an official wind-player (*piffaro*). At various times (1704–6, 1716–19, 1721) he taught at the Pietà.[11] The second, third, and

---

[7] The solo writing appears here in the central part of the period, rather than forming an introduction to the movement as in Op. 5 no. 12.

[8] Instr. mus. i hs. 12:7 and 12:11.

[9] This subject is discussed at greater length in the author's article 'Albinoni's Oboe Concertos', *The Consort*, 29 (1973), 14–22.

[10] 'The Oboe in the Venetian Republic', *Early Music*, 16 (1988), 372–87.

[11] During his first period of teaching (1704–6), when he worked alongside Ignazio Rion, Penati may have been hired to teach recorder rather than oboe.

fourth editions of Vincenzo Coronelli's *Guida de' forestieri sacro profana per osservare il più ragguardevole nella città di Venezia* (1700, 1706, and 1713) all mention him by name among Venice's most distinguished musicians.

The Pietà's first oboe master was in fact another man, Ignazio Rion (possibly a Frenchman), who worked there from 1704 until 1705; in the latter year Rion left for Rome, where he enjoyed a highly successful career. The 1706 and 1713 editions of Coronelli's *Guida* mention him— retrospectively—alongside Penati.[12]

Rion's successor at the Pietà was Ludwig (Lodovico) Erdmann (died 1759), who may be identical with an oboist from Berlin named Erdmann who at the very beginning of the century served at the court in Ansbach of Georg Friedrich, margrave of Brandenburg;[13] Quantz identifies him, at any rate, as a German.[14] In 1706 he was employed at the Pietà to teach the chalumeau (elder cousin of the clarinet), and in the following year he assumed responsibility for the oboe. In 1708 he left Venice for good, moving first to Bologna and finally settling in Florence, where he entered the service of the Tuscan court.

The fourth outstanding oboist active in Venice during Albinoni's lifetime was Ignazio Sieber (died 1761), another German by the sound of his name. Between 1713 and 1716 he was the Pietà's oboe master. Shortly afterwards he must have moved to Rome, since *c.* 1717 Roger brought out a collection of twelve recorder (or flute?) sonatas of which the last six were attributed to a 'Monsieur Sieber demeurant à Rome'. Sieber's activity as a composer is also attested by a set of his *Ariette per il traversiere* formerly in the Lobkowitz collection at Raudnitz.[15] He later returned to Venice, being employed by the Pietà as a flute teacher from 1728 until his retirement in 1757, and succeeding Penati as principal oboist at San Marco until 1760. Sieber's membership of the *Arte de' sonadori* will have given him the opportunity to accept 'extra-mural' engagements in Venice, for example in performances held under the auspices of academies.

There is no information directly connecting any of these virtuosi with the fairly extensive Venetian repertory of sonatas and concertos for oboe composed in the first half of the eighteenth century. Rion and Erdmann were absent during the period leading up to the publication of Albinoni's

---

[12] The *Guida* refers to the celebrated oboist merely as 'Ignazio', thus conceivably Ignazio Sieber instead of Ignazio Rion. One is reminded of the traveller John Ray's observation: 'The *Italians* when they call, speak to, or of one another, use only the christian name, as *Signor Giacomo, Signor Giovanni*, &c. unless it be for distinction's sake; so that you may converse among them, perchance, some months before you hear any man's surname mentioned' (*Travels through the Low-Countries, Germany, Italy and France* . . . , 2nd edn., 2 vols., London, 1738, i. 340).

[13] Information from Alfredo Bernardini, 'The Oboe in the Venetian Republic', p. 379.

[14] 'Herrn Johann Joachim Quantzens Lebenslauf, von ihm selbst entworfen', in Friedrich Wilhelm Marpurg, *Historisch-kritische Beyträge zur Aufnahme der Musik*, 5 vols. (Berlin, 1754–78), i. 231.

[15] See Paul Nettl, 'Musicalia der fürstlich Lobkowitzschen Bibliothek in Raudnitz', *Mitteilungen des Vereins für Geschichte der Deutschen in Böhmen*, 58 (1919), 88–100.

Op. 7, while Penati, who was not a member of the musicians' guild, perhaps did not perform widely outside San Marco and the Pietà. This leaves Sieber as the most likely of the four to have inspired—and perhaps to have given the first performances of—the oboe concertos considered here.

Although oboe playing was much more widespread north of the Alps, it is unlikely that actual concertos for oboe were first written outside Italy, given that the concerto genre took time to implant itself in Germany and did not interest French composers at all until the 1720s. An extant concerto with oboes by Johann David Heinichen, who was visiting Venice at the time, is dated 7 October 1715—thus around the time when Albinoni's Op. 7 was published in Amsterdam. It has not yet been established how old the earliest oboe concertos by Vivaldi are, and one cannot at present exclude that some of them predate Albinoni's collection (the same is true of a few oboe concertos by Telemann and Handel). What is not in doubt, however, is that Albinoni's Op. 7 contained the first examples to appear anywhere in print. Two oboe concertos were included in Vivaldi's Op. 7, which appeared from Roger one or two years later; these appear to be spurious works, like certain violin concertos in the same set, and may even be of non-Italian provenance; otherwise, Vivaldi's first published concertos for oboe are found in his Op. 8 (1725). The Roger anthology *Concerti a cinque* (*c.* 1717), which contains one violin concerto by Albinoni (Co 2), is headed by four oboe concertos, respectively by Giuseppe Sammartini, Alessandro Marcello, and Giuseppe Valentini (two works). Since this collection appears to have been drawn from an assortment of manuscripts already in circulation, the chronological relationship of the oboe concertos in it to those of Albinoni cannot easily be established. This anthology does, however, show that within a couple of years of the appearance of Albinoni's Op. 7 the genre was popular enough to warrant the publication of representative works on the initiative of the publisher alone.

The most straightforward way in which to compose an oboe concerto was to model the oboe part on that of the principal violin in an orthodox violin concerto. This means that the woodwind instrument doubles the first violins in tutti passages, detaching itself in the episodes. The composer must, of course, remember to respect the compass of the instrument, which in baroque times stretched chromatically from c' to d''', omitting $c\sharp'$. He must also bear in mind the instrument's preference for conjunct movement (broken-chord shapes are easier in close than in open position, and cannot be taken too quickly) and the player's need to draw breath periodically. On the whole, Vivaldi assimilates the style of the oboe as much as he dares to that of the violin; it is no accident that the oboe concertos in his authorized published collections name the violin as an alternative solo instrument.

Albinoni's starting premise is different. He models his oboe parts on vocal writing, exploring the lyrical potential of the wind instrument and integrating it fully into the contrapuntal fabric of the work. What passage-work does occur is intricate rather than brilliant, emphasizing the smaller intervals. In his discussion of Venetian compositions for oboe, Alfredo Bernardini has observed, accurately enough, that Albinoni and some other Venetians tend to avoid the low register. He surmises that the combination of reed and oboe that was being used in Venice at the time favoured the high register at the expense of the low one.[16] While this may be so, there are good reasons of a purely stylistic nature for Albinoni's preference. He generally likes the oboe to be heard above the first violin (that is, when it is not engaging in dialogue with it in the same register); in certain cases, he wishes it to imitate florid writing for the trumpet in that instrument's high *clarino* register.

In the outer movements of his single-oboe concertos Albinoni borrows important stylistic elements from the operatic aria, thereby strengthening the equation of the woodwind instrument with the voice. Like the voice, the oboe is excluded from the initial ritornello. It almost invariably enters, at the start of the second period, with a briefly stated solo motto (Riemann's *Devise*), allowing the strings to complete the period with a reference back to the ritornello. (Ironically, by 1715 Albinoni had virtually ceased to employ the *Devise* in his arias.) Then follows a period equivalent to the first vocal period in an aria: the oboe takes up its motto again and this time continues to a cadence in a new key. At this point the strings interpose a short ritornello in that key, usually condensing the opening ritornello in some way.

From this point onwards the close correspondence to an aria disappears. In the remaining portion of the movement Albinoni is likely to visit another related key before rounding off the movement with a series of periods in the home key, paralleling but not exactly repeating those at the beginning. Towards the close Albinoni likes to give the oboe counter-melodies to set against ritornello material or even to allow it to wrest ritornello phrases in a playful spirit from the strings. In true Albinonian style, the movement invariably ends with a repetitive coda for the full ensemble.

During his discussion of the oboe concertos of Op. 7 Schering pointed out with approval the frequently contrasted thematic character of the motto phrase opening the ritornello and the solo motto, each perfectly

---

[16] 'The Oboe in the Venetian Republic', p. 377. Albinoni's avoidance of the oboe's low register is more thoroughgoing than Vivaldi's, the notes c' and eb' being altogether absent.

adapted to its respective instrument.[17] Rather absurdly, he went on to relate this contrast to the thematic dualism of sonata form. In fact, the comparison should once again be made with the vocal aria. The varied forms of relationship Schering is describing are precisely those that we have already encountered in our examination of Albinoni's cantatas in Chapter 5. Whereas in some movements the contrast is striking (Schering takes his example from the first movement of Op. 7 no. 3), in others (e.g. the finale of the sixth concerto, illustrated in Ex. 7 in Chapter 3) the solo motto apes the ritornello note for note.

The slow movements of three of the single-oboe concertos (nos. 3, 6, and 12) make a return to the dignified contrapuntal style of the trio sonata—except that there is now a third voice, the second violin, available for the contrapuntal interplay of the upper parts if the occasion warrants it. In actual fact, the second violin rarely asserts itself unless the oboe is pausing or sustaining long notes, so the counterpoint never becomes too intricate. In certain passages Albinoni suspends the dialogue, allowing the oboe to speak freely without competition. The form of these movements is entirely through-composed in two cases (Concertos VI and XII); in Concerto III the opening theme reappears in the dominant immediately after the cadence in that key, giving the impression of a binary form without repeats.

The slow movement of the ninth concerto rejects the oboe altogether in favour of the familiar series of slowly moving string chords encountered from Op. 2 onwards. On its own terms, it is an inventive movement whose tonal meanderings keep the listener in constant suspense.

Although there is little in these four concertos that is not done on a grander scale and with richer imagination in their opposite numbers in Op. 9 (discounting the question of the scoring of the accompaniment to solo passages, where Op. 7 is certainly more resourceful), they deserve their present-day popularity. Their finely chiselled melodies, their elegant restraint, their *Spielfreudigkeit*, their deft counterpoint, their logical construction: all these are qualities to prize. One should not compare them directly with the oboe concertos of Vivaldi or Marcello and then declare them wanting in virtuosity, for they are clearly intended to be, as Albinoni's title-page so aptly puts it, concertos 'with' oboe rather than 'for' oboe. The woodwind instrument is first among equals, not a dictator. If one also observes that, of all baroque oboe concertos, these are some of the most rewarding for violinists to play, the compliment is meant as genuine and in no sense back-handed.

----

[17] *Geschichte des Instrumentalkonzerts*, p. 77.

The concertos with two oboes mostly follow, in a more concise and often simplified manner, the formal principles adopted in the single-oboe works. In Op. 9 their form will be totally indistinguishable from that of their counterparts with one oboe, from which one may infer that the double concertos in Op. 7 which show most deviation from the 'model' are either early essays in the new genre dating from the time when patterns had not yet crystallized or (perhaps less likely) experimental works which were not judged successful enough to imitate.

Albinoni rarely allows the two oboes to express separate personalities. Their most typical relationship is as a fixed 'team' playing long chains of thirds, although from time to time they are permitted brief snatches of imitation or some other manifestation of contrapuntal independence. Dialogue between the two instruments, a regular feature of Vivaldi's double concertos, is little used. Quite often, they play entirely unaccompanied in a manner familiar from the Sinfonia to Act III of Handel's *Solomon* ('The Arrival of the Queen of Sheba'). When they are joined by a lower part (often a *bassetto* on violins), Albinoni often comes close to the traditional French way of handling a pair of oboes with their bass: the three parts tend to move in note-against-note fashion, and the bass practises a strict contrary motion in relation to the paired upper parts, rising when they fall and vice versa. The similarity may be fortuitous, for this 'concertina effect' (as we may term it) occurs throughout Albinoni's music.

The most substantial of the double concertos is Concerto XI, which is also the closest in form to the single-oboe works. Its first movement is perhaps a little too long for its very simple material, but the others make amends. The Adagio is a perfect example of Albinoni's 'doubled trio' style, in which paired oboes and violins continually toss phrases to each other. Impressive use of syncopation is seen in the finale, which contains perhaps the most remarkable harmonic touch seen in Albinoni's music before Op. 10: in bars 5 and 6 we hear over a tonic (C) pedal first a seven–five chord with the seventh flattened, then a six–four chord with the fourth sharpened, and finally a diatonic five–three chord. The juxtaposition of lowered seventh and raised fourth produces a curious modal effect reminiscent of central and eastern European folk music, which Albinoni would have had an opportunity to encounter at first hand in Venice itself, particularly from the mouths of Dalmatian seamen (the *Schiavoni* after whom the Riva degli Schiavoni is named).

Concertos II and V, likewise in C major, are slighter works, though their slow movements are not insignificant. That of Concerto II, for strings alone, was quoted in Chapter 3 as Ex. 2. Concerto V has an Adagio resembling that of Concerto II. The first movement of Concerto V is

Section	Tonality	Bars
Ritornello 1	D major	1–5
Episode 1	D major modulating to A major	6–9
Ritornello 2	A major	10–14
Episode 2	A major modulating to B minor	15–20/1
Ritornello 3	B minor	20/2–23
Episode 3	B minor modulating to D major	24–33/1
Ritornello 4	D major	33/2–38
Coda	D major	39–40

unusual in that the oboes enter at the very beginning, as in Albinoni's operatic sinfonias with wind instruments.

Concerto VIII is an oddity. Its first movement is regular in form but contains an unusual amount of virtuosic passage-work for the first violin. The second movement, reserved for strings, is exquisitely fashioned in the style of a through-composed sonata movement. But the finale, in jig rhythm, resembles no other movement in the whole of Albinoni's music, for it is quite clearly cast in Vivaldian ritornello form, albeit on a miniature scale. Its form is set out in the table. All the episodes are scored in the same way, with the viola omitted and the unison violins interjecting short motives borrowed from the ritornello. These constant back-references from the violins (which at the same time prepare for the next ritornello) are a device sometimes found in Vivaldi, though they occur regularly in Bach. Another Vivaldian touch is the gradual lengthening of the episodes as the movement proceeds. Only the separate coda betrays Albinoni's authorship. Why he did not go on from this movement to produce others on the same plan is an unaccountable mystery.

Miscellaneous Works in Dresden (*So* 32–4, *Co* 2–5, *Si* 6–7)

The Music Department of the Sächsische Landesbibliothek, Dresden, today possesses the manuscripts of seven Albinoni works (two sinfonias, two violin concertos, and three violin sonatas) unknown from any other source. To these may be added a violin concerto (*Co* 3) destroyed during the bombing of Dresden in 1945, and a sinfonia ('VII, 4a') and two concertos ('VII, 10a' and *Co* 2b) that are variants of works preserved elsewhere.

Three separate groups can be distinguished among these works. The first comprises the sonatas, which are all composition manuscripts (original drafts containing spontaneous corrections). *So 32* was clearly identified as an autograph manuscript from the outset, for its opening page bears the following inscription: 'Sonata a Violino│solo│di me Tomaso Albinoni │Composta p[er] il Sig:ʳ│Pisendel.' The manuscript was almost certainly presented to Pisendel in person during his Venetian sojourn of 1716–17, perhaps as a keepsake or token of appreciation. It forms a close parallel to the autograph manuscripts of six concertos and five sonatas that Vivaldi inscribed to the German violinist. In 1976 the East German scholar Manfred Fechner happened upon the manuscripts of two unattributed chamber sonatas for violin and bass regarded by the Landesbibliothek at the time as anonymous works. Recognizing the hand as Albinoni's and the style as entirely characteristic of him, Fechner was able to make the attribution with confidence. No doubt both sonatas are companion works to the sonata already known, which they complement rather neatly (and perhaps deliberately) by being as emphatically *da camera* in style as the latter is *da chiesa*. All three works belonged to Pisendel's personal collection, which passed on his death in 1755 to the Saxon court and was later amalgamated with the larger collections originating from the *Hofkapelle* and the Catholic *Hofkirche*. [18]

The second group of manuscripts comprises four *Reisepartituren* in Pisendel's hand containing the concertos *Co* 2b, *Co* 4, and *Co* 5, as well as the concerto 'VII, 10a'. [19] As was explained earlier in the discussion of the last work, these are not straightforward copies but arrangements in which (depending on the circumstances) the solo part has been remodelled to increase its quotient of virtuosity, the part-writing has been amended, wind instruments have been cued in, and extra bars have been inserted. These works, too, must date from the time of Pisendel's residence in Venice.

The third group consists of parts formerly belonging to the *Hofkapelle*. It contains three sinfonias (*Si* 4, *Si* 5, and 'VII, 4a') and three concertos (*Co* 2, the lost *Co* 3, and *Co* 4). [20] The hands are various, several of the sets of parts having been prepared by more than one copyist.

Although the date of the works in the third group appears to be the same as that of those belonging to the first two groups, to judge from their style and the date of close concordances, the copies themselves may be somewhat later. Prior to Pisendel's appointment as *Konzertmeister* of the court orchestra in 1728, its repertory had been mainly French-oriented. A recent

---

[18] The inscribed sonata is shelfmarked Mus. 2199-R-1; the unattributed sonatas are Mus. 2199-R-5 (G minor) and Mus. 2199-R-6 (B♭ major).

[19] Mus. 2199-O-2, 3, 4, and 5.

[20] Respectively Mus. 2199-N-1, 2, and 3 (sinfonias), and Mus. 2199-O-2, 1-O-2, and 2199-O-5 (concertos). The former Mus. 1-O-2 was an anthology containing concertos by several composers, hence the absence from the shelfmark of the numerical prefix '2199' pertaining specifically to Albinoni.

study of the Vivaldi sources in Dresden has led to the unexpected conclusion that the *Hofkapelle* started to admit Vivaldi's orchestral works to its active repertory only in the late 1720s.[21] The same may well have been true of Albinoni's concertos and sinfonias. Since we can be fairly certain on musical grounds that the works in the third group are of 1716–17 vintage, we can virtually rule out the possibility that they were ordered from Albinoni during the 1720s, for the composer would hardly have put into circulation works written in a no longer current style. The most likely explanation for the long interval between the date of composition and the date of copying is that the copies are based on originals taken back to Dresden by Pisendel (or one of the other court musicians accompanying the *Kurprinz*) in 1717. In one case, that of *Co* 4, the material in Dresden comprises both a set of parts for the orchestra and a score by Pisendel. The two correspond exactly, except that the pages containing the last movement are missing from the score, which also contains cues for the solo performance of the first violin part (as a 'violino secondo concertato' partnering the principal violin) and for flutes, oboes, and bassoons doubling the orchestral violins. It is possible that the parts were copied directly from this score, to which the cues were added only later. In another case, that of the material in the library folder shelfmarked Mus. 2199-0-2, the score and the parts transmit different versions of the same work (*Co* 2 and *Co* 2b) that are not directly related.

Giazotto briefly describes the lost violin concerto *Co* 3.[22] It was apparently a characteristic but in no way remarkable work with solos in each movement. *Co* 4 and *Co* 5 are strong works that are conceived very similarly. Both have lyrical slow movements in whose central portion the principal violin has a *cantabile* solo part and swift fugal finales in 6/8 a little more generously proportioned than their counterparts in Op. 5. In each of the fugues Albinoni treats the subject cleverly in canon so that it becomes, in effect, a countersubject to itself. Pisendel's hand in the fashioning of the solo episodes is unmistakable. The first movement of *Co* 5 takes the solo violin up to a''', outside Albinoni's normal limit, and includes a passage in *bariolage* (the alternation of an open and a stopped string at the same pitch) over a continuo pedal-note—a device normal in Vivaldi and his followers such as Pisendel but encountered nowhere else in Albinoni's music.

These unusual features might be explained as an attempt by Albinoni to

---

[21] Manfred Fechner, 'Bermerkungen zu einigen Dresdner Vivaldi-Manuskripten: Fragen der Vivaldi-Pflege unter Pisendel, zur Datierung und Schreiberproblematik', in Antonio Fanna and Giovanni Morelli (eds.), *Nuovi studi vivaldiani: Edizione e cronologia critica delle opere* (Florence, 1988), 775–84.

[22] *Tomaso Albinoni*, pp. 252–3. Incipits for all three movements are given in Giazotto's thematic catalogue, p. 348.

'customize' a concerto for the German virtuoso. Two facts make this seem improbable, however. The first is that the sonata *So* 32, most definitely a work tailor-made for Pisendel, attempts nothing special from a purely technical point of view (although its scale and structure are certainly individual). The second is that we have already caught Pisendel tampering with the solo part of a concerto (in the concerto 'VII, 10a', discussed in the previous section) and will do so again in the conspicuous case of another concerto, *Co* 2.

This violin concerto in C major exists, in different versions, in one printed source and five contemporary manuscripts.[23] The source that transmits the earliest, and probably most authentic, version is a set of parts in the Zentralbibliothek, Zürich.[24] A similar version was published under the imprint of Jeanne Roger as Concerto XI of the anthology *Concerti a cinque . . . del* [sic] *Signori G. Valentini, A. Vivaldi, T. Albinoni . . . , c.* 1717. This edition, which was evidently not supervised by the composer, contains many mistakes arising from a misreading of the score. The worst of these is the complete suppression of the second violin part in the third movement; its notes are taken by the first violin, which ought instead to double the principal violin throughout (this movement contains no solo passages).

A comprehensively rescored version of the published text of this concerto that redistributes the material of the original five parts among twelve different parts (four for violin, two for oboe, two for viola, and one each for *basso*, *contrabasso*, *basse de violon*, and *cembalo*, not counting duplicate parts) is preserved in the Sächsische Landesbibliothek. This rather grotesque arrangement shows the lengths to which Dresden musicians would go in adapting music to their local usage.

Two related sources in the University Library, Lund, transmit a slightly different version of the concerto (*Co* 2a), which is attributed there to Vivaldi.[25] The origin of the misattribution is a separate matter which is still unexplained. *Co* 2a differs from *Co* 2 in having six extra bars of conventional passage-work for the soloist inserted into one episode in the first movement. The effect of the addition is to unbalance the movement, and it thus seems unlikely that the six bars originated with Albinoni himself.

The version preserved in Pisendel's score retains those extra bars and, by extending several other solo passages in the same movement, increases the

---

[23] The sources are described and compared more fully in Michael Talbot, 'A Question of Authorship', *Vivaldi informations*, 2 (1973), 17–26.

[24] Shelfmark AMG XIII 1066 & a–d.

[25] Shelfmarks Wensters Samling, Lit. L no. 11, and Engelharts Samling 196 respectively.

total number of bars in it from 71 to 98. In places, the part-writing is rationalized. The slow movement realizes what were previously even semiquavers in *saccadé* fashion (dotted semiquaver plus demisemiquaver) throughout. In the finale Pisendel introduces a long solo episode, obviously believing (unlike Albinoni) that the 'solo' interest in the two outer movements ought—at least minimally—to be comparable.

The six added bars common to *Co* 2a and *Co* 2b establish a mysterious connection between the two variants. Did Pisendel base the more heavily amended version in Dresden on a manuscript containing the Lund text? And could this earlier version also have been his handiwork?

The complexities of the textual criticism surrounding this work should not allow us to overlook its considerable musical virtues. Its opening movement has a powerful unison motto phrase more strongly evocative of Vivaldi than any similar opening in Albinoni's music. Just before the coda Albinoni allows the principal and first violins, playing in thirds, to introduce a delightful counterpoint to the unison theme after the fashion of his oboe concertos. Moser paid the slow movement the compliment of calling it a 'touching (*ergreifend*) duet between principal and first violins'.[26] The finale offers an exceptionally well organized example of binary form, in which both the beginning and the ending of the two repeated sections are matched.

Of the three sinfonias in Dresden the one which adheres most closely to the formal and stylistic model described in the previous chapter is *Si* 6, in B♮ major. One of its bass parts is headed 'Bassono', a word which in Dresden usage signifies the bassoon. To co-opt a bassoon on to the bass line does no great violence to Albinoni's conception; nevertheless, it is doubtful whether Italian practice sanctioned it. *Si* 6 has a separate slow movement, albeit a very brief one, and in its outer movements evidences the same degree of expansion, relative to the sinfonias in Vienna and Stockholm, that we observe in the Op. 7 concertos compared with their predecessors. In both quick movements the interweaving of the two violins and their intricate pattern of cross-rhythms are a delight.

So 7, in G minor, is perhaps the most stormily dramatic orchestral work Albinoni ever wrote. Once again, this sinfonia must have originated as a work for strings in four parts, though the Dresden musicians saw fit to add doubling wind parts—in this case, for two flutes, two oboes, and bassoon. A sinfonia in a minor key is a rarity for this period: were the physiognomy of this work less sinfonia-like in other respects, one might easily suspect it to be an incorrectly titled concerto. The start of its first movement (shown in

---

[26] *Geschichte des Violinspiels*, p. 79.

Ex. 35) illustrates not only its passionate mood but also Albinoni's great skill at handling motivic material. In the opening segment of the period, bars 1–3, the two violin parts present contrasted ideas, that of the first violin (striding quavers preceded by a *tirata*) being dominant; but when the middle segment arrives, in bar 4, the violins exchange figuration, and the semiquavers suddenly come into prominence. Incredibly, this work remains unpublished.

Ex. 35

The third sinfonia, the variant of Op. 7 no. 4 ('VII, 4a'), is clearly inferior in quality to the other two. Even its fugal finale is laboured and clumsy. It has acquired an introductory Grave which gives the two oboes obbligato parts (in the other three movements their role is merely to double the violins following the normal Dresden practice). The anomaly is soon explained. The Grave has been appropriated from a double violin concerto in G major by Telemann, the solo violins being replaced by oboes.[27] Not

[27] The work is listed as 2 V.G(1) in the catalogue of Telemann's concertos contained in Siegfried Kross, *Das Instrumentalkonzert bei G. Ph. Telemann* (Tutzing, 1969), 155.

surprisingly, a copy of this very concerto is found among the manuscripts formerly belonging to the *Hofkapelle*.[28] (It was one of the more questionable practices of the Dresden musicians to create instrumental pasticci from movements belonging to different works, regardless of whether the composer was the same; similar barbarities were inflicted on Vivaldi's concertos.)

The three autograph sonatas are among the very finest Albinoni wrote for the violin. Both a modern critical edition and a facsimile edition exist of the sonata in B♮ major inscribed to Pisendel, *So* 32, which may well be the longest of its kind Albinoni ever wrote.[29] Its two slow movements differ from their counterparts in Op. 6 only by being a little more ornate, but both fast movements break new ground in their different ways. At a superficial level the second movement resembles that of the *Sonata da chiesa* in B minor, *So* 31, being styled as a fugue in two parts. But its long (perhaps slightly over-long) thematically neutral episodes, featuring arpeggiated passage-work on the violin, clearly recall the world of the concerto and must have been introduced to gratify Pisendel. The fourth movement, uniquely in Albinoni's sonatas, adopts the formal design of his concerto allegros, including a distinctive motto. It is worth noting that the introduction of concerto elements into the sonata, temporarily halted during the 'classic' phase represented by Albinoni's Op. 6, is a common feature at the end of the baroque period. The six trio sonatas by Vivaldi preserved among the Turin manuscripts (as distinct from those published earlier in his career in his Opp. 1 and 5) all provide evidence of this trend; Bach's sonata in B minor for flute and obbligato harpsichord (BWV 1030) is another good example.

That the companion chamber sonatas, *So* 33 (in G minor) and *So* 34 (in B♮ major), remain unpublished twelve years after their discovery is perhaps a reflection of the generally low esteem that chamber sonatas enjoy in comparison with church sonatas according to the modern hierarchy of values. As the only sonatas of 'pure' chamber type among Albinoni's solo sonatas—and, moreover, the only examples in his entire œuvre with four rather than the usual three dance-movements—they hold an especial interest. Both observe the sequence Allemanda–Corrente–Gavotta–Sarabanda. In *So* 34 Albinoni has penned in the word 'bis' after the second double bar of the final movement. The instruction is not without ambiguity, for it could either be a reminder to observe the second repeat of

[28] Shelfmark Mus. 2392-O-35.

[29] The critical edition by the present author was published by VEB Edition Peters (Leipzig) in 1975; the facsimile edition, which includes a commentary by the present author, appeared from the Zentralantiquariat der DDR (also Leipzig) in 1980.

the Sarabanda (which would carry the implication that this repeat was often ignored in contemporary performance) or else could indicate a repeat of the entire movement. If the second interpretation is correct, one might in turn consider whether it was normal practice, in the repertory to which Albinoni's balletti belonged, to repeat in their entirety short concluding movements such as gavottes, even in the absence of a specific direction.[30]

The excellence of both sonatas is of a wholly conventional kind, except that their allemandes include a surprising amount of multiple-stopping (other than that, the works make no obvious concessions to Pisendel's virtuosity). The two gavottes both belong to the more modern type with melodic movement in quavers and semiquavers rather than crotchets and quavers.

Sonate a violino solo e basso continuo . . . e uno suario o capriccio a l'imitationo [sic] *del Corelli del Sig. Tibaldi (So 35–9)*

This unauthorized collection, which appeared under the imprint of Jeanne Roger *c.* 1717, is a sequel to the *Sonate da chiesa* of *c.* 1708, with which it has many features in common. The last work in the volume, a set of variations modelled on Corelli's *La folìa* (Op. 5 no. 12) by the Modenese composer G. B. Tibaldi, need not concern us. Nor need the fifth sonata (*So* 39), which, although attributed to Albinoni, contains too many foreign stylistic elements to be credible as an authentic work. (For instance, it opens with a slow movement in binary form, a feature not found in the authenticated sonatas; other unfamiliar features include arpeggiated decorations of cadential chords by the bass in the second and fourth movements, an entirely unaccompanied opening for the violin in the third movement, and a French title, 'Courante', for the last movement.) Ironically, the rhapsodic third movement of this very work was singled out by W. S. Newman to illustrate Albinoni's stylistic evolution. Giazotto had earlier observed: 'Superato è l'Albinoni invece dal Prete Rosso nella frequenza delle emozioni che ormai . . . sono da definirsi romantiche'.[31] Mistaking the passive for the active mood, Newman translated this statement as:

---

[30] In the original printed editions of Op. 3—but not in the later engraved ones—the puzzling instruction 'Si replica al ritornello se piace' (perhaps equivalent to: 'Please repeat from the double bar') appears after the Allemanda of Balletto VII. Since there is no particular feature distinguishing this movement from its counterparts in the other balletti, the reason for the presence of the direction is as hard to fathom as its precise significance. It could be that Albinoni was reminding players to observe the second repeat (which they were apt to ignore) and that his direction is meant to apply to all the movements in binary form in this collection.

[31] *Tomaso Albinoni*, p. 297.

'Albinoni . . . (who) surpasses Vivaldi in the frequency of what are now . . . defined as romantic emotions'—and then proceeded to justify his dubious claim by reference to *So* 39![32] Even if this work were later shown to be absolutely genuine, its degree of deviance from the norm is so great that one would be unwise to draw any general conclusions about Albinoni's music from it.

It is doubtful whether the unquestionably genuine Sonatas I–IV originated in a single manuscript collection, since Sonata III and Sonata IV share a key (A major) and have very similar second movements. The latter is by far the more polished of the two A major works and may be of later date.

The features that link the present group of sonatas to the earlier unauthorized collection (rather than to the *Trattenimenti armonici*, which occupy a chronologically intermediate position) are, first, the exuberance of the writing for violin and, second, the essentially functional, subordinate role of the continuo bass. The four sonatas all contain a good amount of multiple-stopping in both homophonic and contrapuntal passages. They are certainly less elegant than either the Op. 6 works or the sonatas for Pisendel, but they at least avoid the extreme crudities (or gross mistakes of engraving) to be found in the *Sonate da chiesa*.

The first sonata, *So* 35, brings out the essential character of the new set well, since it is merely a new version of the first *Sonata da chiesa* (*So* 26) with a changed third movement. Of note is the fact that in its second movement it reproduces some details of the cognate movement in Op. 6 no. 4. Sonata II (*So* 36) is likewise a refurbished work; it is based on the fifth *Sonata da chiesa* (*So* 30), though its third movement is new and its opening movement considerably recast.

The second movement of *So* 37 provides the first example in Albinoni's music of a fugue in which, by dint of double-stopping, the solo violin successfully simulates the contrapuntal interplay of the two violins in a trio sonata, in which the bass also joins from time to time. (In the episodes between entries, understandably, the move to rapid passage-work usually brings about a temporary suspension of the double-stopping.) The model for Albinoni here, as for countless other composers of violin sonatas, was provided by Corelli's Op. 5 (1700), whose first six sonatas all have second movements of this type.

So 38 possesses not only a similar movement but also a first movement that resorts to another familiar Corellian topos. This Adagio follows two of its principal cadences (in bars 4 and 11) with Presto intercalations taking the

---

[32] 'The Sonatas of Albinoni and Vivaldi', p. 100.

form of a ripple of arpeggios outlining a single chord over a sustained pedal-note on the continuo. The first example of an opening movement in the form of 'adagio with cadenzas' occurs in Corelli's music not in a solo violin sonata but in the last of the trio sonatas in his Op. 3 (1689), also a work in A major. In his Op. 5 set the corresponding example appears in the first work, which is in D major. The choice of D and A major is not fortuitous, since these are the keys in which the arpeggios, which are elaborations of either the tonic or the dominant chord, can best take advantage of the powerful sonority and technical convenience of open strings. So 37 and So 38 end with idealized versions of the corrente and the jig respectively.

Sonata IV (So 38) is by a long way the most skilfully written and satisfying work in the group, though none of the other sonatas is entirely without merit. It would be good to see it published and performed.

Balletti e sonate a tre, Op. 8[33]

This is the only published collection of works by Albinoni to contain not only a letter of dedication but also a preface addressed to the reader ('Al lettore'). Albinoni's purpose in supplying such a preface is less to give advice about performance or explain a difficult point than to pat himself on the back and invite the reader to share his appreciation. A translation of the full text for the preface (whose flowery language defies simplification) reads as follows:

Well you know, gracious and benevolent reader, that if, in the numerous works that I published for your recreation, I ever made myself importunate with my protestations, it was your unfailing approval that impelled and encouraged me to do so. But in the present work, which has cost me more study and toil than any other, I cannot forbear to ask of you one particular and not inconsiderable indulgence. If on other occasions I obtained it from your well disposed nature, this time your generous sense of justice owes it to me; for who does not recognize how great an undertaking it is to compose canons—moreover, canons written in a graceful, singing style—and, much more still, to take the subjects enunciated by the violins into the bass and accommodate them to the structure and length of sonatas. I would like to believe (since I have not seen it adopted by anyone else) that I am the inventor of this procedure; and if such is the case, I would also like to hope that to have undertaken such a labour might earn me a little honour, at least from informed persons. And since I knew that to pass straight from one canon to another

[33] The Roger edition spells the word 'Balletti' with only one 'l'. This form may originate with the composer himself, for Venetians, whose own dialect lacked double consonants, were apt to miss them out when writing the national language. In the autograph chamber sonatas in Dresden we encounter the spellings 'Alemanda', 'Corente', and 'Gavota'.

could perhaps weary you a little on account of the sameness of procedure, I thought it expedient to intercalate after each of them another type of composition in a different taste and style, just as intermezzi are intermingled between the acts of tragedies. I cannot know which pieces will succeed in pleasing you. However, I hope that your approval of this work, which cost me more labour than those others of mine that you received with such generous kindness, will not be any less great. Read, play, consider carefully, and fare well.[34]

The canons to which Albinoni refers with such pride are the two quick movements in each of the six sonatas, which, following a pattern already seen in Op. 2, constitute the odd-numbered works in the set. All have the two violins in strict canon at the unison; the normally undivided bass for cello and keyboard continuo (called 'Cembalo' on the title-page but 'Organo' in the separate partbook) is a free part, although, as Albinoni is quick to bring to our attention, it does its best to become integrated thematically with the canonic parts.

On one point Albinoni's boast was unfounded. Canons 'two in one' over a free bass part were already far from uncommon in sonatas when Op. 8 (published *c.* 1722) was in preparation. Fux and Biber wrote some, and the famous example in the third movement of Bach's Sonata in A major for Violin and Obbligato Harpsichord (BWV 1015) may be slightly earlier. At most, Albinoni's movements were an innovation within the Italian tradition. (Could they perhaps have been intended as a homage to the national taste of the dedicatee, Count Watzdorf?)

Contrary to what this preface implies, the technique of constructing such canons is very straightforward. Having written the part of the 'leading' voice (*dux*) up to the point when the 'trailing' voice (*comes*) enters, the composer then transfers it to the latter and composes a counterpoint to it in the *dux*; this in turn is transferred and receives a new counterpoint. Schematically, the process can be represented as in the first table. However, this basic model needs refinement if it is not to lead to static tonality and an amorphous or haphazard thematic character. Especially in a longer movement, it is necessary to modulate in an orderly fashion and at some point to reintroduce the opening theme (or another theme of the composer's choice). Let us imagine that we wish to bring back the opening theme of the movement in the dominant key (we will call the segment in which this happens 'X') some distance into the movement. The way to do this is very simple but requires a little planning. It entails leaving a temporary gap in the *dux* over the latest segment transferred to the *comes*. 'X' is then supplied to the *dux* in the bars immediately following the gap.

[34] The preface is reproduced as a plate in the author's *Albinoni: Leben und Werk*, p. 107.

	1	2	3	4
dux	A	AB	ABC	ABCD
comes	—	A	AB	ABC

	4	5	6
dux	ABCD	ABCDE	ABCDE X
comes	ABC	ABCD	ABCDE

The scheme is now that shown in the second table. The omitted segment, 'F', is then composed simultaneously against 'E' and 'X', being made tonally and contrapuntally compatible with each. Here the value of a free part becomes especially evident, for the bass can supply harmonic and rhythmic interest or tonal definition in situations where it is expedient to keep one or both upper parts simple (Albinoni exploits as fully as any modern student the fact that rests always make good counterpoint!). Obviously, this method of 'simultaneous composition' can be applied in the course of a movement as often as the composer wishes, and for any number of purposes.

Unfortunately, Albinoni (in contrast to Bach and most other composers of canonic movements) makes very little use of this special technique, employing it once—and once only—in each canonic movement, and then exclusively for the purpose of introducing a da capo restatement of the opening of the movement, which proceeds without any alteration up to the point at which the composer chooses to stop. It is truly astonishing in view of the uncommon length of these movements (up to 127 bars of common time) that they contain no modulation at all apart from incidental modulations built into the first segment and reproduced willy-nilly in nearly all ensuing segments. Without hesitation, one can describe this lack as a basic structural defect that inevitably leads to tedium.

Questions of form and tonality apart, Albinoni's contrapuntal skill remains a potent force. The eight-bar opening segment of the second movement of Sonata II (see Ex. 36) contains fugal entries for the first violin (tonic) and the bass (dominant), to which the second violin provides the complementary third entry when it arrives as the *comes* in bar 9. With such a wealth of subjects and countersubjects already displayed in the opening segment and a free part to act as a port of call for themes that can later pass back, by means of voice-exchange, to the *dux* and thence to the *comes*, Albinoni finds it no real challenge to his permutational skills to reintroduce

Ex. 36

the principal ideas at intervals in all three parts throughout the length of the movement.[35]

Albinoni would not have thanked one for saying so, but the non-canonic slow movements of the sonatas are their saving grace. All six sonatas have two slow movements occupying first and third position except the first, which starts straight away with an Allegro canon. The three-movement plan that results here might perhaps be interpreted as another instance of

[35] Voice-exchange (from German *Stimmtausch*) is the device where two parts swap material (possibly with changes of octave) so that only the distribution of the themes, not the nature of their contrapuntal combination, is altered.

concerto influence, but it may stem merely from a desire to make the most distinctive feature of the collection—the canonic treatment—fully apparent right at the opening, as Giazotto suggests.[36]

Nearly all these movements employ intricate counterpoint involving imitation between the violins or long chains of suspensions. Several of them restate the opening idea, either in a new key (following a modulation) or again in the tonic (to mark the start of the closing section). The third movement (Larghetto) of Sonata VI is unusual for Albinoni in having both a dominant statement of the opening theme and a reprise of it in the home key. This is an embryonic version of the sonata form without repeats that we know from slow movements of the classical period. The third movement of Sonata II, another Larghetto, has perhaps the most independent cello part of any movement in a sonata by Albinoni; on many occasions it parts company with the continuo to become a fourth contrapuntal line. An original touch is seen in the siciliana-like Larghetto separating the two Allegros of the fourth sonata. In this movement a short motto on unison violins immediately echoed by the bass serves to lend emphasis to the cadences at the end of each period (except the third, which assigns this phrase to the bass alone).

The sonatas of Op. 8 provides a salutary lesson of what can happen when a composer departs from tried and tested practices in an attempt to impress his admirers. The canonic movements are, quite frankly, botched: not because they fail in their primary purpose, which is to demonstrate a specific contrapuntal technique, but because too many other vital principles are sacrificed in pursuit of it. Albinoni's single-mindedness has here led to a coarsening of sensibility. All the same, these works deserve an occasional hearing on account of their finely wrought and eloquent slow movements.

The balletti need no such special pleading. They may lack the freshness and élan of their predecessors in Op. 3, but their more elaborate texture and closer attention to detail offer adequate compensation. Dispensing with a prelude, the works follow two alternative sequences: Allemanda–Giga–Sarabanda (nos. 1, 3, and 4) and Allemanda–Corrente–Gavotta (nos. 2, 5, and 6).

The allemandes are very varied in style, but all have an étude-like quality derived from their thoroughgoing development of a short figure heard at the beginning. The most novel is the sixth, in G minor, where the first violin has a notably showy part that includes some percussive multiple-stopping. The correnti and jigs conform to type, but the sarabands and

[36] *Tomaso Albinoni*, p. 189.

gavottes accentuate even more the progressive tendencies found in the chamber sonatas in Dresden. Two of the sarabands (those of Balletti III and IV) are notated in 6/8 metre, which reflects their role as scampering, lightweight final movements. All the gavottes are notated in 2/4 metre, though they are otherwise similar to the Dresden examples. One (no. 6) employs the trisectional form with repeats not seen in Albinoni's music since the finale of the third concerto in Op. 2. The fifth balletto has a gavotte that, with fifty bars, almost attains the scale of an allemande.

To single out any particular balletto in this collection for especial commendation is difficult when their quality is so successfully maintained. Overall, however, the sixth is the most interesting on account of the features just mentioned.

Concerti a cinque, Op. 9

It must remain a matter for conjecture whether, having composed a new collection of concertos on lines very similar to those of Op. 7, Albinoni decided to dedicate Op. 9 to Maximilian Emanuel because he had heard of the excellence of the oboists at the Bavarian court, who had been recruited in the last years of the elector's exile in France, or whether, having chosen the dedicatee, he made a point of including works with oboes, using Op. 7 as a convenient model. Either way, the concertos seem perfectly tailored to the northern European taste of their time (1722), being very substantial in length—on average, between a quarter and a third as long again as their counterparts in Op. 7—and meticulously crafted, with inner parts more active than before. Here and there, a slightly cosmopolitan flavour emerges, reminding one of Italian composers resident at German courts, such as Max Emanuel's own *Konzertmeister*, Evaristo Felice Dall'Abaco (1675–1742). There is more than a hint of the French style, for instance, in the slow movement of Concerto IV, which uses dotted rhythms in a slow 3/4 exactly in the manner of a stately chaconne. To a certain extent, the greater length of their outer movements derives from a more complex structure—the average number of foreign keys visited, hence the number of internal periods, has risen—but it is also a product of the negative tendencies mentioned at the beginning of this chapter, exemplified by long passages of shifting harmonies over pedal-points that seem to have no other function than to delay the arrival of the cadence and also by the prolongation of the period with fussy supplementary cadences following the main cadence.

On the positive side, there is now parity of quality between the four concertos with principal violin (nos. 1, 4, 7, and 10), the four with one oboe

Period	Bars	Key	Thematic content
1	1–40	D	AABC
2	41–69	D–A	ADC
3	70–98	A–b	AEC/FC
4	99–109	b–e	AEC
5	110–26	e–f♯	AEC
6	127–67	D	ABC/DC

(nos. 2, 5, 8, and 11), and the four with two oboes (nos. 3, 6, 9, and 12). There is also more diversity: two of the single-oboe concertos are in minor keys (nos. 2 and 8), and of the double-oboe concertos only two (predictably, nos. 9 and 12, in C and D major respectively) ape trumpet style. A new emphasis has fallen on the slow movements, which now have a much more elaborate internal organization and a longer-breathed style of melody.

All four concertos with principal violin are violin concertos in the true sense that allow this instrument regularly to come forward as a soloist and to display a virtuosity which, although not to be compared with that of Vivaldi's violin concertos, certainly raises it above the level of the orchestral rank and file. The form of the first movements is, at an overt level, not much closer to Vivaldian ritornello form than before, although one notes that in all four cases the first period returns in literal or near-literal form just before the coda, a procedure equivalent to the final statement of a ritornello. More generally, Albinoni seems to have a new-found awareness of the value of thematic economy, both as an aid to unity and as a means of making the distinctive character of a movement more pronounced, for he now quite often brings back material from the middle or closing segments of earlier periods in addition to the opening motto itself.

Two of the finales (those of Concertos I and VII) are written in first-movement form and share the features just mentioned. Both are in 2/4 metre and have long mottoes that are immediately repeated 'piano' at the start of the first period. Repetition of this kind recalls the simple structures of dance-movements (the effect is similar to the repeat of the first vocal period in some of Albinoni's cantata arias)—a deceptive allusion, since the movement, like a Haydn finale that begins similarly with a repeated strain, is likely to develop into a structure no less complex than the companion opening movement. In fact, the finale of Op. 9 no. 7 is more elaborate in its range of modulation and density of thematic cross-reference than any other movement in an Albinoni concerto for strings alone. In the table distinct thematic elements of the third movement are indicated by letters in the order of their appearance. 'A' appears as a motto at the head of each of the six periods, while a standard cadential phrase ('C') brings each to a close. The middle segments of the first and second periods, 'B' and 'D' respectively, both return in the sixth period, which has in consequence a marked recapitulatory character (the diagonal stroke represents a caesura separating the main portion of the period from an extension following the first cadence). The third, fourth, and fifth periods all refer to the same material ('E') in their middle segment. Both 'D' and 'E' accommodate passages of solo writing.

Concertos IV and X end with lengthy fugues very similar to those of the Dresden concertos Co 4 and Co 5. The finale of the fourth concerto introduces one new feature, however: the principal violin has a chance on two occasions to present the subject without support from the orchestral first violins. Although the euphony and effortless flow of both movements are admirable, one feels that technique is beginning to encroach noticeably on the domain of imagination. Albinoni is facing the dilemma of any mature composer—how to profit from acquired experience without stifling the quest for the new—and is opting for the safe solution.

Greater imagination is shown in the slow movements, each of which is cast in an individual form. The Adagio in Concerto I is a short, 'transitional' movement in dotted rhythm that uses solos on the principal violin to provide the links between its disconnected phrases. Concerto IV, which contains no solos, resembles the slow movements of the sonatas in Op. 8. Uniquely in Albinoni's music, it contains not only a reprise of the opening phrase, delightfully reharmonized, but also an earlier false reprise. The Adagio of Concerto X, similar in form, includes several solo passages for the principal violin. These become shorter and more closely spaced as the music proceeds—symbolizing, so to speak, the reconciliation of the solo instrument with its partners. Concerto VII has an Andante in binary form (see Ex. 37) that is strikingly similar to the typical slow movement of an operatic sinfonia (in fact, it resembles the one in Albinoni's surviving opera La Statira, which was written only a few years later). The mode switches to the parallel minor for the first time in a slow movement in Albinoni's instrumental music (discounting the brief transition in Op. 7 no. 2); this is a galant feature that we will meet again in Op. 10. The detached notes of the continuo part, doubled by the cello, are directed to be played 'senza cembalo e il violone pizzigato' (here, Albinoni is undoubtedly referring to the violone grosso, or double-bass). The sinuous melody of the first violins derives its peculiar 'sobbing' quality from the addition of appoggiaturas to its pivotal notes. One should think carefully before describing such a passage as 'typically Venetian', since such remarks tend to

Ex. 37

be based on simple impressions rather than rigorous analysis; moreover, these impressions may derive from a highly selective perception of what is, or is not, Venetian. Nevertheless, the melodic, textural, and harmonic features of this passage seem to conform to a recognizably Venetian topos frequently encountered in the music of Vivaldi, the Marcellos, and Galuppi. No movement in Op. 9 is more forward-looking in style (or more vocally inspired) than this one.

The concerto to which this movement belongs has a good claim to be regarded as the high point in Albinoni's string concertos. The fourth and tenth concertos, notwithstanding the reservations expressed above about their fugues, also deserve to become repertory pieces. Only the first concerto, whose first two movements are a little jejune, falls short of the same standard.

The four concertos with one oboe advance beyond their Op. 7 prototypes in matters of detail rather than substance. They are of course more generously proportioned and wider ranging in modulation, but one is immediately struck by the intricacy of the contrapuntal interweaving between the oboe and the first violin, which share the honours almost equally. The last period of the finale of Concerto VIII (bars 170–207, see Ex. 38) shows to perfection the subtleties of this relationship. Albinoni

Ex. 38

Ex. 38 [CONTINUED]

Ex. 38 [CONTINUED]

begins by restating the *Devise*, heard on the oboe with simple accompaniment from the violins; this is closely related to the motto phrase announced by the violins at the opening of the movement. When the unison violins take over, in bar 176, the oboe, instead of falling silent as before, continues with a shapely counter-melody. In the coda appended to this period, which begins in bar 191, Albinoni returns to the sequence initiated in bar 176 but reassigns the principal melodic part to the oboe, which paraphrases it in accordance with its natural idiom. The violins at first have a discreet accompanying part that moves in tenths with the bass; after bar 198, however, they can no longer resist the temptation to vie for prominence with the wind instrument. Their playful canonic imitation in bars 204–5 comes as an appropriate display of assertiveness just before the movement ends.

Among the slow movements, the most original is the Adagio of Concerto II, whose relaxed key of B♭ major makes a pleasing contrast to the rather dour D minor of the outer movements. In form it resembles the A section of an aria, beginning and ending with an identical ritornello on the strings. The *Devise* is also present. On the other hand, the *Adagio* departs from the normal pattern of an aria by having a reprise of the first solo idea two-thirds of the way through the movement. Whereas the oboe line is *cantabile*, containing several very long notes that lend themselves either to a *messa di voce* or to a 'division' type of embellishment, the first violins have a continuous succession of semiquavers in which broken-chord shapes predominate, the remaining strings proceeding in gently chugging quavers. The mechanical regularity of the accompaniment makes an effective foil to the rhythmic variety of the solo line. Although one must deplore the use of this movement, abstracted from its proper context, as a 'lollipop' in some modern recordings (which bill it, inevitably, as Albinoni's 'Second Adagio'), one understands why it has been singled out. It is indeed highly emotional and sensuous beneath the surface of its calm diatonicism, recalling the slow movement of Alessandro Marcello's Oboe Concerto in D minor. Its spaciousness and perfectly calculated proportions give one the sense of inevitability that one takes for granted in Bach but seldom encounters in his Italian contemporaries.

In their more modest way the other slow movements in the same group are also remarkably fine. In Concerto V the oboe is drawn into a dense web of close imitations that integrate it fully with the other instruments. In the Adagio of Concerto VIII the reprise of the opening is cunningly concealed by a counter-melody on the oboe phrasing over from the preceding bars; to open the coda the oboe takes possession for the first time of the hesitant motive earlier used to accompany it, providing another instance of the give-and-take illustrated in Ex. 38. The slow movement of Concerto IX returns to the 'trio' style familiar from Albinoni's sonatas, first violin and oboe being treated as equal partners, but there is a new finesse in the part-writing and a much more economical use of thematic material than before.

The most impressive of the concertos with two oboes, all modelled in regard to form on the single-oboe works, is unquestionably Concerto III in F major. For the first time in his instrumental music Albinoni writes in 'hunting' style, evoking the braying of natural horns. Since hunting was the pastime *par excellence* of the landed nobility, to include horns in a score or to imitate their characteristic motives in their favourite key of F major can be interpreted in the appropriate context as an act of homage to a noble employer or patron (this special function of the horns is quite overt in Bach's cantata no. 208, *Was mir behagt, ist nur die muntre Jagd*, written for the birthday of Duke Christian of Saxe-Weissenfels). It would have been unfitting for Albinoni to adopt this hunting style in Op. 7, which is dedicated to a minor Venetian patrician who was also a secular priest, but his chance comes in Op. 9, destined for a German elector.

The usable compass of the natural horn lies an octave lower than the most comfortable registers of both the violin and the oboe. In the outer movements of this concerto Albinoni follows the common convention of his time by presenting 'horn' motives an octave higher than they would be played on the original instruments. Both Allegro movements are massive: with 120 bars in common time, the first movement is from two to three times as long as its equivalents in Op. 5. Arguably, Albinoni's style is here a little ponderous, particularly in the lengthy sections in the home key framing the movements. No such criticism can be levelled at the D minor Adagio in the rhythm of a siciliana; here Albinoni shows great sensitivity in knowing when to keep all four upper parts independent for the sake of greater contrapuntal density and when to introduce discreet doubling in the interests of clarity and smoothness.

The sixth concerto, in G major, is less appealing, but contains some interesting features in its outer movements. Already in the opening period of the first movement, and many times subsequently, Albinoni includes phrases for the two oboes in unison over a repeated monotone in quavers on unison strings. These 'drum basses' (to translate Quantz's term *Trommelbass*) may in fact have a military connotation (the oboes supply the fifes), paying homage to Maximilian Emanuel in another of his princely roles. The finale, although marked 'Allegro', is clearly in the rhythm of a minuet. This dance, introduced to Italian music in the late seventeenth century, acquired a new degree of fashionability during the second decade of the new century; in about 1710 Francesco Antonio Bonporti of Trent published as his Opp. 8 and 9 a collection of no fewer than 100 minuets for violin and bass. In Italian concertos of the late baroque period constructed on the three-movement plan the minuet is too short to be employed as the simple dance that we know from the suites of French and German composers; hence it is expanded to become a set of variations or, as here, exchanges its binary form for a more ample design.

Concerto IX is solidly constructed but suffers a little from the blandness that seems—at least in the popular imagination—to be endemic in works written in C major. Its best movement is certainly the finale, which Hutchings, who quotes and analyses the first thirty bars, finds 'pulsating yet urbane'.[37] Concerto XII, in D major, has outer movements that, for Op. 9, are uncharacteristically brief and loosely structured. They are nevertheless lively and witty; the intervening Adagio rivals the slow movement of Concerto III in poignant intensity.

So ends the second phase of Albinoni's mature period. For the next decade he was to desert instrumental music almost entirely and concentrate single-mindedly on a field that had occupied him continuously from the very beginning: opera.

---

[37] *The Baroque Concerto*, p. 159.

8

THE OPERAS AND SERENATAS

The Sources

WHETHER or not we accept as totally accurate Albinoni's claim that *Candalide* (1734) was his eightieth opera—which would make his last opera, *Artamene* (1741), the eighty-first—there can be little doubt that in the course of his career he covered more paper with operatic scores than with all other kinds of music combined. Viewed in this light, the small quantity of his surviving dramatic music may seem puzzling. In complete form we possess today only the following works:

Zenobia, regina de' Palmireni (opera: Venice, 1694)—Washington, Library of Congress, M1500.A72Z4.

Engelberta[1] (opera: Venice, 1709)—Berlin (West) Staatsbibliothek Preussischer Kulturbesitz, Mus. ms. 445; Vienna, Österreichische Nationalbibliothek, Cod. 17713.

La Statira (opera: Rome, 1726)—Vienna, Österreichische Nationalbibliothek, Cod. 18693 (microfilm only).

Pimpinone (comic intermezzi: Venice, 1708)—Vienna, Österreichische Nationalbibliothek, Cod. 18057; Münster, Santini-Bibliothek, Hs. 798.[2]

Il nascimento de l'Aurora (serenata: Venice(?), c. 1710)—Vienna, Österreichische Nationalbibliothek, Cod. 17738.

Il nome glorioso in terra, santificato in cielo (serenata: Venice, 1724)—Vienna, Österreichische Nationalbibliothek, Cod. 17730.

In reality, however, this meagre harvest is quite typical for a baroque composer enjoying in his day an above average but not outstanding reputation. Scores commissioned by the managements of opera houses were usually retained by them as property on the theatre; there is some evidence that composers were often not allowed, according to their terms of contract, to make and retain their own copies.[3] Even if they had the right

---

[1] *Engelberta* was composed jointly with Gasparini, who wrote the music of the fourth and fifth acts.

[2] Only the first intermezzo is contained in the Münster source. Modern writers sometimes use the singular form 'intermezzo' to refer to the set of two or three intermezzi making up the complete work. Since this usage is historically inaccurate and can lead to ambiguity, I have avoided it, even though to refer to *Vespetta e Pimpinone* as a 'set of comic intermezzi' is a little cumbersome.

[3] In a letter of 24 Feb. 1769 to his employer, Karl Eugen, duke of Württemberg, Niccolò Jommelli pleads for the right to be able to make copies of his own compositions lodged with the duke. Vivaldi touches on the same problem in a letter to the *marchese* Guido Bentivoglio d'Aragona of 29 Dec. 1736, where he describes the difficulty of persuading the proprietor of the San Giovanni Grisostomo theatre, Michiel Grimani, to allow the score of Hasse's *Il Demetrio* (performed there in 1732) to be copied for use in Ferrara.

to do so, the cost of copying and, still more, the extreme pressure of time presented obstacles; it was common to put the completed first act of a new opera into rehearsal even before the other acts had been finished. To an operatic management, the intrinsic value of a score was no greater than its commercial value. Once that had disappeared, no compelling reason existed to keep it—which is why, with some notable exceptions, remarkably few of the opera manuscripts from this period that have been preserved can be traced back to the opera houses themselves.

Composers who were personally involved in operatic management had a better than average chance of retaining or repossessing their scores. This is why, for instance, Vivaldi's personal collection, today reunited in the Biblioteca Nazionale, Turin, contains over twenty operatic scores (as opposed to only one score preserved elsewhere). The high rate of preservation of Handel's operas is partly due to similar circumstances. Both of these composers made a practice of borrowing extensively from their earlier music, and it would be interesting to know whether the relatively low incidence of self-borrowing in Albinoni's operas (so far as one can judge from the surviving material) had less to do with any principled objection to the practice than with simple lack of access to his earlier works in that genre.

For Albinoni, as for most of his contemporaries, the majority of the surviving scores are copies made for individual patrons or customers by the *copisteria* engaged by the opera house. This freelance activity, a recognized perquisite of the copying profession, took place in the few weeks that elapsed between the completion of the material required for the production and the return of the score to the theatre management. The scores of *Zenobia*, *Engelberta*, and *La Statira* listed above all belong to this category. A further score of *Zenobia*, whose present ownership is unknown, belonged once to Cardinal Pietro Ottoboni (the coincidence of the opera's date with that of the publication of Albinoni's Op. 1, dedicated to Ottoboni, is probably significant).[4]

To trace Albinoni's development as a composer of opera over a period of thirty-seven years (1694–1741) on the basis of three scores dating from 1694, 1709, and 1726 respectively would be difficult. Fortunately, the survival of separate arias from a dozen or so more operas helps to fill some of the gaps; *Astarto* (1708), *Il tiranno eroe* (1711), *Gli eccessi della gelosia* (1722), *I veri amici* (1722), *L'incostanza schernita* (1727), and *Ardelinda* (1732) are each represented by a large number of arias. In many cases, these aria collections were acquired by collectors from the 'house' copyists who also

---

[4] This score was sold as lot 274 at the auction of the Aylesford Manuscripts held by Sotheby, Wilkinson, and Hodge on 13 May 1918.

supplied complete scores. Some present the arias in fully instrumented form; others omit the instruments apart from continuo in the manner described in Chapter 5 for the 'accompanied' cantata *E dove, Amor, mi guidi*.

Ownership of the scores of comic intermezzi remained with the singers themselves, who usually operated in 'teams' comprising a man and a woman. Although the concept of a stable repertory did not exist at all in *opera seria* of the same period (as distinct from the French *tragédie lyrique*), it characterized the comic intermezzo from the very start. Since responsibility for the choice of intermezzi to be performed with the host work devolved on the *buffo* singers and since so much of the appeal of this genre derived not from the qualities of the individual work but from its interpretation by particular artists, it was logical for them to build up a repertory of tried and tested favourites that they would present over and over again, making incremental modifications as time went on. Whenever one of the singers in a team changed partners, a rôle would acquire a new interpreter; eventually, a popular set of intermezzi such as *Pimpinone* would become widely diffused and form part of the repertory of several such teams operating at the same time.[5] It is therefore certain that performing scores of *Pimpinone* existed in great number during the work's heyday (1708–*c*. 1730). Unfortunately, performing (as distinct from archival) material in manuscript rarely survives today. Moreover, since comic intermezzi had a low literary and musical status, they had less chance than 'serious' operas of becoming collector's items. That *Pimpinone* has been preserved is due to special circumstances. The Vienna score appears ostensibly as an integral part of its host work, a setting of the same *Engelberta* libretto by Antonio Orefici and Francesco Mancini performed at the San Bartolomeo theatre, Naples, in 1709. Naples had a long tradition of including comic scenes within *opera seria* (such scenes were regularly added by local composers to operas 'imported' from Venice), and although the three intermezzi making up *Pimpinone* have no organic connection whatever with *Engelberta*, they are entered into the opera score—perhaps through force of habit—as if they were old-style comic scenes.[6] The score of the first intermezzo preserved in Münster relates to a performance in the private theatre in Rome of Francesco Maria Ruspoli, prince of Cerveteri, in 1711; on this occasion, the intermezzi partnered Caldara's opera *La costanza in amore vince l'inganno*. Highly conscious of his standing as a patron of the arts, Ruspoli seems as a matter of course to have had copies made of

---

[5] On the diffusion of *Pimpinone* see the present author's preface to the edition of the intermezzi (under the title *Pimpinone: Intermezzi comici musicali*) published by A–R Editions, Madison, in 1983 as vol. xliii of the series 'Recent Researches in the Music of the Baroque Era'.

[6] Intermezzo I becomes Scene 15 of Act I; Intermezzo II becomes Scene 20 of Act II; Intermezzo III appears without a scene number after Scene 6 of Act III.

all musical works performed under his auspices, comic intermezzi not excluded.

Serenatas were nearly always commissioned by private individuals, who then became the owners of the scores. *Il nome glorioso in terra, santificato in cielo* and almost certainly also *Il nascimento de l'Aurora* were written for the Imperial (Austrian) ambassador to Venice as a contribution to the annual festivities for the name-day of the Emperor and the birthday of his consort respectively. It was evidently customary for Imperial ambassadors to provide evidence of this kind of homage by despatching copies of the celebratory cantatas to their sovereign, which is why the Österreichische Nationalbibliothek today possesses so many serenatas originally performed outside Vienna. In other circumstances, these works, too, might easily have disappeared.

The Opera System

It is impossible to understand the aesthetic presuppositions of baroque opera—so different from those of today—without appreciating the social and economic conditions in which it functioned. By Albinoni's time opera in Italy had evolved into an integrated system that even, up to a point, embraced opera in the Italian language in distant outposts such as London and Madrid. Because it was such an intricate system that represented such a large number of different interests, it had turned into a highly conservative one whose success depended on strict adherence to custom by all the parties. Although the desired direction of operatic reform had been talked about for decades, it took a non-Italian, Gluck, working in the autocratic environment of the Imperial court, to make the decisive breakthrough with *Orfeo ed Euridice* (1762) and *Alceste* (1767). But even with the example of Gluck's successes before them, the Italians were slow to take up his innovations—a fact that shows how deeply rooted in national life the old conventions had become.

Since this is a book about Albinoni, it would be out of place to devote too much space to a general discussion of Italian baroque opera, a field in which, moreover, an abundance of scholarly literature has appeared in recent years. Nevertheless, it will be useful to introduce at this point an excursus dealing with the social, economic—and also physical—background of Italian opera in Albinoni's day, since this can explain many features of his operatic music that might otherwise be found puzzling.

The economics of Venetian opera around 1730 (but they are generally valid for the whole of Albinoni's career) are well illustrated by two particular sets of documents. The first consists of the balance-sheets relating to the San Giovanni Grisostomo theatre in the Autumn–Carnival season of 1729/30, the San Samuele theatre in the Ascension season of 1730, and the San Giovanni Grisostomo theatre in the Carnival season of 1734.[7] Both theatres were owned by the noble Grimani family, and the three accounts are drawn up in a highly standardized manner that makes their comparative analysis easy. The second source comprises entries relating to opera listed under the heading of 'Spese estraordinaire' (extraordinary expenses) in the household accounts of Girolamo Ascanio Giustinian (1697–1749), the nobleman who wrote the famous series of psalm paraphrases set by Benedetto Marcello.[8] The entries span the years 1729–41 and mostly concern the rental of boxes in various Venetian theatres.

Almost all Venetian theatres were privately owned by patrician families, but their style of management varied. During the period of the Giustinian accounts ultimate control of most theatres remained in the hands of the noble proprietor, who usually left the day-to-day running in the hands of a factor described as an 'agente' or 'procuratore'. This applied to the San Salvatore, San Cassiano, and San Giovanni Grisostomo theatres. The Sant'Angelo theatre, however, was let out every season to an independent impresario, with virtually no continuity of tenure. The smallest theatre, San Moisè, seems also normally to have been under the control of an impresario, though in 1728 Giustinian rented a box directly from the proprietor, his namesake (from a different branch of the clan) Almorò Giustinian.

The difference between control by a proprietor and that by an impresario is important. Impresarios naturally aimed to make a clear profit on the season—which is why, for their purposes, small, unpretentious theatres with comparatively low overheads were the best. Owner-managers, however, regarded breaking even rather than profitability as the criterion of financial success, since they were motivated by other considerations: the prestige gained from providing their fellow nobles and eminent visitors to the city with what was regarded as the highest form of entertainment, and the sheer delight in opera for its own sake. In order to share the risk and provide starting capital other nobles and rich citizens were invited to become subscribers (carattadori) to the season, which

---

[7] Venice, Biblioteca Nazionale Marciana, Cod. It. XI-426, 8 (12142, 8). These documents are briefly discussed in Nicola Mangini, I teatri di Venezia (Venice, 1974), 124 and 143, but the unit of currency is given there erroneously as the ducat instead of the lira.

[8] Venice, Archivio di Stato, Ospedali e luoghi pii diversi, Registro 1004, openings 181, 240, 303, and 347; Registro 1011, openings 173, 221, 241, 277, 322, 400, and 411–13. The accounts were kept by Giustinian's steward Giovanni Andrea Cornelo. That these volumes appear in a series otherwise containing quaderni cassa of the Ospedale della Pietà is strange; perhaps the common factor of size (they are all so large that they can be consulted only in a standing position!) was the determining one.

involved the payment of a fixed subscription (*carato*) and, possibly, a further contribution in the form of a donation (*regalo*).

Breaking even, however, was no easy matter. Foreign visitors liked to recount to their compatriots how desperately uneconomic Venetian opera was. Chassebras de Cramailles, writing in the *Mercure galant* for March 1683, claimed that the noble proprietors must be acting for pleasure rather than profit when they put on operas, since they recouped hardly half of their outlay.[9] However, losses even of this order could be greatly mitigated by cross-subsidies from, first, the gaming houses (*ridotti*) owned by the same noble proprietors, which were popular places of resort after operatic performances had finished, and, second, from the rental of boxes in the theatres themselves, which formed, as Lorenzo Bianconi and Thomas Walker have so rightly said in their seminal article on Italian opera of the seventeenth century, a 'separate economy' and do not appear on operatic balance-sheets.[10] In the last resort, the proprietor himself would have the funds to bail out the enterprise. The three balance-sheets studied show a deficit ranging from just over 3 per cent of total outlay (for Autumn 1729, Carnival 1730, and Ascension 1730 considered together) to just over 10 per cent (for the 1734 season). If we are right to assume that virtually all those persons purchasing entry tickets who did not buy a chair on which to sit in the pit occupied boxes—they could amount to as many as 90 per cent or as few as 35 per cent of those attending—a mere fraction of the box income would have sufficed to erase the deficit. (In theory, members of the audience could have stood in the pit, but there were surely few who had the stamina to do so all the time when performances regularly lasted between four and five hours.)

With this perspective in mind, let us examine in close detail the balance-sheet of the combined Autumn and Carnival of 1729/30 at San Giovanni Grisostomo. This featured four works. *Onorio* (words, Domenico Lalli and Giovanni Boldini; music, Francesco Ciampi) ran for eleven nights in the Autumn season. Carnival opened with *Mitridate* (words, Apostolo Zeno, with revisions by Lalli; music, Giovanni Antonio Giay), which ran for fifteen nights. This was followed by *Idaspe* (words, Giovanni Battista Candi, with revisions by Lalli; music, Riccardo Broschi) for thirteen nights, and *Artaserse* (words, Pietro Metastasio, with revisions by Lalli; music, Johann Adolf Hasse) for eleven nights. Taken together, the

[9] Dated 20 Feb. 1683, the letter appears on pp. 230–309.

[10] The contribution of *ridotto* proceeds to the operatic coffers is mentioned in an anonymous pamphlet entitled *Reflexions d'un patriote sur l'opera françois et sur l'opera italien* (Lausanne, 1754), 6–7. Entitled 'Production, Consumption and Political Function of Seventeenth-Century Italian Opera', the article by Bianconi and Walker appears in volume iv of *Early Music History* (Cambridge, 1984), 209–96. The similarity of the findings published in that article to those presented here serves only to emphasize how durable and stable the general conditions of Italian opera remained in the period 1670–1750.

performances ran for fifty nights; this number naturally fluctuated a little from season to season, given the variation in the date of Easter and hence of Lent, whose beginning marked the official end of Carnival. It is likely that the total number of performances was normally fixed in advance—we find the impresario of Sant'Angelo selling Giustinian a set of 52 entry tickets 'for all the evenings' on 14 October 1728—but it would appear from some extant posters of the time that the date on which one opera was succeeded by the next was often left flexible in order to take account of the public response to each work in turn.

The figures on the balance-sheet (presented below in a form that follows closely the layout of the original, except for the combination of some entries for the sake of brevity) are all expressed in Venetian *lire*, subdivided, where necessary, into twenty *soldi*. For purposes of comparison with English money of the same period, one *lira* can be regarded as approximately equal to fivepence (5*d*.), or a forty-eighth part of a pound sterling. Many of the figures representing contractual payments to individuals are curiously 'unround'. This is because the actual coinage, real or notional, in which payment was to be made added up to a round sum, which subsequent conversion into *lire*, the standard money of account, has rendered less tidy. (A good comparison would be with the conversion of guineas (worth £1 1*s*.) into pounds in the former British monetary system.) Two examples: the 4,340 *lire* paid to the singer Maddalena Pieri are equivalent to 700 ducats, while the 4,400 *lire* paid to her colleague Antonio Castori represent 200 sequins.

The sterling equivalent of the outlay, 145,721 *lire*, 14 *soldi*, lies in the region of £3,035. 17*s*. High as this sum is—and it is probable that San Giovanni Grisostomo operated on one of the highest budgets in Italy—it pales into insignificance before costs incurred by opera in London. The 1729 season of the Royal Academy of Music, managed by Handel and Heidegger, reckoned with an outlay of £11,000 divided into £4,000 for singers, £2,000 for scenery and costumes, £1,000 for the musical director (Handel), and £4,000 for nightly house charges.[11] Small wonder that the most celebrated Italian singers were easily attracted to London, where a leading man or lady could command a fee of £2,000. (Rightly had Mattheson written in 1713: 'Whoever wishes to make a name for himself these days makes for England. One goes to Italy and France in order to learn; one goes to England in order to earn; one stays in the Fatherland in order to waste away most effectively'.)[12]

Nevertheless, the effect of international competition for singers is seen in

---

[11] Judith Milhous, 'Opera Finances in London, 1674–1738', *Journal of the American Musicological Society*, 37 (1984), 588.
[12] *Das neu-eröffnete Orchestre*, p. 211.

Balance-sheet of the expenditure and income of the theatre of San Giovanni Grisostomo according to the accounts of the subscribers in regard to the operatic performances that took place in 1729 [Venetian style, therefore 1729/30]

EXPENDITURE

[*Singers*]

Nicola Grimaldi	12,400
Carlo Broschi [Farinelli]	18,600
Francesca Cuzzoni	22,000
Maria Maddalena Pieri	4,340
Antonio Castori	4,400
Filippo Giorgi and wife [Caterina Giorgi]	9,300
Antonia Negri	2,680
[TOTAL	73,900]

Maestri di musica

Four composers	8,503. 10

Orchestra

Various instrumentalists	11,266

Ballets

Various dancers and the ballet-master [Antonio Ferrari]	7,391

Stage engineers

Giuseppe Valeriani and his brothers	13,516

Wardrobe

Hire of costumes from Nadalin Canciani	7,006

Expenses evening by evening

For 50 performances: lighting, wigs, dressers, ticket sellers, chair vendors, doorkeepers, tuners, prompters, etc., as listed separately	13,045. 5

Miscellaneous expenses

Veils, silk and wool stockings, head-dresses, gloves, boots, ribbons, etc., as listed separately	7,465. 17

Poet

Pietro Metastasio, for libretti	3,300

Copyist

Troian Carpanin, for copies of four operas, ballets, and various canzonets	788. 2
TOTAL	145,721. 14

INCOME

Tickets sold (3,345 + 6,678 + 6,019 + 7,617)	88,721. 5
Chairs (329 + 1,219 + 1,081 + 2,825)	11,565. 16
Profits recovered from Carlo Bonarigo [printer] for the libretti of two operas	1,657. 18
Donation (source unspecified)★	19,840
Subscriptions: 24 @ 868 *lire* each★	20,832
TOTAL	142,616. 19
DEFICIT	3,104. 15

★This income also covers the Ascension opera at San Samuele, so its true value is only about four-fifths of the total.

the remarkably high proportion of expenditure reserved for their fees: around 50 per cent, as compared with 35 per cent in London. Bonlini might well have been thinking of Cuzzoni (making her first appearance in Venice since 1722) when in 1730 he commented, ostensibly in reference to the 1720 Carnival season, when on account of rising costs only San Giovanni Grisostomo among the major Venetian theatres staged opera:

And in truth, liabilities cannot but exceed assets since the custom has arisen of emptying the coffers in order to acquire a singer of some renown. Time was when the payment for a very fine voice was considered exceptional when it exceeded a hundred *scudi* [1,280 *lire*], and it was a matter for wonder and public discussion when 120 *scudi* were offered for the first time. But how can past times be compared with the present, when a fee of over a 1,000 sequins [22,000 *lire*] is becoming almost commonplace among those who can boast some superiority over the others of their profession—an example that has by now led all [singers] to claim inflated fees, and which can only have very bad consequences for the interested parties, when they compete, as happens only too often, to satisfy them in full?[13]

In actual fact, the *primo uomo*, Farinelli, was paid even more than Cuzzoni *pro rata*, since he did not sing in the Autumn opera. His first appearance in Venice the previous year, also at San Giovanni Grisostomo, had been a signal triumph that eclipsed the combined efforts of Faustina Bordoni, Giovanni Paita, and Francesco Bernardi ('Senesino') at San Cassiano; small wonder that attendances shot up in 1730 after his arrival.[14] The famous alto castrato Nicola Grimaldi ('Nicolini', as he was known in

---

[13] *Le glorie della poesia e della musica*, p. 183.

[14] Even if Farinelli had sung in the Autumn opera, attendances would probably still have been somewhat lower than for the Carnival operas, since the number of visitors to Venice always greatly increased after Christmas. An Autumn opera had something of the character of a 'dry run' for a newly assembled cast and was often omitted altogether by Venetian theatres.

England) was paid somewhat less, since he was now in his mid-fifties and possessed a less fine voice than in former years, though his acting ability remained. Pieri, Castori, Filippo Giorgi and Negri were all middle-ranking singers and paid accordingly (Negri's apparently low fee arose from the fact that she sang only in *Mitridate*); Giorgi's wife Caterina was a useful 'bit part' singer (an *ultima parte*, as Italian terminology aptly describes it) needed for *Mitridate*, with its eight roles, *Idaspe*, with seven, and *Onorio*, with six (in the absence of Farinelli), but not *Artaserse*, which with typical Metastasian economy and symmetry reduces the cast to six singers.

Such heavy expenditure on *virtuosi* inevitably led Venetian managers to seek economies elsewhere. The above accounts list no payment for a chorus, and contemporary reports inform us that even when a brief chorus was required by the libretto and score, it was often taken, however incongruously, by the full cast of principals.[15] Evidently, audiences did not mind. The relatively low expenditure on the stage engineers (just over 9 per cent of total outlay for both fees and equipment costs) bears out Luigi Riccoboni's observation in 1738 that this was a common area for retrenchment.[16] It is impossible to identify in the balance-sheet any expenditure on the sliding flats and wings that formed the sets; this is possibly because the theatre already possessed an adequate stock of scenery for conventional sets such as temples, prisons, public squares, palace antechambers, gardens, woods, and so on. In contrast, the singers' specially hired costumes account for almost 5 per cent of total expenditure, not to mention the considerable cost of accessories such as gloves and boots.

The management's policy in regard to libretti kept the interests of economy and novelty in balance. As we learn from Goldoni's autobiography published in instalments as the preface to successive volumes of the first collected edition of his comedies, the Grimani theatres retained Domenico Lalli (pseudonym of Sebastiano Biancardi) as a house librettist or—more often—adapter of old libretti.[17] His collaborator on *Onorio*, Giovanni Boldini, fulfilled a similar role for Grimani; in 1737 we even find him collecting from Giustinian the rental for a half-box at San Samuele.

The adaptation of libretti could take several forms. If it was a matter simply of shortening (or, more rarely, expanding) a text, cuts or insertions

---

[15] French visitors to Italy, accustomed to the presence of a large and frequently employed chorus in their own operas, were surprised by the attenuation or absence of this element in Italian opera. The Seigneur de Fresneuse (Jean Laurent Le Cerf de la Viéville) comments sarcastically: 'When the composer of an opera aspires to the glory of having included a chorus in his work, as a rarity, it is these seven or eight persons [the principals] as a group who form it, all singing together—the king, the clown, the queen, and the old woman' (Brussels, 1704–6: tr. in Oliver Strunk, *Source Readings in Music History*, iii (London and Boston, 1981), 120 n.).

[16] Quoted in Angus Heriot, *The Castrati in Opera* (London, 1956), 75.

[17] *Commedie* (17 vols., Venice, 1761–78), xvii. 10.

could be made. More radical changes could be made to accommodate the number of dramatic roles to the number of available singers. The case of Antonia Negri, brought in specially for one opera, shows that some flexibility in casting was possible, but a theatre less well subsidized than San Giovanni Grisostomo or a travelling company taking opera to the provinces might well have decided instead to eliminate the least essential role. Then it might be necessary to add or subtract arias in order to reflect the relative status of the singers: a *prima donna* would be entitled, quantatively speaking, to parity with the *primo uomo* and superiority over the *seconda donna* and her male counterpart; the latter, in turn, would have the right to superiority over an *ultima parte* (who might not qualify for even a single aria). Substitutions were often made for existing arias. For instance, if a singer were more celebrated for her *arie di bravura* than for arias in a pathetic vein, it would make sense to replace the latter by the former. Singers often travelled from production to production with their favourite *arie di baule* (literally, 'suitcase arias'), which they would make every effort to unpack and display, regardless of context.

The ready manipulability of arias suggests that they were dramatically superfluous. This is largely true: they do not advance the action but rather suspend it in order to comment, through the mouth of one particular character, on the situation in hand or to describe that character's own mental state. Concrete reference (e.g. to named persons) is normally avoided. As Donald Jay Grout succinctly put it, 'Recitative is specific, aria is general'.[18] Like pieces of operatic scenery, arias conformed to a rigid typology that enabled them to be recycled whenever the type of character and type of situation repeated themselves. What a young hero departing for battle sang in one opera was suitable for his opposite number in another opera, usually without any textual modification. Taken to extremes, as in pasticci constructed by picking out arias from a number of pre-existent operas and threading them together with new recitative, this practice could verge on the ridiculous. François Raguenet, normally a strong partisan of Italian music in comparison with French, decries 'airs [that] are like saddles, fit for all horses alike . . . declarations of love made on one side and embraced or rejected on the other, transports of happy lovers or complaints of the unfortunate, protestations of fidelity or stings of jealousy, raptures of pleasure or pangs of sorrow, rage, and despair'.[19]

Although they could not but deplore the mangling of their texts in principle, librettists proved rather tolerant of it in practice. For them, and

---

[18] *Alessandro Scarlatti: An Introduction to his Operas* (Berkeley, Los Angeles, and London, 1979), 13.
[19] *Paralèle des Italiens et des François en ce qui regarde la musique et les opéra* (Paris, 1702), in the English tr. of 1709 attributed to Johann Ernst Galliard quoted in Strunk, op. cit., iii. 114.

for many connoisseurs in the audience, the essential 'drama' did not reside in the *spettacolo* with its added musical and visual dimensions but in the literary work alone, considered in an abstract, ideal sense. In the absence within Italy of a secure tradition of spoken theatre dealing with elevated subjects (of spoken comedy there was plenty), opera became by default the only possible vehicle for tragedy.[20] The response of most poets to this unhappy situation was to resign themselves to the worst as far as the treatment on stage of their drama was concerned but to safeguard their literary reputation by trying to ensure that, in its printed form at least, their 'official' text remained inviolate. Managements were usually willing to respect this wish. In cases of cuts, the excised lines were left in but 'virgulated' (preceded by quotation marks). The original arias could appear in the main text, while substituted or added arias were discreetly removed to an addendum.

In the same spirit, Metastasio's *Artaserse* had the rare privilege, in the 1730 production at San Giovanni Grisostomo, of having its libretto printed in two versions: one in its original form as received from the poet, and the other in its adaptation by Lalli. This measure aimed to satisfy both literary connoisseurs, who would wish to evaluate the new drama as an addition to Metastasio's œuvre, and ordinary opera-goers, who would prefer to have a libretto corresponding to the actual performance. It is a measure of Metastasio's great reputation on the eve of his departure to Vienna to become First Poet to the Emperor that *Artaserse* received near-simultaneous premières in Venice and in Rome, where the poet resided (Leonardo Vinci's setting for the Teatro Alibert opened on 4 February 1730). The payment to Metastasio of 3,300 *lire*, or 150 sequins, would have been within the normal range for a poet of his standing even without reference to his probable earnings from the second première. It exceeds the normal payment to the composer of a new score by about 50 per cent, a typical margin.

What did Grimani's literary workhorses, Lalli and Boldini, earn for their pains? The question is impossible to answer precisely, since neither name appears on the balance-sheet. It is possible that they were entitled to a share of the proceeds from the sale of the libretti, which, being priced at around 30 *soldi* (this figure comes from Nemeitz), would have realized a considerable sum. It is puzzling that the balance-sheet mentions money received from Bonarigo in respect of two libretti only, when five (including the duplicate libretto for *Artaserse*) were printed. We know from Goldoni that Lalli liked to reserve to himself the right to dedicate a

---

[20] 'Tragedy' is used here in the original, Aristotelian sense of a dramatic work whose characters are of exalted rank—not necessarily one with a 'sad' ending.

libretto, hoping thereby to receive the customary *regalo* from the person thus honoured.[21] The thought also occurs that the two men may have been on Grimani's payroll and therefore not entitled to a separate fee in the same way as outsiders. Or they could have been recompensed by being awarded the *dote* (literally, 'dowry') of a few free boxes to rent out as they wished.

The four composers—Ciampi, Giay, Broschi (Farinelli's elder brother), and Hasse—must have received a fee of around 2,000 *lire* each. The great influx of Neapolitan and other non-native composers into the Venetian opera world from the mid-1720s onwards had created a 'buyer's market' for theatre managements, in whose advantage it lay to stimulate rivalry between *maestri* and their respective protectors by spreading commissions around widely. Hasse was probably able to negotiate a higher fee than the others; for the following Ascension opera, *Dalisa*, he was paid 2,380 *lire*. This sum seems quite normal for Venice during the 1730s; Vivaldi reported in 1736 being offered 90 sequins (1,980 *lire*) for providing the final Carnival opera for San Cassiano—a proposition he turned down since he insisted on being paid his usual fee of 100 sequins.[22] It is amazing, by the modern scale of values, that the fees paid to all four composers combined amounted to under 6 per cent of total expenditure, especially when one considers that they will have been expected also to supervise rehearsals and lead the first few performances.

The orchestra bill was slightly larger, that for the *corps de ballet* (probably comprising a ballet-master and six to eight dancers) slightly smaller. The dancers, whose choreography and music were both provided by the ballet-master, performed entr'actes, which, like the functionally similar comic intermezzi, were unconnected with the main work. San Giovanni Grisostomo had a tradition, alone among Venetian theatres, of not admitting comic intermezzi. San Samuele had no such inhibitions, however; in Ascension 1730 it offered hospitality to the well-known *buffo* pair Antonio Ristorini and Rosa Ongarelli, who were jointly paid the very handsome sum of 3,720 *lire*—almost three times as much as the *seconda donna*, Vivaldi's protégée Anna Girò.

The debit side of the balance is completed by the payment to the copying shop of 788 *lire* 2 *soldi*. A typical charge by a Venetian copyist of the period was between three and four *soldi* a page. This payment would therefore represent something in the region of 4,000–5,250 pages, which seems just enough to provide single copies of all the material required for the four operas and the ballets.

On the credit side, the subscriptions and *regalo* account for only just over

<hr>

[21] Goldoni, loc. cit. [22] Letter to Guido Bentivoglio d'Aragona of 3 Nov. 1736.

28 per cent of the official income—23 per cent if the Ascension opera is brought into the reckoning. However, the subscription income must have been vital, giving the management working capital with which, for example, to pay the singers the first instalment of their fee.[23] The most substantial source of income was from the tickets required for entry to the theatre by occupants of boxes and the pit alike. San Giovanni Grisostomo, true to its reputation as the most fashionable and exclusive of the Venetian theatres, had the highest ticket price: 3 *lire* 15 *soldi* (for comparison: in 1721, when Nemeitz visited Venice, Sant'Angelo charged 2 *lire* and San Moisè only 31 *soldi*). By the end of the Autumn–Carnival season in the year under consideration the sale of these tickets had accounted for 62 per cent of total income. The attendance at the three Carnival operas averaged 520 per night.

Eight per cent of the income was realized from the hiring out of chairs in the pit. These were small folding armchairs that Nemeitz describes as coupled together to form ten to twelve rows.[24] San Giovanni Grisostomo had the custom of making the cost of chair-hire equal to the ticket price on the opening night of an opera, presumably because demand was greatest then; thereafter, the charge fell to 36 *soldi* (as compared with 30 and 20 *soldi* at Sant'Angelo and San Moisè respectively).

As we noted earlier, the boxes were administered quite separately. All the Venetian theatres in which opera was performed contained, during Albinoni's time, four to six tightly packed tiers of boxes lining the auditorium in the shape of a horseshoe and in some cases overlapping the stage. San Giovanni Grisostomo, with five tiers, possessed 155 boxes; San Cassiano, with six tiers, had 197 (though the uppermost tier was sometimes closed); Sant'Angelo and San Samuele, both with five tiers, had 145 and 168 respectively; San Moisè, with only four tiers, had 107. As de Brosses and other visitors tell us, the lowest tier (called *pepian*), was unpopular since it brought the occupants of those boxes too close to the groundlings and sometimes allowed their view of the stage to be obscured by the necks of the archlutes in the orchestra, while the highest tier was also avoided by high society, presumably because of its distance from the stage. The first and second tiers (those immediately above the *pepian*) were the fashionable ones.

Individual boxes were treated like apartments in a big *palazzo*. They

---

[23] The private contract drawn up on 13 Oct. 1726 between Vivaldi, as impresario of Sant'Angelo, and the singer Lucrezia Baldini, who was to perform in the final opera of the forthcoming Carnival (Vivaldi's own *Farnace*), provides what must have been a typical agreement with a singer. One third of the fee was to be paid in advance of the opening night, one third half-way through the run, and the last third just before the end of Carnival.

[24] *Nachlese besonderer Nachrichten aus Italien*, i. 74.

Theatre	Type of production	Autumn–Carnival	Ascension
San Giovanni Grisostomo	opera	496–744	
San Samuele	comedy	110–124	
	opera		136.8
San Cassiano	comedy	124	
	opera	248	
Sant'Angelo	opera	124	21
San Moisè	comedy	124	
	opera	155	49.12
San Salvatore	comedy	120	

could be lent or donated to individuals by the proprietor of the theatre, or they could actually be sold as inheritable real estate. For example, in 1745 Anna Girò, nearing the end of her career, bought three second-tier boxes in the San Samuele theatre from Michiel Grimani for 1,000 ducats (6,200 *lire*) apiece.[25] Once bought, boxes, or fractions of them, could be let to third parties. Leases, from the proprietor or the separate owner of a box, could run for several consecutive seasons or be confined to a single season. The Giustinian accounts show that even for a single theatre there was some variability in the rental charge for a box, depending on demand and the position of the box. Again, a differential between the large theatres under the control of proprietors and the small theatres under the control of impresarios is noticeable. So, too, is the contrast in the cost of a box between a season of comedy and one of opera. Typical rental charges (in *lire*) for the period 1729–41 are shown in the table.[26] If one considers that the rental of all the theatre boxes for one combined autumn and carnival season of opera at San Giovanni Grisostomo would have yielded something of the order of 90,000 *lire*, the size of this 'parallel' economy and its potential for cross-subsidizing the 'main' economy appear very considerable indeed. The extent to which the two economies were co-ordinated (if, indeed, they were) is obviously a factor of prime importance to our understanding of the economic basis of early Italian public opera; it is unfortunate how little information on this subject has so far emerged.

The Libretti

It will have become clear how important it is to examine the poetic-dramatic text of a baroque opera or similar composition on its own terms

[25] On Anna Girò's life and this episode in particular see Gastone Vio, 'Per una migliore conoscenza di Anna Girò (da documenti d'archivio)', *Informazioni e studi vivaldiani*, 9 (1988), 26–45.

[26] The figures quoted are for the rental of a whole box from the theatre proprietor, his factor, or the impresario in charge. The figure of 21 *lire* for the rental of a box for an Ascension season at Sant'Angelo (which occurred only in 1733) seems much too low; perhaps it refers to the rental of only a fraction of a box.

before the contribution of the specifically musical component can be fully appreciated. The libretto he receives from the poet 'programmes' the baroque composer to a degree unfamiliar from the practice of later periods. To be sure, he is not denied the opportunity to exercise choice; but this choice is concerned with how to execute the given programme most effectively rather than how to enlarge it or lend it a fresh dimension. It is perhaps unfortunate for our understanding of Italian baroque opera that its greatest musical representative, Handel, is the least conventional in this respect. As Reinhard Strohm has pointed out in a penetrating study of the *opera seria* tradition, the independent dramatic force of the music in Handel's operas arose in response to the difficulty experienced by most members of an English audience in following a 'literary' drama written in a foreign language and their consequent need for extra prompting—special conditions that, needless to say, did not apply in Italy itself.[27]

The literary texts of the five dramatic works by Albinoni that survive complete, or virtually so (leaving aside his part-composition of *Engelberta*), offer a good conspectus of the librettist's art around and just after 1700. *Zenobia, regina de' Palmireni* and *La Statira* are both examples of the *dramma per musica*, the variety of *opera seria* most closely corresponding to classical tragedy. Nearly all Albinoni's operas belong to this species, although we may note among them one pastoral opera (*Aminta*) and another opera that is both pastoral and comic (*L'incostanza schernita*). Pastoral and comic operas of this period differ from tragic (or, better, heroic) ones in style and temper, but not essentially in scale and construction. The text of *Zenobia* (1694) can therefore be taken as representative of libretto writing at the beginning of Albinoni's career—that is, just before the 'reforms' associated with Apostolo Zeno and his circle achieved general currency (although hints of the direction of change can already be seen in *Zenobia*). *La Statira*, which Albinoni set for the Carnival of 1726 in Rome, had received its first setting from Francesco Gasparini twenty years earlier; it is thus a libretto of the 'reform' period in its earliest phase. The comic intermezzi *Pimpinone* (also known as *Vespetta e Pimpinone* and by various other titles) represent this genre in the very first years of its actual existence. The text of one of Albinoni's two serenatas, *Il nome glorioso in terra, santificato in cielo* (1724), is an absolutely typical example of its genre, while the other, *Il nascimento de l'Aurora* (c. 1710), is equally representative in all respects except length.[28]

---

[27] Reinhard Strohm, *Essays on Handel and Italian Opera* (Cambridge, 1985), 99–101.

[28] *Il nascimento de l'Aurora* is described on the title-page of the score as a 'Festa pastorale'. This is a very unusual combination of words, which might easily have been taken to refer to a type of opera rather than serenata. In view of the exceptional length of this work, discussed in more detail later, the description may have been selected quite deliberately in order to suggest a dramatic composition on an exceptionally large scale for a serenata.

Very little is known about Antonio Marchi, the librettist of *Zenobia*, except that he was Venetian and that *Zenobia* was his second drama.[29] The libretto of the 1694 production exists in two impressions, the second of which corrects a few of the very numerous printing errors in the first and, more significantly, changes the title as given at the end of the *Argomento* (Synopsis) from *L'inganno deluso* (Deceit Disappointed) to *Zenobia, regina de' Palmireni*, the form of title found on the title-page and in the preface of both impressions; evidently, the retention in the *Argomento* of the superseded original title had been overlooked at the time of the first impression.[30] The two titles represent two different approaches to naming a baroque opera that between them held near-absolute sway. The first, encountered in about three-fifths of Albinoni's operas, names the drama after the protagonist, the co-protagonist, or both. The second, found in the remaining two-fifths, names it after the theme or moral of the work—what Benedetto Marcello called its 'principal action'.[31] Writing in 1720, Marcello implied that the second type of title was becoming more fashionable than the first; he gives as a witty, oxymoronic example of contemporary practice the invented title *L'ingratitudine generosa* (The Generous Ingratitude), which is almost a conflation of two actual titles belonging to operas set by Albinoni: *L'ingratitudine gastigata* (1698) and *Le gare generose* (1712). Marcello's observation has a bearing on the later fortunes of *Zenobia*, for in Autumn 1717 it was revived at Sant'Angelo in the form of a pasticcio that retained little of Albinoni's original music and was retitled *Il vinto trionfante del vincitore* (The Vanquished Triumphant over the Victor).

According to Groppo's catalogue, the first impression of *Zenobia* was supplied with an addendum of three loose leaves.[32] Unfortunately, none of the surviving examples of the libretto that have been inspected contain this addition, which may have either listed errata or described differences in the sung text as compared with that of the libretto (in addition to the numerous lines already virgulated).

Like most late-seventeenth-century *drammi per musica*, Marchi's libretto opts for a historical rather than mythological subject: the expedition of the Roman emperor Aurelian, who reigned from AD 270 to AD 278, against

---

[29] His first was *Rosalinda* (1692). Albinoni later set his *Zenone, imperatore d'Oriente* (1696), *Radamisto* (1698), and *Alcina delusa da Ruggero* (1725).

[30] The first impression is represented by examples in the Fondazione Giorgio Cini, Venice, the Conservatorio di Musica 'Santa Cecilia', Rome, the Istituto Storico Germanico, Rome, and the Civico Museo Bibliografico Musicale, Bologna; the second impression is held by the University of California at Berkeley and has been reproduced in facsimile as vol. lx of the series *Italian Opera 1640–1770* (= vol. x of the sub-series *Italian Opera Librettos*) published by Garland (New York, 1979).

[31] *Il teatro alla moda*, ed. Andrea D'Angeli (Milan, 1956), 9.

[32] *Catalogo di tutti i drammi per musica*, p. 75.

Zenobia, the queen of the Syrian city of Palmyra. During the period of disorder that had preceded Aurelian's rise to power Zenobia had seceded from the Empire, carving out a substantial kingdom of her own in the Middle East. History records that the queen, defeated in the field by Aurelian, fell back on her stronghold of Palmyra, which was captured only after a long siege; she herself was taken captive and brought back to Rome for Aurelian's triumph, ending her life in a comfortable villa in Tivoli. Marchi, however, is less interested in the *vero*—the factually true—than in the *verosimile*, or fictional but true-to-life. A good half of his *Argomento* is devoted, once the historical background has been sketched and the protagonists Aurelian and Zenobia introduced, to a list of the 'fictions' around which the story is woven—the last of which (the restoration to Zenobia of her kingdom) flatly contradicts historical fact.

It is important to approach this quality of verisimilitude in the spirit of Marchi's contemporaries, who accepted such artifices as the compression of real time into theatrical time or the invention of improbable romantic attachments without question but would object if a character's actions seemed out of keeping with his essential personality. Whereas modern drama favours a dynamic treatment of personality that allows characters to reveal themselves gradually or, indeed, to present different, even contradictory facets of their make-up successively, classical and baroque drama like to give each character a fixed quality or essence (*ethos*) that, although disturbed by transient passions (*pathos*), proves a decisive factor in the resolution of the plot. This *ethos* correlates, though not simplistically, with the social rank of the characters: royal characters on the whole display rarer and more admirable qualities than merely noble ones; confidants, as a class, are a notch above plain servants in terms of morality. Naturally enough, every drama needs to contain at least one character who transgresses the ethical norms appropriate to his station in life (such as a monarch who becomes a tyrant, a general who betrays his sovereign, or a confidant who improperly discloses a confidence). But to show this behaviour as deviant, it is important for dramatists always to include the parallel example of an ethically exemplary character of similar rank. A baroque drama can ultimately be understood as a sophisticated type of morality play, supportive—at least, overtly—of the existing order: one where virtue is seen to triumph over adversity, and vice turns out to be self-defeating. At the end of the drama rewards and penalties are distributed in accordance with the ethical conduct of the characters and in a manner that reflects their social rank.

Marchi's *Zenobia* has parts for eight principal characters (discounting a Messenger and a Soldier, whose roles are so small that they could have been

Zenobia, regina de' Palmireni (A. Marchi): distribution of arias

	Act I	Act II	Act III	TOTAL
Aureliano	6	5	2	13
Zenobia	$\frac{1}{2}$	4	6	$10\frac{1}{2}$
Lidio	$2\frac{1}{2}$	2	4	$8\frac{1}{2}$
Filidea	$1\frac{1}{2}$	3	2	$6\frac{1}{2}$
Ormonte	2	1	2	5
Cleonte	3	1	1	5
Silvio	$1\frac{1}{2}$	0	1	$2\frac{1}{2}$
Liso	0	0	0	0
TOTAL	17	17	18	52

recruited from among the extras, and an allegory of Constancy (La Costanza) who sings one aria during the second of two ballets inserted into the opera). Although the libretto contains no cast-list, which means that individual singers cannot be identified, it is evident from the number of arias allotted to each character which roles were conceived from the start as primary (i.e. for the *primo uomo* and *prima donna*), which as secondary, and which as minor. Just as one would expect, there is a strong correlation between the dramatic importance of each role and the social rank of the character represented.

The primary roles are those of the protagonists Aurelian (Aureliano) and Zenobia. There are four secondary roles, which form two distinct pairs. The first pair, slightly more favoured with arias, comprises the lovers Filidea, daughter of the governor of Palmyra, and Lidio, a Greek prince allied to the Palmyrans. The second pair consists of Cleonte, Aurelian's captain, and Ormonte, Filidea's father. Finally, there are two minor parts for Silvio, Zenobia's young son, and Liso, her servant. Liso, who has no arias at all, is a comic role in the tradition of Venetian seventeenth-century opera. However, since he is the sole comic character in the opera, he interacts perforce only with 'serious' characters; this has the effect both of restraining the comic element (which might have blossomed into farce, had the male servant's traditional comic partner, an old woman (*vecchia*), also been present) and of safeguarding the unity of action.[33] In Marchi's text one can already detect a reticence about mixing the serious and comic genres that was shortly to lead, in the hands of the librettists associated with the 'reform' current, to a total banishment of anything comic from the *dramma per musica*.

The table showing the number of arias sung by each character in each

---

[33] Another example of a *dramma per musica* with a single comic part for a servant is Matteo Noris's *Tito Manlio*, first heard in C. F. Pollarolo's setting (Florence, 1696; Venice, 1697), but better known today in the setting for Mantua (1719) by Vivaldi.

of the three acts illustrates very precisely the stratification of the eight rôles as well as the manner in which arias are distributed for each character across the acts. The fifty-two closed numbers include only two *arie a due* (for Filidea and Lidio in Act I, Scene 6; for Zenobia and Silvio in Act I, Scene 20), counted in the table as 'half' arias for each character. There are no other ensembles and no choruses. Not all Venetian operas of this period promote the solo aria quite so exclusively, although a marked bias in this direction is undeniable. More puzzling is the strong concentration of Aurelian's arias in Act I, Zenobia's in Act III. What, one wonders, did the singer taking the rôle of Zenobia feel when the virtuoso playing opposite her earned plaudits from the audience with aria after aria, while she had nothing but recitative? Would both singers have preferred the spacing of their arias to have been more even in order to give their voices more time to recover between exertions? No convincing answer to these questions can be given, but it seems certain, at least, that the uneven distribution has nothing to do with the construction of the plot: any late baroque opera has more possible 'anchorage points' for arias than it can in practice use, and there are few enough points at which the insertion of an aria becomes an absolute necessity. One could argue that the rising incidence of arias sung by Zenobia mirrors the growing recognition of her moral stature as the opera progresses and corresponds to a shift in dramatic focus away from Aurelian and towards her. But is that perhaps not too modern a way of viewing the matter?

Marchi confesses in his preface that he has no pretensions as a dramatic poet. He will, he avows, be more pleased if his drama is tolerated on the stage by the public than he will be displeased if it is criticized by small cliques of experts. His modesty is not, in an objective sense, false in respect of his poetic gifts, for his verse is rough and awkward, struggling to achieve metrical correctness, let alone elegance. But his handling of the plot is first-rate; it shows not only verve and imagination but also self-discipline and a strong feeling for dramatic cogency. The plot can be summarized as follows:

Act I. As the Romans prepare for their final assault on Palmyra, Aurelian confesses to Cleonte that he is in love. Cleonte is appalled at such inopportune feelings and reminds the emperor of the task in hand. The Romans attack. Hard pressed, the Palmyrans send Ormonte to Aurelian's camp in order to sue for peace. Aurelian refuses to treat, but recognize Ormonte as the father of his secret beloved, Filidea. Cunningly, he offers to marry Filidea and make her empress if Ormonte will come over to his side. Ormonte is finally seduced by the proposal once Aurelian has promised, in addition, to make him his viceroy in the East. He agrees to lead the Roman army into Palmyra via a secret passage provided that his treachery is not revealed.

Meanwhile, the two lovers Lidio and Filidea are shown inside Palmyra. Hearing the sound of battle within the city, Lidio resolves to leave Filidea in order to fight alongside the Palmyrans. But she takes his departure in bad part and vows revenge. Zenobia, fleeing before the Romans from her palace, anxiously asks Liso where Silvio is. Suddenly her son reveals himself on a high balcony. He courageously jumps down into Zenobia's arms, and the three prepare to continue their flight. Their way is barred by Cleonte and a detachment of Roman soldiers, who take them prisoner.

In a public square, awaiting Aurelian's triumph, Ormonte reproaches Filidea for having immodestly wandered the streets during the recent turmoil. Filidea gives a plausible account of her movements (omitting, however, any mention of Lidio) and manages to assuage her father's anger. Ormonte then tells Filidea that Aurelian wants her as his wife. She welcomes this news since she sees an attachment to Aurelian as a way of spiting Lidio. The latter, arriving, is surprised to find Filidea cool towards him. Aurelian and his suite then make a magnificent entrance. Lidio and Ormonte pledge their loyalty to him. Aurelian, in a spirit of generosity, releases his Palmyran captives, who dance a ballet. He announces publicly his intention to marry Filidea. Lidio is horrified, but Filidea makes her eager assent only too plain. At this point Cleonte leads on Zenobia, Silvio, and Liso in chains. Zenobia refuses to swear loyalty to Aurelian, since, as she says, she owes her defeat not to superior force or valour but to treachery. Aurelian is deeply impressed. When Filidea, anxious for attention, addresses him as 'my husband', he becomes angry and sends her away. Feeling love for Zenobia stirring within him, Aurelian orders her release and also that of Silvio and Liso. Zenobia and Silvio immediately resolve to unmask and punish the traitor. Cleonte, left alone on the stage, expresses his wonder at Zenobia's pride and strength of character.

Act II. Aurelian is revealed musing on how hard it is to feign love for one woman while really loving another. When Ormonte, accompanied by Filidea, comes to remind him of their agreement, Aurelian repudiates it. Ormonte angrily accuses Aurelian of breaking his word, not realizing that the emperor has left and Lidio has appeared in his stead. Aware that he may have inadvertently confessed his treachery to Lidio, Ormonte feigns madness. Lidio once more protests his love to Filidea, but she rebuffs him, calling him unfaithful. Indignantly, Lidio asserts his innocence. Left alone, Filidea reasserts her aim to marry Aurelian and punish Lidio.

Meanwhile, Zenobia prays to the gods in her throne-room. She is unreconciled to the thought of no longer being a queen. Liso enters. His intention is to pass a message to Zenobia, but her preoccupations and his timidity make this a laborious business. Eventually, the message gets through: Aurelian wishes to see her. The emperor then enters. A little obliquely, he confesses his love for her and offers his hand. When she eventually understands his proposal, Zenobia defiantly rejects it, fends off his embraces, and leaves. Aurelian ponders whether to put her to death for disobeying him but succumbs to the opposite pull of love. Cleonte enters to tell Aurelian that his soldiers are restive and wish to continue the campaign to win back the East. But all Aurelian can do is to sing of love. Cleonte then philosophizes on the power of love, that can lay low even the strongest.

Ormonte and Filidea decide to waylay Aurelian for a second time in order to hold him to his promise but are prevented from doing so by the arrival of Lidio, which forces Ormonte to renew his pretence of madness and leave, followed by his daughter. Lidio asks Aurelian for permission to marry Filidea, which is (naturally) granted. He is elated.

In another room in the palace Zenobia and Silvio vow to each other to be steadfast. Aurelian then arrives with Liso. With the servant's connivance, Silvio hides. Once again, Aurelian makes advances to Zenobia, which she repulses. The emperor then instruct Liso to act as his proxy. A mixture of timidity, loyalty, and decency (with his knowledge of Silvio's concealed presence an added complication) reduces Liso to comic impotence. Aurelian furiously renews his suit in person and assaults Zenobia, who again resists him stoutly. Silvio comes to her aid. Eventually, Aurelian tires of his efforts and leaves. Mother and son comfort each other. A *macchina* descends, bearing Constancy, whose followers dance a ballet.

Act III. Cleonte tells Aurelian that he can get his way through threatening the life of Silvio if Zenobia does not assent. Ormonte and Filidea, who overhear him from the next room, are appalled (but only out of self-interest). When Aurelian encounters them, he once again dismisses their case, saying that Filidea cannot have two husbands. Lidio opportunely arrives, and Aurelian makes his meaning clear by joining the hands of the two former lovers. Ormonte is incensed and begins to think of revenge. Filidea remains cool to Lidio, and asks for time to consider her position. Lidio, alone, confesses that he loves Filidea regardless of her behaviour towards him.

Meanwhile, Zenobia, alone in a grand mausoleum, nostalgically contemplates pictures of her earlier victories over the Romans. Silvio joins her, and is instructed in the significance of the pictures. Liso then bursts in to say that Cleonte is on his way, accompanied by soldiers. The queen is resigned to her fate and bids Silvio farewell. Cleonte arrives to announce the ultimatum. After a poignant inner struggle, Zenobia decides to place her honour higher than her son's life—in which she is supported by Silvio, who declares himself unafraid of death. Silvio is led off by Cleonte. Zenobia is then visited by Ormonte, who promises to restore her to the throne and return Silvio to her unharmed. Before he can reveal his plan, Aurelian arrives. Noticing that the queen looks unexpectedly cheerful, he decides to hide in order to overhear the conversation. Ormonte advises Zenobia to feign love for Aurelian and stab him with a knife when they embrace. Zenobia adamantly refuses to do this and recognizes Ormonte as the one who earlier betrayed her. After Zenobia has left, Aurelian reveals himself and has Ormonte arrested.

Elsewhere in the palace, Lidio decries love. Filidea joins him. To his surprise, she protests her love for him (he naturally does not know that this sudden rekindling of her affection is connected with the planned removal by assassination of Aurelian). It is now his turn to be unmoved and ask for time.

Cleonte arrives with Silvio, Aurelian with Zenobia. To general amazement, Aurelian commands Zenobia's restoration to her throne and Silvio's release. Liso and Lidio enter, then Ormonte in chains. Aurelian lets the newly crowned Zenobia decide on Ormonte's fate. The contrite governor appeals to Zenobia, Silvio, and Lidio in turn for mercy: he receives none. Suddenly, Filidea enters to plead eloquently for her father's life. Zenobia passes the judgement back to Aurelian, who is moved by Filidea's entreaties and commutes the expected sentence of death to one of exile. The wedding of Lidio and Filidea is confirmed, and the opera ends with a short expression of happiness by Zenobia.

The plot hinges, as do those of so many baroque operas with a happy ending, on a double 'catastrophe' (to use this term in its original sense of an abrupt reversal of fortune in either direction). The first is Ormonte's betrayal of Zenobia; the second is his attempted betrayal of Aurelian, which is thwarted by Zenobia's refusal to support him even before Aurelian himself intervenes. The two catastrophes are linked by being the result of the same moral choice: between honour and ambition. Ormonte allows the second to prevail and ultimately pays the price; Zenobia allows the first to prevail and through her noble decision overcomes adversity. (Providence, as usual, is shown to be self-correcting.) From the viewpoint of a contemporary critic, Marchi's drama easily passes the test of 'probability', for the actions of all its characters flow naturally from their personalities. Admirable, too, is the close adherence to the 'principal action' in all the parts of the drama.

Each act contains three or four stage sets. Nearly all are conventional in nature, and many must have been designed to employ scenery belonging to the permanent stock of the theatre. The sets include some (like the 'small room' in the middle of Act III) that would have worked well as *scene corte*, or scenic arrangements confined to the front of the stage, as opposed to *scene lunghe* with their deep perspective. Shallower sets were particularly useful, as they enabled the rear part of the following set to be prepared in advance and so facilitated changes—in particular, the very rapid type of change known as a 'transformation' (an example occurs near the end of Act III, where the small room suddenly becomes a 'sumptuous amphitheatre'). The opening set for Act III is a bipartite one showing two rooms side by side. Marchi deploys his characters on stage skilfully in order to exploit its possibilities.

The three acts are divided into twenty-one, twenty-one, and twenty-four scenes respectively.[34] The criterion for a scene change is a purely formal one: that there is a change in the characters on stage. This means that if a character goes off stage, a new scene ensues. Whereas the departure of a character is always a clear-cut event, the arrival of a character is sometimes hard to pinpoint—particularly where several characters arrive in quick succession—and can lead to uncertainty. Most of the numerous discrepancies in scene division between the published libretto and the text as it stands in Albinoni's score can be accounted for by this factor.

Modern commentators on late baroque opera often draw attention to the fact that the majority of arias occur in 'exit' position, at the end of a scene. Given the custom of allowing the singer to sweep off the stage after singing an aria and acknowledging the audience's applause, the preponderance of the 'exit' aria is a foregone conclusion. One might even say that it is as much the aria that determines the position of the scene as the reverse. Nevertheless, a good many arias in *Zenobia* are not followed by the character's departure and hence occur in opening or middle position. As against thirty-five 'exit' arias, there are nine 'entry' arias and six 'medial' ones.[35] It is noticeable that many of the arias not in 'exit' position have short texts—the poet's way of inviting the composer to be brief so as not to hold up the action too much in mid-flow. Many of the shorter aria texts cannot be divided into two semistrophes, which therefore precludes in principle a da capo setting. In regard to the aria texts as a whole, those prescribing a da capo setting (through repetition of the incipit of the first semistrophe followed by '&c.' after the last line) are in a clear majority; this majority may in fact be even greater than is apparent, since in several cases the repetition of the incipit seems to have been omitted inadvertently by

---

[34] Act III has 2 consecutive scenes numbered 'VII' in the libretto, so the scene numbers rise only to 23.

[35] Act III, Scene 7*bis*, is a soliloquy for Zenobia comprising only an aria. This stanza is thus an 'entry' and an 'exit' aria rolled into one.

Marchi or his printer. The *Zenobia* libretto represents a stage in Italian operatic history where the da capo form has established itself as the norm in more weighty arias but as not yet entirely supplanted through-composed and strophic forms in lighter, more incidental ones.

Coincidentally, the story of *La Statira* is also one of female fortitude rewarded. The conception of its libretto belongs to Apostolo Zeno (1668–1750), the doyen of Italian dramatic poets in the first quarter of the eighteenth century. A Venetian patrician, Zeno wrote nearly fifty *drammi per musica* between 1695 and 1734; his early operas were mostly conceived for the stage of his native city, while his later works received their first performances in Vienna, where Zeno served Charles VI as court poet and historian from 1718 to 1729. Zeno was closely involved with the 'purifying' goals of Italian literary academies around the turn of the century—he was the founder of the Accademia degli Animosi in Venice and a member of the Roman Arcadia—and he rigorously excluded the comic and the absurd from his operas. His scruples as a historian somewhat inhibited his imagination as a dramatist; it has been aptly said that his dramas were more the result of study and taste than of inspiration and enthusiasm.[36] Nevertheless, the solidity and rationality of Zeno's plots deserve praise.

His major weakness was as a versifier. He had the good sense, however, often to enlist the assistance of a fellow *letterato*, Pietro Pariati (1665–1733), precisely for this purpose. Pariati had been born in Reggio, in the duchy of Modena, but had been exiled in 1699 for gross misconduct while in Modenese government service and had taken refuge in Venice, which as a fiercely independent republic offered a safer haven than most cities to refugees from Italy's princely states. Zeno took Pariati under his wing, and between 1705 and 1709 the two men produced eleven collaborative works. In 1714 Pariati was appointed as a court poet in Vienna on his mentor's recommendation; after Zeno himself arrived in Vienna the collaboration was occasionally revived.

Pariati's part in the joint works seems to have been to fashion the verse according to a detailed scenario provided by Zeno. His lines are fluent and use relatively unstilted language. Perhaps his greatest merit is as a constructor of dialogue; Pariati is a master of stichomythia, the technique of giving two characters alternate lines or hemistiches so as to produce a lively cut and thrust effect.

La Statira has seven characters. The two primary roles are those of Statira, the daughter of the recently deceased Persian king Artaxerxes

---

[36] This view is expressed in Tullo Concari, *Il Settecento* (Milan, n.d.), 60.

La Statira (A. Zeno and P. Pariati): distribution of arias

	Act I	Act II	Act III	TOTAL
Statira	3	2	2	7
Arsace	2	3	2	7
Barsina	3	2	1	6
Oronte	2	1	2	5
Dario	1	1	1	3
Idaspe	1	1	1	3
Oribasio	0	1	0	1
TOTAL	12	11	9	32

(Artaserse), and Arsace, a Persian prince chosen as her future husband by
Artaxerxes when alive. The principal secondary roles are those of Barsina,
the daughter of Cyrus (Ciro), the deposed Persian king who preceded
Artaxerxes, and Oronte, the king of Scythia who, having been refused
Statira's hand by Artaxerxes, has gone to war with him and killed him in
battle. There are two subsidiary roles: Dario, a Persian captain, and Idreno,
a prince of Issedon whose father has also been slain by Oronte and who is
seeking revenge under the assumed identity of Idaspe. The *ultima parte*
belongs to Oribasio, a Persian nobleman who is Barsina's champion and
suitor; his participation in the story is fairly limited, and his main *raison
d'être* seems to be to provide a counterweight to Arsace in the early stages of
the drama.

In the original Roman production of Albinoni's setting (1726) all the
rôles were taken by male singers, as papal legislation required. When the
opera was revived for performance in Venice at Sant'Angelo in 1730, the
casting was more conventional, save that two male rôles were taken by
female singers (Maria Santina Cattanei as Idaspe and Dorotea Lolli as
Oribasio).

As the table shows, the distribution of arias, compared with that of
Zenobia, is both more finely nuanced in accordance with the character's
(and the singer's) importance and more evenly spaced. Only once does a
singer have two arias in succession (Barsina, in Act I, Scenes 5 and 6). The
arias are much less numerous than those of the earlier opera, but since they
are generally more substantial in length (all include the da capo) and are
shared out among a slightly smaller number of singers, the relative weight
of the aria component is preserved. In addition, Act III has a duet for
Barsina and Arsace (Scene 4), a terzet for Statira, Barsina, and Oronte
(Scene 13), and a concluding quintet (the conventional chorus of
celebration) for Statira, Barsina, Arsace, Oronte, and Dario. There are no
ballets, but comic intermezzi for the characters Malsazio and Fiammetta,
for which Albinoni also wrote the music, were inserted between the acts

and probably also at a suitable point towards the end of Act III (such as occurs before Scene 15). The story proceeds as follows:

Act I. Statira and Barsina are revealed in the Persian camp by Tauris, close to the border with Scythia, quarrelling over the succession following Artaxerxes' death. Barsina claims the throne since her father Cyrus was born a king; Statira claims it since her father Artaxerxes, who replaced Cyrus, ended his life as one. Oribasio and Arsace enter to declare themselves the champions of the respective pretenders. Barsina, who knows Arsace's valour, confesses in an aside that with him against her, success is unlikely. Dario enters bringing the news that the Scythians have renewed their attack. He begs the princesses to set aside their internecine differences before the common foe. Statira is willing to have the Persian Senate decide the issue, but Barsina rejects this option. They decide to settle their dispute by single combat between Arsace and Oribasio. The champions depart. Dario reproaches Statira for leaving Artaxerxes still unburied. Statira, feeling guilty for this omission and also for putting Arsace's life at risk, likewise leaves. Dario then declares his love for Barsina. Barsina responds by asking him to support her efforts to gain the throne. Honourable soldier that he is, Dario demurs. Sending him away angrily, Barsina, now alone, confesses her willingness to take extreme measures in order to become queen.

Oronte, addressing his soldiers in his pavilion, tells them that with the Persians in a state of civil war, his victory is assured. Idaspe (Idreno) arrives. Oronte is surprised to see him, believing him to be a captive of the Persians, and asks him how he has managed to escape. Idaspe, who is on a private mission to kill Oronte in revenge for his father's death, explains that he has been released in order to deliver a letter to Oronte. This letter, from Barsina, asks the Scythian king to support her claim to the throne. The request is firmly rejected by Oronte, whose love for Statira is indeed the *casus belli*. The king commands his army to attack and take Tauris.

Statira and Arsace are revealed outside the royal palace in Tauris. They declare their mutual love, and Arsace reassures the princess that he is willing to risk his life in her cause. Statira leaves as Oribasio arrives. The two champions begin to fight but are stopped by Dario, who informs them that the Scythians have broken into the city and are close at hand. Arsace immediately goes off to fight. Oribasio, whose concern is more limited, considers going to Barsina's defence. Before he can do so, Oronte arrives together with Statira, Barsina, and Idaspe. He declares that he does not wish to take the Persian notables captive. Statira is defiant in defeat, Barsina more pliable. Oronte instructs Idaspe to tell his soldiers to cut short the sack of the town. He states his intention of making himself the arbiter of the succession to the Persian throne. Statira declares her refusal to accept the decision of a foreign enemy: only the Senate can decide. Oronte secretly admires her courage and high principle. After Statira's departure Barsina tells Oronte that, unlike her rival, she wishes nothing better than to accede to his wishes. Made anxious, Oribasio and Dario interpret this insinuation as expedient flattery. Unmoved, Oronte sends Barsina away and declares his willingness to let the Senate decide the succession. Oronte having departed, Oribasio and Dario consider the situation. Both agree that the Senate is likely to favour Statira. Dario is prepared to accept the Senate's verdict, while Oribasio is unreconciled to the probable outcome out of personal loyalty to Barsin. When Oribasio leaves, Dario points out the contrast between his own principled attitude and Oribasio's opportunism.

Act II. Arsace meets Statira in a room in the palace with a secret door. The prince tells her that he is anxious to renew his contest with Oribasio but lets slip his fear of Oronte as a possible rival in love. Statira, while praising Oronte's magnanimity, denies that the Scythian has shown her any affection. Idaspe comes, bearing the message that Oronte wishes to see Statira. In order to dispel Arsace's doubts, the princess tells him to hide and overhear her conversation with Oronte. Arsace does this. Oronte's purpose is, indeed, to declare his love and ask for Statira's hand. Statira turns him down on account of her father's memory and her engagement to Arsace. Oronte is angered by her refusal and vows revenge before leaving. When Arsace emerges from hiding, Statira urges him to find a securer place within the palace in order to escape Oronte's wrath. The secret door leads to a passage that will take him to safety. After some hesitation, Arsace takes her advice and leaves along the passage. Statira, alone, prays to the gods to succour and protect her.

In another part of the palace Barsina confers with Idaspe, who tells her that Oronte has responded unfavourably to her letter. Barsina, angered, asks Idaspe to kill him for her sake. Since Idaspe, unknown to Barsina, also wishes to do this on his own account, he readily agrees. Idaspe decides to make his way to the room where Oronte is resting, kill him with a sword, and escape. As fate would have it, the secret passage along which Arsace has travelled, with Statira following close behind, ends in the vicinity of Oronte's quarters. Just as they emerge, they hear Oronte approaching in a state of high agitation. Arsace draws his sword in anticipation of having to defend himself. When Oronte appears, he is seen to be bleeding from a wound as a result of a failed assassination attempt. Arsace is naturally identified by Oronte as the obvious assailant. He rebuts the accusation by saying that, as a prince, he is incapable of such a base action; Statira supports him. Idaspe, unsurprisingly, does not come to Arsace's defence, and his search on Oronte's instructions for a possible culprit yields no new suspect. Arsace suspects that Oronte has manufactured the accusation out of jealousy. He is persuaded to give up his sword and be taken to prison. Statira is now left alone with Oronte, who summons Barsina. She arrives with her allies Dario and Oribasio. Barsina, giving a further hint of a suppressed love for Arsace, expresses her certainty of his innocence; Oribasio is more inclined to believe in his guilt, again from personal motives. Oronte, who is intent on observing all the legal niceties in order to show that a Scythian 'barbarian' can be civilized, tells the princesses that since one but not both of them will be queen, they will each have to sign Arsace's death warrant; Dario will have the duty of bringing the warrant to the prisoner, Oribasio of informing him (Oronte) of the sentence. After Oronte has left, Dario urges a delay in the signing; he wishes to visit Arsace in prison in order to learn more. Both Statira and Barsina decide to do likewise. Oribasio's attempt to persuade Barsina to sign immediately is rebuffed. This surprises and dispirits him. He would, he says, prefer a feigned expression of love to such coolness.

Act III. In his underground prison Arsace is visited by Dario, who promises to do his best for him within the law. After Dario has departed, Arsace resigns himself to dying for Statira's sake—on the assumption that she will become Oronte's queen. He is interrupted by Statira, who is horrified to hear him speak in such terms. She declares that she will willingly give up the throne if his life can thereby be spared. Barsina arrives just in time to hear this renunciation of ambition. She declares her love to Arsace, explaining that she had concealed it earlier since she did not consider herself beautiful enough to merit his affection. Barsina gives Arsace an ultimatum: if he responds to her expression of love, she will pardon him; if he spurns it, he will die. Arsace replies by proclaiming his continuing fidelity to Statira. Oronte then joins them. Statira informs him that she is unwilling to sign the warrant. Barsina, after eliciting the same response from Arsace, tells Oronte that she will indeed sign. Oronte then says that as a result, Barsina will be queen. Barsina departs in triumph. Making a final attempt to succeed in his main design, Oronte offers Arsace his life if he will release Statira to marry him and become queen of both Persians and Scythians. Arsace refuses to yield. Oronte then declares his intention to put him to death and send Statira into exile. Statira resolves to go to Barsina and pleads for Arsace's life despite his willingness to die for her sake. This leaves Arsace confused, for Statira's constancy is now becoming a weapon against his honour.

Oribasio comes to tell Barsina, in her apartments, that the Senate has acclaimed her as queen. She replies that to win her love, he will have to conceal himself and then arrest Statira when she leaves after the audience. Statira arrives to tell Barsina that if she will save Arsace's life, she (Statira) will renounce her claim to the throne. Barsina replies that, as a result of the Senate's decision, she has no need to make bargains. Oribasio enters to arrest Statira, who is led off to prison. Oronte arrives. Barsina, who wishes Statira dead but Arsace alive, proposes that her rival die in his stead, since she was the prime mover behind the assassination attempt. This Oronte (who still loves Statira) will not have. Oronte commands Arsace to be brought before him; Barsina summons Statira. When the captives arrive, both Barsina and Oronte draw swords. The princess threatens Statira's life if Arsace is harmed; the king threatens Arsace's life if Statira is harmed. Oronte demands of Statira her love if Arsace is to be spared; Barsina demands of Arsace his love if Statira is to be spared. Meanwhile, the captives remain resolutely faithful to each other. The deadlock continues as Idaspe arrives, bringing the news that, urged on by Dario, the people have risen to demand that Statira be queen, that Arsace live, and that Oronte die. In their alarm Oronte and Barsina are about to kill their respective captives when Arsace seizes Idaspe's sword and attacks Oronte, who defends himself. Seeing Arsace on the point of being overpowered, Statira pleads with Barsina to assist him and offers to give him up to her rival. Arsace is recaptured. Oronte instructs Idaspe to fetch the Senate so that it can be present at Arsace's punishment. Arsace is led off. Oronte remits Statira to Barsina's custody. In vain Statira pleads once again for Arsace's life. Left alone on the stage, Idaspe is troubled by his conscience and resolves to confess his crime.

In a hall inside the palace Oronte is visited by Oribasio, who tells him that the Senate has acceded to the will of the people and now wishes Statira to be queen. This is a great shock for Barsina, who arrives next, particularly on account of Dario's rôle. Dario justifies himself by saying that love cannot override honour. Oronte declares that he will accept the Senate's final verdict, provided that Arsace is executed. Statira is unwilling to become queen under these conditions, even though Arsace begs her to. Oronte finally loses patience and declares that Barsina instead shall be queen and that the faithful lovers shall both be punished. Barsina, however, is still unwilling to punish Arsace. Oronte finds a way out of the impasse by ordering his own soldiers to carry out the prince's execution. At this fateful juncture Idaspe confesses and reveals his true identity. Oronte thinks initially of punishing Idaspe but then decides to reward his obedience to conscience by pardoning him. In a continuing spirit of magnanimity he declares Statira queen of Persia and Arsace her consort. Statira proposes that Barsina reign beyond the Euphrates with Dario as her consort. This, too, is instantly agreed. Statira declares perpetual peace between Persia and Scythia, and a chorus celebrates the victory of love over war.

The plot of *La Statira* is typical of its time in including a highly topical element in its subject. The question of whether it was legitimate to depose a monarch on account of his conduct (as had happened to Barsina's father, Cyrus) and, further, whether this deposition should affect his descendants' right of succession was very pertinent when the libretto was first published in 1706, less than twenty years after the Glorious Revolution in England. Indeed, the War of the Spanish Succession, which was to decide whether members of the Habsburg or Bourbon dynasties would rule in Spain and in the event changed the whole political complexion of Italy, was in full swing at the time. To the society for which Zeno and Pariati wrote, the Ancient World, though of course less well understood in strictly historical terms than is the case today, was a good deal closer in ethical and, in a broad sense, cultural respects; it therefore provided a credible setting, inoffensive because of its remoteness in time (and often space), for the articulation of political and moral issues of current concern.[37]

As in *Zenobia*, the plot of this opera is organized around a double 'catastrophe': Idaspe's initial refusal to own up to the attempt on Oronte's life, which allows the blame to fall on Arsace, and then his much later confession, which undoes the damage. The idea of making a single character the instrument of both catastrophes is neat and satisfying, for if Idaspe's behaviour in the first crisis expresses well his *pathos* (his overriding desire for revenge—motivated by filial piety, which makes it a little less reprehensible), his courageous admission in the second vindicates his princely *ethos*, which is the stable, definitive element of his personality. The triumph of *ethos* over *pathos* is perhaps the dominant motif in all of baroque opera.

It must be pondered, however, whether *La Statira* and the hundreds of musical dramas constructed on the same 'reform' principles do not suffer from a surfeit of neatness. The trouble with rationality operating within fixed and narrow parameters is that the result is apt to be very uniform, so that arid 'formula writing' is encouraged. The perfectly symmetrical state of immobilization in which Oronte and Barsina find themselves when each holds a hostage whose life is protected by the threat on the other is certainly ingenious, but is inspired more by the artificiality of a geometrical pattern than by the complexity of real human relations. Marchi's *Zenobia* text,

---

[37] It is doubtful, for example, whether the thought-provoking debate on the relative merits of republican and autocratic forms of government found in Metastasio's drama *Catone in Utica* (1728) would have been allowed past the censors in most states, had it been transposed to a contemporary setting.

poetically far inferior, is a more engaging drama on this plane precisely because of its structural asymmetries, not to say vagaries. Something was lost as well as gained when the reformers took over.

In the more technical aspects of its style of production and musical setting the libretto of *La Statira* shows some movement away from the practice of *Zenobia*. While the number of sets per act remains similar $(3 + 2 + 3)$, the scenic transformations (and presumably the stage machinery needed to effect them) have gone; spectacle in its most striking form—*la meraviglia*—has been sacrificed to dramatic purity and perhaps also to the bill for the singers. All the closed numbers are in exit position, and all the aria texts save one prescribe the da capo; the exception, Arsace's aria 'A quel ben che voi perdete' in Act III, Scene 2, is a budding da capo aria cut short by Statira's entrance and immediate riposte. The da capo aria has thus reached the stage of maturity where it can be treated as a background against which divergent foreground designs can be profiled. It is interesting—and perhaps the most conspicuous instance of asymmetry in the whole libretto—that the ensemble numbers (the duet, the terzet, and the quintet-chorus) all occur in the final act. Given that such movements are inevitably few in number compared with arias, their concentration here is beneficial since it produces a feeling of climax.

When we move to consider the text of *Pimpinone*, we are confronted with an entirely different kind of dramaturgy. These particular intermezzi have been the most studied among the first generation of Venetian comic intermezzi (which is how one may describe the approximately twenty sets performed in Venice between 1706 and 1709, mainly at the San Cassiano theatre).[38] *Pimpinone* stands out not merely because it became one of the most widely diffused of the group—the list of cities in which Albinoni's setting was produced includes Munich (1722), Brussels (1728), Moscow (1731), and Ljubljana (1740), not to mention countless Italian provincial centres—but even more because it is one of the very few early works in this genre for which both a librettist and a composer can be identified reliably.[39] Pariati's name appears on none of the libretti for productions using Albinoni's music, and we would not be able to give him credit for its creation had the work not been revived in Vienna in 1717 in partnership with the opera *Sesostri*, for which Pariati also wrote the text. The composer

[38] These intermezzi are listed in Charles Troy, *The Comic Intermezzo: A Study in the History of Eighteenth-Century Italian Opera* (Ann Arbor, 1979), 36–7.

[39] As we shall see later, the attribution to Albinoni is not unproblematic, but the attributions of the same music that have been made by modern scholars to four other composers (Buini, Caldara, Gasparini, and Ziani) seem to rest on the mistaken assumption that whoever composed the music for the opera did the same for the accompanying intermezzi, regardless of whether those intermezzi were receiving their first performance.

of the music to both works was Francesco Conti. Since the music for the intermezzi was being composed again from scratch, it was logical to base the text not on its primitive form as underlaid to Albinoni's music (and subsequently modified incrementally as the performing tradition continued) but on its polished 'literary' form first published at the time of the original production in Autumn 1708.[40] The Vienna libretto, uniquely among the original literary and musical sources, claims Pariati as the author—which one can believe without difficulty, since the text has the liveliness and mastery of quickfire dialogue that, as shown also in *La Statira*, is the hallmark of his style.[41] One can hardly imagine that *Pimpinone* was the only work in its genre written by Pariati (who otherwise produced about fifty dramatic works of various kinds), but so far no certain attributions to him of any other comic intermezzi have been made.

The reason why the author of early comic intermezzi is so rarely named is presumably because the genre had low status, reflecting little credit on the dramatist, and, moreover, was more than usually liable to arouse the wrath of the censors.[42] In October 1707, just before the opening of the second season of the cultivation of comic intermezzi in Venice, the state officials responsible for the suppression of blasphemy (*Signori Esecutori sopra la Bestemmia*) decreed that intermezzo texts, which had formerly been left in manuscript state, would in future have to be printed, so that they could be scrutinized by the censors in the same way as ordinary opera libretti—and so that what was printed on the page could be compared with what was sung on the stage.[43] Ironically, the fact that intermezzo texts were now regularly printed tended slightly to raise the genre's literary standing; in 1723 we even find an two-volume anthology of intermezzi published under a pseudonym in Milan (the publisher, trying to throw the censors off the scent, has substituted 'Amsterdam' in the imprint!).[44]

The sudden emergence of comic intermezzi, which remained a popular adjunct to opera in most theatres for over fifty years (though in rivalry with ballets, which eventually supplanted them in public favour), was a direct response to the 'reform' of *opera seria*. They were a means of preserving the

[40] In the version of the libretto set by Conti the role of Vespetta is renamed 'Grilletta': the wasp turns into a cricket.

[41] Pariati's authorship is confirmed by the augmented edition of Lione Allacci's *Drammaturgia* (Venice, 1755), col. 629; the editors, who included Giovanni Cendoni, Giovanni Degli Agostini, and possibly Zeno himself, may either have derived the identification from the Vienna edition of the libretto or have had 'inside' information.

[42] After his entries for the year 1706 in his opera catalogue Bonlini allows himself a brief disquisition in which he gives his reasons for not including comic intermezzi in the catalogue and makes his low regard for the genre very evident.

[43] A copy of this decree is preserved in Venice, Museo Civico Correr, MS P.D. 348, fol. 23.

[44] Ipigeo Lucas [pseudonym] (ed.), *Raccolta copiosa d'intermedj* (2 vols., Amsterdam [Milan], 1723). *Pimpinone* appears in i. 410–21.

art of comic singing (and the livelihood of the specialized comic singer). The pair, or sometimes trio, of comic singers were given a self-contained work consisting of between two and four (normally three) extended scenes. Each scene involved all the characters and could include several closed numbers, including the obligatory duet or ensemble that formed its climax. The libretti of comic intermezzi rarely describe the requirements for scenery. This is understandable since 'spectacle' plays no part in the entertainment. Intermezzi could no doubt make do with whatever simple background, borrowed from the scenery for the opera, was available.

Most intermezzi take over the stereotypes popularized in the scenes reserved for comic characters in seventeenth-century opera, particularly Neapolitan opera. The combination of the *servetta* and the *vecchio* (or, in its reversal of the sexes, the *paggio* and the *vecchia*) was an old favourite since it contained within itself so many universal antitheses that could be exploited for comic effect: youth versus age, comeliness versus ugliness, guile versus gullibility, boldness versus cowardice. However, the fact that the intermezzi had been detached definitively from the opera proper meant that they were free to move out of a historically remote setting into a familiar time and place: Venice (or anywhere else) in the early eighteenth century. In fact, they had to break completely loose from the world of any one opera in order to become compatible with all the different operas to which they would be juxtaposed during their life in the repertory of the comic singers. This gave them the opportunity, denied to the old-style comic scenes, of including undisguised topical elements that could be treated in satirical fashion.

Pariati's *Pimpinone* is one of the first intermezzo texts—perhaps the very first—to emphasize the topical element and exploit its comic potential. As well as being a fable about a cunning servant-girl (as vespine as her name suggests) and a foolish old man, it is a satire on class and social custom. During the seventeenth century the Venetian patriciate began to go into demographic decline (partly because of self-imposed restrictions on marriage designed to keep the family patrimony undivided) and saw the citizenry begin to rival it in wealth. The new possibility of buying one's way into the patriciate, as Marco Ottoboni did, further weakened the barrier between the nobles and the rest of the population, adding to their collective unease. In this unstable context, the question of what we would today call 'life-style' assumed great importance. If nobility was no longer merely a matter of purity of blood, it could at least be expressed by custom and usage. The *parvenu*—the person aping noble manners without the title to them—became an object of hostility (if successful) or ridicule (if unsuccessful). What makes the character of Vespetta so delightfully outrageous is that, not content to marry from below into the bourgeoisie, she aspires to the noble life-style above it, ignoring the sober habits of her husband, who, foolish though he is in personal matters, provides a model of social decorum. That Vespetta belongs by origin not to the social layer immediately below the patriciate (the *cittadini*) but to the lowest social layer of all (the *popolani*) is not fortuitous: to have made the *parvenue* an authentic member of the middle class would have been dangerously near the bone. It cannot be stressed enough that, although the comic intermezzo, like the *opera buffa* of the second half of the eighteenth century, draws its characters from the middle and lower social orders, it is not yet 'middle-class' entertainment. The Venetian audience that heard *Pimpinone* in 1708 was no different from the one which came to hear *Astarto*, the host work; it was dominated in spirit, and perhaps even in numbers, by the nobility. Overtly, at least, Pariati wishes his audience most of the time to laugh at, rather than with, his comic characters.

The plot of the little work is simplicity itself. In Intermezzo I Vespetta seeks employment as a maid. She inveigles Pimpinone, a rich bachelor, into engaging her by complaining of the spendthrift ways and loose morals of her former employer (thus implying that her own conduct is exemplary on both counts). Greatly impressed by her apparent competence and honesty, Pimpinone looks forward to having her as his housekeeper. For her part, Vespetta flatters his vanity (but expresses her contempt for him in asides).

Intermezzo II begins with Vespetta giving notice. When Pimpinone asks her anxiously for the reason, she answers that she cannot tolerate his lack of economy. However, she abandons that line of argument when she learns that the jewels that Pimpinone has just bought for twenty *scudi* are intended for her. She then gives as her reason for wanting to leave the gossip that she has heard about her relationship with her master. Pimpinone sees a way out: marriage. But he first has to assure himself that his bride-to-be will not engage in immodest or idle behaviour such as sporting a low neckline, going out to supper parties, balls, and the theatre, playing cards, reading books about love, receiving visits from admirers, and going about masked. Vespetta, feigning the innocent, agrees. Pimpinone promises to provide the dowry from his own pocket. The two sing of their impending happiness (Vespetta spicing her expressions of bliss with cutting asides).

As Intermezzo III begins, Pimpinone reproaches Vespetta, now his wife, for going out without his permission. Vespetta is indignant at his thought of restraining her: she wishes to go out to visit her lady friend and considers herself perfectly entitled to do so. Pimpinone pleads with her to return early. She refuses to countenance it. When her husband tells her that she should attend more to the home, she demands the right to enjoy to the full the theatre, parties, card games, dancing, and social calls: all the things, in fact, that she has earlier foresworn. When Pimpinone asks her what she would think of him if he acted similarly, she reponds that her type of life-style is for ladies only. He then mentions the possibility of chastizing her with a stick. She threatens him with a divorce and a demand for the return of her dowry if this act is ever carried out. At this point Pimpinone caves in: he is, he admits, too much in love with her despite all to risk a rupture. In a final duet Vespetta roundly abuses him while he takes his medicine humbly (but in asides rues the day he set eyes on her and warns men to be careful).

Each intermezzo except the first contains an aria for each character and a concluding duet. The first intermezzo, however, lacks an aria for Pimpinone. This puzzling asymmetry was remedied in the performing tradition, from 1715 if not earlier, by the insertion of the aria 'Ella mi vuol confondere', whose text and music probably owed nothing to either Pariati or Albinoni. Many other additions and substitutions were made in the course of the work's transmission.[45]

Before discussing the literary text of Albinoni's two surviving serenatas, it will be useful to clarify the nature of the serenata genre, which is frequently not recognized as a distinct genre at all in modern writings on baroque vocal music. Some writers seem to regard a serenata as an oversized cantata, while others see it as a miniature opera. (The confusion is readily apparent from a consultation of work-lists for different composers in *The New Grove*, where serenatas are grouped now with operas, now with cantatas.) In reality, the genre is quite well defined, although in their purely literary form its texts go by a great variety of descriptions (*poemetto drammatico*, *applauso musicale*, *festa teatrale*, etc.) But this is no different from the genre we are pleased to call 'opera', with its *drammi per musica*, *favole pastorali*, *tragicommedie per musica*, and so on.[46]

The first recognizable serenatas appear to have been written in Italy just after the middle of the seventeenth century—in other words, shortly after the emergence of the chamber cantata as a distinct genre. The serenata is a dramatic cantata for upwards of two voices (more than six are rare) with instrumental accompaniment. Such works were often performed at night

---

[45] These are described in some detail in the preface to the modern edition (see n. 5 above), which also contains a complete 'literary' edition of the text with a parallel English version in prose.

[46] I examine the nature of the serenata genre more fully in 'The Serenata in Eighteenth-Century Venice', *[RMA] Research Chronicle*, 18 (1982), 1–50, and in 'Vivaldi's Serenatas: Long Cantatas or Short Operas?', in Lorenzo Bianconi and Giovanni Morelli (eds.), *Antonio Vivaldi: Teatro musicale, cultura e società* (Florence, 1982), 67–96.

in the open air: hence their name, which derives from Italian *sereno*, meaning a clear sky. Serenatas were privately commissioned works usually performed on significant occasions for rejoicing such as births, marriages, birthdays, name-days, anniversaries, visits by important guests, and military victories. They rarely constituted in themselves the complete celebration but formed part of a complex entertainment that might also contain, for example, a banquet, a pageant, and a fireworks display.

Serenatas have points in common with operas, oratorios, and cantatas alike. They deploy in their music the full vocal and instrumental resources of opera and are stylistically hardly distinguishable, except that, being works performed before an invited audience rather than a ticket-buying public, they are sometimes more refined or 'erudite' than the typical opera in both poetic and musical respects. Most serenatas employ no chorus—but, as we have already seen, that was not untypical of contemporary Italian opera either. Serenatas resemble oratorios of the same period by being divided into two 'parts' rather than three or more acts and having a similar length, often corresponding to just over one act of a three-act opera. The break was functional: where an oratorio might have a sermon, a serenata would commonly have an intermission for refreshments. Another feature shared by the oratorio and serenata genres is that both like to adopt an overtly moralizing tone, exemplified by the presence of allegorical characters taking the form of personifications of qualities such as glory, fame, and virtue. The link with the chamber cantata is found in the pastoral, sometimes frankly Arcadian, *mise en scène*, and the emphasis on feeling rather than action.

Serenatas are 'dramatic' only in the classical, Aristotelian sense: their characters all speak in their own voices, and there is no separate narrator in the manner of the *testo* in oratorio. Despite the length of the compositions, they are nearly always devoid of a plot. They commonly take the form of an extended debate among the several characters. These debates often resemble the proceedings of contemporary learned academies, which were in fact among the sponsors of serenatas. Despite the dissensions that emerge during the debate, the tone is always moderate, and when the time ultimately comes to devote all energies to singing the praises of the person or persons who are the subject of the serenata, pure consensus reigns. A serenata text, however tangential its initial connection with the subject may be, always homes in on it well before the end. Two particular topoi may be identified. The first we may call the 'dispute' (the French scholar Jacques Joly has coined for this type the expressive phrase 'joûte oratoire'—oratorical tourney), the second the 'quest'. In the 'dispute' opposing viewpoints are reconciled or synthesized by reference to the subject of the serenata.[47] In the 'quest' the characters are led by stages towards a person who is finally identified as the subject.[48]

The manner in which serenatas were performed reflected the often improvised nature of the indoor or outdoor auditorium and the great haste with which preparations usually had to be made. The singers read from music, sometimes in a seated position. They might wear a form of costume, but this was not a normal requirement. Scenery was often limited to a simple scenic background that remained unchanged for the duration of the performance.

The more conventional of Albinoni's two serenatas, *Il nome glorioso in terra, santificato in cielo*, was written in 1724 as part of the annual *festa* held by the Imperial ambassador to Venice, Johann Baptist von Colloredo-Wallsee, in celebration of the name-day (4 November) of his master Charles VI. The author of the text was Vincenzo Cassani, a Venetian man of letters of whose life virtually nothing is known. Between 1711 and 1736 Cassani wrote the libretti of six operas produced in Venice; Albinoni provided the music for three of them (*Il tiranno eroe*, 1711; *Cleomene*, 1718; *L'incostanza schernita*, 1727).[49] Cassani was equally active as a purveyor of serenata texts; six are known to have been produced by him during the period 1705–27.[50] *Il nome glorioso in terra, santificato in cielo* was preceded earlier in the year by *I tre voti* (music by Antonio Pollarolo), a serenata commissioned by the same ambassador for the birthday of Empress Elisabeth Christine.

Il nome glorioso in terra, santificato in cielo is for three voices. These are cast in the roles of two nymphs—Climene (soprano) and Cidippe (contralto)—and a shepherd, Florigello (tenor). The first part of the serenata, which contains five closed numbers (four solo arias and a concluding terzet), is modelled on the 'quest' formula. Florigello realizes from the magnificence of the dawn that the day is a very special one; the nymphs rescue him from his rustic ignorance by identifying the person whom the heavens are honouring (Charles VI) and the saint (St Charles Borromeo) to whom the day is dedicated.

---

[47] Serenatas with the words 'gara' or 'contesa' (both meaning 'contest') in their title are the most easily identified representatives of this type, to which Girolamo Baruffaldi's text for Albinoni's lost serenata *Il concilio de' pianeti* (Venice, 1729) also belongs.

[48] Domenico Lalli's text for Giovanni Porta's serenata *Il ritratto dell'eroe* (Venice, 1726) in honour of Cardinal Ottoboni is a classic example of this type; another is Lalli's *La Sena festeggiante*, set by Vivaldi around the same time.

[49] Cassani's last known opera libretto, *Le nozze di Psiche*, was set to music by Santo Giambattista Serini for a performance in Venice in an unknown location in 1736; its three acts are adapted from an undated serenata libretto entitled simply *Psiche* which Benedetto Marcello set. A comparison of the two versions shows very clearly the essential differences between the opera and serenata genres.

[50] The six texts are listed as nos. 40, 67, 68, 73, 75, and 181 in the catalogue of works contained in my article 'The Serenata in Eighteenth-Century Venice' (see n. 46).

In the second part the three make their own contribution to the celebration by outlining the course of political and military events during Charles's reign up to that point. The most favourable gloss is naturally put on each event mentioned, and the major set-backs (such as the renunciation of Charles's claim on the Spanish throne) are simply omitted. The account begins with the Archduke Charles's return from Spain in 1711 to become emperor in succession to his elder brother Leopold I. The recovery by Austria of its 'ancient patrimony' (principally, the former Spanish territories in Italy), as ratified by the treaties of Utrecht, Rastatt, and Baden, is proudly related. Cassani next describes in idyllic terms the short period of peace following the end of the War of the Spanish Succession. This is soon over, however, for the 'Dragon of Pontus' (the Ottoman Empire) goes to war with Venice (the 'famous Lion'); Cassani's metaphors are typical of the highly stylized form of language required by Arcadian convention. Austria intervenes selflessly on Venice's side. Cassani mentions victories on the battlefield by Prince Eugene, commander of the Imperial forces, and his capture of the cities of Temesvár and Belgrade. The war ends on favourable terms to the Christian powers (through the Treaty of Passarowitz, 1718): Austria gains Hungary and some Balkan territories, while Venice strengthens her frontier in Dalmatia—her loss of the Peloponnese is of course not mentioned. (The flattering references to Venice are an obvious attempt to gratify those members of the audience who were Venetian subjects and, more generally, a way of calling attention to the good state of relations between the Empire and Venice obtaining at the time.) Cassani then recalls with bitterness the 'stab in the back' of the Spanish Bourbons, who launched an invasion of Italy in order to regain some of their lost territories while the war with the Turks was still in progress. The settlement of this new conflict through the Treaty of the Hague (1720) brought Austria Sicily, which Cassani proudly mentions (and the cession to Savoy of Sardinia, which he prudently does not). This brings the account up to date, leaving time for a final outburst of praise for the saint and the emperor that ends with another terzet. The second part is slightly longer than the first, containing five arias.

In serenatas it is common for the roles to be absolutely equal in importance. When this is the case, arias are often distributed in a series of 'rounds', each such round containing one aria for each singer (naturally, the order in which the singers make their contribution varies from round to round). *Il nome glorioso in terra, santificato in cielo* is less regular in this respect, for Climene has four arias, Cidippe three, and Florigello only two. The disparity was doubtless not accidental and conformed to the singers' expectations. However, the arias exhibit one feature that is very typical of serenatas: five out of nine of them (including all four in Part I) are allotted to a character who has not sung the passage of recitative immediately preceding. This procedure would be rather unusual in an opera, where an aria is, so to speak, a florid continuation of recitative. The reason why it is so common in serenatas is that the characters, however many debating points they score over one another, are entirely of one mind where praise of the subject is concerned; when the sentiment expressed in recitative by one character is clinched in an aria sung by another, the universal quality of that praise is symbolized.

Il nascimento de l'Aurora, like *I tre voti*, celebrates Elisabeth Christine's birthday (28 August). The text refers to her presence in Spain, which narrows down the date of the composition to the period between her arrival in Barcelona (1 August 1708) and her departure for Vienna (19 March 1713). It is unlikely that a serenata would have been commissioned in 1708, when the archduchess would have had little time to consolidate her presence in Spain in advance of her birthday, and since there is no mention of her husband's new status as emperor, the year 1712 can be all but excluded. This leaves a choice of 1709, 1710, and 1711.

No printed libretto is extant. The score identifies neither the librettist nor the circumstances of performance; it does, however, describe the work as a 'festa pastorale', an unusual term hinting at the large scale of the composition (the term 'festa' was also used for full-scale operas). There are no indications where the performance took place. Spain itself can be ruled out, for the text makes it clear that the home of the archduchess lies to the west. Since pressure of time meant that the music for serenatas was usually commissioned from a local composer, one would imagine that the performance took place in Venice at the residence of the Imperial ambassador who preceded Colloredo-Wallsee, Prince Filippo Ercolani. But a performance in another Italian city such as Milan or Rome is a distinct possibility.

The text of *Il nascimento de l'Aurora* is quite extraordinarily long for a serenata, being equivalent to two acts of an opera.[51] Remarkably, there is no division into two parts; nor is there any obvious point at which such a division could conveniently be made. It contains twenty-six closed numbers, of which the first, third, and last are 'cori' for the quintet of singers (no. 3 is in fact a restatement of no. 1 a tone lower); the rest are solo arias.

The five characters are taken from classical mythology. They comprise the river-god Peneius (Peneo), the god Apollo, the wood-nymph Daphne,

[51] In a recording by Claudio Scimone with I Solisti Veneti a slightly abridged version of the work, which retains all the arias but removes many passages of recitative, lasts almost 2 hours.

Character		round 1		round 2	round 3	round 4	round 5
Peneo	2		8			17	22
Daphne		4		9	13	18	23
Flora		6		10	14	19	24
Apollo		5		11	15	20	25
Zeffiro		7		12	16	21	

the wind-god Zephyr (Zeffiro), and the goddess Flora. The place is Tempe, a valley in northern Thessaly through which the Peneius flows.

The text assumes a knowledge of the story of Apollo and Daphne related in the first book of Ovid's *Metamorphoses*. Cupid has made Daphne (who is Peneius's daughter) averse to love by wounding her with a lead-tipped arrow. Apollo, however, has been wounded by Cupid with a gold-tipped arrow, which makes him amorous. He pursues Daphne, who flees from him. When Daphne is on the point of being caught, she prays to her father to turn her into a tree. Her wish is granted, and she becomes a laurel. In consolation, Apollo makes a laurel wreath for himself from her leaves.

The story of Zephyr and Flora is related in Ovid's *Fasti*. Flora, the goddess who exhales flowers, is the former earth-nymph Chloris, whom the wind-god, her lover, turned into her new form. Zephyr and Flora thus stand for chaste love, Apollo for unchaste love, and Daphne for the repudiation of love. These divergent attitudes are brought out very amusingly at many points in the text.

The serenata divides into five episodes, each containing a 'round' of arias for Daphne, Flora, Apollo, and Zephyr. Peneius stands somewhat apart from his companions: using a device very common in serenatas, the librettist makes him a kind of 'chairman' whose purpose is to keep order and sum up at intervals.[52] His four arias (nos. 2, 8, 17, and 22) are all placed at the start of an episode or between episodes. The only irregularity occurs between the second and third rounds, where he has no aria.[53] Daphne is always the first singer of an aria in a round; then come Flora and Apollo (in that order, except in the first round, where Apollo leads); Zephyr's arias come last (except in the fifth round, where no aria for him is included). This pattern, shown in the table, is much more rigid at the level of the individual round than one is accustomed to find in a serenata; perhaps the poet's underlying motive was to space out the arias for each character as evenly as

[52] A perfect example of such a 'chairman' is the character Apollo in Antonio Grossatesta's *L'unione della Pace e di Marte* (music by Vivaldi), performed outside the residence of the French ambassador to Venice on 14 Aug. 1727.

[53] Since the sole extant source for the text is found in the musical score, one cannot exclude the possibility that in its original, literary form the serenata contained one or more arias that Albinoni either did not set or set but later excised.

possible in order to conserve the singer's stamina—a wise precaution in such a long work.

The topics treated in the five episodes are as follows. The first begins with a summons to all the inhabitants of Tempe to celebrate the birthday of the dawn-goddess Aurora. Daphne, Apollo, Flora, and Zephyr then debate the value of love, chaste or otherwise. In the next episode each character promises to make an offering to Aurora: Daphne will offer a lily (symbol of purity), Flora a rose (symbol of majesty), Apollo a song on his lyre, and Zephyr some sweet, cooling breezes.

The third episode is a true *jeu d'esprit*, a game played by the same four. Each chooses the name of a flower. The rest of the instructions are as given by Daphne:

Ogni di voi ben si ricordi il fiore	Each of you must remember the flower
che scelto fu; quand'io dirò, 'Che manca	you chose; when I say: 'What does
al gelsomin, degli altri fiori un fregio?'	the jasmine lack that adorns another flower?'
allor il fior chiamato	then the named flower
così dica di sé verso d'un altro.	has to compare itself with another.
Chi tosto non risponde o mal risponde,	Whoever fails to reply quickly or replies badly,
o'l nome obblia de' fiori o dà il nome	or forgets the name of his flower, or gives the name
d'un fior che non fu scelto,	of a flower that was not picked,
ei tosto de l'Aurora	will straightaway have
canti le lodi. Io già incomincio: attenti!	to sing Aurora's praises. I'll start: ready!
'Sarebbe pur più bello il gelsomino,	'The jasmine would be prettier
se avesse il bel pallor de la viola'.	if it had the lovely pallor of the violet'.

The errors, and the resultant arias, soon arrive. Daphne forgets that she is the jasmine; Flora does not respond to the mention of the rose; Apollo, his thoughts distracted by an unexpected reference by Daphne to love, fails to identify the violet as his flower; Zephyr brings up for comparison the amaranth, forgetting that it is not one of the chosen flowers.

From the delightful banter of this episode Peneius steers the serenata round to its true destination. By coincidence, just as Aurora in the east is celebrating her birthday, so too Elisa (Elisabeth) in the west, her equal in everything, is celebrating hers. The other characters then express in turn their birthday wishes for Elisa, including (characteristically for the age) the

wish that she become pregnant and provide her husband with an heir. In
the final episode Daphne turns herself into a laurel. This time her purpose is
not to escape Apollo's attentions but to adorn the brows of Aurora and
Elisa. Flora and even Apollo applaud this act of self-sacrifice, and the
serenata ends with general rejoicing.

The Music

Zenobia, regina de' Palmireni is illustrative equally of Albinoni's operatic
style in its earliest phase and of the general state of Venetian opera in the last
decade of the seventeenth century. At that time an orchestra in the modern
sense—a large instrumental ensemble with doubled string parts in all
registers—was still relatively new to the Italian opera house; one is
therefore not surprised to find that Albinoni handles it both sparingly and
cautiously.[54] To place *Zenobia* in context one must also bear in mind that
although the da capo aria was firmly established as the dominant aria form,
it tended to retain the terse expression of the older aria forms (such as
strophic form) that it had replaced; in comparison with the da capo aria of
the high baroque, that of the 1690s appears condensed and short-winded.
The brevity and frequency of the arias cause the musical interest to be
diffused widely throughout the work rather than concentrated at a few
selected climactic points.

The surviving score of *Zenobia* in the Library of Congress presents a
form of text that differs in important respects from that transmitted by the
printed libretto. There are many slight but significant textual variants, in
addition to a much larger number of trivial differences of a purely
orthographic nature. The more conspicuous differences probably go back
to Marchi himself and represent the 'primitive' form of the text as supplied
in manuscript to the composer.

When compared with the libretto, the score, which to the eye contains
very few corrections and alterations, reveals a great number of cuts as well
as one addition. Seeing that the score is a secondary copy rather than the
composer's original draft, it is likely that many of these alterations had not
been made when the opera opened but were introduced in the course of the
production. Act I loses, predictably, the virgulated aria 'Vengan pur falangi
cento' (Ormonte, Scene 15).[55] Remarkably, Albinoni turns the two *arie a
due*—'Se tu m'ami, mio diletto' (Lidio and Filidea, Scene 6) and 'Crudel,

---

[54] On the constitution of the instrumental ensemble in Italian opera houses during the 17th century
see Neal Zaslaw, 'When is an Orchestra not an Orchestra?', *Early Music*, 16 (1988), 483–90.

[55] The scene numbers to which reference is made are those of the libretto, from which the score often
deviates.

crudel, crudel' (Zenobia and Silvio, Scene 20)—into solo arias for Filidea and Zenobia respectively by omitting one stanza in each case.[56] Contrary to the poet's obvious expectation that the stanzas would be set in through-composed fashion, Albinoni opts for da capo form. It is impossible to know why the participation of two characters in these arias was rejected; the reason was presumably a practical one. The music for the ballet of freed Palmyran captives in Scene 18 is not included in the score. This is to be expected since the responsibility for the composition of such insertions normally lay with the ballet-master, not with the composer of the opera.

A major cut was made towards the end of Act II; it entails the loss of Aurelian's aria 'Care, vaghe mie pupille' closing Scene 19, the whole of Scene 20, and all of Scene 21 except Zenobia's final aria 'Ha un'alma d'eroe'. The excised lines mainly comprise the semi-farcical episode in which Aurelian instructs the reluctant Liso to make advances to Zenobia on his behalf. It seems likely that the cut was made as a result of objections on the grounds of taste or decency. The result is to deprive the opera of its only substantial opportunity for comic acting. It is certain that the cut was made after Albinoni had completed the setting, for the final cadence of the recitative preceding the cut, which is in F major, does not match the key of Zenobia's aria, which is A major. In compensation, Aurelian receives an extra aria, 'Bella, ti baccerò' (Scene 2). As before, the ballet music, which includes an aria for La Costanza, is omitted.

In Act III cuts have been applied with such severity that only eight arias out of an original eighteen survive; from Scene 13 (when Aurelian overhears Ormonte's proposal to Zenobia that she assassinate him) until Scene 20 (the dénouement) very little is retained, and there are further excisions of arias in Scenes 12 and 22. The main loss to the drama is Filidea's unsuccessful wooing of Lidio, which ironically mirrors his unsuccessful wooing of her earlier. This time, the reason for the cuts seems to have been a compelling wish to shorten the opera very considerably by any means possible.

Of the forty surviving arias sixteen (two-fifths) are set by Albinoni as simple continuo arias. In style and form they are hardly distinguishable from the 'lighter' arias in his cantatas. They include nine movements without an introductory ritornello, four employing the *Devise*, four with ostinato elements in the bass, and two with elements of binary form in the A section. Particularly noteworthy is his setting of the short aria for Aurelian opening Act II, Scene 13. Marchi's lines open as follows.

---

[56] Rather surprisingly, Filidea appropriates the stanza that was originally intended to be sung by her lover.

AUR. Sì, spero di goder   Yes, I hope to enjoy
    a tuo dispetto, Amor,   despite your efforts, Love,
    con prospera fortuna.   with prosperous fortune.
ORM. Cesare.   Caesar.
FIL. Augusto.   Augustus.
AUR. Giunge l'importuno.   The importunate one arrives.

The pattern of indentation (reproduced from the libretto) shows that Marchi had in mind a complete through-composed aria for Aurelian. In order to add realism to the interruption, however, Albinoni sets the three lines as a truncated da capo aria. Lines 1 and 2 provide the text for a highly condensed A section, while line 3 is used for the aborted opening of the B section. This initiative illustrates how a little freedom of manœuvre remained available to the composer within the generally constraining parameters laid down by the poet. Very soon, of course, the 'truncated' da capo aria became part of the librettist's stock-in-trade as well; La Statira, as we saw, contains an example.

In addition, there are seven continuo arias preceded or followed by a ritornello for orchestral strings, which include separate alto and tenor violas (as in nearly all Albinoni's instrumental music up to Op 5). The four that have the ritornello written out before the aria may have required it to be restated at the end as well, thus forming a kind of frame around the movement.[57] It is interesting to see that in three cases the aria has a separate continuo ritornello following the orchestral one. In this context the orchestral ritornello acquires the character more of a self-contained interlude than an integral part of a larger movement.

The remaining seventeen arias are orchestrally accompanied, having ritornelli not only at both ends of the A section but also in the middle (separating the two full statements of the A text). The extent to which the orchestral instruments remain active during the vocal passages varies greatly—many arias dispense with their use altogether. Paramount in the composer's mind is the desire to avoid 'swamping' the voice. If middle parts are retained, they play in a light, detached style, as in a concerto accompaniment. There is no thought of strengthening the vocal line by doubling it instrumentally. All these features are very normal in operas of the time.

The two most common orchestra textures are 'a 5' (employing the full string ensemble) and 'a 4' (the same, with the violins united). A few arias have the violins alternately united and divided. Two arias, both for Aurelian in an appropriately martial mood, add a trumpet to the strings,

---

[57] In similar arias in Vinaccesi's oratorio Susanna (also 1694) the da capo indication is followed by an instruction to repeat the orchestral ritornello at the close.

recalling the instrumentation of the introductory Sinfonia (Si 1). Perhaps the most enterprising piece of scoring occurs in Filidea's aria of revenge 'Saprò, barbaro, vendicarmi' (Act I, Scene 8), in which the violas are suppressed and the violins remain in unison during the ritornelli (see Ex. 39). The lightening of the texture that results allows Albinoni to write with uninhibited zest for the violins, employing repeated notes in time-honoured fashion to suggest fury and passion.

It is not possible to identify with certainty Albinoni's criteria for deciding what kind of accompaniment to use for a given aria. On the whole, however, it appears that an orchestral accompaniment is preferred for the representation of strong or less common *affetti* (defiance, anger, courage), whereas conventional expressions of tenderness or amorous delight generally call for plain continuo.

The quality of Albinoni's arias in *Zenobia* is uneven. Many of the continuo arias are trite and inconsequential, though more than a few display the qualities of elegance and melodic shapeliness encountered in his similarly scored cantatas. Of the orchestrally accompanied arias the most memorable are that for Filidea singled out above and Zenobia's magnificently defiant 'Ha un'alma d'eroe' concluding Act II. Engaging, too, are the many arias written in a simple, popular style and often evocative of the dance (Filidea's 'Se tu m'ami, mio diletto', from Act I, Scene 6, is in an unmistakable gavotte rhythm). At times Albinoni puts his counterpoint on display: the orchestral ritornello preceding Silvio's 'S'armi il ciel, s'armi il terra' (Act I, Scene 12) takes the form of a brief fugato. In general, the music of *Zenobia* bears out the comment about Venetian opera made by the contemporary Bolognese commentator Francesco Maria Zambeccari, who blamed the failure of Alessandro Scarlatti's opera *Mitridate Eupatore* at San Giovanni Grisostomo in 1707 on the Venetian predilection for 'roba allegra e saltarelli' (lively stuff and saltarellos).[58] *Zenobia* does, however, have one impressive aria in slow tempo: the heroine's prayer 'Sommi dèi, ch'in ciel regnate' (Act II, Scene 6). Unfortunately, the end of the A section of this aria is missing from the Washington score. From the dimensions of the aria as a whole one would guess that the missing portion occupied two pages. Since the quiring is entirely regular (all the gatherings comprise four leaves) and the catchwords at the end of each gathering always correspond to the first word of text in the next gathering, it is clear that no part of the manuscript has been lost. The most likely explanation for the omission is that the copyist inadvertently turned over two pages of his exemplar at once.[59]

---

[58] Bologna, Biblioteca Universitaria, It. 201 (92), Busta IV, n. 8, letter 7 (16 Apr. 1709).

[59] Marcello (*Il teatro alla moda*, p. 63) refers to this hazard when he writes that copyists 'lascieranno facciate intere' (will skip entire openings).

Ex. 39

Albinoni's approach to the expression of the words is perhaps over-restrained. Some *affetti* elude him altogether: the aria in which Ormonte feigns madness ('Mirate, mirate') sounds merely cheerful, and the one in which Zenobia bids farewell forever (as she believes) to Silvio, 'Ti lascio, e resta in pace', conveys no hint of poignancy. In this, his first opera, Albinoni is still thinking too often in abstract, 'instrumental' terms.

His lack of experience in writing operas comes out most strongly in the recitative, however. Operatic recitative has to achieve vitality and create a sense of direction in a different way from cantata recitative. The pace at which it moves precludes lingering over details in the melodic line, and the need for all the sung parts to be committed to memory encourages the composer to build up the melodic line from familiar modules rather than invent new turns of phrase. The main responsibility for giving coherence to the music thus falls to the continuo, which, by its choice of chord progressions, its rate of harmonic change, and its pattern of modulation, is able to mirror even small changes in the emotional climate of the drama.

Later in his career Albinoni will master this skill. But in *Zenobia* the recitative is organized haphazardly in melodic, harmonic, and tonal respects, revealing an unfortunate lack of control. In addition, the composer betrays a lack of expertise (or is it an excess of nonchalance?) in his word-setting, in which many stresses are misplaced and many caesuras go unrespected.

Between *Zenobia* and *La Statira* no score of a complete Albinoni opera survives. Nevertheless, the three acts Albinoni contributed to *Engelberta* (1709) show clearly the path he and his colleagues working for the Venetian stage were travelling in the intervening years.

The most striking change concerns the instrumentation of the arias, all eighteen of which (in Acts I–III) feature the da capo. Only seven have a plain continuo accompaniment, and it is significant that six of them bring in the strings for an initial or concluding ritornello. The remaining eleven are orchestrally accompanied. They differ from their counterparts in *Zenobia* by employing the orchestral strings much more extensively during vocal passages. However, some pruning of the texture generally takes place at these points: the bass instruments or the viola (now a single part) may drop out, and the violin parts are occasionally given to solo instruments. Most orchestrally accompanied arias now have two alternating 'modes' of instrumental scoring—the heavier for the ritornelli, the lighter for the vocal sections. In one aria ('Selvagge amenità' from Act I, Scene 2) Albinoni allows the voice to be doubled throughout by a violin part. This is an early instance of a practice that was to become almost universal in his later operatic scores. It functions as a kind of safety device, ensuring that the vocal line will stand out regardless of the activity of the remaining instruments.

A third of the arias still retain the *Devise*. This represents a slightly smaller proportion than in *Zenobia*. From now on, it will become less common in Albinoni's operatic arias; by the 1720s it is almost extinct.

The eclipse of the *Devise* is confirmed by *La Statira*, where it makes only one appearance in thirty-two solo arias.[60] The arias in this score confirm the growing importance of the orchestra. Opening ritornelli are now of a length to justify cutting when they return. It is interesting to observe that Albinoni is entirely conventional in his method of applying cuts to aria ritornelli—usually by removing the front portion—since in his concertos it is this segment (the motto) that invariably survives at the expense of the following ones. It is now common for the orchestra to be given not only full ritornelli but also short interludes while the voice pauses; the most common points for such insertions are near the end of the second vocal period of the A section (after the first cadence in the tonic) and mid-way through the B section.

In the accompaniment of the arias high voices (soprano and alto) are doubled routinely by whichever violin part is more suitable. When the voice is singing, violas either drop out or double the bass. The bass line itself is usually thinned by eliminating one or two of its components (harpsichord, cello, double-bass), a practice we have already noted in Albinoni's later concertos. For example, Statira's aria 'Sento Amor che sospirando' (Act III, Scene 7) strips the bass down to a cello and a double-bass playing pizzicato. The occasional use of wind instruments lends some variety to the scoring. In Arsace's aria 'Vien con nuova orribil guerra' (Act III, Scene 8) the full complement of two trumpets and two oboes joins the strings for the first and only time since the sinfonia; three further arias call for a pair of oboes, and one employs a single trumpet. Oribasio's aria 'Almen vorrei che'l labbro', which closes Act II, has parts for two horns, which were possibly played by the trumpeters.

A few arias include near the end of the A section a fermata marking the point where the singer is expected to insert a cadenza; some of these occur over a six–four chord in the manner of the 'classical' cadenza. The musical style shows the first stirrings of a *galant* sensibility: appoggiaturas are frequent, and triplet semiquavers make a few appearances.

Albinoni's ability to hit the right *affetto* is now consolidated. The depiction of Arsace's hesitation at the thought of leaving Statira in the aria

---

[60] In the case of *La Statira* the text underlaid to Albinoni's music corresponds very accurately to the text printed in the libretto (whose aria texts differ considerably, however, from those of the original libretto of 1706).

'Parto . . . oh Dio! Partir non so' (Act II, Scene 4) is achieved in masterly
fashion by the use of rests. Diminished sevenths are employed to good
effect in order to suggest horror in Statira's aria 'Non creder, no, che
sia | D'orrore all'alma mia' (Act III, Scene 10). Statira is in fact telling
Barsina that her threat to imprison her does not hold any terrors (horrors).
But faced with a choice between illustrating the individual word and
bringing out the more complex—here, actually contradictory—sense of
the statement to which it belongs, Albinoni opts, as most of his Italian
contemporaries would have done, for the easier solution. In certain arias
Albinoni puts his contrapuntal expertise to good use. The most
conspicuous show of counterpoint occurs, however, in the terzet from Act
III, Scene 13. Whereas the parts for Barsina and Oronte move much of the
time in parallel intervals, symbolical of their 'ganging up' against Statira,
that of the heroine herself remains defiantly aloof in contrapuntal
opposition to the other two.

The most characteristically 'Albinonian' music, now as before, is
represented by the many arias in a tender, lyrical vein. Their expression
may be rather neutral in character, but the sheer beauty of the melody and
the logic with which it unfolds can offer ample compensation. A
particularly fine example of this type of aria is Statira's 'Pensa che sei | Il sol
degl'occhi miei' from Act I, Scene 10. It is in fact a contrafactum,
transposed down a tone, of the aria 'Troppo mi sei | Sole degl'occhi miei'
(Niceta, Act I, Scene 5) in Albinoni's *I veri amici* (Munich, 1722). The first
vocal period is shown in Ex. 40.

During the period of more than thirty years since *Zenobia* Albinoni's
handling of recitative has achieved competence and occasionally rises
above that level. Zeno's—or should one say Pariati's?—brilliant opening
scene for Statira and Barsina which uses lively dialogue in stichomythia in
order to carry out the task of a dramatic exposition receives a fitting
response from the composer. Lines 10–13 are instructive. The text runs:

BAR. Ei nacque re,	He was born a king.
STA. Ma da tiranno è morto.	But he died a tyrant.
BAR. Re non nacque Artaserse.	Artaxerxes was not born a king.
STA. Chi re muore è più re di chi vi nasce.	He who dies a king is more so than he who is born one.

Albinoni organizes the bass in two stepwise ascending phrases, each
corresponding to a statement by Barsina and the riposte to it by Statira. The
close connection between the two couplets, which express exactly the same
argument from different angles, is emphasized by the substitution of the
note *b* for the expected *d* after 'morto'; the resulting 'interrupted' cadence

Ex. 40

both assists continuity and preserves the linear style of movement of the bass. The second rising phrase reaches a higher note ($c\sharp'$) than the first (b); this conveys the rising tension of the exchanges between the two princesses and matches the triumphant sweep of Statira's last phrase up to $f\sharp''$, a third higher than her corresponding earlier phrase. Another telling stroke in the vocal line is the quaver rest after 'muore', which does not derive from any caesura in the poetry. In Ex. 41 Albinoni is realistically imitating a person who begins a statement confidently but then has to pause in order to formulate a satisfactory conclusion to it.

Ex. 41

The numerous arias from other operas surviving singly or in groups add little to what we have learnt from the complete scores. *I veri amici* is worth singling out, however, since it contains two arias with notable obbligato parts. Amasi's 'Cerco l'oggetto del mio furor' (Act II, Scene 13) has an elaborate solo line for oboe, in dialogue with the tenor voice, that may have been performed at the celebrated performance in Munich by a member of Maximilian Emanuel's orchestra to whom a solo part in the Op. 9 concertos (dedicated to the elector) had been entrusted only a few months earlier. The cellist who took the equally demanding obbligato part in Tilame's 'Avrò in petto un doppio cor' (Act III, Scene 5) was presumably the one much praised by Mattheson's correspondent from Regensburg.[61]

The slightly problematic nature of the attribution to Albinoni of the original (and in its day most widely performed) setting of the comic intermezzi *Pimpinone* was mentioned earlier. Strange to say, none of the

---

[61] See Chapter 1 n. 10.

literary or musical sources confirms his authorship.[62] The presumption in modern reference works that Albinoni wrote the music rests on a generalization (which is probably true) that whoever composed the music of the host work also composed that of the accompanying intermezzi— assuming, of course, that both were new. Naturally, a generalization of this kind cannot be assumed valid a priori for individual cases. In the end, one has to make the attribution to Albinoni principally on grounds of style, whatever one's misgivings about the reliability and methodological acceptability of this criterion.

When we consider the music of *Pimpinone*, we have to bear in mind that the comic intermezzo was at that time a newly forged genre still in the process of defining its essential stylistic identity. In Venice, where the specialization in, and segregation of, the comic element in opera was less well developed than in Naples (which can be regarded as the 'capital' of the comic style in Italian opera around the turn of the century), there was initially a tendency to regard the style of a comic intermezzo as an adaptation of the heroic style rather than its negation. This is the perspective from which to view the following, rather harsh, comments on the early Venetian intermezzo made by Gordana Lazarevich:

The text underlay in the intermezzi of Gasparini and the early 18th-century Venetian composers . . . was not so successful a union of text and music as in the Neapolitan intermezzo. The Venetian form seldom created a true buffo line in which the rhythms and shape of the melodic motives are guided by the inflections of the words . . . Most of the arias in the Venetian intermezzo were merely set in dance-like patterns which created a lighter effect. Consequently, musical characterization was not so successful in the Venetian as it was in the Neapolitan intermezzo. The duets were no more than *arie a due*. . . . The arias that were not in dance rhythm were frequently square cut and devoid of grace.[63]

The description of the arias in the Venetian intermezzo as 'square cut' certainly applies to *Pimpinone*. Both the vocal periods and the ritornelli tend to be shorter than their counterparts in *opera seria*, and antecedents and consequents are often of equal length, producing a naïve symmetry. It is also true that the musical inflections are rather abstractly conceived and do not possess an intimate relationship with either the rhythm or the meaning

[62] A set of parts for the first aria of Intermezzo I ('Chi mi vuol? Son cameriera') in the Mecklenburgische Landesbibiliothek, Schwerin (Hs. 4721) identifies it as 'dell' opera Sign. Albinoni'. However, given the clear distinction in 18th-century minds between the genres 'opera' and 'intermezzo', it is quite possible that the description applies to the opera with which *Pimpinone* was performed rather than to the intermezzi themselves.

[63] Gordana Lazarevich, 'The Role of the Neapolitan Intermezzo in the Evolution of Eighteenth-Century Musical Style: Literary, Symphonic and Dramatic Aspects 1685–1735', dissertation (Columbia University, 1970), 353.

of the text. Now and again, however, Albinoni's musical characterization hits the mark. The opening aria for Vespetta, 'Chi mi vuol? Son cameriera', creates a delightfully waspish effect with its jagged rhythms and the playful darting in and out of the violin parts.

The most impressive numbers in Albinoni's little work are the three duets. Most definitely, these are not *arie a due* but genuine duets with contrapuntal interest and some effective differentiation of the two characters. Albinoni's penchant for non-imitative counterpoint has been mentioned earlier. It certainly stands him in good stead in these duets, where thematically unrelated, overlapping phrases for the two characters give an accurate impression of the disorderliness of real conversation—and especially of furious argument, as in the final duet (music shown in Ex. 42):

VES.	Se mai più . . .		If ever again . . .	
PIM.		(Sia maledetto . . .)		(Cursed be . . .)
VES.	Che! Che dici?		What! What are you saying?	
PIM.		Niente, niente.	Nothing, nothing,	
VES.	Se mai più noi la vedremo, romperemo il matrimonio.		If ever again we quarrel like this, that will be the end of our marriage.	
PIM.	(Maledetto quando mai m'intricai con tal demonio.)		(Cursed be the day when I got involved with such a devil.)	

In its simple way, this duet looks forward to the mature *buffo* style of the later part of the century exemplified by Mozart's operas on libretti by Lorenzo Da Ponte. Its 'parlando' style of word-setting, in which expansion is achieved by the immediate repetition of words and phrases rather than the use of melismas, characterizes all the arias and duets to a high degree.

The variable scoring of the accompaniment broadly follows the pattern of the nearly contemporary *Engelberta*, except that the *Devise* is totally absent. Its absence is logical, given that this is a resource used to lengthen an aria and increase the sense of formality—both effects being inappropriate in a comic genre.

The two serenatas differ noticeably from each other in their musical approach. Whereas *Il nome glorioso in terra, santificato in cielo* is operatic through and through, *Il nascimento de l'Aurora* modifies the operatic character by a generous infusion of the kind of counterpoint found in instrumental works such as the Op. 5 concertos. The first movement of its sinfonia is a lengthy four-part fugue, the only fugal first movement found anywhere in Albinoni's music. Imitation informs a number of the arias, notably Daphne's 'Perché un giglio è nel candore' and later her 'Questa fronda'; the second aria, an Adagio movement in F minor, is perhaps the most beautiful example of Albinoni's elegiac vein in all his music.

Ex. 42

The quintets (i.e. choruses), though largely homophonic, are skilfully written pieces in da capo form. On its first hearing, 'Goda Tempe e su l'amena' (which is repeated after one intervening aria) functions as a substitute for the expected final movement to the sinfonia, which has only two movements. The notion of dovetailing the overture and the main body of the work in this manner was certainly not Albinoni's own discovery, but it can at least be claimed to illustrate the exceptional degree of care and thought that went into the composition of this work.

The incidence of arias accompanied only by continuo with and without introductory orchestral ritornelli, of the employment of the *Devise*, and of the doubling of the voice by a violin remains close to the norm seen in *Engelberta*. However, two features point to the future: the doubling of the bass by viola on octave higher in 'Perché un giglio', and the frequent reduction of the bass during vocal passages to solo cello. Apollo's aria 'Con cetra più sonora' summons up the lyre in the form of an archlute, which has an elaborate and highly idiomatic obbligato part.

For the couplets making comparisons between flowers during the 'game of flowers' described earlier Albinoni finds an original and successful solution. Each couplet is set to a paraphrase, adapted to the vocal register of each character, of the four-bar tune first given out by Daphne at the end of her explanation of the rules of the game. We join the game at the point where it is resumed after Daphne's aria.

DAF.	È vago il gelsomin, ma tal non sembra	The jasmine is fair, but it does not seem so
	perché non ha il color del bel giacinto.	because it is not coloured like the lovely hyacinth.
PEN.	È ver, ma di ostro e d'or come veggo	That is true, but it is not sheathed in gold and purple
	la rosa ei non è cinto.	as I see the rose to be.
FLO.	La rosa ha l'oro e l'ostro,	The rose has gold and purple,
	ma la viola è in umiltà più bella.	but the humility of the violet is more becoming.

If the style of *Il nascimento de l'Aurora* can be situated quite precisely around the time of *Engelberta* and *Pimpinone*, that of *Il nome glorioso in terra, santificato in cielo* belongs to the period of *La Statira*. One feature that the two later works have in common is the preponderance of major tonalities in the arias. The serenata has no closed numbers in a minor key at all, while the opera has only three out of a total of thirty-five movements. To some extent this represents a secular trend that is more marked in opera and the concerto, less marked in the cantata and the sonata. 'Public' music inclines towards the major mode, 'private' music towards a greater parity between

Ex. 43

the modes. To the extent that, during this period, music as a whole assumes a increasingly 'public' character irrespective of genre, the supremacy of the major mode is progressively reinforced until, around the middle of the century, the minor mode comes to occupy quite a marginal position, being reserved for movements of exceptional pathos or emotional turbulence. (For comparison: *Zenobia* has seven solo arias out of forty in a minor key, *Il nascimento de l'Aurora* five out of twenty-three; among Albinoni's solo cantatas the two modes are almost equally represented.)

The music of *Il nome glorioso in cielo, santificato in cielo* possesses great charm and grace but is not free from insipidity. Whereas the earlier serenata seems to have posed the composer a challenge that he eagerly took up, here all is routine and technique. As regards the instrumentation, one notes the use of a solo trumpet in the introductory sinfonia and the two terzets, and a transverse flute for a lyrical obbligato part in one aria ('Al mirar l'aquile Auguste'). The presence of a flute here is of some historical interest because it provides the earliest evidence so far uncovered of the use of this instrument in Venice (its next known appearance, in Vivaldi's opera *Orlando furioso*, comes over two years later).

We cannot leave Albinoni's dramatic music without considering whether it deserves—and has any practical prospect of—revival on the stage, in the concert hall, and in recordings. To a great extent the problems are not those of the individual works themselves; they are common to all Italian baroque opera. The first hurdle is that of the language itself, which in a certain sense is 'foreign' even to the modern native speaker of Italian. Then one has to confront the very unfamiliar climate of baroque opera, the aesthetic and dramaturgical conventions governing it. For *opera seria*, at least, one has to find some means of replicating or providing a satisfactory equivalent of the visual spectacle. The acting and gesture of the singers has to strive for an approach which is both authentic and convincing. Perhaps most difficult of all: one has to find a producer less concerned with the kind of originality that will make him or her talked about than with fidelity to the more humdrum practices of baroque production as contemporaries once experienced them.

Zenobia, unfortunately, is not suitable for a staged revival. In the first place, the version preserved in the Washington score is severely mutilated; in the second place, the quality of the recitative is too low. *La Statira*, however, is possibly worth reviving, with the caution that the music rarely attains the level of Handel or Vivaldi at his best.

Pimpinone would at first sight seem the ideal candidate for revival, being short, lively, and humorous. But here we encounter a problem that is not of Albinoni's making. In 1725 Telemann made a setting of a new version of

THE OPERAS AND SERENATAS · 249

Pariati's text by Johann Philipp Praetorius that retained the arias in their original Italian but made a paraphrased translation into German of the recitatives. The result was a masterpiece that outshines Albinoni's pioneer setting in every musical and dramatic respect while requiring no additional instruments or resources. A comparison of Albinoni's setting of Pimpinone's aria in Intermezzo III, 'So quel che si dice', with that of Telemann leaves one in no doubt of the superiority of the later setting. Whereas Albinoni mimics the two gossiping women that are the subject of this aria with a timid excursion into the tenor region, Telemann goes boldly into falsetto and, moreover, differentiates the two female speakers by register (one is a soprano, the other a contralto). His greater enterprise and skill is shown in countless other ways. Deservedly, Telemann's work has already established itself in the modern repertory, and it will be hard to promote Albinoni's intermezzi in competition with it except on the grounds of historical interest.

The two serenatas, which do not require a staged performance, offer the best prospects for revival. *Il nascimento de l'Aurora* is by far the more interesting work, though its exceptional length might sometimes cause problems.

Thought might also be given to the possibility of performing small groups of arias (for a common character, voice-type, or instrumentation) in recitals or recordings. This would make available not only the pick of the arias in the six works (including *Engelberta*) that survive complete but also many fine examples from the incompletely preserved works.

9

THE LATE INSTRUMENTAL WORKS
(FROM 1723)

ONLY sixteen indisputably authentic surviving instrumental works (including two sinfonias that have presumably become detached from the dramatic works they once introduced) can be assigned to the period in Albinoni's career following Op. 9. Their small quantity can be attributed to a gradual waning of the composer's creative powers, perhaps aggravated in his last years by old age and infirmity, to a slackening of demand for his instrumental music, and, during the early part of the period, to an increased involvement with opera. The existence of instrumental works by Albinoni postdating Op. 9 went almost unrecognized until the late 1960s; no mention of them occurs in the discussions of his music by Schering, Giazotto (leaving aside the discussion of spurious works), Newman, or Hutchings. In the case of the two published collections from this period, Op. 10 and the *Six Sonates da camera a violino solo*, the delay in recognition must have been due to the very small number of preserved examples (which may accurately reflect their degree of popularity in their own day) and their location in less well known or inaccessible collections.

It must be admitted frankly that not only the quantity but also the average quality of these late works evidences an all too noticeable decline. From the mid-1720s onwards Albinoni had to contend with two crises: one generated internally, the other externally. The 'internal' crisis resulted from the inability of his cherished formal structures to respond adequately to the needs of an evolving style. A less obstinate or more enterprising composer would have resolved this problem satisfactorily. In contrast, the 'external' crisis affected not only Albinoni but also every other north Italian composer of his generation who was still active. As we saw in Chapter 3, the finely nuanced 'Neapolitan' style, spearheaded by alumni of the Neapolitan conservatories, swept all before it. To remain in fashion a Venetian composer had to appropriate the graceful, singing style of composers such as Leo, Porpora, and Vinci, and deck his melodies out with Lombard rhythms, appoggiaturas both long and short, chains of triplet semiquavers, syncopations, and all the other hallmarks of the *stile galante*. In itself, this proved no problem for Albinoni, who assimilated the purely melodic components of the *galant* style with great gusto—in fact, in a much more throughgoing manner than either Vivaldi or Dall'Abaco, despite his seniority to both. But the *galant* style also implies a new type of phrasing and a new approach to harmony. The music becomes more segmented, relying less on *Fortspinnung* (extension through motivic repetition) and more on symmetrical phrase-grouping as seen in Domenico Scarlatti's harpsichord sonatas; the harmony emphasizes primary triads (tonic, dominant, and subdominant) at the expense of triads on other scale-degrees. These changes are to some extent resisted by Albinoni. The result can be a curious discrepancy between melodic and harmonic intentions: the melody may suggest a simple harmonization that is, however, belied by the tortuous, sometimes almost perverse, series of chords chosen to accompany it.

Take, for instance, the opening of the third concerto of Op. 10. In bars 1–3 the harmonization conforms in essence to one's natural expectations (except that only Albinoni would have allowed the second violin to circle around the first violin with such freedom or would have insisted on making the quavers of the bass move about so fussily). But in bar 4 the third and fourth beats are harmonized in an old-fashioned sequential manner as II–VI in preference to the more obvious V^7–I. His desire to avoid consecutive fifths in the outer parts leads the composer to end bar 4 very awkwardly with a curious-sounding first inversion of the A minor chord. The harmonization of the fourth and fifth bars is eccentric, to say the least. Most composers, following the implications of the melody, would have maintained a G major chord during the whole of bar 4 and supplied a seven–four–two chord (G–A–C–F♯) for the first half of bar 5, returning to the chord of G in the second half. Instead, Albinoni launches into a bizarre series of seven–five, six–four, and five–three chords over his pedal-note. This passage (shown in Ex. 44) is an extreme case of a tendency that, in milder form, characterizes much of Albinoni's later music.

One consequence of the advent of the *galant* style is that the metronomic value of the note representing the beat is now susceptible to greater variation, for a given tempo marking, than in the previous period. Whereas an allegro in common time in a concerto written around 1715 moves at the same kind of pace whether it occurs in a work by Vivaldi, Albinoni, or Valentini—the unifying factor is the even flow of semiquavers against a background of quavers and crotchets—an allegro of the late 1720s or the 1730s may have a considerably slower beat, if it has to find room for a profusion of shorter note-values (or, conversely, a faster one, if its effective metre is alla breve). Significantly, it is during this period that Vivaldi begins to make great use of 'nuanced' markings such as 'allegro non molto' and

Ex. 44

'allegro ma poco'.[1] Albinoni remains content with simple directions such as 'allegro' and 'adagio', but their meaning is now less uniform.

Spurious Works

So far, we have passed over in silence the numerous works attributed in contemporary sources to Albinoni but clearly not by him. My catalogue in *Albinoni: Leben und Werk* lists thirty such works, which are preceded by the prefix *Mi* (for 'Miscellaneous') and ordered by key. In most cases, source criticism based on non-textual data such as paper-type, staving, hand-writing, and previous ownership cannot be brought into play to determine their authenticity, simply because there is no suitable context in which these factors can acquire significance. Even when a concordant source for one of these works exists—and possibly an attribution there to another com-poser—non-textual data can in practice rarely clinch an argument for authorship. So we are left with an evaluation of style as the best method of arriving at a conclusion. In Albinoni's case the homogeneity of style in the authenticated works is very considerable, and their musical language is very distinctive. It becomes easy, therefore, to pronounce a work bearing his name spurious on the grounds of its stylistic incompatibility. In strict logic, this approach could be accused of begging the question: the prior assumption of stylistic homogeneity is used to debar from the Albinonian canon works that would belie it. But its great virtue, in pragmatic terms, is to err (if it does err) on the side of caution. On balance, the consequences of considering as genuine a work that is in reality spurious are more serious than the reverse.

It is not surprising that most of the sources containing instrumental works misattributed to Albinoni coincide chronologically with the later part of his career, for it was precisely then that his production of new works (other than operas) began to fall off—long before his popularity as a composer had declined to a similar extent. In other words, a 'gap' in the market opened up for others to exploit. Two particular groups of works misattributed to Albinoni require mention here: the first, because it forms part of a published anthology; the second, because it was long considered genuine by some authorities and has been the object of considerable discussion on account of its 'progressive' features.

The anthology in question was the collection of six concertos brought

---

[1] See Karl Heller, 'Tendenzen der Tempo-Differenzierung im Orchesterallegro Vivaldis', in Eitelfriedrich Thom (ed.), *Die Blasinstrumente und ihre Verwendung sowie zu Fragen des Tempos in der ersten Hälfte des 18. Jahrhunderts: Konferenzbericht der 4. Wissenschaftlichen Arbeitstagung Blankenburg/Harz, 26.–27. Juni 1976* (Magdeburg and Leipzig, 1977), 79–84.

out by Walsh and Hare in 1728 under the title *Harmonia Mundi: The 2ᵈ Collection*. All the concertos except the second are attributed to a named composer. That of Concerto I is Giuseppe Matteo Alberti;[2] Albinoni is specified as the composer of the third and fourth concertos (*Mi* 14 and *Mi* 19); Vivaldi, of the fifth concerto (RV 456); Tessarini, of the sixth concerto. The first, third, and sixth works are scored for principal violin, violins 1 and 2, viola, and united *violoncello* and *organo*; the second concerto is for two *concertino* and two *ripieno* violins with bass as before; the fourth and fifth concertos are for solo oboe, two violins, viola, and bass.

The violin concerto in F major (Concerto III) attributed to Albinoni appears to have been composed by a not very imaginative follower of Vivaldi. The outer movements exhibit a rudimentary ritornello form, and their episodes, unlike those of Albinoni's genuine concertos with principal violin, accompany the solo instrument with only a single strand, by turns on continuo and orchestral violins.

The oboe concerto in G major (Concerto IV) departs from Albinonian precedent by featuring a fugal opening movement prefaced by a slow introduction. It is very clearly a concerto 'for' rather than 'with' oboe, and in that sense entirely contradicts Albinoni's approach as revealed in Opp. 7 and 9.

Circumstantial evidence suggests that one is wise to be suspicious, for the *Harmonia Mundi* concerto attributed to Vivaldi is also regarded by scholars as being of uncertain authorship.[3]

The other group of misattributed works is a set of six sinfonias for two violins, viola, and bass formerly preserved in the Hessische Landes- und Hochschulbibliothek, Darmstadt (shelfmark Hs. 3003). The manuscript parts themselves were destroyed by fire during the Second World War, but a microfilm of them remains. The works already appear in a manuscript catalogue of the music belonging to the former Hessian court library dating from the middle of the eighteenth century (the so-called *Kupferkatalog*, Hs. 2591). Giazotto claimed to have information of a manuscript inventory in the British Library that listed works taken back to Darmstadt in 1735 by Prince Philip of Hesse-Darmstadt, Governor of Mantua, who was recalled in that year.[4] The entry in this inventory relating to the sinfonias is quoted by Giazotto as: 'Sei sinfonie a violino primo e secondo[,] viola che si raddoppia e violoncello del Signore [deletion] Albinoni veneto scritte per il principe di d'Armstadt.' Unfortunately, this inventory cannot be tracked

---

[2] The concerto is identified as 'vn4G₂' in the author's 'A Thematic Catalogue of the Orchestral Works of Giuseppe Matteo Alberti (1685–1751)', *RMA Research Chronicle*, 13 (1976), 1–26.

[3] See Peter Ryom, *Répertoire des œuvres d'Antonio Vivaldi: Les Compositions instrumentales* (Copenhagen, 1986), 550.

[4] *Tomaso Albinoni*, pp. 260–1.

down—Giazotto states that his information about it is at second hand and that his informant omitted to supply a shelfmark. Nevertheless, the sinfonias must be regarded, irrespective of their appearance in the *Kupferkatalog* and this elusive inventory, as prima facie candidates for Albinoni's authorship, since, as the microfilm shows, the manuscripts themselves name him as the composer.

All six sinfonias adopt the four-movement plan typical of the classical symphony (fast movement—slow movement—minuet and trio—fast movement) except the third and fifth, which omit the slow movement. This is itself would be extraordinary for an orchestral work of Italian provenance, since in the Italian late baroque and early classical traditions the minuet, if it appears at all, is employed as a finale, often in the shape of a theme and variations. The style of the sinfonias is emphatically 'early classical', resembling that of composers born around 1700 such as Giuseppe Sammartini. In fact, the only point in common with Albinoni's genuine instrumental music is the composer's willingness to let the two violin parts cross freely.

Giazotto, like the Italian scholar Fausto Torrefranca before him, accepts the genuineness of the sinfonias unquestioningly. Regarding them as authentic specimens of Albinoni's 'late style', he subjects them to a painstaking descriptive analysis occupying thirty-one pages.[5] Since they are very attractive works, this close attention is not in itself undeserved. Only: they cannot be by Albinoni. Until uncontested examples of Albinoni's style of writing during the 1730s belatedly emerged, it was arguably reasonable to admit the possibility that, overnight, the composer's style underwent a sea-change, but the rediscovery of Op. 10, a collection of indisputable authenticity exactly contemporary with the Darmstadt sinfonias, effectively shut the door on this hypothesis. To their credit, most scholars were reluctant from the first to subscribe to Giazotto's view. As early as 1951 Bernhard Paumgartner voiced his disbelief in the genuineness of the sinfonias in his article on Albinoni for the encyclopaedia *Die Musik in Geschichte und Gegenwart*, describing them as 'dubious on account of their *galant* thematic substance'.[6] Nevertheless, in 1961 Ricordi published the third and fifth sinfonias under Albinoni's name in an edition prepared by Giazotto himself, and these still appear today in recital programmes as ostensibly genuine works.[7]

    [5] Ibid. 262–92.
    [6] Friedrich Blume (ed.), *Die Musik in Geschichte und Gegenwart* (14 vols., Kassel, etc., 1949–68), i, col. 298.
    [7] Another spurious work frequently performed under Albinoni's name is a concerto in C major (*Mi* 3) for solo trumpet, three oboes, and bassoon from the Fürstenberg collection; in an edition by Johannes Wojciechowski it was published by Sikorski in 1966.

Two Sinfonias (*Si* 8–9)

Certain points of style enable two sinfonias for four-part strings preserved in Swedish collections to be assigned tentatively to the period following Op. 9. The sinfonia in G major, *Si* 8, survives in manuscripts found in Stockholm and Uppsala;[8] that in F major, *Si* 9, comes from Lund.[9]

Si 8 opens with a rather ponderous Allegro leading straight into a brief Larghetto; the 'fusion' of the first and second movements is a feature we have already seen in many of Albinoni's earlier sinfonias. The fast section is a perfect example of the 'strepitoso' approach to the sinfonia genre in which sonorous unisons, percussive violin chords, and long chains of busy semiquavers all contribute to a rather synthetic kind of excitement. The 3/8 finale, a compressed binary-form movement, manages to find room for some deft handling of thematic material in its forty-eight bars. Its opening idea recurs in the dominant key at the end of the repeated first section, in the same key (though in a lower octave) at the beginning of the second section, and in the tonic key at the close of the second section: three times in all. This kernel from which 'monothematic' sonata form will later grow is encountered again in some of the Op. 10 finales.

Si 9 is perhaps the best instrumental work to have survived from Albinoni's late period. In style it is more like a *concerto a quattro* than a typical sinfonia; its slow movement, though very brief, is detached, and its surprisingly long finale eschews binary form in favour of Albinoni's standard first-movement form. The opening Allegro has a pleasing rhythmic variety—the 'chattering' repeated semiquavers in the violin parts are a device associated with *opera buffa* that belongs quintessentially to this period—while the bouncy finale, in 2/4 metre, recalls similar movements in Op. 9.

Concerti a cinque, Op. 10

It is ironic that just at the time when Albinoni's grip on harmony and part-writing should be showing signs of weakening, he should begin to display a heightened sensitivity for dynamics and texture. Yet this is all part of the puzzle of Op. 10, which is both fastidious and ham-fisted, forward-looking and regressive. Although the collection often reminds one of Locatelli or Tartini—as the composer no doubt intended it to do—it can also reach back forty years to recover and serve up again a turn of phrase characteristic

---

[8] Shelfmarks respectively Orkester/Rar. and Instr. mus. i hs. 12:12.
[9] Engelharts Samling 260.

of Albinoni's music in the 1690s. Its curious *mélange* of the old and the new must have disconcerted contemporary players and listeners.

Contrasts of 'forte' and 'piano' are encountered in many of the movements. While 'piano' is normally used in a conventional way for echo-effects and for 'enclaves' in the parallel minor key, it occasionally acquires a new function: to distinguish a consequent (soft) from its antecedent (loud). Perhaps originally inspired by dialogue in comic opera, this usage will later enjoy great popularity in the classical period. In bar 93 of the first movement of Concerto IV Albinoni introduces for the first and only time in his instrumental music the direction 'piano piano' (equivalent to 'pianissimo'); it is applied to the orchestral violins and cello accompanying the principal violin.

The most striking thing about the instrumentation of Op. 10 is Albinoni's readiness to suppress the continuo for long stretches at a time, leaving the cello to sustain the bass line unaided. Whereas the omission of the continuo usually coincides, in the concertos of Vivaldi and other contemporaries, with the elimination of the bass register altogether, this is rarely the case here. The slow movements of the fifth, tenth, and twelfth concertos dispense with continuo all the way through, adopting a 'pure' four-part or five-part string texture. Albinoni often reinforces the cello line with delightful effect by doubling it a few notes at a time in the viola or second violin part, one octave higher. In the outer movements of Concerto III, which in other respects is a typical *concerto a quattro*, a solo cello, accompanied by (or accompanying) two violin parts, is allowed a few florid excursions—which collectively fall far short, however, of what one would expect of a full-blown cello concerto. At the start of a passage beginning in bar 7 of the first movement of Concerto I the unusual direction 'cimbalo senza contrabasso' appears in the *organo* part; this instructs the harpsichord to keep playing while the double-bass pauses (and also confirms the point made in Chapter 3 that the double-bass always reads from the continuo, not the cello, line).

The odd-numbered concertos of Op. 10 all have the principal violin in strict unison with the first violin throughout; in other words, these are works without a soloist. The incidence of solo writing in the even-numbered concertos varies immensely. Concertos VIII, X, and XII all have extensive solo passages in their outer movements; the eighth and twelfth concertos have an ornate solo line throughout the slow movement, while the tenth concerto reverts to 'tutti' scoring. The outer movements of these three concertos all feature one interesting novelty: the second period opens with a statement of the motto phrase by the lightly accompanied principal violin (in earlier concertos with a solo part for principal violin this statement is always reserved for the tutti). Perhaps the innovation was inspired by those movements in Albinoni's oboe concertos in which the oboe's opening phrase echoes that of the tutti period just concluded. Solo participation in the remaining even-numbered concertos (nos. 2, 4, and 6) is more sporadic and can be regarded as little more than a colouristic effect.

All the opening movements and seven of the finales (in nos. 2, 5, 8, 9, 10, 11, and 12) are cast in Albinoni's characteristic form organized around regular restatement of a motto. If one compares these movements with their equivalents in Op. 9, one sees that Albinoni now tends to employ fewer periods within each movement but in compensation increases their average length (the 'real' increase in length is even greater if one takes into account the generally slower pulse). To expand these periods to the required length Albinoni resorts to prolongation techniques of various kinds: major–minor shifts, sequences, pedals, interrupted cadences, phrase-repetitions, and the like. All too often, the result is unnatural and unconvincing. To compound the problem, the little counter-melodies and bridging phrases in the second violin that proved so successful in the composer's earlier music now often appear fussy intrusions that merely make it more difficult to follow the main melodic line.

A curiosity: in the first movement of Concerto XI Albinoni makes a brave but rather gauche attempt to pay a compliment to the Spanish dedicatee of the collection, Don Patiño, by imitating the sound of the guitar. In the passage quoted in Ex. 45 (bars 59–66 in the principal and first violin parts) a melodic-harmonic cliché identified with flamenco music is heard three times.

The slow movements are on the whole more successful. The only stumbling block to their full acceptance is the eccentric harmonization of certain passages and some infelicities of part-writing. As the opening of the second movement of Concerto II shows (see Ex. 46), Albinoni can still

Ex. 45

Ex. 46

produce a superbly shaped melody, fragrant and haunting, however much
he may stumble over the lower parts.

Four of the slow movements, following the prevalent trend of the
period, are in binary form. Those in the second, fourth, and seventh
concertos have repeats marked; that in Concerto V has a clear caesura
separating the two strains but no repeat sign. The remaining movements
are through-composed in the manner familiar from Albinoni's Op. 1
onwards. In the third and sixth concertos Albinoni steps back in time,
composing in a solidly contrapuntal 'trio' style. The slow movement of
Concerto IX is similar but attempts, with very odd results, to give the two
upper parts *galant* rhythms characterized by constant reverse-dotting.

It is left to the five finales in binary form to salvage something of
Albinoni's reputation. Their very lack of pretension prevents the composer
from ruining them with heavy-handedness or an excess of decorative zeal.
Two of them (in the first and sixth concertos) adopt the monothematic
approach described earlier in connection with the sinfonia *Si* 8. The finale
of the third concerto is in the fashionable style of a minuet. But the
movement that perhaps comes closest to the ideal of the 1730s, represented
by Pergolesi's comic intermezzi, is the finale of Concerto VII, shown in
Ex. 47. Its amiable garrulousness, momentarily relieved by a touch of

Ex. 47

wistfulness (in bars 21–3), goes to the very heart of the Italian *buffo* style.

In restrospect, one may wonder why it took so long for Op. 10 to come to the notice of modern scholars. Le Cène listed it in his catalogue of 1736, and Michel Corrette even included extracts from the eighth and twelfth concertos in a treatise on violin-playing.[10] The first of the three known surviving examples of the edition, that in the De Geer collection in Leufsta Bruk, Sweden, was brought to light by Albert Dunning in 1966;[11] the other examples are found in the André Meyer collection, Paris, and the Musicological Institute of the Rijksuniversiteit, Utrecht. In 1968 a recording of the complete set played by I Musici was brought out by Philips as part of a large recording project devoted to Albinoni's instrumental music, but since then Op. 10 seems to have left the musical world quite cold. Only the first concerto has so far appeared in a modern edition. It is sad that what could easily have been a discovery of major importance has turned out—for quite understandable reasons, as we have seen—to be a damp squib.

Six Sonates da camera a violino solo col basso cimbalo, 'Op. post.' (So 40–5)

Since the rise of Paris as a centre of music publishing during the 1730s came at the very end of Albinoni's career, one would not have expected him to abandon Le Cène and entrust his music to a Parisian house. Both Op. 10 (1735/6) and the lost Op. 11 consisting of six trio sonatas (1739) were sent, following the pattern of earlier collections, to Amsterdam. Rather surprisingly, none of the collections brought out by Estienne and Jeanne Roger or Le Cène was 'pirated' in Paris. There may, however, be a special reason for this connected with the system of 'privileges' (i.e. licences) that governed music publishing in France under the *ancien régime*.

In order to print or engrave music, the interested party (who might be a printer, an engraver, a bookseller, a composer, or an independent entrepreneur) had to apply for a privilege. This document took the form of a standard text that specified, among other things, the name of the privilege-holder, the work or works covered by the privilege, and its duration (usually from three to fifteen years). Applications for privileges were filed in official registers, which have been preserved.[12] Once a

[10] *L'Art de se perfectionner dans le violon* (Paris, 1782), 13.

[11] Albert Dunning, 'Die De Geer'schen Musikalien in Leufsta', *Svensk tidskrift för musikforskning*, 47 (1966), 187–210.

[12] The privileges relating to music for this period are discussed and transcribed in Michel Brenet, 'La Librairie musicale en France de 1653 à 1790 d'après les registres de privilèges', *Sammelbände der Internationalen Musik-Gesellschaft*, 8 (1906–7), 401–66, and Georges Cucuel, 'Quelques documents sur la librairie musicale au XVIIIᵉ siècle', *Sammelbände der Internationalen Musik-Gesellschaft*, 13 (1911–12), 385–92.

privilege was granted, its text was engraved and appeared as a separate page in every publication issued by the privilege-holder.

Privileges were of two kinds: a *permission simple* allowed the applicant to bring out the works in question but did not prevent others from doing the same; a *privilège général*, on the other hand, conferred a monopoly on the privilege-holder. Successive generations of the house of Ballard had held a *privilège général* for music printed from movable type ever since 1522, which effectively removed all competition in this sphere. No such monopoly existed for engraved music, although in the late 1730s the two Le Clerc brothers, music sellers and publishers, between them managed effectively to corner the market in works by Italian composers already published in Amsterdam. Jean-Pantaléon Le Clerc, the elder brother, was Le Cène's Parisian agent and stocked virtually the entire catalogue of the Amsterdam house. Charles-Nicolas Le Clerc, the younger brother, obtained in 1736 a *privilège général* valid for fifteen years that covered nearly everything currently being imported from Holland by Jean-Pantaléon. It would appear that Charles-Nicolas had no intention of publishing more than a fraction of the music governed by his privilege; his real purpose was almost certainly to pre-empt the publication by others of the imported music that his brother was selling—in other words, to protect an existing monopoly.

This meant that any works by Albinoni engraved in Paris were destined to lie outside the series of 'authorized' publications stretching from Op. 1 to Op. 10. In 1723 an anonymous applicant obtained a three-year *permission simple* to publish unspecified music by Albinoni, but no publications issued under this licence have been uncovered. Then in 1737 a certain Marchand (perhaps identical with Jean-Noël Marchand, a 'tambour de l'Écurie') took out a nine-year privilege covering the Opp. 13 and 14 of Vivaldi, the Op. 10 of Valentini, and the Op. 10 of Albinoni, all of which were to be 'pour la musette et vielles' (the bagpipes (musette) and hurdy-gurdy (vièle) were two quasi-pastoral instruments that were enjoying a vogue in the rococo atmosphere of court life in the 1730s). To judge from the so-called Op. 13, *Il pastor fido*, that Marchand issued *c.* 1737 under Vivaldi's name, the intention of the privilege-holder was to concoct a mixture of pastiche and simple forgery purporting to be the most recent work of the named composer. A similar 'Op. 10' by Albinoni seems not to have materialized, perhaps because the genuine Op. 10 had reached Paris in the mean time.

Finally, in November 1737 a noted engraver, Louis Hue, took out a six-year *privilège général* for 'plusieurs pièces de musique'. Among these miscellaneous works was a set of six violin sonatas that appeared towards 1740 under Albinoni's name as an ostensibly posthumous collection

('Œuvre postume'). Only one example of the collection appears to have survived. It was formerly in the private collection of the musicologist Marc Pincherle, who in 1947 referred to it in a review of Giazotto's *Tomaso Albinoni* published in the *Revue de musicologie*.[13] After Pincherle's death in 1974 the volume passed to the British Library.

To say that at least two and possibly four of the sonatas are probably spurious should by now almost be tantamount to a statement of normality. The two whose authorship can be contested most strongly are the third (*So* 42) and fifth (*So* 44), both of which are described as playable on the transverse flute ('La 3.e et la 5.e sonate peuvent se jouer sur la flûte allemande'). They have obviously been written originally for the violin, for *So* 42 contains some instances of triple-stopping, while both sonatas descend below the compass of the flute to *b*. The two works are alike in having an allemande as the second movement and a jig as the finale, each preceded by an abstract slow movement. Their short-winded melodic style, from which sequence is conspicuously absent, is wholly untypical of Albinoni; certain melodic and harmonic inflections suggest a French composer writing in an Italian vein.

The case of the first (*So* 40) and fourth (*So* 43) sonatas is more problematic. Hitherto, I have always regarded both as genuine, but a re-examination of them convinces me that my acceptance was premature. Their modulations and proportions, their rhythms and ornaments, are decidedly un-Albinonian. The 'Minueto' ending the first sonata (following a Giga) would, if genuine, be the only fifth movement in the whole of Albinoni's instrumental music. The heading 'Tempo di corrente' (rather than plain 'Corrente') for the last movement of the fourth sonata is equally uncharacteristic. All the same, one cannot deny the authenticity of these two sonatas with absolutely categorical assurance.

Unless the compiler of the set was a pasticheur of uncommon skill and resourcefulness, the second (*So* 41) and sixth (*So* 45) sonatas are certainly genuine, for they are close in spirit, and more than once in actual notes, to works belonging to the accepted canon. Neither seems significantly more advanced in style than the works in the 1717 collection. The explanation must be either that the language of Albinoni's sonatas remained static (while that of the concertos advanced) or that Hue took the works from manuscripts that were already quite old. The second hypothesis seems the more likely.[14]

So 41, in A minor, is a finely wrought work that deserves occasional

---

[13] *Revue de musicologie*, 26 (1947), 101.

[14] The case of the six cello sonatas by Vivaldi published by Charles-Nicolas Le Clerc *c.* 1740 is strikingly similar, for these, too, appear to be works composed about 20 years earlier.

performance. Its second movement, unusually for Albinoni, is a jig; the concluding fourth movement is a *perpetuum mobile* in 6/8 metre. Both slow movements have expressive harmony that exploits the poignancy of the Neapolitan Sixth at climactic moments.

So 45 models its two opening movements very closely on those of the fourth sonata in the 1717 collection (*So* 38), which is in the same key of A major. The Adagio has two 'presto' interpolations over pedal-points à la Corelli; these are a little more exuberant than in the earlier work, ascending as high as a″′. The following Allegro is a fugue in which the single violin simulates the contrapuntal interplay of the two violins in a trio sonata. Its subject is a more compact version of that in *So* 38. But the resemblance in fact goes further, since the second episode in *So* 45 (bars 26–31) presents in strict alternation two motives taken from separate episodes (bars 12–14 and 49–53 respectively) in the earlier movement. Most surprisingly, the thirteen bars of coda are derived from a much earlier A major movement: the second movement of the trio sonata Op. 1 no. 3 (similarly, the closing phrase of the brief finale of *So* 45, which is in binary form, echoes that of the fourth movement of Op. 1 no. 3). It is ironic that in the last work of Albinoni to be published there should be a clear reference to one of his first works, dating back almost half a century, and that no incongruity of style should arise. This case of borrowing symbolizes the essential continuity of the composer's style, which, having matured early, never sought to depart from its original vision.

10

CONCLUSION

MANY people draw a distinction between 'good' music and 'great' music. The distinction is not a very profound one and in any case has a relative rather than absolute force. By good music people mean music that scores highly in terms of technique and expression and proves (or promises to prove) a rewarding listening experience. It is immaterial, by this yardstick, whether the music in question or its composer are well known or utterly obscure: analysis of the score suffices to qualify the music as 'good'. 'Great' music, however, can be understood as music that has exerted a seminal force on the evolution of musical culture and the musical language. No little-known music, however good, can qualify as great; on the other hand, there can be works (for instance, the operas of Lully) whose greatness far outstrips their 'good' qualities. What constitutes good music is open to personal interpretation and rarely commands universal agreement. What constitutes great music, however, is—or ought to be—a matter of historical record. Imperfectly known as they are, the influences exerted by composers on their musical environment and that of their successors are amenable to objective investigation and can therefore provide the basis for an informed consensus on 'greatness'. Whatever our personal view of the merit of the works of Handel, Beethoven, Brahms, or Stravinsky, we cannot deny that they, and their composers, are great in this sense.

Viewed in this perspective, Albinoni, unlike Vivaldi, can make only a feeble claim to greatness. If we ask ourselves whether, if he had not existed, the course of musical history might have been different, we cannot give a unequivocally positive answer. It is true that his concertos popularized the three-movement plan; that they introduced a simplified harmonic language emphasizing tonic and dominant harmonies;[1] that they pioneered the use of fugue in combination with writing for a solo instrument; that they provided models for the light accompaniment of a solo instrument by the full ensemble; that they were forward-looking in absorbing some of the features of the operatic sinfonia; that their themes possessed a new urgency; that they were among the first orchestral works to admit a wind instrument (the oboe) to a *concertante* role; and many other things. But in none of these

---

[1] Eleanor Selfridge-Field (*Venetian Instrumental Music*, p. 218) goes so far as to speak of a 'harmonic reform' expressed by 'the ceaseless emphasis of tonic and dominant'.

cases can we be sure that Albinoni was the only composer involved—and most of the developments were of such a simple nature that they would have arisen spontaneously regardless. To draw a simple parallel: one does not call Domenico Alberti 'great' merely because he was an early— perhaps, indeed, the earliest—exponent of a once popular style of accompaniment that today bears his name. At most, we will be able to say that certain instrumental collections of Albinoni (Opp. 2, 5, 6, and 7) were influential in the years immediately following their first publication.

How good Albinoni's music is can be assessed by asking a similar provocative question: if all of it were to disappear tomorrow, would our musical experience, actual and potential, be impoverished? Here, the answer must be an emphatic 'yes'. Its chief virtue is its individuality, which in a sense overrides any of its particular merits and demerits. But certain elements of Albinoni's musical language deserve respect by any standards: the highly developed sense of formal balance,[2] the superb feeling for melodic line, the knack of obtaining strong rhythmic effects by simple means, the ability to mirror words subtly in music.

Albinoni's achievement as a contrapuntist is more controversial. Many scholars have praised him for his fugues and canons—in other words, for types of contrapuntal writing based on imitation of a prescribed subject. To the present writer, Albinoni's handling of imitative counterpoint appears fairly unremarkable and certainly rather unambitious. His contrapuntal gifts are found in a different and rather unusual sphere: the simultaneous combination of entirely different melodic strands, divergent in phrasing and rhythmic make-up.

His part-writing has been praised, sometimes extravagantly, as in Hutchings's claim that 'Albinoni's harmony is consistently careful, as though sensitive part-writing were as natural to him as it was to Handel or Mozart'.[3] In fact, when composing in more than three real parts, Albinoni achieves good part-writing only with obvious effort and with variable success. To be sure, Italian composers of earlier generations who were thoroughly trained in the *stile antico*—men like Legrenzi, Stradella, Colonna, and Alessandro Scarlatti—mastered easily the manipulation of large numbers of contrapuntal parts. But Albinoni, like so many others of his generation, lacked this depth of grounding; he prefers to simplify the counterpoint by reducing the 'structural' voices to two (treble and bass) or three (two trebles and bass), which means that any extra voices have to be content with gathering up the leavings. In two-part or three-part textures,

---

[2] Arthur Hutchings (*The Baroque Concerto*, pp. 156–7) writes that Albinoni's music is 'shaped in clear and readily understood ideas and extended into almost perfect forms'.
[3] Ibid. 163.

however, he is completely at home and sometimes obtains impressive results.

Special effects of instrumentation and timbre seem to have interested him only sporadically. Attention has been drawn in particular to the variegated slow movements of the Op. 5 concertos, to obbligato instruments employed in his dramatic music, and to the lightening of the bass in Opp. 9 and 10. While this evidence protects Albinoni against a charge of being indifferent to these matters, it hardly adds up to a strong case for regarding him as an innovator on the same level as Vivaldi (or even Bach).

In the final analysis, Albinoni's status as an artist rises above his demonstration of artistry. To many—including this writer—he appears more significant than a dispassionate technical analysis of his music would suggest. This belief seemed to be general during the 1960s and 1970s, when the instrumental works were frequently published, programmed, and recorded. The present lull reflects a weakening of this conviction. Perhaps the 250th anniversary of his death, which falls in the year 2001, will stir the musical world once more into activity on his behalf. Before then, however, there is much preparatory work to be done. It is important during this critical phase that his vocal music, especially the solo cantatas, is vigorously promoted, and that a more discriminating approach to the revival of his instrumental music is taken. So much good music by him has not yet had a chance to make itself heard in modern times that there is a real possibility of a 'second' rediscovery, which would be the best anniversary present of all.

A SHORT CATALOGUE OF ALBINONI'S WORKS

INTRODUCTORY REMARKS

THREE thematic catalogues of Albinoni's instrumental works are in existence. The earliest occupies pp. 318–51 of Giazotto's *Tomaso Albinoni*, published in 1945. It lists 127 works, of which the first 102 are Opp. 1–9 including the six sonatas published by Roger in 1708 as an ostensible Op. 4. Giazotto's catalogue can be faulted both for omitting several works whose existence in major European libraries was easily ascertainable at the time of its compilation and for including several works whose authenticity has later been disproved or questioned with good reason. Its thematic incipits also contain numerous errors. Nevertheless: as the only easily accessible catalogue to include incipits for every movement, it can still be a useful source of reference today.

The second volume of the present writer's unpublished dissertation 'The Instrumental Music of Tomaso Albinoni', completed in 1968, also contains a thematic catalogue (pp. 1–99) with incipits for every movement. The number of works listed is 179, including spurious compositions identified as such.

Finally, a thematic catalogue of the instrumental works appeared in *Albinoni: Leben und Werk* (pp. 207–44). This includes only first-movement incipits except in cases where those of later movements are needed to distinguish between variants. The system of reference adopted in that catalogue has been followed in the present book and is described below. Its principles of organization are straightforward. Works that originally appeared in collections bearing an authentic opus number are given a code beginning with a Roman number corresponding to the opus number and ending with an Arabic number corresponding to the work's position in the collection. Thus 'VII, 3' is Op. 7 no. 3. In cases where works of two different kinds alternate within a single collection the original titles of individual works usually bear numbers different from those of the respective codes; thus 'II, 3' is Sonata II from Op. 2, 'II, 2' being Concerto I. The few variants of these works contained in contemporary manuscripts are distinguished from the published version by the addition of a letter to the Arabic number; thus 'VII, 4a' is the sinfonia in Dresden closely related to Concerto IV in Op. 7.

Works, printed or manuscript, not contained in Opp. 1–10 are organized in four separate lists with appropriate prefixes. Nine sinfonias preserved separately from their parent works appear as *Si* 1–9; five concertos appear as *Co* 1–5; forty-five sonatas and balletti appear as *So* 1–45. Thirty spurious ('miscellaneous') works belonging to a variety of genres appear as *Mi* 1–30. The works in the *Si*, *Co*, and *So* series are listed in approximate chronological order; those in the *Mi* series follow the ascending key-sequence of Bach's '48' but within each key are grouped arbitrarily. A problem arises in the case of spurious works appearing alongside genuine ones in 'unauthorized' sonata collections. It has been thought least confusing to retain them in the *So* series among the genuine works, while making a note of their doubtful attribution, rather than transfer them to the *Mi* series.

Since the publication of *Albinoni: Leben und Werk* in 1980 no new indisputably genuine works have come to light. A spurious flute concerto is preserved in a set of parts in the Biblioteca Comunale of Montecatini-Terme (near Pistoia). Then there are the four anonymous works contained in manuscripts preserved in Durham Cathedral Library which are likely, on stylistic grounds, to be early works by Albinoni.

A non-thematic catalogue of the cantatas was included in the present writer's article 'Albinoni's Solo Cantatas', published in 1972.[1] Substantially the same list, corrected and updated, appears on pp. 203–5 of *Albinoni: Leben und Werk*. However, Carlo Guaita's unpublished dissertation 'Le cantate di Tomaso Albinoni (1671–1751): Studio storico-critico e bibliografico' (1986) contains, on pp. 356–419, not only a thematic catalogue of forty-eight cantatas but also a valuable series of indexes concerning their poetic texts.

Apart from brief work-lists in dictionaries, the only previous catalogue of Albinoni's dramatic music (operas, comic intermezzi, and serenatas) is that in *Albinoni: Leben und Werk*. It comprises in fact two lists: one presenting the works chronologically according to the date of their first performance (pp. 193–202); the other organized alphabetically by title (pp. 203–5). Neither list includes thematic incipits.

The present catalogue will not attempt to reproduce, still less to enlarge on, the information on individual works contained in my earlier book. Its main purpose is to provide a basis for simple statistical analysis and facilitate identification. In addition, it functions as an index to references to individual works in the text of the present book—the column on the far right in each section lists page numbers.

Albinoni's works are listed in the following order: operas, comic intermezzi, serenatas, oratorios, sacred vocal music, solo cantatas, instrumental works with authentic opus number, sinfonias (*Si* series), concertos (*Co* series), sonatas (*So* series), spurious works (items from the *Mi* series mentioned in the present book), four anonymous works in Durham.

ABBREVIATIONS

A	Autunno (Autumn)
b	basso
bc	basso continuo
BOF	Bologna, Teatro Formagliari
BOM	Bologna, Teatro Marsigli Rossi
BRN	Brescia, Nuovo Teatro
bs	bassoon

C	Carnevale (Carnival, Winter)
cem	cembalo
con	concerto
E	Estate (Summer)
FEC	Ferrara, Teatro da Santo Stefano
fl	flute
FLC	Florence, Teatro di via del Cocomero
GEF	Genoa, Teatro del Falcone
MUH	Munich, Hoftheater
NAB	Naples, Teatro di San Bartolomeo
ob	oboe
org	organo
P	Primavera (Spring)
PAO	Pavia, Teatro Omodeo
PID	Piacenza, Teatro Ducale
pr	principale
PRS	Prague, private theatre of Count Franz Anton Sporck
ROC	Rome, Teatro Capranica
S	Sensa (Ascensiontide)
SGA	San Giovanni in Persiceto, Teatro degli Accademici Candidi Uniti
ten	tenore
tpt	trumpet
TRD	Treviso, Teatro Dolfin
VEA	Venice, Teatro di Sant'Angelo
VEC	Venice, Teatro di San Cassiano
VEG	Venice, Teatro di San Giovanni Grisostomo
VEM	Venice, Teatro di San Moisè
VEP	Venice, Teatro dei Santi Giovanni e Paolo
VES	Venice, Teatro di San Samuele
VIG	Vicenza, Teatro delle Grazie
vl	violin
vla	viola
vlc	violoncello
vle	violone
vtta	violetta

CATALOGUE

OPERAS

Title	Librettist	First performance	State of preservation	Pages
Alcina delusa da Ruggero[1]	A. Marchi	VEC, 1725A	lost	207 n.
Aminta	A. Zeno	FLC, 1703A	lost	36, 206
Amor di figlio non conosciuto (L')	D. Lalli	VEA, 1716C	lost	
Antigono, tutore di Filippo, re di Macedonia[2]	G. Piazzon	VEM, 1724C	lost	8
Ardelinda	B. Vitturi	VEA, 1732A	five arias	192
Artamene	B. Vitturi	VEA, 1741C	lost	40, 191
Arte in gara con l'arte (L')	F. Silvani	VEC, 1702C	lost	
Astarto	A. Zeno and P. Pariati	VEC, 1708A	several arias	192, 225
Candalide	B. Vitturi	VEA, 1734C	lost	7, 191
Ciro	P. Pariati	VEC, 1710C	lost	9
Cleomene	V. Cassani	VEA, 1718C	lost	37, 228
Didone abbandonata	P. Metastasio	VEC. 1725C	lost	19
Diomede punito da Alcide	A. Aureli	VEA, 1700A	lost	
Due rivali in amore (Le)	A. Aureli	VEM, 1728A	lost	
Eccessi della gelosia (Gli)[3]	D. Lalli	VEA, 1722C	several arias	37, 192
Elenia	L. Bergalli	VEA, 1730C	lost	
Engelberta[4]	A. Zeno and P. Pariati	VEC, 1709C	extant	8, 154, 191, 192, 206, 238–9, 244, 246, 249
Ermengarda (L')	A. M. Lucchini	VEM, 1723A	lost	
Eumene	A. Salvi	VEG, 1717A	one aria	
Eumene	A. Zeno	VEM, 1723C	two arias	
Fede tra gl'inganni (La)	F. Silvani	VEA, 1707C	lost	
Fortezza al cimento (La)	F. Silvani	PID, 1707	lost	
Gare generose (Le)	A. Zaniboni	VEC, 1712A	five arias	207
Giustino (Il)	N. Beregani, rev. P. Pariati	BOF, 1711P	lost	
Griselda[5]	A. Zeno	FLC, 1703C	three arias	5, 36

[1] Revived under the new title of *Gli evenimenti di Ruggero* (VEM, 1732C).
[2] Written in collaboration with Giovanni Porta.
[3] Revived under the new title of *La Mariane* with most music replaced by that of Giovanni Porta (VSA, 1724A and 1725C).
[4] Fourth and fifth acts composed by Francesco Gasparini.
[5] Revived under the new title of *L'umiltà esaltata* (NAB, 1734).

Title	Librettist	First performance	State of preservation	Pages
Incostanza schernita (L')[6]	V. Cassani	VES, 1727S	several arias	192, 196, 228
Inganno innocente (L')[7]	F. Silvani	VEA, 1701C	several arias	18
Ingratitudine gastigata (L')[8]	F. Silvani	VEC, 1698C	lost	10, 207
Laodice	A. Schietti	VEM, 1724A	two arias	
Lucio Vero	A. Zeno	FES, 1713P	lost	
Meleagro	P. A. Bernardoni	VEA, 1718C	lost	
Merope[9]	A. Zeno	PRS, 1731A	lost	
Più infedel tra gli amanti (Il)	A. Schietti	TRD, 1731A	lost	
Primislao, primo re di Boemia	G. C. Corradi	VEC, 1697A	lost	
Prodigio dell'innocenza (Il)	F. M. Gualazzi	VEP, 1695C	lost	
Prosperità di Elio Sejano (La)	N. Minato	GEF, 1707C	lost	
Radamisto	A. Marchi	VEA, 1698A	lost	207 n.
Rivali generosi (I)	A. Zeno	BRN, 1725	lost	
Scipione nelle Spagne	A. Zeno	VES, 1724S	lost	
Statira (La)	A. Zeno and P. Pariati	ROC, 1726C	extant	7, 73–4, 184, 191, 192, 206, 215–22, 223, 238, 239–42, 246, 248, 286
Stratagemmi amorosi (Li)	F. Passerini	VEM, 1730C	lost	
Tigrane, re d'Armenia (Il)	G. C. Corradi	VEC, 1697C	lost	4, 36
Tiranno eroe (Il)	V. Cassani	VEC, 1711C	several arias	192, 228
Tradimento tradito (Il)	F. Silvani	VEA, 1709C	lost	
Trionfo d'amore (Il)[10]	P. Pariati	MUH, 1722A	lost	
Trionfo di Armida (Il)	G. Colatelli	VEM, 1726A	lost	
Veri amici (I)	F. Silvani and D. Lalli	MUH, 1722A	several arias	viii, 5, 192, 240, 242
Zenobia, regina de' Palmireni[11]	A. Marchi	VEP, 1694C	extant	4, 43, 67, 81, 95, 191, 192, 206, 207–15, 216, 221, 222, 233–8, 239, 240, 285, 286

[6] Revived under the new titles of Filandro (VSM, 1729C) and L'infedeltà delusa (VIG, 1729E).

[7] Revived under the new title of Rodrigo in Algeri with additions by Giovanni Battista Stück (NAB, 1702).

[8] Revived under the title Alarico (PID, 1712).

[9] Music described in the libretto as 'in large part' by Albinoni.

[10] This is not a full-scale opera but a short componimento poetico.

[11] Text and some of the music used for the pasticcio Il vinto trionfante del vincitore (VSA, 1717A).

Title	Librettist	First performance	State of preservation	Pages
Zenone, imperator d'Oriente	A. Marchi	VEC, 1696A	lost	207 n.

COMIC INTERMEZZI

Title	Librettist	First performance	State of preservation	Pages
Malsazio e Fiammetta[12]	unknown	ROC, 1726C	lost	216–17
Satrapone (Il)[13]	A. Salvi	PAO, 1729	lost	
(Vespetta e) Pimpinone[14]	P. Pariati	VEC, 1708A	extant	10, 16, 59–60, 191, 193, 206, 222–6, 242–4, 246, 248–9, 286

SERENATAS

Title	Solo voices	Librettist	Occasion	Place, date	State of preservation	Pages
Concilio de' pianeti (Il)	3	G. Baruffaldi	dauphin: birth	Venice 16 Oct. 1729	lost	11, 228 n.
Nascimento de l'Aurora (Il)	5	unknown	Elis. Christine von Habsburg: birthday	c. 1710	extant	viii, 11, 48–50, 72, 155, 191, 194, 206, 230–3, 244–6, 248, 249, 286
Nome glorioso in terra, santificato in cielo (Il)	3	V. Cassani	Emperor Charles VI: name-day	Venice 4 Nov. 1724	extant	11, 74, 191, 194, 206, 228–30, 244, 246, 248, 286

ORATORIOS

Title	Solo voices	Librettist	Sponsor	First performance	Pages
Trionfi di Giosuè (I)[15]	5	G. P. Berzini	Compagnia di San Marco	Florence, 1703	36
Maria annunziata	6	F. Silvani	Compagnia di San Marco	Florence, 1712	11, 36

[12] These intermezzi were first performed together with *La Statira*.

[13] The libretto of the original production does not identify Albinoni as the composer of the music, but his name appears in that of a revival (PRS, 1729A).

[14] These intermezzi were first performed together with *Astarto*. They were revived under the new title of *La serva astuta* (BOF, 1717P; SGA, 1725; BOM, 1728C).

[15] Pasticcio. This oratorio was revived by the Compagnia di San Sebastiano in Florence *c.* 1710 under the new title *Giosuè in Gabaon*.

SACRED VOCAL MUSIC

Messa a tre voci (Tenors 1–2, Bass)	28, 41, 65
Magnificat in G minor for voices and strings (spurious)	41

SOLO CANTATAS

First lines	Voice[16]	Tonality[17]	Op. 4	Pages
Al fin m'ucciderete, o miei pensieri[18]	S	a		118
Amarissime pene	S	c		
Amor, sorte, destino	S	B♭	no. 1	
Bel fantasma tu fosti al mio pensiero	S	G		
Bella, perché tu forsi	S	c		140
Biondo crin, occhio nero, e sen d'avorio	S	a		
Che ne dici, che risolvi	S	G		
Chi non sa quanto inhumano	A	A	no. 12	
Clori nel ciel d'amor lucida stella	S	B♭		134 n.
Crudelissimo amore[19]	A	F		
Da l'arco d'un bel ciglio	A	g	no. 2	117, 126, 137
Del chiaro rio	S	C	no. 3	
Di tante ree sciagure	S	g		
Donna illustre del Latio	S	E♭		33, 125
Dove sei, che fai cor mio	S	F		
Dubbio affetto il cor mi strugge[20]	S	C		125, 141
E dove, Amor, mi guidi[21]	S	F		118, 193
Fatto bersaglio eterno	A	e		141
Fileno, caro amico[22]	S	a		117, 125, 127 n.
Filli, chiedi al mio core	A	g	no. 6	125, 139
Già del mar sorgea l'alba	S	D		
Già tornava l'aurora[23]				
Il bel ciglio d'Irene	S	B♭		125

[16] A = alto, S = soprano; unless otherwise stated the accompaniment is for continuo alone.

[17] Capitals for major tonalities, lower case for minor tonalities.

[18] Although all four extant sources name Albinoni as the composer of this cantata, its style is so uncharacteristic as to suggest a misattribution.

[19] This work is attributed to Albinoni only in the Breitkopf catalogues (Part VI, 1765, p. 28). The source in Naples, Conservatorio di Musica 'San Pietro a Majella' (Cantate 265, fols. 67–9), has no attribution; that in Milan, Conservatorio di Musica 'Giuseppe Verdi' (Fondo Noseda, o 43-14) attributes it to Domenico Sarri. Its style is typically Albinonian.

[20] This cantata has the separate title *Amante timido*.

[21] This cantata has an instrumental accompaniment of which only a violin ritornello for the final aria (included in the vocal part only as a cue) survives.

[22] This cantata exists in two distinct versions having different text and music for the second aria. One version is found in West Berlin, Staatsbibliothek Preussischer Kulturbesitz (Mus. ms. 447, 13); the other in Ostiglia, Biblioteca Musicale Greggiati (B. 260, 6).

[23] This cantata is reported to be preserved in Sondershausen (GDR), Stadt- und Bezirksbibliothek (M 2, p. 161), but no further details are available.

First lines	Voice	Tonality	Op. 4	Pages
Il penar senza speranza	S	b		
In alta rocca, ove d'un genio amico	S	e		33
Io che per colpa sol del fato rio [24]	S	d/f		118
Io non amo altri che voi	S	A		118, 125
Là dove il nobil Giano	S	E♭		116, 118
Lontan da te, mia vita	S	a		126–34 passim, 137
Lontananza crudel, mi squarci il core	S	b	no. 5	
Mi dà pena quando spira	A	C	no. 8	125
Ove rivolgo il piede	S	d	no. 7	
Parti, mi lasci	S	e	no. 9	
Per un volto di gigli e di rose [25]	S	A		117–18
Poiché al vago seren di due pupille	S	c	no. 11	
Quanta pietà mi date, o mesti fiori	S	B♭		
Questa è l'ora fatale [26]	S	g		117
Riedi a me, luce gradita	A	D	no. 4	
Rivolse Clori un giorno	S	C		
Senti, bel sol, deh senti	S	a		134 n.
Senza il core del mio bene [27]	S/A	e/c		117
Son qual Tantalo novello	A	F	no. 10	
Sorgea col lume in fronte [28]	S	b		33, 142
Sovra letto d'erbette	S	E♭		
Sovra molle origliere	S	B♭		
Volto caro del mio bel sole [29]	S	c		118
Vorrei che lo sapessi	A	C		
Vorrei scoprir l'affanno [30]	S	F		115, 125

[24] This cantata is in D minor in Naples, Conservatorio di Musica 'San Pietro a Majella' (Cantate 3, fols. 192–7), but in F minor in its other source, Brussels, Conservatoire Royal de Musique (F15, 154). Which tonality was the original one is unclear.

[25] This cantata is attributed to Albinoni in West Berlin, Staatsbibliothek Preussischer Kulturbesitz (Mus. ms. 30136, 5), but to Alessandro Scarlatti in London, Royal Academy of Music (MS 37), and to Francesco Antonio Pistocchi in Vienna, Österreichische Nationalbibliothek (EM 178). The rather bland style neither supports nor calls into question the attribution to Albinoni.

[26] This cantata exists in two versions having slightly different texts and (except for the first aria) different music. One version is found in West Berlin, Staatsbibliothek Preussischer Kulturbesitz (Mus. ms. 447, 11); the other in Ostiglia, Biblioteca Musicale Greggiati (B 260, 3).

[27] This cantata is in E minor, for alto, in Naples, Conservatorio di Musica 'San Pietro a Majella' (Cantate 18, fols. 53–5), but in C minor, for soprano (with some musical differences), in Ostiglia, Biblioteca Musicale Greggiati (B 260, 7).

[28] Words by Antonio Ottoboni. A literary source for the poetic text, which has the separate title Partenza di Filli, exists in Venice, Museo Civico Correr (Cod. Correr 466, p. 47).

[29] An ms in Vienna, Österreichische Nationalbibliothek (EM 178, 13), names Albinoni as the composer, but the work is attributed more plausibly to Giacomo Antonio Perti in Assisi, Biblioteca del Convento di San Francesco (Mss. N. 304/3).

[30] Publ. by Breitkopf & Härtel in 1911 as no. 5 of the series Ausgewählte Kammer-Kantaten der Zeit um 1700, ed. by Hugo Riemann.

INSTRUMENTAL WORKS WITH AUTHENTIC OPUS NUMBER

[12] *Suonate a tre*, Op. 1 (1694):   6, 12, 22, 28, 32, 62, 77, 78, 82, 85–9, 94, 111, 144,
vl 1, vl 2, vlc, org.   192, 259, 266, 283–4, 287

I, 1	Sonata I	d	86, 89
I, 2	Sonata II	F	86, 87, 111
I, 3	Sonata III	A	21, 87, 89, 264, 283
I, 4	Sonata IV	g	83, 94
I, 5	Sonata V	C	89
I, 6	Sonata VI	a	86, 87, 94, 283–4
I, 7	Sonata VII	G	86
I, 8	Sonata VIII	b	21, 86, 284
I, 9	Sonata IX	D	61, 86
I, 10	Sonata X	f	86, 87, 284
I, 11	Sonata XI	e	86, 284
I, 12	Sonata XII	B♭	13, 21, 60, 86, 89, 284

[6] *Sinfonie e* [6] *concerti a cinque,*
Op. 2 (1700): concertos—vl 1, vl di
con, alto vla, ten vla, vlc, bc;
sinfonias (sonatas)—same, minus
vl di con.   6, 12, 13, 17, 22, 34, 35, 68, 69, 72, 77, 78, 81, 90–2,
                                        94, 96, 103–8, 146, 157, 160, 166, 178, 284, 287

II, 1	Sonata I	G	91, 92, 284
II, 2	Concerto I	F	105
II, 3	Sonata II	C	91–2, 103, 284
II, 4	Concerto II	e	20, 105–6, 108
II, 5	Sonata III	A	284
II, 6	Concerto III	B♭	104, 105, 107, 182
II, 7	Sonata IV	c	56, 59, 68, 91, 92, 146, 284
II, 8	Concerto IV	G	103, 105
II, 9	Sonata V	B♭	91, 92, 284
II, 10	Concerto V	C	103, 104, 105, 107
II, 11	Sonata VI	g	284
II, 12	Concerto VI	D	13, 103, 105–6, 108

[12] *Balletti a tre*, Op. 3 (1701): vl 1,
vl 2, vlc, cem.   viii, 12, 13, 17, 19, 36, 67, 71, 72, 80, 85, 110, 144–5,
                                        175 n., 284, 287

III, 1	Preludio I	C	58, 145, 284
III, 2	Allemanda II	e	144, 284
III, 3	Preludio III	G	145, 284
III, 4	Preludio IV	A	284
III, 5	Allemanda V	d	144, 284
III, 6	Preludio VI	F	145, 284
III, 7	Preludio VII	D	61, 62, 145, 175 n.
III, 8	Allemanda VIII	c	144, 145
III, 9	Preludio IX	g	144, 145

III, 10   Preludio X   E
III, 11   Allemanda XI   a   63, 64, 144, 145
III, 12   Preludio XII   B♭

[12] *Concerti a cinque*, Op. 5 (1707):
vl 1, vl di con, vl 2, alto vla, ten vla,
vlc, cem.   12, 13, 22, 36, 69, 71, 72, 96, 104, 107, 146–9, 157,
                                              160, 170, 190, 244, 266, 267, 284, 287

V, 1   Concerto I   B♭   146, 147, 148
V, 2   Concerto II   F   66, 68, 146–7, 148
V, 3   Concerto III   D   146, 148, 284
V, 4   Concerto IV   G   146, 147, 148
V, 5   Concerto V   a   66, 68, 146, 148
V, 6   Concerto VI   C   146, 148
V, 7   Concerto VII   d   47, 146, 148
V, 8   Concerto VIII   F   66, 68, 146, 148, 284
V, 9   Concerto IX   e   146, 148, 284
V, 10   Concerto X   A   146, 148
V, 11   Concerto XI   g   66, 146, 147–8
V, 12   Concerto XII   C   146, 147, 148

[12] *Trattenimenti armonici per camera*,
Op. 6 (*c.* 1711): vl, vlc, cem.   12, 13, 22, 32, 36–7, 71, 85, 144, 151–3, 174, 176, 266,
                                              284, 287 n.

VI, 1   Sonata I   C   284
VI, 2   Sonata II   g   145, 153
VI, 3   Sonata III   B♭
VI, 4   Sonata IV   d   74, 150, 176, 284
VI, 5   Sonata V   F   284
VI, 6   Sonata VI   a   20, 153, 284
VI, 7   Sonata VII   D   284
VI, 8   Sonata VIII   e   75, 76
VI, 9   Sonata IX   G
VI, 10   Sonata X   c
VI, 11   Sonata XI   A   284
VI, 12   Sonata XII   B♭

[12] *Concerti a cinque*, Op. 7 (1715):
nos. 1, 4, 7, 11—vl 1, vl 2, alto vla,
vlc, bc; nos. 2, 5, 8, 11—same, plus
ob 1, ob 2; nos. 3, 6, 9, 12—same,
plus ob 1.   13, 17, 32, 37, 56, 67, 68, 104, 148, 157, 158, 160–8,
                                              172, 182, 185, 189, 254, 266, 284

VII, 1   Concerto I   D   158–9, 160–1, 284
VII, 2   Concerto II   C   53, 54, 160, 167, 184
VII, 3   Concerto III   B♭   160, 162, 166
VII, 4   Concerto IV   G   74, 75, 155, 160, 161, 284

VII, 5	Concerto V	C	160, 167–8
VII, 6	Concerto VI	D	57–8, 160, 166
VII, 7	Concerto VII	A	160, 161, 284
VII, 8	Concerto VIII	D	160, 168
VII, 9	Concerto IX	F	160, 166
VII, 10	Concerto X	B♭	63, 73, 161–2, 284
VII, 11	Concerto XI	C	160, 167
VII, 12	Concerto XII	C	160, 166
VII, 4a	Sinfonia[31]	G	74, 75, 155, 168, 169, 173, 285
VII, 10a	Concerto	B♭	161, 168, 169, 171
VII, 10b	Concerto[32]	B♭	162

[6] *Bal[l]etti e* [6] *sonate a tre*, Op. 8
(1722): vl 1, vl 2, vlc, org.   23, 37–8, 56, 60, 67, 71, 110, 157, 177–82, 184, 284–5

VIII, 1	Sonata I	B♭	180–1, 285
VIII, 2	Allemanda I	d	181, 285
VIII, 3	Sonata II	A	179, 181
VIII, 4	Allemanda II	F	181
VIII, 5	Sonata III	C	
VIII, 6	Allemanda III	D	181, 182
VIII, 7	Sonata IV	g	181, 285
VIII, 8	Allemanda IV	B♭	181, 182, 285
VIII, 9	Sonata V	F	
VIII, 10	Allemanda V	C	181, 182
VIII, 11	Sonata VI	c	181
VIII, 12	Allemanda VI	g	181, 182

[12] *Concerti a cinque*, Op. 9 (1722):
nos. 1, 4, 7, 11–vl 1 pr, vl 1 di con,
vl 2, vtta alto, vlc, bc; nos. 2, 5, 8,
11—same, plus ob 1, minus vl 1 di
con; nos. 3, 6, 9, 12—same, plus ob
1, ob 2, minus vl 1 di con.   16, 37, 38, 67, 104, 148, 157, 160, 166, 167, 182–90,
                                     242, 249, 254, 256, 258, 267, 285

IX, 1	Concerto I	B♭	182, 183, 184, 285
IX, 2	Concerto II	d	183, 188–9, 285
IX, 3	Concerto III	F	183, 189–90, 285
IX, 4	Concerto IV	A	182, 184, 285
IX, 5	Concerto V	C	183, 189
IX, 6	Concerto VI	G	103, 183, 190
IX, 7	Concerto VII	D	56, 182, 183–5, 285
IX, 8	Concerto VIII	g	183, 186–8, 189
IX, 9	Concerto IX	C	51, 183, 190, 285
IX, 10	Concerto X	F	58, 182, 184, 285

[31] The original scoring of VII, 4a appears to have been: vl 1, vl 2, vla, b (the source in Dresden has extra parts for ob 1, ob 2, and bs).
[32] Unlike VII, 10, VII, 10b has no solos for vl pr included in the vl 1 part.

IX, 11	Concerto XI	B♮	183, 189
IX, 12	Concerto XII	D	183, 190

[12] *Concerti a cinque*, Op. 10
(1735/6): vl pr, vl 1 di con, vl 2, alto,
vlc, org. viii, 13, 17, 39, 52, 56, 62, 68, 104, 157, 167, 184, 249, 255, 256–61, 262, 267, 285

X, 1	Concerto I	B♭	257, 259, 285
X, 2	Concerto II	g	65, 258, 259
X, 3	Concerto III	C	251, 257, 259
X, 4	Concerto IV	G	257, 258, 259
X, 5	Concerto V	A	257, 258, 259
X, 6	Concerto VI	D	258, 259
X, 7	Concerto VII	F	259–61
X, 8	Concerto VIII	g	257–8, 261
X, 9	Concerto IX	F	56, 57, 258, 259
X, 10	Concerto X	C	257–8
X, 11	Concerto XI	c	258
X, 12	Concerto XII	B♮	257–8, 261

SINFONIAS

The original instrumentation is vl 1, vl 2, (alto) vla, b, unless otherwise stated. (Some manuscript sources add doubling parts for other instruments.)

Si 1	'Sonata di concerto à VII vocibus', 'Sinfonia a 6', 'Sonata con violini e tromba a 6'; also sinfonia to Act I of *Zenobia, regina de' Palmireni* (1694)—tpt, vl 1, vl 2, alto vla, ten vla, vlc, vle/cem.	D	67, 78, 80–1, 95–6, 97, 102, 285
Si 2	Sinfonia to Act I of *Engelberta* (1709)	F	154
Si 3	Sinfonia	A	154–5, 160
Si 3a	Sonata III in *VI Sonates ou concerts à 4, 5 & 6 parties* (1709–12)—vl 1, vl 2, alto vla, vlc/org.	A	15, 155, 285
Si 4	Sinfonia used in *Croesus* (1714)	D	15, 154–5, 160, 169
Si 5	Sinfonia	A	154–5, 160, 169
Si 6	Sinfonia	B♮	172, 285
Si 7	Sinfonia	g	172–3, 285
Si 8	Sinfonia	G	256, 259
Si 9	Sinfonia	F	256, 285

CONCERTOS

The original instrumentation is vl pr, vl 1, vl 2, (alto) vla, b, unless otherwise stated. (Some manuscript sources add doubling parts for other instruments.)

Co 1	Concerto—vl pr, vl 2, vl 3, alto vtta, vle, bc.	D	16, 78, 81–2, 98, 102–3, 285
Co 2	Concerto XI in *Concerti a cinque* (c. 1717)	C	7 n., 22, 67, 169, 170, 171, 285

Co 2a	Concerto	C	171–2
Co 2b	Concerto	C	168, 169, 170, 171–2
Co 3	Concerto (lost)	D	168, 169, 170, 285
Co 4	Concerto	G	169, 170, 184, 285
Co 5	Concerto	A	169, 170, 184, 285

SONATAS

Works thought spurious are indicated with an obelus (†).

So 1	Sontata a sei con tromba—tpt, vl 1, vl 2, [alto vla], ten vla, vla (= vle), org.	C	78, 95, 103, 285, 286

Balletti a cinque: vl 1, vl 2, alto vtta, ten vtta, vlc, org.			15, 69, 78, 79–80, 82, 108–12, 113, 114, 144, 286
So 2	Introduzione I	B♮	111
So 3	Introduzione II	g	111
So 4	Introduzione III	e	94, 111
So 5	Introduzione IV	f	79, 80, 111
So 6	Introduzione V	A	80, 111
So 7	Introduzione VI	F	111

Balletti a quattro: vl 1, vl 2, alto vtta, bc.			69, 78, 79, 110, 112–14, 286
So 8	[Balletto] I	G	113, 114
So 9	[Balletto] II	b	
So 10	[Balletto] III	D	53, 55, 96, 112, 114
So 11	[Balletto] IV	A	
So 12	[Balletto] V	C	113
So 13	[Balletto] VI	e	
So 14	[Balletto] VII	F	112
So 15	[Balletto] VIII	a	94, 114
So 16	[Balletto] IX	B♮	113
So 17	[Balletto] X	d	114
So 18	[Balletto] XI	E	114
So 19	[Balletto] XII	g	114

Sonate a tre: vl 1, vl 2, vlc, org.			81, 89–90, 91, 92
So 20	Sonata I	C	89, 286
So 21	Sonata II	˙B♮	91, 286
So 22	Sonata III	F	
So 23	Sonata IV	D	
So 24	Sonata V	G	91
So 25	Sonata VI	A	

Sonate da chiesa, 'Op. 4': vl, vc/bc.   14, 19, 74, 149–51, 175, 176, 285

So 26	Sonata I	*d*	150, 176
So 27	Sonata II	*e*	150–1
So 28	Sonata III	B♭	151
So 29†	Sonata IV	*g*	14, 145, 149, 150, 151
So 30	Sonata V	*g*	150, 151, 176
So 31	Sonata VI	*b*	67, 151, 174

Sonatas in Dresden, Sächsische Landesbibliothek: vl, b.   15, 42 n., 168–9, 174–5, 176, 286, 287 n.

So 32	*Sonata a violino solo*, composta per il Sig. Pisendel	B♭	viii, 169, 171, 174, 286
So 33	'Solo'	*g*	110, 169, 174–5, 286
So 34	'Solo'	B♭	110, 169, 174–5, 286

Sonate a violino solo e basso continuo: vlc, bc.   14, 74, 175–7, 263, 285–6

So 35	Sonata I	*d*	150, 176, 286
So 36	Sonata II	*g*	54–6, 176
So 37	Sonata III	*A*	176, 177
So 38	Sonata IV	*A*	176–7, 264
So 39†	Sonata V	*e*	14, 24, 175–6

Six Sonates da camera, 'Op. post.': vl, cem; *So* 42 and *So* 44 alternatively fl, cem.   14–15, 249, 261–4, 285

So 40†	Sonata I	F	263
So 41	Sonata II	*a*	263–4
So 42†	Sonata III	E	263, 285
So 43†	Sonata IV	*d*	263
So 44†	Sonata V	D	263, 285
So 45	Sonata VI	*A*	263, 264

SPURIOUS (MISCELLANEOUS) WORKS

This list is restricted to works individually mentioned in the text of the present book.

Mi 1	Sinfonia I (Darmstadt)	C	254–5
Mi 3	Concerto	C	255 n.
Mi 5	Sinfonia II (Darmstadt)	D	254–5
Mi 6	Sinfonia IV (Darmstadt)	D	254–5
Mi 7	Sinfonia V (Darmstadt)	D	254–5
Mi 12	Concerto	*e*	286 n.
Mi 13	Sinfonia VI (Darmstadt)	F	254–5
Mi 14	Concerto III (Harmonia Mundi)	F	15, 254
Mi 17	Sinfonia III (Darmstadt)	G	254–5
Mi 19	Concerto IV (Harmonia Mundi)	G	15, 254
Mi 26	Adagio per archi e organo	*g*	v, 24, 157

FOUR ANONYMOUS WORKS IN DURHAM

THESE works are thought to be by Albinoni, principally on grounds of style. The list gives the work identification in Brian Crosby, *A Catalogue of Durham Cathedral Music Manuscripts* (Oxford, 1986), followed by the shelfmarks and page nos. in Durham Cathedral Library, and then the original title, tonality, and instrumentation. The thematic incipit of the first movement of each work is quoted and the tempo, metre, and number of bars of each succeeding movement are described.

ANON 93, MS M175, pp. 19–22.

[Sonata a cinque], *D*: tpt, vl 1, vl 2, vla, b.

Presto, C, 34 bars (see Ex. 48 for incipit)—Adagio e spiccato, C, 2 bars—Presto, 3/4, 35 bars—Adagio, C, 3 bars—[Allegro], 12/8, 28 bars. Ex. 48.

Ex. 48

ANON 97, MS M175, pp. 59–68; MS M193/2, 3, 4, 6, 7, pp. 14–15.

Sonata a cinque, *g*: vl 1, vl 2, alto vla, ten vla, b.

[Adagio], C, 17 bars (see Ex. 49 for incipit); [Allegro], C, 51 bars; [Grave], C, 18 bars; [Allegro], 3/4, 107 bars. Ex. 49.

Ex. 49

ANON 98, MS M175, pp. 69–88; MS M193/2, 3, 4, 6, 7, pp. 20–1.

[Sonata a sei], *D*: tpt, vl pr, vl di con, vl 2, alto vla, vlc, b.

[Allegro], 3/4, 67 bars (see Ex. 50 for incipit); [Grave], C, 3 bars; [Allegro], 12/8, 32 bars. Ex.50.

Ex. 50

ANON 99, MS M175, pp. 89–93; MS M193/2, 3, 4, 6, 7, pp. 22(–3).

'Serenatto', *D*: tpt, vl 1, vl 2, alto vla, ten vla, b.

[Allegro], C, 40 bars (see Ex. 51 for incipit—[Adagio], C, 3 bars—[Presto], C, 9 bars—Adagio, C, 2 bars—[Allegro], 3/4, 36 bars. Ex. 51.

Ex. 51

MODERN EDITIONS OF ALBINONI'S WORKS

THE appendices of my earlier book, *Albinoni: Leben und Werk*, provide details of modern editions of Albinoni's works. Since 1980, when it was published, surprisingly few new editions have appeared, although the newcomers include a certain number of critical editions, a category that prior to 1980 was poorly represented in regard to Albinoni's music. Rather than provide a simple, though comprehensive, listing, as in my earlier book, I have chosen to offer here a guide to performers and scholars who wish to gain access to the music. As an editor myself, I have been reluctant to be too censorious of my *confrères*, although where there is an obvious practical problem with the use of a particular edition or series of editions, I have pointed it out. I have also taken the opportunity to draw attention to works that deserve to appear in a modern edition but have not so far done so, in the hope that someone will take steps to fill the gap.

There exists, in progress, a collected edition of Albinoni's instrumental works edited by the Austrian scholar Walter Kolneder.[1] This is a series that derives its cohesion from having the same editor rather than the same publisher, for volumes in it have appeared variously from Schott (1958–1964), Eulenburg, later Kunzelmann (1973–), and Amadeus (1974–).[2] These are all simple performing editions with only a brief preface and no critical apparatus. Longer works such as concertos are always published in individual volumes, shorter works sometimes in twos or threes. In most cases—particularly in that of works with opus number from Op. 7 onwards—the text is reliable and will generally satisfy performers. Kolneder's continuo realization for harpsichord is more problematic: the added parts always lie at an unusually great distance from the bass, often requiring the use of leger lines above the treble stave, so that a thin, jangly sound may result if the chords are played exactly as written. Performers intending to use Kolneder's realization as a basis for their own should be prepared to redistribute the upper parts in order to bring treble and bass closer.

As one would expect, the instrumental works with opus number have received the closest attention from modern editors and publishers. The best work in Op. 1, Sonata III in A major, was picked out early by Nagels Archiv and published in an edition by Walter Upmeyer in 1929. The sixth sonata was edited by Erich Schenk

---

[1] The series is described as a 'Gesamtausgabe der Instrumentalmusik' (complete edition of the instrumental music), but since no programme of publication has been announced, the degree of 'completeness' envisaged is not known.

[2] The volumes published by Schott are not described as part of the *Gesamtausgabe* project but are related to it in the sense that their editorial method and styling are exactly the same; significantly, none of the music they contain has been duplicated in the later volumes from Amadeus, Eulenburg, and Kunzelmann.

for Österreichischer Bundesverlag in 1951. Kolneder provided Schott with nos. 10–12 in 1959. Bärenreiter issued no. 8 in 1987 in an edition by Stefan Altner (Hortus Musicus 240). There are thus six sonatas still awaiting publication.

The six concertos from Op. 2 have so far been totally ignored by publishers, but five sonatas have appeared. Nagel were first, in 1956, with the powerful G minor sonata (II, 11), edited by Franz Giegling; the A major sonata (II, 5) was published in 1959 in an edition by Remo Giazotto which makes many tacit alterations and needs to be compared with an original source before use. The C minor sonata (II, 7), edited by Günter Kehr, followed in 1970. Kolneder's edition, under the Kunzelmann imprint, has so far issued the first three sonatas (II, 1, 3, 5). The fifth sonata still remains.

Kolneder edited the first three sonatas of Op. 3 for Schott in 1964 and has continued with the next group of three for Amadeus (1974). Because of the quality of these Balletti a tre, one hopes that the remainder will not be long delayed.

Nine of the Op. 5 concertos have already appeared from Edition Kunzelmann in Kolneder's edition. Of the missing three (nos. 3, 8, and 9), no. 8 has been published in a critical edition by Martin L. Shapiro that also includes Op. 5 no. 8 and Op. 7 nos. 7 and 10; the volume was published by Theodore Presser in 1976. The ninth concerto was published by Boosey & Hawkes in 1954 together with Op. 7 no. 1 in an edition by Bernhard Paumgartner.

Individual sonatas from Op. 6 have quite frequently appeared. Walter Upmeyer edited the first and eleventh in a common volume for Nagels Archiv in 1928 (reissued 1958). The sixth sonata was published by Nagel separately in 1934 (reissued 1956) in the version for recorder preserved in the Biblioteca Palatina, Parma; the editor was Ludwig Schäffler. In 1959 the Zurich publisher Hug brought out the fourth, fifth, and seventh sonatas in an edition by Willi Reinhart; ten years later the fourth sonata was brought out by Heinrichshofen in an edition by Frederick Polnauer. The manuscript copy of the sixth sonata with a continuo realization by Heinrich Nikolaus Gerber corrected by J. S. Bach, which is preserved in the library of the Gesellschaft der Musikfreunde, Vienna (IX 45276), has been published no fewer than three times: by Bernhard Paumgartner for Hug (1951); by E.-F. Callenberg for Moeck (1957); by W. Weismann for Peters of Leipzig (1965). The present writer is in the process of bringing out a critical edition in three volumes of the complete set published by European Music Archive; the first two volumes, containing the first eight sonatas, have already appeared (1979, 1986).

Op. 7 has now been issued complete in twelve volumes by Edition Kunzelmann. Concerning earlier modern editions of individual concertos from this set, note should be taken of the contemporary arrangement of the fourth concerto for flute, two violins, and bass preserved in a Stockholm manuscript, which has appeared as an ostensibly authentic version in editions from Deutscher Ricordi Verlag (1956) and Sikorski (1957).

Op. 8 is blessed with almost a surfeit of modern editions. The most reliable and attractively produced is the critical edition in two volumes for A–R Editions by

C. David Harris (1986). Kolneder has edited the whole set in three volumes for Edition Kunzelmann, while individual sonata-balletto pairs have appeared from Österreichischer Bundesverlag (Sonata IV and Balletto IV: 1952) and Theodore Presser (Sonata I and Balletto I: 1977).

Op. 9 is the collection that has been most extensively mined. Only the first and third concertos have so far appeared in the collected edition, but both of these and all the rest except, strangely, no. 4 can be found in the lists of other publishers. Musica Rara have brought out all the single and double oboe concertos in the set except no. 2 in critical editions by Franz Giegling; these can be recommended with the caution that Giegling has assumed that the double-bass should play with the cello rather than the continuo (an assumption which, as I have argued earlier in this book, conflicts with the evidence). Concerto II is available in editions by Fritz Kneusslin (Edition Kneusslin, 1955) and Remo Giazotto (Suvini Zerboni, 1953). Concerto I has appeared from Süddeutscher Musikverlag (1976), Concerto VII from Edition Kneusslin (1973), and Concertos IX and X from Ricordi (1959, 1961).

For Op. 10 the only modern edition so far is that of the first concerto (by Kolneder for Edition Kunzelmann).

We turn now to the works lying outside the collections with opus number. Three sinfonias are available in print. Si 1, the overture to *Zenobia, regina de' Palmireni*, was published by Musica Rara in a critical edition by the present writer in 1970. At that time I had knowledge of the four separately preserved sources that describe the work variously as a sonata, a 'sonata di concerto', and a sinfonia, but was not yet aware of its presence at the head of the *Zenobia* score. This explains why the work was published as 'Sonata no. 2' (following the earlier publication by Musica Rara of the trumpet sonata *So* 1 as 'Sonata no. 1'). Two sinfonias from the Dresden collection, *Si* 6 and the variant of Op. 7 no. 4 identified as 'VII, 4a', were published by Schott in 1958 and 1959 respectively in editions by Kolneder. This leaves a further seven sinfonias (eight, if *Si* 3a is regarded as a separate work) still to be published. *Si* 7 and *Si* 9, which are among the very best Albinoni works of any kind preserved only in manuscript, deserve early consideration.

Of the miscellaneous concertos, *Co* 2, the violin concerto in C major published in the Jeanne Roger anthology *Concerti a cinque*, was published by Vieweg as early as 1930 in an edition by Upmeyer. *Co* 5, the A major violin concerto in Dresden, was brought out by Schott in 1974 in an edition by Friedrich Wanek. Since *Co* 1 is a primitive, unsatisfactory work and *Co* 3 disappeared during the Second World War, it remains only to bring out the excellent G major violin concerto in Dresden, *Co* 4.

The violin sonatas from the three 'unauthorized' collections have received some attention. In 1974 Kolneder's edition of the 1708 set (the so-called *Sonate da chiesa*, 'Op. 4') appeared from Amadeus in two volumes. The six sonatas published in Paris as 'Op. post.' (*So* 40–5) have appeared more recently from the same editor and publisher in three volumes, one of which contains the two spurious sonatas designated alternatively for flute (*So* 42 and *So* 44). Surprisingly, the 1717 collection published by Jeanne Roger (*So* 35–9) has so far been ignored, except for the publication of the first sonata by Schott *c.* 1909 in an edition by Alfred Moffat.

The Dresden sonata inscribed to Pisendel in the composer's autograph manuscript (*So* 32) has been published twice: first, in a critical edition by the present writer for Peters of Leipzig (1975); second, in a facsimile edition brought out by Zentralantiquariat der Deutschen Demokratischen Republik in 1980. The time is ripe for publication by either method of the two splendid chamber sonatas for violin (*So* 33 and *So* 34) unearthed by Manfred Fechner in the Sächsische Landesbibliothek in 1976.

Mention has been made above of the critical edition by Edward H. Tarr of the trumpet sonata in Vienna *So* 1, which appeared from Musica Rara in 1968. For this edition the missing *alto viola* part has been skilfully reconstructed by the editor. A more recent edition by Walter Kolneder for Edition Kunzelmann also exists. The first two trio sonatas from the manuscript set of *Sonate a tre* (*So* 20–5) in the same Este collection of the Österreichische Nationalbibliothek were published by Theodore Presser in 1977 in an edition by Frederick Polnauer.[3] So far, none of the early *Balletti a cinque* (*So* 2–7) and *Balletti a quattro* (*So* 8–19) have appeared in print. It would be as well to be rather selective if and when their publication is considered, for their quality is very uneven.

The publishing history of the vocal music is more briefly told. Of the cantatas for solo voice, only the twelve in Op. 4 are available; these were published by A–R Editions in 1979 in a critical edition by the present writer. Since these represent just over a quarter of the extant cantatas by Albinoni, and in view of the uniformly high quality of the composer's works in this genre, there is a strong case for publishing the best of the remainder, perhaps in one volume for soprano and another for contralto (one recognizes, naturally, the particular difficulty, in present-day conditions, of making the publication of early vocal chamber music economic).

The comic intermezzi *Pimpinone* were published by A–R Editions in a critical edition by the present writer in 1983. Neither of the extant *opere serie* (*Zenobia, regina de' Palmireni* and *La Statira*) is available in an edition suitable for performance, but the first exists in a facsimile edition brought out by Garland Publishing in 1979 as vol. 18 of the series *Italian Opera 1640–1770*. It would probably not be worthwhile to issue either opera in a performing edition. A much better case can be made for the two surviving serenatas, *Il nascimento de l'Aurora* and *Il nome glorioso in terra, santificato in cielo*; the first of these, which has been recorded, is a work of great appeal.[4]

In years to come one can expect the appearance of facsimile editions of the instrumental collections engraved during Albinoni's lifetime. Now that an increasing number of continuo players are able to improvise an accompaniment

---

[3] Theodore Presser have also issued under Albinoni's name a violin concerto in E minor (*Mi* 12) attributed to him in the Este manuscript EM 110c in the Österreichische Nationalbibliothek. The style of this work casts strong doubt on Albinoni's authorship.

[4] A performance directed by Claudio Scimone was recorded in 1983 on Erato 75153–4.

without reference to a written-out realization, it makes sense for modern performers specializing in the baroque repertory to use a reproduction of the original performing material. Because of the high standard of accuracy of most of the early engraved editions of Albinoni's music, such facsimiles will provide a reliable basis for performance. There is, however, one possible source of danger. The four instrumental collections (Opp. 1, 2, 3, and 5) that appeared first in editions by Giuseppe Sala printed from movable type—editions unlikely to be reproduced in facsimile, since the modern performer finds them much harder to read than their engraved counterpart—contain fewer bass figures than Roger's 'pirated' editions. A keyboard player or lutenist using the Roger text would be well advised, therefore, to keep an open mind about the figures, or, better still, to consult the printed originals.[5]

[5] Although there exist no earlier Italian editions for Albinoni's Op. 6 and the 'unauthorized' collections of violin sonatas issued by Jeanne Roger and Louis Hue, one may be fairly certain that Albinoni's original figuring, probably rather sparse (to judge from the autograph violin sonatas in Dresden), has been augmented by the publishers for the convenience of amateur musicians north of the Alps. The same caution therefore applies.

BIBLIOGRAPHY

THE present list is intended as a short guide to modern literature dealing mainly or in substantial part with Albinoni and his music. It excludes most writings (such as opera catalogues and general histories of music) that deal with the composer as part of a larger project but includes some items of secondary literature that have not been referred to earlier. Dates given are always those of the first edition.

GENERAL STUDIES (LIFE AND WORKS)

Giazotto, Remo, *Albinoni* (Brescia, La Scuola, [1953]).
—— *Tomaso Albinoni: 'musico di violino dilettante veneto' (1671–1750)* (Milan, Bocca, 1945).
Talbot, Michael, *Albinoni: Leben und Werk* (Adliswil, Edition Kunzelmann, 1980).
—— 'The Instrumental Music of Tomaso Albinoni', dissertation (University of Cambridge, 1968).

BIOGRAPHY

Talbot, Michael, 'Albinoni: The Professional Dilettante', *The Musical Times*, 112 (1971), 538–41.
Vio, Gastone, 'Per una migliore conoscenza di Tomaso Albinoni: documenti d'archivio', *Recercare*, i, 1988, forthcoming.

INSTRUMENTAL MUSIC (GENERAL)

Moser, Andreas, *Geschichte des Violinspiels* (Berlin, Hesse, 1923).
Selfridge-Field, Eleanor, *Venetian Music from Gabrieli to Vivaldi* (Oxford, Blackwell, 1975).
Solie, John E., 'Aria Structure and Ritornello Form in the Music of Albinoni', *The Musical Quarterly*, 63 (1977), 31–47.
Talbot, Michael, 'Vivaldi and Albinoni', *Vivaldi informations*, 1 (1971–2), 23–7.
Wasielewski, Wilhelm Joseph von, *Die Violine und ihre Meister* (Leipzig, Breitkopf & Härtel, 1869).

SONATAS

Newman, William, *The Sonata in the Baroque Era* (Chapel Hill, University of North Carolina Press, 1959).
—— 'The Sonatas of Albinoni and Vivaldi', *Journal of the American Musicological Society*, 5 (1952), 99–113.

CONCERTOS

Hutchings, Arthur, *The Baroque Concerto* (London, Faber and Faber, 1961).

Schering, Arnold, *Geschichte des Instrumentalkonzerts* (Leipzig, Breitkopf & Härtel, 1905).

Shapiro, Martin L., 'Form in the Violin Concertos of Tomaso Albinoni', dissertation (University of California at Santa Barbara, 1971).

Solie, John E., 'Form in the Concertos and Sinfonias of Tomaso Albinoni', dissertation (University of Chicago, 1974).

Talbot, Michael, 'A Question of Authorship', *Vivaldi informations*, 2 (1973), 17–22.

—— 'Albinoni's Oboe Concertos', *The Consort*, 29 (1973), 14–22.

—— 'The Concerto Allegro in the Early Eighteenth Century', *Music & Letters*, 52 (1971), 8–18, 159–72.

CANTATAS

Guaita, Carlo, 'Le cantate di Tomaso Albinoni (1671–1751): Studio storico-critico e bibliografico', dissertation (University of Milan, 1986).

Schmitz, Eugen, *Geschichte der weltlichen Solokantate* (Leipzig, Breitkopf & Härtel, 1914).

Talbot, Michael, 'Albinoni's Solo Cantatas', *Soundings*, 5 (1975), 9–28.

OPERAS

Wolff, Hellmuth Christian, 'Neue Quellen zu den Opern des Tommaso Albinoni', *Studi musicali*, 8 (1979), 273–89.

—— '*Pimpinone* von Albinoni und Telemann—ein Vergleich', *Hamburger Jahrbuch für Musikwissenschaft*, 5 (1981), 29–36.

—— 'Zur Neuausgabe von Tommaso Albinonis Oper *Zenobia* (1694)', *Die Musikforschung*, 36 (1983), 79–82.

INDEX

THIS index is a general one containing personal names, places, titles, and subjects. The names indexed include those of authors and editors but exclude those of publishers except when the latter have a place in the argument of the book. The names of fictional characters in cantatas, serenatas, and operas are also excluded, although any historical persons whose name they share duly appear; hence Aurelian (in Italian, Aureliano), the character in *Zenobia, regina de' Palmireni*, is not indexed, but Aurelian, the Roman emperor, is. Similarly, there are no entries for places appearing merely in bibliographical references or titles. The titles of books, periodicals, and articles are normally omitted, but those of musical, poetic, or dramatic works by authors other than Albinoni are included as a matter of course; entries and page references for individual compositions by Albinoni and the collections containing them do not appear in the index; they are found in appendix A earlier.

The alphabetization of headings and subheadings follows the word-by-word system (treating hyphens and apostrophes between words as non-existent); thus 'D'Astorga, Emanuele' precedes '*da capo* aria'. Initial definite articles in titles are ignored, although the article is left in its normal place, giving, for example, '*Il ritratto dell'eroe* (Porta)' (following 'ritornello form') rather than '*Ritratto dell'eroe, il* (Porta)'. In the alphabetization of subheadings short initial particles such as 'in' are discounted.

For the sake of brevity the name 'Tomaso Albinoni' has been shortened to 'A' in qualifying expressions and subheadings.

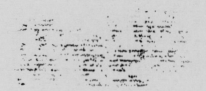

DATE DUE

ILL 6-15-92			

Demco, Inc. 38-293